Favorite Recipes® of Home Economics Teachers

Salads and Vegetables

Cookbook

Revised

Library of Congress Cataloging in Publication Data
Main entry under title:
Salads and vegetables cookbook.
   "Revised and combined edition of . . . the 1964 salads cookbook and the 1966 vegetables cookbook."
   Includes index.
   1. Salads.   2. Cookery (Vegetables)   I. Favorite recipes of home economics teachers, salads including
appetizers.   II. Favorite recipes of home economics teachers, vegetables edition, including fruits.   III. Title:
Favorite recipes of home economics teachers.
TX807.S28 1979   641.8'3   79-17866
ISBN 0-87197-126-7

Dear Homemaker,

This is a nutrition-conscious, calorie-counting age, and more than ever, families are getting "back to the basics" of wholesome, nutritious eating. So, what could be more appropriate than an all-new SALADS*VEGETABLES Cookbook from Home Economics Teachers?

Yet, you will find that this is not just any new cookbook. Its emphasis is on making the most of what nature's glorious bounty has to offer in the form of bright, gleaming vegetables and fruits, with all their color, sparkle and fresh flavor. Moreover, it is a revised and combined edition of 2 all-time great Home Economics Teachers cookbooks—the 1964 SALADS Cookbook and the 1966 VEGETABLES Cookbook, updated to include over 200 brand new recipes.

In this edition, then, you will find the best of the old along with the best of the new, plus an up-to-the-minute Nutrition Labeling Chart and hints on dealing with the Energy Crunch. But, old or new, every recipe is tried and true, home-tested, and then personally signed and submitted by each Home Economics Teacher.

Getting back to the basics with a SALADS*VEGETABLES Cookbook doesn't mean the recipes are plain. Far from it! Instead, you will find that you can build beautiful menus around these recipes, and each will be as simple to prepare as it is appetizing!

Enjoy your new cookbook and share it with others—Home Economics Teachers are sure it will bring endless cooking pleasure into every kitchen.

Mary Jane Blount
Cookbook Editor

BOARD OF ADVISORS

RUTH STOVALL, *Chairman*
Alabama Department of Education
(Retired)

CATHERINE A CARTER
Consultant, Consumer Homemaking
   Education
Illinois Division of Vocational
   and Technical Education

BARBARA GAYLOR
Supervisor, Consumer and Homemaking
   Education
Michigan Department of Education

JANET LATHAM
Supervisor, Home Economics Education
Idaho State Board of Vocational Education

BETTY ROMANS
State Advisor, Texas Association
   Future Homemakers of America
Consultant, Homemaking Education
Texas Education Agency

FRANCES RUDD
Supervisor, Home Economics Education
Arkansas Department of Education

ANNE G. EIFLER
Pennsylvania Department of Education
(Retired)

ODESSA N. SMITH
Louisiana Department of Education
(Retired)

Contents

Our sincere appreciation to all who submitted recipes. We regret we were unable to incorporate all of the recipes due to similarity and lack of space.

Nature's Glorious Bounty

"More, please!"

The request you most love to hear at mealtime. It is all the assurance you need to know that you have scored a hit—whether it's with a savory meat entree, delicious homemade rolls, or a scrumptious dessert.

But, what about your salad, vegetable and fruit dishes? Is it *"away with"* salads and vegetables in your home at mealtime, or do you have *"a way"* with them that keeps everyone asking for more?

Hopefully, you have "a way" with salads and vegetables because they are a clever cook's dream foods. Truly reflecting the bounty of nature, they add the greatest variety of color and flavor to mealtime, as well as an abundance of vitamins and minerals not found in other foods. Moreover, vegetables and fruits are so easily prepared into an exciting array of flavorful and tempting accents that they put an end to menu monotony.

SALADS: Salads have been a part of mealtimes since before the birth of Christ. But, unlike the many varieties of salads we are familiar with today, those early salads were most likely made with fresh herbs, oil and a small amount of cabbage or spinach leaves. And, they were probably served more as an appetizer than as a part of the meal.

The term "salads" apparently originated in Rome, and is derived from the Roman word for salt. Many of the salad ingredients we take for granted today were unheard of then, or considered inedible. Fruits were common—such as grapes, figs, dates, wild pears, apples, and others—but they were served fresh for dessert, or stewed and not in salad form.

By the 14th Century, "sallets" were part of the nobleman's diet, and were very rich concoctions, indeed. Typically called "macedoines" after the melting-pot country of Macedonia, ingredients could include several herbs, raisins, olives, oranges and lemons, sugar, cauliflower, spinach, lettuce, and even nuts and some flowers. Peasants and other poor people rarely ate vegetables and fruits, especially in salad form.

Thomas Jefferson was known to be quite partial to salads and grew all sorts of herbs, fruits and vegetables, and even exotic sesame seeds to use in his salads. And, several well-known restaurants were listing salads on their menus during the 1860's.

But, salads could never have become so popular or available an item on the modern menu if it had not been for men like Luther Burbank in California. His, and the work of other horticulturists, revolutionized fruit and vegetable agriculture in America. He grafted orange trees to lemon trees, cross-pollinated one variety of fruit with another, thus introducing nearly 100 new types of vegetables, fruits and nuts.

The secret to successful salads, then, is the imaginative and generous use of the bounty that nature provides. Try unexpected flavor combinations, make use of color and freshness, and serve a different salad as often as possible. The possibilities are virtually endless, and your family will be saying "More Please!" to your heart's content!

VEGETABLES: If you have ever had a hard time encouraging your family to eat their vegetables, you are certainly not the first! For centuries people believed certain vegetables to be not only unwholesome, but even poisonous or evil.

Tomatoes and potatoes were thought to cause leprosy and weakness. In some lands, the tomato was called "the love apple" because it was thought to be a powerful aphrodisiac. And, even just a few generations past it was considered totally unfit for ladies to eat unless boiled for several hours. And, there was a time when, if you had wanted to eat an onion in India, you would have had to leave the city to do so.

Artichokes, with their intriguing cluster of leaves, have also had an interesting history. Early Greeks considered the artichoke a "monster" created by the earth, unfit to eat. But, in 2nd Century Rome, the artichoke was among the most popular and highly priced of vegetables.

It took an aristocratic fad to popularize green peas. They had been "commoner's" food since the Stone Ages, and they were eaten uncooked, pod and all. Then, according to a letter written by a member of the French Court in 1696, some ladies, after eating cooked, shelled peas at the Royal table, would hurry home to eat peas again!

Spinach is one of the most abused as well as one of the most praised vegetables. Even though it has long been popularized in the comics by Popeye the Sailor Man, most children and many adults turn their noses at the mere mention of spinach as a "wholesome green for any age or condition, especially for youths. It's juice cureth any wound received of a scorpion, and is therefore of much request in Italy."

Historical writings prove that vegetables, including peas, turnips, cauliflower, broccoli, lettuce, beans, cucumbers, and many others have been around for several thousand years. Why, then, were they distrusted for so long, and still are not as popular as their beauty and flavor might demand?

First of all, cooks have been overcooking vegetables for generations, in order to make them "safe to eat." As a result, most vegetables were considered mushy, tasteless and colorless foods. Secondly, only in the past 75 to 100 years have we come to know the nutritional value of vegetables and how to cook them to preserve their flavor, color and texture. The secret to successful vegetable cookery, as the Chinese learned long ago, is to cook them quickly in little or no water. Lacking an abundance of cooking fuel, the Chinese developed this cooking technique out of necessity. But, as more and more modern homemakers are serving nature's full array of flavorful vegetables, cooked just right and seasoned to perfection, families are requesting "More, please!" as never before. Vegetables are to be eaten with gusto, and not just because "they are good for you," but because they are just plain good!

APPETIZERS & ACCOMPANIMENTS: The early Greeks and Romans have long been famous for their love of great cooking and lavish feasts. Their love for good food quickly taught them the value of serving zesty, aromatic foods to tantalize the appetite prior to the meal. Now, three thousand years later, Italians still serve *antipasto,* and the Greeks their *mezethakia,* or appetizers, to "tease the appetite" before the meal.

The use of appetizers appear all through food history, even early Chinese and Japanese writings mention appetizers. Today, appetizers are an integral part of almost every modern cuisine. The appetizers we know today apparently began in the Scandinavian countries. It is their custom to serve small bits of piquant foods and small, savory sandwiches with drinks before dinner. This custom spread to Russia in the form of "little bits," or *zakuski* served with vodka, and then to Europe to become *hors d'oeuvres* in France, *vorspeisen* in Germany. The "Unsinkable" Molly Brown has been given credit for popularizing appetizers for Americans, bringing the idea back with her from trips to Europe.

Accompaniments are the many pickles, relishes, preserves, jams, jellies and conserves that embellish main-course foods, adding a touch of color and spicy flavor to any food they accompany. Food preservation is as old as man's need for food—especially to ensure a food supply on long journeys or during the cold of winter. But not until about 150 years ago had food preservation advanced much farther beyond salted or smoked meats, dried fruits and vegetables, or some foods kept in brine.

Then, when Pasteur's findings about bacteria became known, and food processing had been perfected by the late 1800's, canning finally became a reliable, convenient and popular way to preserve foods. Canning is perfect for preserving fruits and vegetables in the form of accompaniments because it makes the most of their beauty and their adaptability to a great variety of seasonings, herbs and spices. As a result, the cook can add her own personal touch to her family's favorite breads, meats, seafood, salads and desserts.

"More, please!" It's a request you can hear whenever you serve salads, vegetables, fruits, accompaniments and appetizers. The following collection of recipes bring out all the exciting aspects of SALAD*VEGETABLE cookery, and will give your family a new appreciation for some of nature's most nutritious gifts.

YOUR KITCHEN and the ENERGY CRUNCH

Salads and Vegetables are energy savers—more important than ever before in this energy-conscious age. Served at their very best, they require little or no cooking, which also saves the cook's energy. But, like most foods, the storage and preparation of salads and vegetables make use of all the major kitchen appliances—the stove top, the oven and the refrigerator. So, there is every reason to be careful and conserving with kitchen appliances. The following energy-saving tips are easy and timesaving, as well, because they are efficient.

8

The Refrigerator:

—Locate the refrigerator and/or freezer away from heat source, such as the oven, heaters, and direct sunlight.

—Defrost the freezer section when the frost builds to ¼-inch thick.

—Remove and replace items as quickly as possible, or several at the time to avoid the door being open for any length of time.

—Make it part of your regular housekeeping routine to clean the motor, coils and drip pan of the refrigerator or freezer.

—Set the refrigerator at about 40°F., the freezer no lower than 0°F.

—Replace worn door gaskets, as it acts as "weatherstripping" for the appliance.

—Allow very hot foods to cool before placing them in the refrigerator.

The Stove-top:

—Use small amounts of water when cooking in a saucepan. It will take less time and energy to come to a boil, and is perfect for vegetable cookery because it protects flavor, color and nutritive value.

—Cover saucepans and other cooking pans with tightfitting lids to keep the heat and steam in the pan and out of the kitchen.

—Choose saucepans to fit the size of the electric burner.

—Turn the electric burner off a few minutes before the end of cooking time as the heat will continue to cook the food for a short while longer.

—Never allow gas to flame up the sides of the pan.

—Remember that the water boils and simmers at the same temperature, so once the contents begin to boil, reduce the temperature to a simmer.

—Use a pressure cooker whenever possible, as it cooks quickly at a low heat.

The Oven:

—Preheat the oven only to the temperature needed. It accomplishes nothing to turn the oven up very high and then reduce it to the proper temperature.

—Preheating is not necessary for foods that take longer than one hour to cook.

—Open and close the oven door as little as possible. Use the oven window, if there is one, or use a timer to check the progress of cooking.

—When possible, prepare an entire meal in the oven, including the vegetables. Vegetables cook best at 325° to 375° F. For higher oven temperatures, add 1 extra tablespoon of water.

Turn the oven off just a few minutes before the food is finished cooking. Leave the door closed and the food will cook properly with the heat retained in the oven.

When baking, use the oven to its full capacity, and freeze extra foods for later use.

—Invest in a small toaster oven if you do not regularly use the range oven to its full capacity. It also saves energy to prepare toast in a toaster instead of the oven.

—DO NOT line your oven with aluminum foil, as it tends to interfere with the proper flow of heat.

Other Kitchen Appliances:

—Always run a full load of dishes in the dishwasher. Studies have shown that a dishwasher uses approximately 15 gallons of water, while washing the same amount of dishes by hand uses 20 gallons of water.

—After the final dishwasher rinse, open the door, pull out the dish racks and allow the dishes to "drip dry," saving the energy used by the drying element.

—Run cold water through the disposal unit, except for an occasional hot rinse to cut grease and food buildup.

The Salad Bar

Salad making is an art, and the salad maker today is blessed with an almost limitless number of delicious ingredients to work with. And, the creative results are defined by imaginative combinations and the wise additions of seasonings and dressings.

Vegetable salads most often begin with crisp salad greens—from familiar Iceberg lettuce to the lesser known escarole and dandelion greens. To these are added any combination of colorful, *very* fresh vegetables, including mushroom slices, perky cauliflowerets and pepper rings, as well as pieces of carrots, beets, radishes and broccoli—just to begin. Complementary additions include relishes, pickles, sliced hard-cooked eggs, and of course, the flavorful salad dressing. For eye appeal, salad ingredients may be layered in a clear bowl, or creatively tossed and garnished to display colors and shapes.

Fruit salads include many delicious dishes that can be varied according to the season and the menu. They can serve as a first course, a main course, or as a refreshing dessert after a sumptuous dinner. On lunch or dinner menus, fruit salads are appetizing and especially appealing to calorie counters. Fruit salads complement almost any meat, and are especially delicious with poultry and game birds. As variety is the spice of life, prepare fruit salads with a flair for contrasting textures and colors—such as blueberries and nectarines, strawberries and avocados, apricots and pears, blackberries and pineapple— the combinations are endless. Congealed salads are a most desirable addition to any meal and they can be prepared ahead of time! Decorative shapes lend elegance to any occasion.

Try new salad ideas as often as possible. If you are thinking thin but craving a pizza, create a pizza salad! On a bed of romaine or other salad greens, layer sliced mozzarella cheese, black olives, tomato slices, fresh mushrooms, chopped onion, pepperoni slices—all your favorite pizza toppings—lightly drizzled with a zesty Italian dressing. Pronto— pizza!

Or, surprise your sweet tooth with a Banana Split Salad. But, instead of calorie-laden ice cream, chocolate syrup, nuts and whipped cream, dress up your banana slices with scoops of yogurt or cottage cheese, garnished with fresh blueberries, strawberries and peach slices, sprinkled with granola or sunflower seeds. Delicious!

Begin today creating your own salad masterpieces with the delightful array of Home Economics Teachers salad recipes featured on the following pages. Your creative salad artistry will delight your family and add unlimited interest to all your menus.

Salad Seasoning Chart

Adding herbs, spices and cheeses to salads gives them a tasty lift. But remember, use your seasonings in only one dish per meal to get the most out of its flavor. The chart below will guide you in using seasonings to complement salads with a flair.

Store herbs and spices in tightly covered containers away from heat. They keep best in a cool, but not cold, place. As soon as herbs and spices lose their delicate, distinctive aroma they should be replaced because they have also lost their flavor.

Refrigerate cheeses for long lasting freshness. Serve them, however, at room temperature to bring out their flavor. Cream, cottage and Neufchatel cheeses should be chilled when served.

THESE HERBS	ADD ZEST TO
BASIL	Tomato and green salads; fresh tomato slices
CARAWAY	Coleslaw; beet and potato salads
CHIVES	Potato, cucumber, mixed vegetable and green salads
DILLSEED	Coleslaw; potato and cucumber salads
MARJORAM	French dressing; mixed green and chicken salads
MINT	Fruit, cabbage and celery salads; coleslaw
MUSTARD	Potato salad; French and oil/vinegar dressings
OREGANO	Potato, mixed green and seafood salads; tomato aspic
PARSLEY	Greens, vegetables, shellfish salads; garnish for all salads
ROSEMARY	French dressing or mayonnaise for chicken or potato salads
SAVORY	Mixed green, green vegetables, potato and tomato salads; aspic
TARRAGON	Chicken, seafood, vegetable and mixed green salads; oil/vinegar dressings
THYME	Aspic; tomato and beet salads; mayonnaise and herb dressings

THESE CHEESES	ARE BEST WITH
AMERICAN CHEDDAR	Tossed and main dish salads, dressings, appetizers
BLEU	Tossed salads, dressings, appetizer spreads
BRICK	Salads, appetizers
CAMEMBERT	Fruit salads, appetizer spreads
COTTAGE	Fruit, vegetable salads
CREAM	Fruit, vegetable salads, dressings, appetizer spreads
GORGONZOLA	Salads, dressings
GOUDA	Appetizers
MUENSTER	Raw vegetable appetizers
NEUFCHATEL	Salads, in dips
PROVOLONE	Appetizers
RICOTTA	Salads, appetizers
ROQUEFORT	Dressings, appetizers
SWISS	Fruit, vegetable and main dish salads

THESE SPICES	BRING LIFE TO
ALLSPICE	Fruit salads; fruit salad dressings
GINGER	Pear salads, chicken salad
MACE	Whipped cream dressings for fruit salads
PAPRIKA	French dressings, garnish for green salads
CAYENNE PEPPER	Salad dressings; meat, fish and vegetable salads

APPLE-CARROT SALAD

3 apples, diced
2 carrots, grated
½ c. chopped pecans
3 tbsp. sugar
½ c. mayonnaise
⅓ c. raisins

Combine apples, carrots and pecans; mix in sugar and mayonnaise. Add raisins. Refrigerate until ready to serve. Yield: 6-8 servings.

Mrs. Mildred Bullard, Fike Sr. H. S.
Wilson, North Carolina

APPLE-CIDER SALAD

2 pkg. unflavored gelatin
2½ c. cold cider
¼ tsp. salt
1 c. chopped apples
½ c. chopped celery
1 tbsp. chopped parsley
¼ c. chopped nuts

Soften gelatin in ½ cup cider for 5 minutes. Bring remaining cider to a boil. Pour into gelatin mixture; stir until dissolved. Stir in salt. Cool until partially congealed. Stir in remaining ingredients; pour into individual molds. Chill until firm. Unmold on beds of watercress; serve with French dressing, cooked salad dressing or mayonnaise. Yield: 6 servings.

Dianne J. MacPherson, Garden Spot H. S.
New Holland, Pennsylvania

APPLESAUCE SALAD

1 can applesauce
1 pkg. strawberry, raspberry or cherry Jell-O
1 sm. bottle of 7-Up

Bring applesauce to a boil. Pour Jell-O into apple-sauce. Add 7-Up; mix well. Pour into mold. Refrigerate until firm.

Mrs. Louise P. Hughes, Mountain Heritage H. S.
Burnsville, North Carolina

APPLE-CRANBERRY SALAD

2 c. ground cranberries
1 orange, ground
1 c. sugar
2 pkg. strawberry gelatin
2 c. ground apples
1 c. chopped pecans

1 sm. can pineapple
1 c. marshmallows

Combine cranberries, orange and sugar; let stand until juicy. Dissolve gelatin in 3 cups boiling water; chill until partially congealed. Stir in all ingredients. Chill until firm. Yield: 15 servings.

Ethel Spradling, Bixby H. S.
Bixby, Oklahoma

DRESSED WALDORF SALAD

1 c. mayonnaise
1 c. sour cream
2 tbsp. honey
3 c. diced apples
2 c. diced celery
1 c. chopped walnuts
2 c. seeded halved red grapes

Combine mayonnaise, sour cream and honey for dressing. Combine apples, celery, walnuts and grapes; fold in dressing. Garnish with unpeeled apple slices. One-half cup sliced dates may be added, if desired. Yield: 10 servings.

Mrs. Ethel Moons, Artesia H. S.
Artesia, California

APRICOT-CHEESE DELIGHT

1 lg. can apricots
1 lg. can crushed pineapple
1 lg. package orange gelatin

Drain fruits, reserving juices. Chop apricots. Chill fruits. Dissolve gelatin in 2 cups hot water; add 1 cup reserved juices. Chill until mixture begins to thicken. Fold in fruits. Pour into large serving dish. Chill until firm.

Cheese Topping:

½ c. sugar
3 tbsp. flour
1 egg, slightly beaten
1 c. reserved apricot and pineapple juice
2 tbsp. butter
1 c. whipped cream
¾ c. grated cheese

Combine sugar, flour and egg. Add juices. Cook until thick, stirring constantly. Remove from heat; add butter. Cool. Fold in whipped cream. Spread over congealed layer. Sprinkle cheese over top. Yield: 24 servings.

Judy Carter, Soddy-Daisy Jr. H. S.
Daisy, Tennessee

AMBROSIA SALAD

2 bananas, sliced
¾ c. diced orange
½ c. seedless grapes
¼ c. chopped dates or raisins
¼ c. flaked coconut
⅓ c. broken nuts
3 tbsp. lemon juice
¾ c. whipping cream
2 c. mayonnaise

Combine first 6 ingredients. Sprinkle with lemon juice. Chill thoroughly. Whip cream until stiff; whip in mayonnaise. Stir carefully into fruit mixture. Chill until served. Yield: 4-6 servings.

Catherine B. Anthony, Courtney H. S.
Yadkinville, North Carolina

MOLDED WALDORF SALAD

1 env. unflavored gelatin
⅓ c. sugar
½ tsp. salt
¼ c. vinegar or lemon juice
2 c. diced tart apples
½ c. diced celery
¼ c. chopped pecans

Combine gelatin, sugar and salt in small saucepan. Add ½ cup water. Stir over low heat until gelatin is dissolved. Remove from heat; stir in 1 cup water and vinegar. Chill until partially congealed. Fold in apples, celery and pecans; chill until firm. Yield: 6 servings.

Lucille Whitney, Thetford Academy
Thetford, Vermont

CREAMY APRICOT SALAD

1 6-oz. package apricot gelatin
1 No. 2 can crushed pineapple
¾ c. sugar
1 c. apricot puree or 2 sm. jars strained baby food apricots
1 8-oz. package cream cheese, softened
1 lg. can evaporated milk
⅔ c. finely chopped nuts

Combine gelatin and pineapple in saucepan; bring to boiling point. Add sugar, apricot puree and cream cheese; simmer until cream cheese melts, stirring constantly. Remove from heat to cool. Chill until partially congealed. Chill milk in freezer tray until icy crystals form around edge. Whip until stiff peaks form. Fold into apricot mixture; pour into 9 x 13-inch

pan. Chill until firm. Sprinkle nuts over top. Yield:15 servings.

Patricia C. Harker, Waynesburg H. S.
Waynesburg, Pennsylvania

APRICOT PARFAIT SALAD

1 11-oz. can mandarin oranges
1 1-lb. can apricot halves
1 3-oz. package apricot gelatin
1 pt. vanilla ice cream
1 c halved seeded grapes
¼ c. broken walnuts

Drain oranges and apricots; reserve juices. Chop apricots. Add enough water to reserved juices to measure 1½ cups liquid; pour into saucepan. Bring to a boil. Add gelatin; stir until dissolved. Add spoonfuls of ice cream; stir until melted. Chill until partially congealed. Stir in fruits and walnuts; pour into 9-inch square pan. Chill until firm. Yield: 9 servings.

Ruth Anderson, Home Economics Advisor
Norristown, Pennsylvania

APRICOT SALAD DELUXE

1 6-oz. package apricot Jell-O
1 sm. can crushed pineapple, drained
2 lg. bananas, sliced
½ c. chopped pecans (opt.)
½ c. sugar
2 tbsp. flour
1 egg
2 tbsp. margarine
1 3-oz. package cream cheese, softened
1 pkg. Dream Whip

Mix Jell-O according to package directions. Pour into a 7½ x 12-inch dish. Drain pineapple juice, reserving ½ cup for topping. Add pineapple, bananas and pecans to gelatin mixture. Chill until set. Combine sugar, flour, egg, margarine, pineapple juice and cream cheese in a saucepan. Cook on medium-low heat until thick. Set aside to cool. Mix Dream Whip according to package directions. Fold into topping mixture. Spread over gelatin. Chill until served.

Debby H. Ellis, Jo Byrns School
Cedar Hill, Tennessee

PAT'S APRICOT SALAD

1 No. 2 can crushed pineapple
¼ c. sugar
2 packages apricot Jell-O
1 8-oz package cream cheese, softened

1 c. chopped celery
1 c. nuts
1 lg. can evaporated milk, chilled

Bring pineapple and sugar to a boil. Add Jell-O, mix well. Add cream cheese; mix well. Add cup ice water, celery and nuts. Chill until partially set. Whip evaporated milk until stiff. Fold into Jell-O mixture. Chill until firm.

Pat Whitson, Mountain Heritage H. S.
Burnsville, North Carolina

DRESSED APRICOT SALAD

1 lg. can apricots
2 tbsp. flour
¾ c. sugar
2 eggs, beaten
Juice of 1 lemon
½ lb. cheese, grated
Chopped nuts

Drain apricots; reserve juice. Chop apricots. Combine flour and sugar; stir into eggs. Pour into top of double boiler; stir in lemon juice and reserved apricot juice. Cook over hot water until thick, stirring constantly. Cool dressing thoroughly. Combine apricots, cheese and nuts; spread in shallow mold. Pour dressing over top; chill thoroughly. Cut into squares to serve. Yield: 8 servings.

Mrs. Berniece Wiginton, Big Sandy H. S.
Big Sandy, Texas

AVOCADO-GRAPEFRUIT SALAD

2 3-oz. packages lime gelatin
2 grapefruit, peeled and sectioned
2 avocados, sieved
½ c. mayonnaise

Dissolve gelatin according to package directions; chill until partially congealed. Remove membranes from grapefruit sections; arrange sections in 8 x 12-inch pan. Pour half the gelatin over grapefruit; chill until firm. Pour remaining gelatin into mixer bowl; add avocados and mayonnaise. Beat until light and frothy. Pour over grapefruit layer; chill until firm. Cut into squares; serve, frothy side up, on lettuce leaf. Garnish with whipped cream and a maraschino cherry, if desired. Yield: 10 servings.

Mrs. Helen D. Andrus, Beaverhead County H. S.
Dillon, Montana

AVOCADO MOUSSE

1 package unflavored gelatin
1 tsp. salt

1 tsp. onion juice
2 tsp. Worcestershire sauce
2 tbsp. lemon juice
2 c. mashed avocado
½ c. heavy cream, whipped
½ c. mayonnaise

Soften gelatin in ½ cup cold water; dissolve in ½ cup boiling water. Add salt, onion juice, Worcestershire sauce, lemon juice and avocados; chill until partially congealed. Fold in whipped cream and mayonnaise; turn into oiled mold. Chill until firm. Yield: 8 servings.

Mrs. Mary Belle Nutt, Cotulla H. S.
Cotulla, Texas

AVOCADO RING MOLD

1 pkg. lemon gelatin
2 ripe avocados, mashed
¼ c. sour cream
2 tbsp. white wine
⅛ tsp. salt
1 c. heavy cream, whipped

Dissolve gelatin in 1 cup boiling water. Add avocados, sour cream, wine and salt; beat until smooth and fluffy. Chill until partially congealed. Fold in whipped cream; pour into ring mold. Chill until firm. Unmold onto crisp salad greens. Yield: 6 servings.

Dorothy E. Brevoort
State Department of Education
Trenton, New Jersey

MOLDED AVOCADO ASPIC

1½ tbsp. unflavored gelatin
2½ c. tomato juice
2 bay leaves
5 whole cloves
¼ c. chopped onion
½ tsp. salt
⅛ tsp. pepper
3 drops of Tabasco sauce
2 avocados, peeled and diced
½ c. chopped celery

Soften gelatin in ¼ cup cold water for 5 minutes. Combine tomato juice, bay leaves, cloves, onion, salt, pepper and Tabasco sauce in saucepan. Boil for 5 minutes; strain. Add gelatin; stir until dissolved. Cool until partially congealed. Add avocados and celery. Pour into 8 individual molds; chill until firm. Yield: 8 servings.

Mrs. LeArta Hammond, West Side H. S.
Dayton, Idaho

FRANCES' AVOCADO SALAD

1 pkg. lemon Jell-O
1 3-oz. pkg. cream cheese
½ c. mayonnaise
1 avocado, peeled and mashed
½ c. diced celery
1 tbsp. onion juice (opt).
¼ c. diced green pepper

Prepare Jell-O according to package directions. Chill until partially set. Combine cream cheese, mayonnaise and avocado. Mix until smooth. Add celery, onion juice and green pepper. Fold into Jell-O. Pour into a 9-inch square glass pan. Chill until firm. Cut into squares. Place on lettuce leaf. Top with a dollop of mayonnaise. Serve with assorted crackers. Yield: 9 servings.

Frances Stewart, Congress Jr. H. S.
Denton, Texas

BANANA-COCONUT SALAD

4 bananas
Lemon juice
½ c. mayonnaise
½ c. whipped cream
1 c. toasted coconut or chopped nuts

Cut bananas in half lengthwise, then crosswise. Coat bananas with lemon juice immediately to prevent discoloration. Combine mayonnaise and whipped cream. Roll bananas in mayonnaise mixture; dredge with coconut. Serve on crisp salad greens. Yield: 4 servings.

Mrs. Shirley Leslie, J. D. Leftwich H. S.
Magazine, Arkansas

FROZEN BANANA SALAD

1 8-oz. package cream cheese, softened
2 tbsp. milk
½ tsp. baking powder
1 tsp. vanilla extract
¼ c. confectioners' sugar
1 No. 3 can fruit cocktail, drained
2 bananas, sliced
¼ c. chopped pecans

Cream softened cream cheese with mixer. Add milk, baking powder, vanilla and confectioners' sugar; mix well. Fold in fruit cocktail and bananas. Place in rectangular dish. Sprinkle with pecans. Freeze until firm. Let stand at room temperature for 5 minutes before slicing into squares to serve.

Carolyn Cauthorn, Richardson West Jr. H. S.
Richardson, Texas

FROZEN BANANA-STRAWBERRY SALAD

2 c. miniature marshmallows
1 No. 2½ can crushed pineapple
4 bananas, sliced
1 c. sliced strawberries
1 c. diced peaches
½ c. salad dressing
½ c. whipped cream

Combine marshmallows and pineapple in saucepan; cook over low heat until marshmallows are melted, stirring frequently. Let cool until slightly thickened. Stir in bananas, strawberries and peaches; add salad dressing. Fold in whipped cream. Freeze until ready to serve. Yield: 8 servings.

Mrs. Marjorie Stewart, Hartford H. S.
Hartford, Kentucky

CREAMY BANANA SALAD

1 tbsp. lemon juice
1 tsp. salt
2 tbsp. mayonnaise
2 3-oz packages cream cheese, softened
2 tbsp. crushed pineapple
½ c. quartered maraschino cherries
½ c. chopped nuts
½ c. whipped cream
3 ripe bananas, cubed

Combine lemon juice, salt and mayonnaise; stir into cream cheese. Add pineapple, cherries and nuts; fold in whipped cream. Add bananas. Freeze until ready to serve. Yield: 10 servings.

Mrs. Betty Hastings, Cloverleaf Sr. H. S.
Lodi, Ohio

BLACKBERRY DELIGHT

1 pkg. blackberry gelatin
1 c. sugar
1 3-oz. package cream cheese, softened
1 carton frozen blackberries
¼ c. chopped nuts

Dissolve gelatin and sugar in 1 cup boiling water. Pour ¼ cup hot gelatin over cream cheese; mix until smooth. Add frozen blackberries, nuts and softened cream cheese to gelatin; mix carefully. Refrigerate until firm. Yield: 8 servings.

Mrs. Clarice I. Snider, Unicoi County H. S.
Erwin, Tennessee

CREAMY BLUEBERRY SALAD

1 pkg. lemon gelatin
1 c. boiling blueberry juice
1 c. pineapple juice
1 c. whipped cream
1 banana, mashed
1 c. drained blueberries

Dissolve gelatin in blueberry juice; stir in pineapple juice. Refrigerate until partially congealed. Fold in whipped cream, banana and blueberries. Spoon into large mold or individual molds. Chill until firm. Yield: 8 servings

Bettye Robinson, LaPuente H. S.
LaPuente, California

ELEGANT BLUEBERRY SALAD

1 lg. package raspberry Jell-O
1 can blueberry pie filling
1 8-oz. package cream cheese, softened
1 sm. carton sour cream
½ c. sugar
½ c. chopped pecans

Dissolve Jell-O in 1 cup boiling water. Add pie filling and 2 cups cold water. Pour into serving dish. Chill until firm. Combine cream cheese and sour cream. Blend with sugar. Spread over Jell-O mixture evenly. Sprinkle with pecans. Chill.

Mrs. Ella Jo Adams, Allen H. S.
Allen, Texas

IRENE'S BLUEBERRY SALAD

1 can blueberries
1 med. can crushed pineapple
2 pkg. raspberry Jell-O
1 c. chopped pecans

Drain blueberries and pineapple, reserving juice. Place in saucepan with enough water to measure, 3½ cups. Bring to a boil. Pour over Jell-O, stirring constantly until dissolved. Pour into large serving dish. Chill until partially set. Add blueberries, pineapple and pecans. Chill until firm.

Creamy Topping:

1 sm. carton sour cream
2 c. Cool Whip
1 c. sugar
Chopped pecans

Combine sour cream, Cool Whip and sugar; mix well. Spread over congealed layer evenly. Sprinkle with chopped pecans. Chill. Cut into squares; serve on lettuce leaf. Yield: 20 servings.

Mrs. Ronnie Strickland, Home Economics Teacher
Potts Camp, Mississippi

LINDA'S BLUEBERRY SALAD

1 lg. package black cherry Jell-O
1 can blueberry pie filling
1 sm. can crushed pineapple
½ pt. sour cream
2 sm. packages cream cheese
½ c. sugar
½ tsp. vanilla extract
½ c. chopped nuts

Dissolve Jell-O in 1 cup hot water. Add 1 cup cold water. Add pie filling and crushed pineapple. Pour into long dish. Refrigerate until firm. Mix sour cream, cream cheese and sugar with mixer until blended well. Add vanilla and nuts. Spread over top of salad. Chill until ready to serve.

Linda Jones
Woodville, Texas

BUFFET FRUIT PLATTER

1 lg. banana
Lemon juice
1 lg. apple, cut into wedges
1 3-oz. package cream cheese, softened
½ c. chopped pecans
Lettuce
1 med. pink grapefruit, sectioned
4 canned peach halves
Green grape clusters
4 canned pear halves
Cranberry-orange relish
1 egg, beaten
½ c. honey
Dash of salt and ground mace
1 c. sour cream

Score banana lengthwise with tines of fork; cut diagonally into crosswise slices. Pour a small amount of lemon juice over bananas and apple wedges to prevent discoloring. Chill. Blend cream cheese until smooth. Shape into small balls; roll in pecans. Arrange fruits on bed of lettuce. Top pears with cheese balls; spoon relish into peach halves. Combine egg, honey and ¼ cup lemon juice in saucepan. Cook, stirring constantly, over low heat until thick. Blend in salt and mace; cool. Fold in sour cream. Chill. Serve Honey-Lemon Dressing over fruit platter.

Mrs. Louise D. Edwards, Hancock Central H. S.
Sparta, Georgia

ANNE'S FRESH FRUIT SALAD

1 No. 202 can fruit cocktail
1 sm. can mandarin oranges, drained
4 bananas, sliced
3 oranges, peeled, cubed
2 grapefruit, peeled, cubed
3 red apples, cubed
1 liter 7-Up, chilled

Combine all ingredients except 7-Up; mix well. Chill. Add 7-Up just before serving; mix well.

Anne E. Shadwick, Seneca H. S.
Seneca, Missouri

BRIAN'S CITRUS SALAD

Iceberg lettuce
Romaine
1 can mandarin oranges, chilled
4 or 5 thin slices sweet onion
Fresh mushrooms, sliced
2 tbsp. toasted sesame seeds
½ c. olive oil
2 tbsp. tarragon vinegar
2 tbsp. sugar
½ tsp. salt
½ tsp. dry mustard
½ tsp. celery salt
1 tsp. grated onion

Tear lettuce and romaine into salad bowl. Combine with oranges, onion, mushrooms and sesame seeds. Combine remaining ingredients in container with cover; shake well. Combine all ingredients with lettuce. Toss to coat.

Bette Jahrmarkt, Chaparral H. S.
Scottsdale, Arizona

BRIDE'S SALAD

½ pt. whipping cream
Sugar
1 pkg. miniature marshmallows
1 sm. can crushed pineapple, drained
12 maraschino cherries, chopped
1 3-oz. package cream cheese, softened
2 tbsp. mayonnaise
½ c. chopped pecans, (opt.)

Beat whipping cream until stiff, adding ⅓ cup sugar to sweeten. Combine marshmallow and pineapple in separate bowl. Blend cherries, cream cheese, 2 tablespoons sugar and mayonnaise until creamy in separate bowl. Add cherry mixture to pineapple mixture. Fold whipped cream carefully into cherry-

pineapple mixture. Add pecans. Pour into glass bowl. Chill for several hours. Yield: 6-8 servings.

Mrs. Barbara Pinkston, Clear Lake H. S.
Houston, Texas

AGGIE'S SALAD

1 can sweetened condensed milk
1 can cherry pie filling
1 can crushed pineapple, drained
1 8-oz. carton Cool Whip

Combine first 3 ingredients; mix well. Fold in Cool Whip. Chill until set.

Helen Bunfill, Barnesville H. S.
Barnesville, Ohio

TASTY CHERRY SALAD

1 can cherry pie filling
1 lg. carton Cool Whip
1 c. crushed pineapple, drained
1 can sweetened condensed milk
1 c. pecans

Combine all ingredients; mix well. Chill for several hours before serving.

Barbara Gray Clement, Lexington H. S.
Lexington, Tennessee

CHERRY-PECAN SALAD

1 pkg. cherry gelatin
1 pkg. lemon gelatin
1 c. sugar
1 can crushed pineapple with juice
1 can tart pie cherries with juice
2 c. pecan halves

Dissolve gelatins and sugar in 2 cups boiling water; chill until partially congealed. Stir in pineapple and cherries; place pecan halves on top. Chill until firm. Yield: 6 servings.

Hilda S. Wright, Hanceville H. S.
Hanceville, Alabama

CHERRY-PINEAPPLE SALAD

1 16-oz. can red tart cherries
1 20-oz. can crushed pineapple
1 c. sugar
2 3-oz. packages cherry Jell-O

1 6½ oz. bottle of Coca-Cola
1 c. chopped nuts

Drain cherries and pineapple, reserving juices. Mix sugar, ½ cup water, and reserved juice in a saucepan. Bring to a boil. Combine Jell-O and cherries. Add boiled mixture; stir well. Let stand in refrigerator for 15 minutes. Add pineapple, Coca-Cola and nuts; mix well. Chill until firm. Yield: 8 servings.

Judy H. Fentress, Springfield H. S.
Springfield, Tennessee

CHERRY DELUXE SALAD

2 c. crushed pineapple
1½ c. sugar
1½ pkg. unflavored gelatin
1 3-oz. package cream cheese, softened
12 maraschino cherries
2 tbsp. cherry juice
2 tbsp. lemon juice
½ c. chopped pecans
1 c. whipped cream

Heat pineapple and sugar together until sugar is melted. Soften gelatin in ¼ cup cold water; add to pineapple mixture. Stir in cream cheese until smooth. Let cool. Add cherries, juices and pecans; fold in whipped cream. Pour into mold; Chill until firm. Yield: 10 servings.

Mrs. Marie Slover, Springlake H. S.
Earth, Texas

CHERRY WALDORF SURPRISE

1 3-oz. package cherry Jell-O
2 c. diced apples
¾ c. chopped celery
½ chopped nuts
¼ c. shredded coconut
2 tbsp. chopped maraschino cherries

Prepare Jell-O according to package directions. Add remaining ingredients. Chill until set. Fruit quantities may be adjusted as desired.

Nancy J. Stoos, Union Academy Jr. H. S.
Bartow, Florida

FROZEN CHERRY SUPREME

1 No. 303 can Royal Anne cherries
1 No. 303 can Bing cherries
2 cans mandarin oranges
1 No. 2 can crushed pineapple

1 8-oz. package cream cheese, softened
2 tbsp. milk
⅓ c. mayonnaise
½ c. chopped maraschino cherries
½ c. chopped pecans
1 c. whipped cream

Drain Royal Anne cherries; remove seeds. Drain Bing cherries, oranges and pineapple. Blend cream cheese with milk. Add mayonnaise; blend until smooth. Add fruits and pecans; fold in whipped cream. Freeze until ready to serve. Yield: 18 servings.

Mrs. W. G. Frazior, Nederland H. S.
Nederland, Texas

CHRISTMAS FRUIT SALAD

1 c. sliced peaches
1 c. pineapple chunks
1 c. sliced bananas
1 c. orange sections
½ c. fresh grapefruit sections
½ c. seedless grapes
½ c. strawberries
½ c. diced apple
1 c. chopped pecans
1 c. sugar
1 tsp. vanilla flavoring
1 tsp. lemon flavoring
2 c. whipped cream

Combine fruits, pecans and ½ cup sugar. Stir remaining sugar and flavorings into whipped cream; fold in fruit mixture. Chill thoroughly. Garnish with maraschino cherries. Yield: 12 servings.

Mrs. Harlan Hawkins, Waldron School
Waldron, Arkansas

CLOUD-NINE CREAM

1 sm. can crushed pineapple
1 8-oz. package cream cheese, softened
1 2-oz. package Dream Whip
3 tbsp. sugar
½ c. pecans
½ c. maraschino cherries

Drain pineapple, reserving juice. Beat cream cheese until creamy. Gradually add reserved juice; beat until smooth. Prepare Dream Whip according to package directions. Fold in cream cheese, pineapple, sugar, pecans and cherries; cover. Chill for 3 hours.

Beverly Plyler, Glenwood H. S.
Glenwood, Arkansas

NANCY'S COCA-COLA SALAD

2 10-oz. bottles Coca-Cola
1 3-oz. box cherry Jell-O
1 sm. can crushed pineapple
1 c. chopped nuts

Bring 1 bottle Coca-Cola to a boil. Dissolve Jell-O in boiling Coca-Cola. Add remaining Coca-Cola. Stir in remaining ingredients. Pour into glass dish. Chill. Cut into squares. Serve on lettuce with desired dressing.

Nancy Milner Bugg, Corry Jr. H. S.
Memphis, Tennessee

BERRY-FRUIT FREEZE

2 3-oz. packages cream cheese, softened
2 tbsp. sugar
2 tbsp. mayonnaise or salad dressing
1 16-oz. can whole cranberry sauce
¾ c. crushed pineapple, drained
½ c. chopped walnuts
1 c. whipping cream, whipped
4 drops of red food coloring

Beat cream cheese with sugar and mayonnaise. Stir in cranberry sauce, pineapple and nuts. Fold in whipped cream and food coloring. Pour into 8½ x 4½ x 2½ inch loaf pan. Freeze until firm. Let stand at room temperature for 10 to 15 minutes before serving. Unmold, slice and serve. Yield: 8-10 servings.

Mary Spradley, Nacogdoches H. S.
Nacogdoches, Texas

CRANBERRY-MARSHMALLOW STAR

1 pkg. raspberry gelatin
2 tsp. lemon juice
1 1-lb. can whole cranberry sauce
2 oranges, sectioned and chopped
⅓ c. chopped walnuts
¾ c. miniature marshmallows

Dissolve gelatin in 1 cup boiling water. Add lemon juice; stir in cranberry sauce. Cool until partially congealed. Fold in oranges, walnuts and marshmallows. Pour into star-shaped mold; refrigerate until firm. Yield: 8 servings.

Arlene Trautman, Arickaree School
Anton, Colorado

CRANBERRY MEDLEY

1 8-oz. can apricots
2 3-oz. packages cream cheese, softened
2 tbsp. salad dressing
2 tbsp. sugar
1 1-lb. can whole cranberry sauce
16 seedless grapes, halved
½ c. chopped nuts
1 c. whipped cream

Drain and slice apricots. Combine cream cheese, salad dressing and sugar. Add cranberry sauce, apricots, grapes and nuts; fold in whipped cream. Freeze until firm. Let stand at room temperature for about 15 minutes before serving. Yield: 8-10 servings.

Mrs. Walter D. Owen, San Marcos H. S.
San Marcos, Texas

CRANBERRY SALAD FOR COMPANY

3 env. unflavored gelatin
1 c. boiling orange juice
2 c. sugar
1 qt. cranberries, ground
2 Delicious apples, ground
2 lg. oranges, sliced
2 c. chopped pecans

Soften gelatin in ¾ cup cold water; dissolve in orange juice. Stir in sugar until dissolved; let cool. Combine fruits and pecans; fold into gelatin mixture. Chill until firm. May be frozen. Yield: 20 servings.

Mrs. Helen D. Jones, Buckatunna H. S.
Buckatunna, Mississippi

CRANBERRY SOUFFLE SALAD

1 env. unflavored gelatin
2 tbsp. sugar
¼ tsp. salt
½ c. mayonnaise
2 tbsp. lemon juice
1 tsp. grated lemon rind
1 1-lb. can whole cranberry sauce
1 orange, peeled and diced
¼ c. chopped walnuts

Combine gelatin, sugar and salt in small saucepan. Add 1 cup water. Stir over low heat until gelatin is dissolved. Remove from heat; stir in mayonnaise, lemon juice and lemon rind. Beat with rotary beater until mayonnaise is dissolved. Pour into refrigerator tray; quick chill in freezing unit for 10 to 15 minutes or until firm about 1-inch from edge. Pour into mixing bowl; beat until fluffy. Fold in remaining ingredients; pour into oiled mold. Chill until firm. Serve with mayonnaise. Yield: 6 servings.

Dora C. Fleming, Centerville H. S.
Sand Coulee, Montana

CREAMY CRANBERRY SALAD

1 sm. can crushed pineapple
1 3-oz. package cherry Jell-O
2 c. ground cranberries
1 3-oz. package cream cheese, crumbled
1 c. chopped pecans
1 orange, cut up
1 c. sugar

Drain pineapple, reserving juice. Combine juice with enough water to measure 2 cups liquid. Boil a portion of the liquid. Stir in Jell-O and remaining liquid. Chill until partially set. Add remaining ingredients. Chill until firm. Yield: 12 servings.

Barbara S. Forbes, South Caldwell H. S.
Hudson, North Carolina

FESTIVE CRANBERRY SALAD

1 14-oz. can sweetened condensed milk
¼ c. lemon juice
1 16-oz. can whole cranberry sauce
1 20-oz. can crushed pineapple, drained
½ c. chopped walnuts
1 9-oz. container frozen nondairy whipped
   topping, thawed

Combine sweetened condensed milk and lemon juice in a large bowl. Stir in cranberry sauce, pineapple and walnuts. Fold in whipped topping. Spread in 13 x 9-inch baking dish. Freeze until firm. Remove from freezer 10 minutes before serving. Serve on lettuce leaves. May be refrozen. Cover and store frozen until ready for use. Yield: 15 servings.

Zona Beth Cates, Marcos de Niza H. S.
Tempe, Arizona

SPICED CRANBERRY SALAD

1½ c. cranberry juice
¼ tsp. oil of cinnamon
9 whole cloves
1 pkg. lemon gelatin
1 7-oz. can whole cranberries
¼ tsp. dry horseradish
2 c. sour cream

Combine cranberry juice, oil of cinnamon and cloves in saucepan; bring to a boil. Strain out cloves. Dissolve gelatin in hot mixture. Cool; chill until partially congealed. Fold in cranberries; chill until firm. Combine horseradish and sour cream; serve over salad. Yield: 8 servings.

Elizabeth A. M. Mitchell, Bridgeville H. S.
Bridgeville, Delaware

EASTER FRUIT SALAD

1 16-oz. can fruit cocktail
1 15-oz. can crushed pineapple
1 pkg. orange Jell-O
1 c. whipping cream, whipped
1 3-oz. package cream cheese, softened
3 c. colored marshmallows

Drain fruits, reserving juices. Dissolve Jell-O in 1 cup hot water. Pour into a 2-quart mold or a 9 x 13-inch glass dish. Add reserved juice. Refrigerate until well thickened. Combine whipped cream and cream cheese; mix well. Beat Jell-O until light and fluffy. Fold in whipped cream mixture. Add fruits and marshmallows. Refrigerate until ready to serve. Cool Whip or Dream Whip may be used in place of whipping cream. Yield: 12 servings.

Linda A. Becker, Hendersonville H. S.
Hendersonville, Tennessee

EASY FRUIT SALAD

1 lg. can fruit cocktail, drained
1 lg. can pineapple chucks, drained
1 can mandarin oranges, drained (opt.)
2 or 3 apples, chopped
2 or 3 bananas, sliced
1 can peach pie filling

Combine all ingredients; mix well. Chill for several hours. Yield: 6-8 servings.

Mrs. Doris S. Johnson, Atlanta H. S.
Atlanta, Texas

FROZEN COCKTAIL CUPS

2 3-oz. packages cream cheese, softened
1 c. mayonnaise
1 No. 2½ can fruit cocktail, well drained
½ cup drained maraschino cherries, quartered
2½ c. miniature marshmallows
1 sm. carton Cool Whip
2 or 3 drops of red food coloring (opt.)

Blend cream cheese and mayonnaise. Stir in fruit cocktail, cherries and marshmallows. Fold in Cool Whip. Tint if desired. Pour mixture into paper-lined muffin tins or a freezer container. Freeze until firm, 6 hours or overnight. Serve on lettuce and garnish with cherries. Yield: 10-12 servings.

Mrs. Linda S. Martin, Land O' Lakes Sr. H. S.
Land O' Lakes, Florida

FAVORITE GOOSEBERRY SALAD

1 c. sugar
Dash of salt
2 c. drained gooseberries
1 pkg. lemon gelatin
3 bananas, sliced
1 c. finely cut marshmallows
½ c. chopped nuts

Combine sugar, salt and gooseberries in saucepan; heat slowly until sugar melts, stirring frequently. Let cool. Dissolve gelatin in 2 cups boiling water; chill until partially congealed. Combine all ingredients; pour into mold. Chill until firm.

Mrs. Austin Noblitt, Rockville H. S.
Rockville, Indiana

FIVE-CUP SALAD WITH PECANS

1 c. well-drained pineapple tidbits
1 c. flaked coconut
1 c. well-drained mandarin oranges
1 c. miniature marshmallows
1 c. sour cream
1 c. chopped pecans

Combine all ingredients; chill for several hours or overnight. Garnish with maraschino cherries. Yield: 6-8 servings.

Kay M. Goldsworthy, Southwest Jr. H. S.
Melbourne, Florida

FRUIT SALAD FOR A BUNCH

3 No. 303 cans pineapple chunks
3 cans mandarin oranges
5 Bananas, sliced
1 qt. peaches
2 red apples, unpeeled
2 boxes fresh strawberries
1 Jr.-size jar baby food fruit dessert

Drain canned fruit into bowl, reserving juice. Slice fresh fruit into reserved juice to prevent discoloration. Drain fresh fruit. Combine all ingredients; mix well. Chill until ready to serve.

J. Jean Robertson, Collegedale Academy
Collegedale, Tennessee

GREEN GRAPE SALAD

¼ c. mayonnaise
1 3-oz. package cream cheese, softened

Garlic salt to taste
1 lb. Thompson seedless green grapes

Whip mayonnaise into cream cheese; season with garlic salt. Fold grapes into cheese mixture. Chill until ready to serve. Yield: 4-6 servings.

Mrs. Emma L. Flake Van Laningham
Walnut Springs H. S.
Walnut Springs, Texas

GREEN PARTY SALAD

¼ lb. marshmallows
1 c. milk
1 3-oz. package lime gelatin
6 oz. cream cheese, softened
1 No. 2 can crushed pineapple
1 c. whipping cream, whipped
⅔ c. mayonnaise
1 c. chopped pecans (opt.)

Melt marshmallows in milk in top of double boiler. Pour hot mixture over lime gelatin; stir until dissolved. Stir in cream cheese until well blended. Add pineapple; cool. Blend in whipped cream, mayonnaise and pecans. Pour into glass dish. Chill until firm. Yield: 12 servings.

Olga M. Decker, Little Elm H. S.
Little Elm, Texas

HEAVENLY HASH

1 3-oz. package strawberry gelatin
1 pt. whipping cream
1 tsp. vanilla extract
4 tbsp. sugar
2 lg. bananas, sliced and cut into fourths
½ c. marshmallows, cut finely
1 c. pecans, finely broken
1 c. crushed pineapple, drained

Dissolve gelatin in 1½ cups hot water. Let cool until partially set. Whip cream, adding vanilla and sugar slowly. Set aside. Whip gelatin. Add whipped cream, bananas, marshmallows, pecans and pineapple; mix well. Pour into a serving dish. Chill until set. Yield: 10-12 servings.

Melinda Kinney, Moore Central Mid-H. S.
Moore, Oklahoma

LIME AND PINEAPPLE SALAD

1 3-oz. package lime Jell-O
12 marshmallows

1 3-oz. package cream cheese, softened
1 sm. can crushed pineapple
1 5-oz. can evaporated milk, chilled

Dissolve Jell-O in 1 cup hot water. Melt 12 marshmallows and cream cheese over low heat. Add cream cheese and marshmallow mixture to Jell-O; stir well. Add pineapple. Whip evaporated milk. Fold into fruit mixture. Chill until set. Yield: 6-8 servings.

Rachel Farmer, Springfield H. S.
Springfield, Tennessee

MULTITUDE-OF-SINS SALAD

1 pkg. lime Jell-O
2 c. miniature marshmallows
1 c. grated cheese
1½ c. chopped celery
1 No. 2 can crushed pineapple, drained
1 c. chopped nuts
2 tbsp. lemon juice
½ pt. whipping cream, whipped
⅓ c. mayonnaise

Stir Jell-O and marshmallows in 2 cups hot water until dissolved. Chill until mixture begins to thicken. Add cheese, celery, pineapple, nuts and lemon juice; blend well. Combine whipped cream and mayonnaise; blend into fruit mixture. Pour into 8 x 12 x 2-inch glass dish. Refrigerate at least 12 hours. Cut into squares to serve.

Betty C. Nutt, Lewis County H. S.
Hohenwald, Tennessee

NECTARINE SALAD

1 No. 2½ cans peeled nectarines
Juice of 4 lemons
Juice of 2 limes
1½ c. sugar
2 env. unflavored gelatin
2 3-oz. packages cream cheese, softened
½ c. chopped nuts
Mayonnaise

Drain nectarines, reserving juice. Heat juice in saucepan. Add sugar; stir until dissolved. Add lemon and lime juice. Pour ½ cup water over lemon and lime peelings; rub together. Strain; add gelatin. Add to hot mixture; stir until dissolved. Cool. Cream the cheese. Add nuts and enough mayonnaise to blend. Shape into balls. Place in center of each nectarine half. Place in individual salad molds with the smooth side of nectarine down. Fill each mold with gelatin mixture. Chill until firm. Unmold and place on a leaf of lettuce. Serve with additional mayonnaise on each

salad. Peach or apricot halves may be used instead of nectarines. Yield: 12 servings.

Mrs. Joe H. Rainey, Chester County H. S.
Henderson, Tennessee

MARY'S PINK SALAD

1 8-oz. carton lowfat cherry yogurt
1 9-oz. carton Cool Whip
1 c. miniature marshmallows
1 sm. can crushed pineapple, drained
½ c. chopped pecans

Combine all ingredients; mix well. Pour into glass serving dish. Chill until serving time. Yield: 4-6 servings.

Mary Fuller, John Tyler H. S.
Tyler, Texas

COMPANY FRUIT SALAD

1 c. cubed cantaloupe
1 c. cubed honeydew
1 c. cubed watermelon
3 bananas, sliced
1 c. salad dressing
½ c. frozen strawberries or raspberries, thawed

Combine fresh fruits in bowl. Mix salad dressing and frozen strawberries in mixer or blender. Spoon over fruit. Yield: 6 servings.

Lynn Knight, Marcos de Niza H. S.
Tempe, Arizona

FRESH FRUIT PARTY SALAD

1 ripe cantaloupe
1 grapefruit, sectioned
2 seedless oranges, sectioned
Endive or lettuce
½ c. fresh strawberries, blackberries, or sweet cherries

Cut cantaloupe into ½-inch rings. Chill grapefruit and orange sections. Arrange endive on salad plates. Place cantaloupe rings on endive. Arrange remaining fruits attractively in the center. Serve with French or fruit dressing. Yield: 4 servings.

Mrs. Edna M. Crawford,
Lamar County Comprehensive H. S.
Barnesville, Georgia

BEST-EVER SUMMER SALAD

½ watermelon
1 cantaloupe
1 honeydew melon
Chunk pineapple, grapes and strawberries
  (opt.)
½ c. sugar
1 tbsp. grated lemon rind
1 tbsp. grated orange rind
3 tbsp. lemon juice
2 tbsp. lime juice

Scoop balls from melons; toss fruits together. Combine remaining ingredients and ⅓ cup water in saucepan; bring to a boil. Boil for 5 minutes or until thickened, stirring constantly. Let cool thoroughly. Pour over fruits; let stand in refrigerator for several hours before serving. Serve in peeled melon rings, in lettuce cups or as centerpiece in watermelon shell. Yield: 10-15 servings.

Mary Jo Thompson, Ardmore H. S.
Ardmore, Alabama

SUMMER FRUIT TOSS

1 cantaloupe
1 bunch white seedless grapes
1 sm. can pineapple chunks, drained
2 lg. bananas, chunked
¼ c. honey
⅛ c. fresh lime juice
Dash of salt

Scoop balls from cantaloupe; toss fruits together. Combine remaining ingredients for honey dressing; beat until well mixed. Pour over fruits; toss carefully. Yield: 4 servings.

Mrs. Cilicia H. Burden, Butler County H. S.
Morgantown, Kentucky

NECTARINE FLUFF DELIGHT

1 env. unflavored gelatin
1 tsp. vanilla extract
¼ tsp. salt
½ c. sugar
3 egg whites
1 c. diced fresh nectarines
Creamy Fruit Sauce:

Soften gelatin in ¼ cup cold water; dissolve in ¾ cup boiling water. Stir in vanilla, salt and sugar. Chill until partially congealed. Add egg whites; beat until thick. Fold in nectarines; pour into 8½ x 4½-inch pan. Chill until firm. Serve with Creamy Fruit Sauce;

garnish with nectarines, if desired. Yield: 4-6 servings.

Creamy Fruit Sauce

½ c. butter
3 egg yolks, slightly beaten
½ c. sugar
¼ tsp. salt
⅓ c. light cream
1 tbsp. grated lemon rind
2 tbsp. lemon juice
2 c. diced nectarines

Melt butter in top of double boiler. Combine egg yolks, sugar, salt and cream; stir into butter. Cook, stirring constantly, until thick. Remove from heat; add lemon rind and juice. Stir in nectarines. Chill thoroughly.

Lucille Johnson, Dunlap Township H. S.
Dunlap, Illinois

CHEESEY-ORANGE SALAD

1 sm. can crushed pineapple
1¼ c. sugar
1 3-oz. package orange Jell-O
¾ c. Cheddar cheese, grated
¾ c. chopped pecans
½ pt. whipping cream, whipped

Combine crushed pineapple with sugar and 1 cup water in a saucepan. Bring to a boil. Mix with Jell-O. Stir until dissolved. Pour into mold or glass dish. Chill until partially set. Add grated cheese, pecans and whipped cream; Mix well. Chill until firm.

Mrs. Willene Bott, East Bernard H. S.
East Bernard, Texas

ALMA'S ORANGE SALAD

2 3-oz. packages orange Jell-O
1 lg. can crushed pineapple
1 can mandarin oranges
1 pkg. lemon instant pudding mix
1 pkg. Dream Whip

Dissolve Jell-O in 1½ cups hot water. Drain pineapple and oranges, reserving juices. Add 1½ cups reserved juices to Jell-O; stir well. Pour into 9 x 12-inch Pyrex dish. Chill until slightly thickened. Add pineappple and oranges. Chill until firm. Prepare pudding mix and Dream Whip according to package directions. Combine pudding and Dream Whip; blend well. Spread over salad. Chill for several hours. Cut into squares to serve. Yield: 8-12 servings.

Alma C. McGimsey, McDowell H. S.
Marion, North Carolina

GOLDEN FRUIT FREEZE

1 11-oz. can mandarin oranges
1 8-oz. can crushed pineapple
¼ c. sugar
1 c. small-curd cream cottage cheese
1 2-oz. package dessert topping mix
½ c. milk
1 tsp. vanilla extract
⅓ c. mayonnaise

Combine fruit and sugar. Combine cottage cheese, dessert topping mix, milk and vanilla; beat until smooth. Fold in fruit and mayonnaise. Turn into 8 x 8 x 2-inch pan. Freeze. Let stand at room temperature for 15 minutes. Cut into squares. Serve on lettuce.

Sharon Coward, Ocean Springs H. S.
Ocean Springs, Mississippi

MANDARIN ORANGE SALAD DELUXE

2 cans mandarin oranges
1 med. can crushed pineapple
2 sm. packages Jell-O
1 sm. can frozen orange juice
1 pkg. instant lemon pudding mix
1 c. milk
1 sm. package Dream Whip

Drain oranges and pineapple, reserving juice. Dissolve Jell-O in 2 cups hot water. Stir in reserved juice, orange juice, pineapple and oranges. Pour mixture into 9 x 13-inch glass dish or mold. Chill until firm. Combine pudding mix with milk, mix well. Prepare Dream Whip according to package directions. Combine 2 mixtures; mix well. Spread topping over Jell-O layer. Chill until set. Yield: 8-10 servings.

Helen Borders, Burns Sr. H. S.
Lawndale, North Carolina

MY MAN'S SALAD

1 3-oz. package orange Jell-O
1 9-oz. package Cool Whip
1 8-oz. carton sour cream
1 c. coconut
2 8-oz. cans mandarin oranges, drained
1 6-oz. can pineapple chunks, drained
½ c. chopped pecans

Blend Jell-O, Cool Whip, sour cream and coconut in large bowl. Add oranges, pineapple and pecans to Cool Whip mixture. Fold gently until all ingredients are blended. Chill. Yield: 6-8 servings.

Karen Love, J. L. Williams Jr. H. S.
Copperas Cove, Texas

ORANGE-AVOCADO SALAD

1 pkg. lemon gelatin
2 tbsp. sugar
1 tsp. vinegar
1 can mandarin oranges, drained
1 avocado, diced
1 tbsp. diced pimento
1 tbsp. grated lemon rind
1 tsp. grated orange rind

Dissolve gelatin in 1 cup boiling water; add ⅔ cup cold water, sugar and vinegar. Chill until partially congealed. Add remaining ingredients; chill until firm. Yield: 8 servings.

Mrs. Alma Martin, St. Maries H. S.
St. Maries, Idaho

ORANGE DELIGHT

1 3-oz. package orange gelatin
1 c. vanilla ice cream
3 tbsp. orange juice
1 9-oz. can crushed pineapple with juice
½ c. chopped pecans
1 can mandarin oranges, drained

Dissolve gelatin in ¾ cup boiling water; stir in ice cream and orange juice. Chill until partially congealed. Stir in pineapple and pecans; pour into 1-quart mold. Chill until firm. Garnish each serving with mandarin orange sections. Yield: 6 servings.

Doris C. Sporleder, Hall H. S.
Spring Valley, Illinois

ORANGE SALAD SUPREME

1 lg. package orange Jell-O
1 6-oz. can frozen orange juice
1 lg. can crushed pineapple, drained
2 cans mandarin oranges, drained
1 c. whipping cream, whipped
1 c. milk
1 pkg. vanilla instant pudding mix
Ground pecans

Dissolve Jell-O in 2 cups boiling water. Add orange juice, pineapple and oranges. Pour into mold or pyrex dish. Chill until firm. Combine whipped cream, milk and pudding mix. Spread over Jell-O layer. Garnish with pecans. Chill.

Mrs. Barbara McCoy, Booneville H. S.
Booneville, Mississippi

TEN-MINUTE ORANGE FRUIT SALAD

2 pkg. orange gelatin
1 pkg. lemon gelatin
2 6-oz. cans frozen orange juice concentrate
1 8-oz. can crushed pineapple with juice
3 bananas, mashed
2 c. whipped cream

Dissolve gelatins in 1½ cups boiling water. Add orange juice concentrate; stir until dissolved. Stir in pineapple. Chill until partially congealed. Fold in bananas and whipped cream. Chill until firm. Yield: 12 servings.

Ruth E. Kuhn, La Conner H. S.
La Conner, Washington

PEACH GLOW

1 No. 2 can peaches
1 pkg. orange gelatin
½ tsp. almond extract

Drain peaches; reserve juice. Dice peaches. Add enough water to reserved peach juice to measure 1 cup liquid. Dissolve gelatin in 1 cup boiling water; stir in peach juice and almond extract. Chill until partially congealed. Fold in peaches. Chill until firm.

Claudia Bringle, University H. S.
Iowa City, Iowa

SPICED PEACH MOLD

2 lg. jars spiced peaches
2 pkg. orange or lemon gelatin
2 cans white seedless grapes, drained
1 No. 2 can pineapple tidbits, drained
1 c. chopped almonds or pecans

Drain peaches; reserve juice. Dice peaches. Bring 2½ cups reserved peach juice to a boil. Pour into gelatin; stir until gelatin is dissolved. Chill until partially congealed. Combine peaches, grapes and pineapple; stir into gelatin. Add almonds; pour into mold. Chill until firm. Yield: 10-12 servings.

Myrtis L. McAlhany, St. George H. S.
St. George, South Carolina

STUFFED PEACH SALAD

1 3-oz. package cream cheese, softened
½ c. mayonnaise
½ c. chopped pecans
¼ c. chopped maraschino cherries
1 c. whipped cream

12 peach halves
Red food coloring
6 whole cloves

Combine cream cheese, mayonnaise, pecans and cherries; mix well. Fold in whipped cream. Fill centers of half the peaches with cream cheese mixture; top with remaining peaches to make 6 whole peaches. Mix a small amount of food coloring with water; brush over part of each peach to produce a blush. Insert 1 clove in each peach for stem. Chill until ready to serve. Yield: 6 servings.

Mrs. Willie Fay Spurlock, M. C. Napier H. S.
Hazard, Kentucky

FRESH PEAR SALAD AND DRESSING

2 tbsp. flour
½ c. sugar
2 tbsp. lemon juice
2 c. diced fresh pears
1 c. diced celery
⅓ c. chopped pecans

Combine flour, sugar and lemon juice in saucepan. Cook over low heat until dressing is thick and clear. Cool thoroughly. Stir pears and celery into dressing; add pecans. Serve on salad greens; garnish with maraschino cherries. Yield: 4 servings.

Mrs. Margaret Thornton, Thorndale H. S.
Thorndale, Texas

PEAR-CHEESE SALAD

3 pkg. lime gelatin
1 lg. package cream cheese, crumbled
1 lg. can pears with juice
1 c. chopped pecans

Mix gelatin and cream cheese together. Add 3 cups boiling water, beat with electric mixer at low speed until cream cheese is melted. Chill until partially congealed. Beat pears with electric mixer; stir pears and pecans into gelatin mixture. Chill until firm. Yield: 10-12 servings.

Mrs. Roceil Graves, Leakey H. S.
Leakey, Texas

CONGEALED PEAR SALAD

1 No. 303 can pear halves
1 sm. package lime Jell-O
1 8-oz. package cream cheese, softened
6 to 8 maraschino cherries
½ c. pecans

1 sm. package Dream Whip
½ c. milk

Drain pears. Add enough water to pear juice to measure 1 cup. Bring to a boil. Dissolve Jell-O in boiling liquid. Blend in cream cheese until smooth. Chill until thickened. Add chopped pears, cherries and pecans. Prepare Dream Whip with milk according to package directions. Fold into pear mixture. Chill until set.

Anita Stubblefield, Rivercrest H. S.
Bogata, Texas

PEAR-PINEAPPLE SALAD

1 lg. can chunk pineapple
1 lg. can pears, diced
1 c. sugar
4 tbsp. flour
3 egg yolks
1 egg
1 lg. Cool Whip
1 c. grated cheese

Drain fruit, reserving juice. Combine sugar and flour. Beat eggs together. Add sugar mixture; mix well. Stir into juice in saucepan. Bring to a boil, stirring constantly. Cool. Pour over fruit in glass dish. Top with Cool Whip and cheese. Chill. Yield: 8 servings.

Antoinette H. Kincade, Lake Local Schools
Millbury, Ohio

PINK-LADY-DAY SALAD

1 c. crushed pineapple, drained
1 lg. package strawberry Jell-O
1 sm. package miniature marshmallows
1 c. small-curd cottage cheese
1 c. chopped pecans

Drain pineapple, reserving juice. Add enough water to juice to measure required amount of liquid for dissolving Jell-O. Dissolve Jell-O in saucepan according to package directions. Add marshmallows to mixture. Place saucepan over medium heat; stir until marshmallows are melted. Allow mixture to cool for 10 minutes. Add remaining ingredients; mix thoroughly. Pour mixture into mold. Chill until set.

Gracie Marie Yarbrough,
Robertson County Vocational Center
Springfield, Tennessee

CREAMY PINEAPPLE LOOPS

1 3-oz. package cream cheese, softened
¼ c. mayonnaise

2 tbsp. pineapple juice
1 banana, sliced
4 maraschino cherries, cut in fourths
¼ c. chopped nuts
8 pineapple slices, drained

Blend cream cheese, mayonnaise and pineapple juice until smooth. Fold in bananas, cherries and nuts. Arrange 2 pineapple slices by making a slit thru ring, looping into the other on a bed of crisp greens. Pile cream cheese-fruit mixture to one side or place 1 spoonful in the center of each ring. Yield: 4 servings.

Mrs. Marjorie Little, Silver Lake Regional H. S.
Pembroke, Massachuetts

FRENCH PINEAPPLE SALAD

1 lg. pineapple
Sugar to taste
1 lg. orange, peeled and sectioned
2 peaches, sliced
1 banana, sliced diagonally
1 apple, sliced
1 pt. strawberries, hulled and sweetened
1 c. pecan halves

Cut pineapple in half lengthwise, keeping frond intact. Scoop out fruit; set shells aside. Cut pineapple into cubes; sprinkle lightly with sugar. Combine pineapple cubes with remaining ingredients; chill for 30 minutes. Pile pineapple mixture lightly into pineapple shells. Yield: 6-8 servings.

Mrs. Marvel E. Wax, Bel Air H. S.
El Paso, Texas

TABASCO-FRUIT SALAD

1 lg. pineapple
2 tbsp. frozen orange juice concentrate,
    thawed
¾ tsp. salt
½ tsp. sugar
¼ tsp. Tabasco
1 tbsp. lemon juice
½ c. mayonnaise
½ c. sour cream
3 or 4 oranges, sectioned
1 sm. grapefruit, sectioned
Strawberry halves or raspberries
1 or 2 bananas, sliced
Melon balls (opt.)

Halve pineapple lengthwise through the green top. Scoop out fruit; cut into cubes. Blend orange juice concentrate, salt, sugar, Tabasco and lemon juice into mayonnaise. Stir in sour cream. Arrange fruit in pineapple halves. Serve with sour cream dressing. Yield: 6-8 servings.

Photograph for this recipe on page 51.

HAWAIIAN FRUIT SALAD

1 c. fresh pineapple cubes
1 c. white seedless grapes
1 c. cubed cantaloupe
1 c. fresh shredded coconut
½ c. whipped cream

Combine pineapple, grapes, cantaloupe and coconut. Toss lightly with whipped cream. Yield: 8-10 servings.

Mrs. Daisy Massey, Fredericksburg H. S.
Fredericksburg, Texas

PINEAPPLE BOATS

4 fresh pineapples
2 oranges, sectioned
2 bananas, sliced diagonally
1 pt. whole strawberries
1 8-oz. package cream cheese, softened

Cut pineapples in half lengthwise, keeping fronds intact. Scoop out fruit, leaving ½-inch shells. Discard cores; dice pineapple, reserving juice. Combine fruits; fill shells; garnish with mint. Stir cream cheese and reserved juice together until smooth; serve with pineapple boats. Yield: 8 servings.

Mrs. Harriett S. Reed, Milltown School
Milltown, Indiana

PISTACHIO SALAD

1 sm. package pistachio instant pudding mix
1 No. 2 can crushed pineapple
1 med. carton Cool Whip
1 sm. package marshmallows
1 c. coconut
1 c. chopped pecans

Combine all ingredients in order listed. Chill for several hours. Yield: 10-12 servings.

Bettye T. Pate, Weston H. S.
Jonesboro, Louisiana

WATERGATE SALAD

1 sm. package instant pistachio pudding mix
20 oz. crushed pineapple and juice
9 oz. Cool Whip
1 c. chopped nuts
1 c. miniature marshmallows

Combine all ingredients; mix well. Chill for 2 to 3 hours before serving.

Kay Hepler, Pine Tree H. S.
Longview, Texas

RASPBERRIES AND MELON BALLS

2 10-oz. packages frozen raspberries, thawed
2 pkg. raspberry gelatin
½ c. lemon juice
1 c. watermelon balls

Drain raspberries; add enough water to raspberry syrup to measure 1½ cups liquid. Dissolve gelatin in 2 cups boiling water; stir in raspberry syrup, lemon juice and raspberries. Chill until partially set. Add melon balls. Pour into individual molds or 9-inch square pan. Chill until firm. Yield: 9 servings.

Mrs. Stephanie T. Mulford, Salem, H. S.
Salem, New Jersey

RED RASPBERRY SALAD

2 3-oz. packages raspberry gelatin
2 pkgs. frozen red raspberries
1 c. crushed pineapple
1 banana, sliced
1 pt. sour cream

Dissolve gelatin in 2 cups hot water. Add frozen raspberries. Comtinue stirring until raspberries are thawed and gelatin begins to congeal. Add crushed pineapple and banana. Place layer of gelatin mixture in mold. Chill until set; cover with layer of sour cream. Place remaining gelatin on top. Chill until set. Unmold to serve. Yield: 10-12 servings.

Nelle Alspaugh, Eastbrook H. S.
Marion, Indiana

PINK DELIGHT SALAD

1 3-oz. package raspberry gelatin
1 8-oz. package cream cheese, softened
1 1-lb. can crushed pineapple
1 c. broken walnuts

Dissolve gelatin in 1 cup boiling water. Blend in cream cheese thoroughly. Add pineapple and walnuts. Refrigerate until set. Yield: 8 servings.

Joyce Skidmore, Alvin H. S.
Alvin, Texas

RED RASPBERRY RING

1 10-oz. package frozen raspberries, thawed
2 3-oz. packages red raspberry gelatin
1 pt. vanilla ice cream
1 6-oz. can frozen pink lemonade concentrate, thawed
¼ c. chopped pecans

Drain raspberries; reserve syrup. Dissolve gelatin in 2 cups boiling water. Add ice cream by spoonfuls, stirring until melted. Stir in lemonade concentrate and reserved raspberry syrup. Chill until partially congealed. Add raspberries and pecans; turn into 6-cup ring mold. Chill until firm. Yield: 8-10 servings.

Mrs. Eugene Romsos, Barron Sr. H. S.
Barron, Wisconsin

SPECIAL SALAD

2 pkgs. lemon Jell-O
1½ c. diced apples
3 bananas, diced or sliced
1 sm. can crushed pineapple
2½ tbsp. cornstarch
½ c. sugar
Juice of 1 lemon
1 c. pineapple juice
1 c. whipping cream, whipped

Prepare Jell-O according to package directions using 3¾ cups water. Chill until slightly set. Add apples, bananas and crushed pineapple. Place in glass dish; chill until set. Combine cornstarch, sugar, lemon and pineapple juices in top of double boiler. Cook until thickened. Cool. Fold in whipped cream. Place over Jell-O layer. Cool completely. Cut in squares and serve. Yield: 10-12 servings.

Carol Robinson, Berea H. S.
Berea, Ohio

SURPRISE SALAD

1 head lettuce, shredded
1 c. chopped celery
1 tbsp. minced parsley
2 green onions and tops, sliced
1 or 2 cans mandarin oranges, drained
½ tsp. salt
2 tbsp. vinegar
¼ c. oil
¼ tsp. Tabasco sauce
6 tbsp. sugar
Dash of pepper
½ c. slivered almonds, blanched

Combine lettuce, celery, parsley, green onions and oranges in a large salad bowl. Combine salt, vinegar, oil, Tabasco sauce, 2 tablespoons sugar and pepper. Melt 4 tablespoons sugar in a heavy skillet over low heat. Add almonds. Heat sugar until melted and slightly brown. Stir to coat almonds well. Cool on foil. Break apart when cool. Add caramelized almonds to lettuce mixture just before serving. Toss with dressing. Yield: 6 servings.

Betty Sievert, Tartan H. S.
St. Paul, Minnesota

CREAMY STRAWBERRY SALAD

1 3-oz. package strawberry gelatin
1 10-oz. package frozen strawberries, thawed
1 pt. strawberry ice cream
1 c. whipped cream
½ c. chopped pecans
3 bananas, sliced

Pour 1 cup boiling water over gelatin; stir until dissolved. Add strawberries; chill until partially congealed. Beat ice cream until smooth. Add gelatin; mix well. Fold in whipped cream until just blended. Add pecans and bananas; pour into 9 x 13-inch dish or into individual molds. Chill until firm. Yield: 15 servings.

Mrs. Estella Hottel, Dimmitt H. S.
Dimmitt, Texas

JESSI'S STRAWBERRY SALAD

1 8-oz. can pineapple
2 pkg. strawberry Jell-O
2 10-oz. packages frozen strawberries
1 c. chopped pecans
1 carton sour cream
1 pkg. Dream Whip, prepared

Drain pineapple, reserving juice. Add enough water to juice to measure 1 cup. Bring juice to a boil. Dissolve Jell-O in that juice. Add strawberries, pineapple and pecans. Pour half the mixture in a glass dish. Chill until set. Spread sour cream over Jell-O. Pour remaining Jell-O over sour cream. Chill until set. Serve topped with Dream Whip.

Jessi Casto, Church Hill H. S.
Church Hill, Tennessee

KAY'S STRAWBERRY SALAD

2 pkgs. strawberry Jell-O
2 10-oz. packages strawberries, frozen
1 sm. can crushed pineapple and juice
2 bananas, sliced
1 8-oz. carton sour cream

Prepare 1 package Jell-O, using 1 cup hot water and half the fruit. Let stand until congealed. Spread on sour cream layer. Prepare remaining package of Jell-O, using 1 cup hot water and remaining fruit. Pour over sour cream. Chill until firm.

Kay H. Worsham, Chattooga H. S.
Summerville, Georgia

STARLA'S STRAWBERRY SALAD

1 15-oz. can crushed pineapple
1 pkg. strawberry Jell-O
1 8-oz. carton (large-curd) cottage cheese
1 med. carton Cool Whip

Pour pineapple with juice into a saucepan. Bring to a boil. Dissolve Jell-O in hot mixture. Refrigerate until slightly thick. Stir in cottage cheese and Cool Whip. Pour into serving dish. Chill until set. Yield: 12-15 servings.

Starla Kizer, North Side Jr. H. S.
Jackson, Tennessee

STRAWBERRY-BANANA SALAD

1 lg. package strawberry-banana Jell-O
2 10-oz. packages frozen sliced strawberries, thawed
5 or 6 bananas, mashed
1 tbsp. lemon juice
1 c. chopped pecans
1 sm. can crushed pineapple
1 pt. sour cream

Dissolve Jell-O in 2 cups hot water. Let cool. Add strawberries, bananas, lemon juice, pecans and pineapple. Pour half the mixture into 13 x 9 x 2-inch glass dish. Chill until firm. Spread with sour cream. Pour remaining mixture on top. Chill until firm. Yield: 12 servings.

Marialice Tatom, Dougherty Jr. H. S.
Albany, Georgia

JANICE'S STRAWBERRY-BANANA SALAD

1 lg. package strawberry Jell-O
1 10-oz. package strawberries
1 sm. can crushed pineapple
4 bananas, mashed
1 pkg. chopped pecans
1 8-oz. carton sour cream

Combine Jell-O and 1½ cups hot water until dissolved. Combine remaining ingredients except sour cream; mix well. Pour ½ of the mixture into 8-inch square glass dish. Freeze for 45 minutes. Whip sour cream. Spread over frozen mixture. Pour remaining Jell-O over sour cream. Refrigerate until set. Yield: 8 servings.

Janice Schaffer, Hudson Sr. H. S.
New Port Richey, Florida

STRAWBERRY DELIGHT

1 6-oz. package strawberry Jell-O
1 20-oz. can crushed pineapple
1 pkg. frozen strawberries
1 c. sour cream

Dissolve Jell-O in 2 cups boiling water. Add frozen berries. Stir until thawed. Add pineapple. Pour half the mixture into a mold. Refrigerate until firm. Spread sour cream over Jell-O layer. Add remaining Jell-O mixture. Refrigerate until firm.

June Fallon, St. Mary's H. S.
Phoenix, Arizona

STRAWBERRY LAYER SALAD

1 3-oz. package strawberry Jell-O
1 10-oz. package frozen sliced strawberries, partially thawed
1 8¼-oz. can crushed pineapple, drained
2 med. bananas, mashed
½ c. finely chopped pecans
½ pkg. cheesecake filling mix
¾ c. milk

Stir gelatin in ¾ cup boiling water until dissolved. Stir in fruits and pecans. Pour half the gelatin mixture into 8 x 8-inch pyrex pan. Chill until firm. Store remaining gelatin mixture at room temperature. Mix cheesecake filling mix with milk; mix well. Spoon cheesecake filling over congealed fruit mixture. Spoon remaining gelatin mixture over filling. Chill until firm. Cut into squares to serve. Garnish with lettuce leaf. Yield: 9 servings.

Mrs. Katherine Knippers, Many H. S.
Many, Louisiana

STRAWBERRY-NUT SALAD

2 3-oz. packages strawberry gelatin
2 10-oz. packages frozen sliced strawberries
1 1-lb. 4-oz. can crushed pineapple, drained
3 med. bananas, mashed
1 c. chopped nuts
1 pt. sour cream

Combine gelatin with 1 cup boiling water in large bowl, stirring until dissolved. Fold in strawberries with juice, pineapple, bananas and nuts. Turn half the strawberry mixture into 12 x 8-inch dish. Refrigerate until firm. Spread with sour cream and remaining strawberry mixture. Chill until set.

Sandra Ford, Northeast Mississippi, Jr. College
Booneville, Mississippi

STRAWBERRY WHIRL SALAD

3 sm. packages strawberry Jell-O
2 c. miniature marshmallows
1 c. crushed pineapple and juice
2 pkg. frozen strawberries
1 c. chopped pecans
3 tbsp. mayonnaise

Dissolve Jell-O in 2 cups boiling water. Add marshmallows; stir until melted. Add 5 ice cubes, stirring until melted. Chill until slightly thick. Add pineapple, strawberries, pecans and mayonnaise. Spooon into 9-inch mold. Chill until firm. Yield: 8-10 servings.

Mrs. Willie Dean McLaurin, South Leake H. S.
Walnut Grove, Mississippi

SANDRA'S STRAWBERRY SALAD

2 sm. packages strawberry Jell-O
1 10-oz. package unsweetened frozen
  strawberries
3 bananas, mashed
1 sm. can crushed pineapple
1 sm. carton sour cream

Dissolve Jell-O in 2 cups boiling water. Add frozen strawberries; stir until thawed. Add bananas, crushed pineapple; mix well. Pour half the mixture into bowl. Chill until set. Spread with sour cream. Pour remaining mixture over all. Refrigerate until set. Cut into squares to serve.

Sandra Bell, William James Jr. H. S.
White Bluff, Tennessee

THREE-FRUIT STRAWBERRY SALAD

2 3-oz. packages strawberry gelatin
2 10-oz. packages frozen strawberries
1½ c. crushed pineapple
2 bananas, diced
2 tbsp. lemon juice
1½ c. sour cream

Dissolve gelatin in 2 cups boiling water. Add strawberries; stir until thawed. Add pineapple, bananas and lemon juice. Pour into 7-cup mold. Chill until firm. Remove from refrigerator. Spread sour cream thinly over top. Yield: 8 servings.

Oleta Hayden, Milford H. S.
Milford, Texas

ASHEVILLE SALAD

4 pkg. unflavored gelatin
2 8-oz. packages cream cheese
2 cans tomato soup
1 c. finely chopped celery
1 c. finely chopped onion
1 c. finely chopped green pepper
½ c. chopped pecans
1 c. mayonnaise

Soften gelatin in ⅛ cup cold water. Heat cream cheese and soup together until cheese is melted. Add gelatin; stir until dissolved. Chill until partially congealed. Stir in remaining ingredients; pour into large ring mold or individual molds. Chill until firm. Serve on lettuce, topped with mayonnaise, if desired. Yield: 16 servings.

Mrs. Alice Harvard, Effingham County H. S.
Springfield, Georgia

ARTICHOKE-GRAPEFRUIT SALAD

1 head green lettuce
1 bunch endive
1 can artichoke hearts, drained
2 onions, sliced and separated into rings
2 grapefruit, sectioned
Garlic French dressing or Roquefort dressing

Make a nest of lettuce and endive. Place artichoke hearts, onion rings and grapefruit sections in nest. Pour dressing over top. Yield: 6 servings.

Monna S. Ray, George Washington H. S.
Alexandria, Virginia

ARTICHOKE-MUSHROOM SALAD

1 8-oz. can artichoke hearts, drained
2 c. sliced fresh mushrooms
1 c. diagonally sliced celery
½ c. pitted green olives
¼ c. cider vinegar
1 tsp. salt
¼ tsp. pepper
½ tsp. sugar

Cut artichoke hearts into bite-sized pieces. Combine with remaining vegetables. Mix vinegar and seasonings. Pour over vegetables; toss lightly. Refrigerate for at least 1 hour. Serve on romaine leaves. Yield: 6 servings.

Marjory M. Peters, Talawanda H. S.
Oxford, Ohio

GREEN GODDESS SALAD BOWL

1 pkg. lime gelatin
1½ tsp. garlic salt
Dash of pepper
¾ c. sour cream
¼ c. mayonnaise
1 tbsp. vinegar
1 2-oz. can anchovies, minced
1 9-oz. package frozen artichoke hearts
1 grapefruit, sectioned
1 c. diced tomatoes
½ c. sliced olives
¼ c. chopped green onions
3 qts. torn salad greens
1 c. French dressing

Dissolve gelatin and garlic salt in ¾ cup boiling water. Add pepper, sour cream, mayonnaise, vinegar and anchovies; beat with rotary beater until well blended. Pour into loaf pan; chill until firm. Cook artichoke hearts according to package directions; drain. Cut each artichoke heart in half; chill. Combine grapefruit, tomatoes, olives, green onions and salad greens; chill thoroughly. Combine artichoke hearts and salad greens mixture; toss lightly with French dressing. Cut gelatin into 1-inch cubes; arrange on top of salad to serve. Yield: 10 servings.

Betty Pate, Clinton H. S.
Clinton, Arkansas

ASPARAGUS-RADISH SALAD

Fresh green asparagus
3 tbsp. olive oil
1 tbsp. vinegar
1 tsp. salt
Freshly ground pepper to taste
1 sm. clove of garlic, crushed
20 to 25 radishes, thinly sliced
Salad greens

Cook asparagus until tender; chill thoroughly. Combine oil, vinegar, salt, pepper and garlic. Add radishes; marinate for 2 to 3 hours. Place asparagus on salad greens; arrange radishes over asparagus. Spoon marinade over radishes; serve immediately. Yield: 4 servings.

Mrs. Aussie A. Miller, Newton H. S.
Newton, Texas

ASPARAGUS WITH ALMONDS

1 pkg. unflavored gelatin
1 can asparagus
1 tsp. salt
2 tbsp. lemon juice
½ c. mayonnaise
1 c. almonds
½ c. whipped cream

Soften gelatin in ¼ cup cold water. Drain asparagus; reserve juice. Add enough water to reserved juice to measure 1 cup liquid; pour into saucepan. Bring to a boil. Add gelatin; stir until dissolved. Stir in salt, lemon juice and mayonnaise; chill until partially congealed. Add asparagus and almonds. Fold in whipped cream. Pour into mold; chill until firm. Serve with mayonnaise mixed with a small amount of lemon juice, if desired. Yield: 8-10 servings.

Mrs. J. W. Gant, White County H. S.
Sparta, Tennessee

ASPARAGUS SALAD MOLD

1 tbsp. unflavored gelatin
1 c. hot asparagus liquid
2 tbsp. minced onion
2 tbsp. lemon juice
1 tsp. salt
½ tsp. Accent
Few drops of Tabasco sauce
2 c. diced asparagus
1 c. chopped celery
4 hard-cooked eggs, chopped
1 c. sour cream or mayonnaise

Soak gelatin in ½ cup cold water. Dissolve gelatin in asparagus liquid. Add onion, lemon juice, salt, Accent and Tabasco sauce. Chill until mixture begins to thicken. Add asparagus, celery, eggs and sour cream. Pour into ring mold or large cake pan. Chill until firm. Unmold and serve on bed of lettuce. Yield: 12 servings.

Jane L. Fieldcamp, Alief Ind. School District
Alief, Texas

GUACAMOLE SALAD

2 lg. avocados
1 lb. tomato, peeled
1 lg. onion, diced
3 tbsp. mayonnaise
1 tbsp. salad oil
2 tsp. chili powder
2 tsp. sugar
Salt and pepper to taste
4 dashes of Tabasco sauce

Peel and mash avocados; chop and drain tomato. Combine avocados, tomato and onion in bowl. Add remaining ingredients; mix well. Serve immediately on shredded lettuce. Yield: 4 servings.

Mrs. Joyce Nance, Nixon H. S.
Nixon, Texas

AVOCADO SALAD SUPREME

1 pkg. lime Jell-O
1 c. mashed avocado
¼ c. finely diced cucumber
½ c. whipped cream
¼ c. mayonnaise
½ c. honey
½ c. lime juice
Pinch of ginger (opt.)

Dissolve Jell-O in 2 cups boiling water. Chill until partially congealed. Stir gently; add next 4 ingredients. Combine remaining ingredients; mix well. Pour honey dressing over salad. Garnish with mandarin oranges.

Janet K. Alvord, Gilmanton H. S.
Gilmanton, Wisconsin

TOSSED AVOCADO SALAD

2 lg. tomatoes, chopped
3 avocados, sliced
1 sm. onion, diced
1 tsp. salt
½ tsp. pepper
½ tsp. garlic salt
1 head lettuce, torn into bite-sized pieces
2 tbsp. oil
2 tbsp. vinegar

Toss first 7 ingredients in large salad bowl. Combine oil and vinegar; mix well. Pour over salad. Toss lightly. Serve immediately. Yield: 6 servings.

Sandra Tanner, Troy H. S.
Troy, Texas

CREAMY WAX BEAN SALAD

2 No. 303 cans wax beans
4 hard-cooked eggs
¼ c. minced green pepper
¼ c. minced onion
1 tbsp. vinegar
1 tbsp. cream
¾ c. mayonnaise

Drain beans; dice 3 of the eggs. Place beans, green pepper, onion and diced eggs in bowl. Combine remaining ingredients; mix well. Pour over bean mixture; toss carefully. Chill until ready to serve. Garnish with slices of remaining egg. Yield: 4-6 servings.

Elaine Kirkpatrick, T. L. Handy H. S.
Bay City, Michigan

CRUNCHY BEAN SALAD

1 No. 303 French-style green beans
1 No. 303 can tiny green peas
1 No. 303 can Chinese vegetables
1 sm. can water chestnuts, sliced
3 c. vinegar
1 c. sugar
1 tsp. salt
Pepper to taste
1½ c. chopped celery
3 med. onions, sliced

Drain vegetables, reserving liquids. Add vinegar, sugar, salt and pepper to reserved liquids. Combine all ingredients; mix well. Refrigerate overnight before serving. Will keep for several days in refrigerator.

Mary N. Vaughn, Connelly Jr. H. S.
Lewisburg, Tennessee

FOUR-BEAN SALAD

1 can green beans, drained
1 can wax beans, drained
1 can kidney beans, rinsed and drained
1 can garbanzo beans, drained
1 lg. purple onion, sliced in rings
1 green pepper, sliced in rings
⅓ c. vinegar
½ c. oil
⅔ c. sugar
Salt and pepper to taste

Mix beans together in bowl. Place onion and green pepper slices on top of beans. Combine vinegar, oil, sugar, salt and pepper; pour over beans. Let stand overnight. Yield: 12 servings.

Verona Wegley, Beach H. S.
Beach, North Dakota

CHILLED LIMA BEAN SALAD

2 pkg. frozen baby lima beans
2 tbsp. garlic vinegar
2 tbsp. salad oil
2 tsp. sugar
2 tbsp. chopped parsley or parsley flakes
2 tsp. salt
1 c. sour cream

Cook lima beans according to package directions, omitting salt. Drain well. Add remaining ingredients in order listed to hot beans. Chill overnight. Serve from lettuce-lined bowl. Yield: 8 servings.

Faye Quinley, Corsicana H. S.
Corsicana, Texas

GREEN BEAN SALAD WITH BACON

1 lb. fresh or canned green beans
4 slices bacon, fried and crumbled
1 sm. red onion, sliced
2 tbsp. vegetable oil
1 tbsp. sugar
½ tbsp. pepper
⅛ tsp. thyme
3 tbsp. cider vinegar

Cut beans crosswise into 1-inch pieces. Cook in 1 inch boiling water until tender-crisp, about 7 minutes. Do not salt. Drain; cool. Mix beans, bacon and onion slices, reserving a small amount of bacon and onion for garnish. Measure remaining ingredients into a small bowl. Mix until sugar is dissolved. Toss with bean mixture. Place in serving bowl; cover. Refrigerate for 1 hour. Toss again just before serving. Garnish with reserved bacon and onion.

Marcia Barkemeyer, Granger H. S.
Granger, Texas

OVERNIGHT GREEN BEAN SALAD

⅔ c. vinegar
⅔ c. cooking oil
⅔ c. sugar
1 No. 2 can French-style beans, drained
1 No. 2 can bean sprouts, drained

Combine vinegar, oil and sugar in saucepan; bring to a boil. Add beans and bean sprouts; bring to a boil. Simmer for about 5 minutes. Cool. Let stand in dressing overnight. Drain before serving. Yield: 6 servings.

Mrs. W. B. Killebrew, Port Neches Jr. H. S.
Port Neches, Texas

BEAN TRIO SALAD

1 No. 2 can wax beans
1 No. 2 can green beans
1 No. 2 can red kidney beans
1 lg. white onion, cut into rings
⅓ c. salad oil
¾ c. white vinegar
¾ c. sugar
1 tsp. salt
1 tsp. pepper

Drain beans well. Combine beans with onion rings. Combine oil, vinegar, sugar, salt and pepper. Pour over bean mixture. Marinate in refrigerator overnight. Yield: 6 servings.

Jo Helen Akins, Lexington H. S.
Lexington, Tennessee

IDA LOU'S BEAN SALAD

1 c. chopped celery
1 can English peas, drained
1 can French-style green beans, drained
1 c. chopped onion
1 green pepper, chopped
1 can water chestnuts, drained and sliced
¾ c. vinegar
¾ c. sugar
½ tsp. salt
½ c. salad oil

Combine vegetables. Bring vinegar, sugar, salt, salad oil and ¼ cup water to a boil; cook for several minutes. Pour over vegetables. Marinate for 24 hours in refrigerator. Bring to room temperature 1 hour before serving. Yield: 8 servings.

Ida Lou Pentecost, Jackson Central-Merry H. S.
Jackson, Tennessee

LYNNE'S THREE-BEAN SALAD

1 No. 2 can cut green beans
1 No. 2 can wax beans
1 15½-oz. can red kidney beans, rinsed and drained
½ c. diced celery
1 med. onion, diced
¾ c. sugar
1 tsp. salt
½ tsp. pepper
½ c. salad oil
½ c. white vinegar

Mix the first 5 ingredients. Set aside. Mix the remaining ingredients with ⅓ cup water. Add to first mixture. Chill for several days, stirring occasionally. Drain before serving. Serve in a lettuce-lined bowl.

Lynne M. Reindl, Wausau East H. S.
Wausau, Wisconsin

TWENTY-FOUR HOUR BEAN SALAD

1 1-lb. can green beans, drained
1 1-lb. can wax beans, drained
1 1-lb. can red kidney beans, drained
¾ c. sugar
¼ c. vinegar
¼ c. wine vinegar
½ c. salad oil
1 tsp. salt
Pepper to taste
1 med. red onion, sliced
½ c. sliced green pepper
1 tsp. celery seed

Toss all ingredients to mix well. Cover tightly. Refrigerate for at least 24 hours before serving.

Linda Haines, New Richmond Exempted Village New Richmond, Ohio

PATIO BEAN SALAD

4 15-oz. cans kidney beans
8 hard-cooked eggs, diced
1 c. chopped onion
2 c. diced celery
1⅓ c. pickle relish
2 c. shredded sharp Cheddar cheese
2 c. sour cream

Rinse and drain beans. Combine beans, eggs, onion, celery, pickle relish and cheese. Add sour cream; toss lightly. Serve on lettuce; garnish with additional hard-cooked eggs, if desired. Yield: 20 servings.

Mrs. Mary Frances B. Wilson, Cherokee County H. S. Centre, Alabama

MEXICAN BEAN SALAD

2 c. cooked pinto beans
½ c. diced celery
3 green hot chili peppers, minced
2 cucumber pickles, chopped
½ onion, chopped
2 tbsp. prepared mustard
6 tbsp. cream or evaporated milk
Salt and pepper to taste

Combine first 5 ingredients in bowl; mix thoroughly. Mix mustard and cream together; stir into bean mixture. Season with salt and pepper. Serve on lettuce; sprinkle with chili powder, if desired. Yield: 6-8 servings.

Lelia Cook Greenwald, Socorro H. S. Socorro, New Mexico

CARDINAL SALAD

1 pkg. lemon gelatin
¾ c. beet juice
3 tbsp. vinegar
½ tsp. salt
1 tbsp. prepared horseradish
2 tsp. grated onion
¾ c. diced celery
1 c. diced cooked beets

Dissolve gelatin in 1 cup boiling water. Add beet juice, vinegar, salt, horseradish, and onion. Chill

until partially congealed. Fold in celery and beets; pour into molds. Chill until firm. Yield: 6-8 servings.

Mrs. Roberta Britton, Socastee H. S. Myrtle Beach, South Carolina

FINNISH BEET SALAD

1 c. diced cooked beets
2 c. diced cooked potatoes
¾ c. diced cooked carrots
2 tbsp. minced onion
¾ c. anchovies or herring
¼ c. vinegar
Salt to taste

Combine all ingredients; mix carefully. Chill for 2 to 4 hours. Serve in lettuce cups; garnish with hard-boiled egg slices, if desired. Yield: 6 servings.

Mrs. Fred Lamppa, Chisholm Sr. H. S. Chisholm, Minnesota

FRESH BROCCOLI SALAD

1 lb. fresh broccoli
2 tbsp. vinegar
1 tbsp. soy sauce
1 tbsp. sesame oil
1 tsp. sugar
1 tbsp. sesame seed, toasted

Cut broccoli stalks lengthwise into uniform spears, following branching lines. Halve spears, crosswise. Cook in 1 inch boiling salted water for 10 to 15 minutes, or until tender. Drain. Chill. Combine vinegar, soy sauce, sesame oil and sugar in screw top jar; cover. Shake to mix well. Drizzle vinegar mixture over broccoli. Toss gently. Sprinkle with toasted sesame seed. Yield: 4-6 servings.

Carol J. Brown, Ft. Jennings H. S. Ft. Jennings, Ohio

CONSOMMED BROCCOLI SALAD

1 env. unflavored gelatin
2 c. hot beef consomme
2 pkg. broccoli, cooked
4 hard-cooked eggs, chopped
½ c. mayonnaise
Dash of Tabasco
Dash of Worcestershire sauce

Dissolve gelatin in consomme; chill until partially congealed. Mash broccoli. Add broccoli and remaining ingredients to gelatin; pour into oiled molds. Chill until firm. Yield: 6-8 servings.

Dionetta K. Talley, Demopolis H. S. Demopolis, Alabama

BROCCOLI VINAIGRETTE

2 10-oz. packages frozen chopped broccoli
1 bottle Italian salad dressing
2 hard-cooked eggs, chopped
1 2-oz. jar pimentos, chopped
8 pitted black olives, chopped

Cook broccoli according to package directions; drain and chill. Toss broccoli with Italian dressing. Add eggs, pimentos and olives; toss again. Yield: 6 servings.

Dorothy L. Anderson, Princeton H. S.
Princeton, Minnesota

INDIVIDUAL BROCCOLI SALADS

1 pkg. frozen broccoli spears
1 env. unflavored gelatin
1 can hot beef consomme
1 c. mayonnaise
1 tsp. onion juice
1 tsp. Tabasco sauce
Juice of 1 lemon
1 tsp. Worcestershire sauce
½ tsp. salt
6 hard-cooked eggs

Cook broccoli according to package directions; cool and cut into small pieces. Soften gelatin in ¼ cup cold water; dissolve in hot consomme. Stir in all ingredients except broccoli and eggs; chill until partially congealed. Add remaining ingredients; pour into 6 individual molds. Chill until firm. Yield: 6 servings.

Mrs. Frances E. Poole, Mary Persons H. S.
Forsyth, Georgia

ATHENIAN SALAD

¼ lb. black Greek olives
1 lg. cucumber, sliced
4 stalks celery, minced
2 green peppers, cut into rings
5 radishes, thinly sliced
3 med. tomatoes, cut in wedges
4 scallions, thinly sliced
6 tbsp. olive oil
2 tbsp. wine vinegar
¼ tsp. oregano
¼ tsp. pepper
½ tsp. salt
½ lb. feta cheese, diced

Combine olives, cucumber, celery, green pepper, radishes, tomatoes and scallions in a large salad bowl. Place olive oil, vinegar, oregano, pepper and

salt into a screw-top jar; shake well. Toss salad with dressing. Sprinkle cheese on top. Yield: 6-8 servings.

Janet L. DeWilde, Nauset Regional Middle Sch.
Orleans, Massachusetts

CABBAGE LIME DELIGHT

1 pkg. lime gelatin
12 lg. marshmallows, quartered
2 tbsp. salad dressing
1 c. finely shredded cabbage
1 c. drained crushed pineapple
½ c. chopped pecans

Dissolve gelatin in 2 cups boiling water. Add marshmallows; stir occasionally until marshmallows are melted. Chill until partially congealed. Mix in remaining ingredients; chill until firm. Yield: 6 servings.

Mrs. Harry N. Young, Holgate Local H. S.
Holgate, Ohio

CABBAGE-PINEAPPLE-NUT SALAD

3 c. shredded cabbage
1 c. drained crushed pineapple
½ c. chopped nuts
6 to 8 maraschino cherries, chopped (opt.)
½ 3-oz. package cream cheese, softened
3 tbsp. mayonnaise
3 tbsp. pineapple juice
⅛ tsp. salt

Place cabbage, pineapple, nuts and cherries in salad bowl. Combine remaining ingredients; mix well. Pour dressing over salad; toss to mix well. Chill until ready to serve. Garnish with maraschino cherries, if desired. Yield: 6-8 servings.

Mrs. Gladys Jo Ridgeway, Moselle Sch.
Moselle, Mississippi

CALICO CABBAGE SALAD

1 med. onion
2 c. shredded green cabbage
2 c. shredded red cabbage
2 sm. unpared apples, sliced
½ c. salad oil
¼ c. vinegar
1 tsp. celery seed
1 tsp. salt

Slice half the onion into rings; chop remaining half. Combine chilled cabbage with chopped onion in large bowl. Arrange row of chilled apple slices and onion rings on top. Combine salad oil, vinegar, celery seed and salt. Pour over salad; toss to mix well. Serve immediately. Yield: 6-8 servings.

Norma Wallace, Marion Sr. H. S.
Marion, Virginia

OLD-FASHIONED PEANUT-CABBAGE SALAD

2 tbsp. flour
¾ c. sugar
Salt and pepper to taste
2 eggs, beaten
½ c. vinegar
3 tbsp. prepared mustard
1 lg. head cabbage, shredded
½ c. broken peanuts

Sift flour, sugar, salt and pepper together. Combine eggs, 1½ cups water, vinegar and mustard; mix well. Stir into sugar mixture. Pour into saucepan; cook until dressing is thick and smooth. Let cool. Combine cabbage and peanuts in salad bowl. Toss with dressing to mix well. Yield: 10 servings.

Katie B. Whorton, Cabot H. S.
Cabot, Arkansas

CALYPSO COLESLAW

4 c. shredded cabbage
1 12-oz. can whole kernel corn with sweet peppers, drained
½ c. finely chopped onion
1 c. mayonnaise
2 tbsp. sugar
2 tbsp. vinegar
4 tsp. prepared mustard
½ tsp. celery seed

Combine first 3 ingredients in large bowl. Combine remaining ingredients in a small bowl. Toss 2 mixtures together; mix well. Yield: 6 servings.

Winn Williams, Lake Hamilton H. S.
Pearcy, Arkansas

COLESLAW SOUFFLE SALAD

1 sm. package lemon Jell-O
½ c. mayonnaise
2 tbsp. vinegar
¼ tsp. salt
1½ c. shredded cabbage
½ c. shredded radishes
1 carrot, shredded
½ c. diced celery

2 to 4 tbsp. sweet pepper
1 or 2 tbsp. chopped onion

Dissolve Jell-O in 1 cup hot water. Mix mayonnaise, ½ cup cold water, vinegar and salt. Add to Jell-O; blend well. Chill until partially set. Beat until fluffy. Add vegetables; mix well. Pour into molds or a small glass dish. Chill until set. Serve on a lettuce leaf. Yield: 6-8 servings.

Dorothy H. Hamrick, Crest Sr. H. S.
Shelby, North Carolina

FOOD-PROCESSOR COLESLAW

¼ c. salad oil
¼ c. vinegar
¼ c. sugar
½ tsp. salt
¼ tsp. celery seed
1 head cabbage, cut up
1 onion, quartered
1 carrot, peeled
Dry parsley
Paprika

Combine salad oil, vinegar, sugar, salt and celery seed. Process cabbage and onion, using slicing disc in food processor. Process cabbage core and carrot, using grating disc, packing tightly into tube. Toss dressing mixture with processed vegetables; mix well. Sprinkle lightly with dry parsley and paprika.

Lois Paquette, Chippewa Falls Sr. H. S.
Chippewa Falls, Wisconsin

GERMAN RED CABBAGE SLAW

6 strips bacon, diced
1 2-lb. head red cabbage, shredded
1 apple, diced
¼ c. sugar
2 tsp. salt
Pepper to taste
6 to 8 tbsp. vinegar or red wine

Brown bacon in heavy saucepan. Add cabbage, apple and ¼ cup water. Cover tightly; steam slowly for about 1 hour, stirring frequently to prevent burning. Stir in sugar, salt, pepper and vinegar. Serve warm. Will keep in refrigerator for several days. Yield: 8 servings.

Margaret S. Yoder, Upper Perkiomen H. S.
East Greenville, Pennsylvania

MAMA'S FAVORITE SLAW

1 lg. cabbage, shredded
1 lg. onion, chopped
1 med. green pepper, chopped
½ c. fresh parsley, chopped
½ c. oil
¼ c. white vinegar
2 tsp. white pepper
1 tbsp. sugar
1 tbsp. salt

Mix cabbage, onion, green pepper and parsley. Mix oil, vinegar, white pepper, sugar and salt in separate bowl; mix well. Pour dressing mixture over cabbage mixture. Let stand in covered dish in refrigerator for several hours or overnight. Stir and serve.

Lynn C. Smith, South Caldwell H. S.
Hudson, North Carolina

RINA'S CABBAGE SLAW

½ c. sugar
1 tbsp. prepared mustard
¼ c. vinegar
1 tsp. salt
¾ c. salad oil
1 med. head cabbage, shredded
3 lg. carrots, grated

Combine sugar, mustard, vinegar, salt and oil; mix well. Pour over cabbage and carrots; mix well.

Karen Orsak, Hull H. S.
Hull, Massachusetts

CARROT-COCONUT SALAD

1 c. flaked coconut
1½ c. shredded carrots
¼ c. seedless raisins
2 tbsp. lemon juice
½ tsp. ground ginger
¼ c. mayonnaise

Combine all ingredients; mix well. Chill thoroughly. May serve on crisp lettuce with additional mayonnaise and garnish with mandarin orange sections, if desired. Yield: 4-5 servings.

Sandra M. Cuchna, La Farge H. S.
La Farge, Wisconsin

CARROT CONCOCTION

⅓ c. raisins
1½ c. grated carrots
½ c. drained crushed pineapple
¼ c. salted peanuts
½ c. cooked dressing
½ tsp. prepared mustard
1 tbsp. sugar
2 tbsp. cream

Soak raisins in water until plump. Drain well. Combine raisins, carrots, pineapple and peanuts; refrigerate for 1 hour. Combine dressing, mustard, sugar and cream; mix until smooth. Toss carrot mixture with dressing to mix well; let stand for 15 minutes before serving. Yield: 6 servings.

Catherine Nelson, Jeffers Public School
Jeffers, Minnesota

FOURTEEN-CARROT GOLD SALAD

1 pkg. orange gelatin
1½ tsp. vinegar
½ tsp. salt
Grated onion to taste
1½ c. coarsely grated carrots
1 red apple, diced or chopped radishes
¼ c. shredded cabbage
½ sm. can crushed pineapple

Dissolve gelatin in 1½ cups boiling water. Add vinegar, salt and onion. Chill until partially congealed. Add remaining ingredients; pour into oiled 1-quart mold or individual molds. Chill until firm. Unmold onto salad greens to serve. Yield: 6 servings.

Mrs. Doris Gustafson, Brethren H. S.
Brethren, Michigan

COPPER PENNY CARROTS

1 can tomato soup
½ c. salad oil
1 c. sugar
¾ c. vinegar
1 tsp. prepared mustard
1 tsp. Worcestershire sauce
2 lb. carrots, sliced
1 med. green pepper, sliced
1 med. onion, sliced

Bring the first 6 ingredients to a boil. Let cool. Cook carrots in salted water until tender-crisp. Rinse in ice or very cold water. Arrange layers of carrots, peppers and onions in tightly-sealed container. Pour dressing over vegetables. Seal tightly. Refrigerate for several hours or overnight. Will keep for weeks. Liquid may be drained and used as a salad dressing. Yield: 2 quarts.

Sammie Krietzer, Dickson Jr. H. S.
Dickson, Tennessee

LEMONED CARROTS

12 small carrots, peeled
1 6-oz. can frozen lemonade concentrate
6 whole cloves

Boil carrots in small amount of water until tender; drain well. Combine carrots, lemonade concentrate and cloves in saucepan; simmer for 5 minutes. Let cool; chill thoroughly. Drain carrots; remove cloves. Serve on lettuce. Yield: 4 servings.

Mrs. Doveta Hunt, Pecos H. S.
Pecos, Texas

CAULIFLOWER-AVOCADO SALAD

1 lg. head cauliflower, cut into sm. pieces
4 lg. avocados, mashed
1 16-oz. carton sour cream
½ can ripe olives, sliced
Garlic salt to taste
Lettuce
2 lg. tomatoes, wedged

Combine first 4 ingredients; mix well. Season with garlic salt. Place on bed of lettuce. Garnish with tomato wedges.

Kay Manning, Pottsboro H. S.
Pottsboro, Texas

CRUNCHY CAULIFLOWER SALAD

1 sm. head cauliflower, thinly sliced
3 unpeeled red apples, diced
1 c. sliced celery
3 sm. green onions, sliced
¾ c. chopped parsley or 1 sm. bunch
  watercress, chopped
1 clove of garlic, cut
½ tsp. salt
¼ c. red wine vinegar
¼ c. salad oil or olive oil
Pepper to taste

Chill cauliflower, apples, celery, onions and parsley. Rub salad bowl with cut garlic clove and salt. Combine vinegar, oil and pepper in jar; cover tightly. Shake vigorously. Pour over cauliflower mixture; toss lightly. Yield: 6 servings.

Mrs. Ruth S. Park, Bend Sr. H. S.
Bend, Oregon

CAULIFLOWER-OLIVE SALAD

1 fresh cauliflower, uncooked
3 green onions, chopped
½ c. chopped ripe olives
½ c. chopped green olives
1 c. Hellmann's mayonnaise

Pull cauliflower apart into flowerets; chop into bite-sized pieces. Combine with remaining ingredients; mix well. Store in covered container in refrigerator overnight. Yield: 6-8 servings.

Mrs. Rachel Pearce, Castleberry H. S.
Fort Worth, Texas

CAULIFLOWER SALAD DELUXE

1 med. head lettuce
1 lg. onion
1 med. head cauliflower, cut fine
1 lb. bacon, fried
¼ c. sugar
2 c. mayonnaise
⅓ c. Parmesan cheese
Salt and pepper to taste

Cut lettuce, onion and cauliflower into a large container. Add bacon. Mix sugar and mayonnaise together. Pour over all ingredients. Add cheese, salt and pepper. Let set overnight. Mix before serving.

Ruth E. Brown, Manchester H. S.
Manchester, Ohio

CELERY-CHEESE SALAD

1 pkg. lemon gelatin
1 c. mayonnaise
1 c. cottage cheese
Pinch of salt
1 c. chopped celery
2 tbsp. minced onion
¼ c. chopped green pepper
Green food coloring (opt.)
Chopped pimento (opt.)

Dissolve gelatin in 1 cup boiling water; let cool. Stir in mayonnaise, cottage cheese, and salt. Chill until partially congealed. Stir in remaining ingredients; pour into mold. Chill until firm. Yield: 6-8 servings.

Virginia L. Langston, State Department of Education
Baton Rouge, Louisiana

CHINESE SALAD

1 can water chestnuts
1 16-oz. can mushroom slices
2 16-oz. cans French-style green beans
1 16-oz. can Chinese vegetables
1 16-oz. can green peas
2 c. chopped celery
1 c. chopped onion
1 sm. jar chopped pimentos, drained
1 c. vinegar
1 c. sugar
Dash of salt

Drain all canned vegetables well. Stir together. Add remaining vegetable ingredients; stir well. Heat vinegar, sugar and salt together until sugar melts; stir well. Pour over combined vegetables while hot. Chill for several hours in refrigerator before serving. Keeps for days in refrigerator.

Mrs. Nancy D. Stubblefield, Warren County Sr. H. S.
McMinnville, Tennessee

CHRISTMAS SALAD

1½ c. sugar
½ c. vinegar
½ c. vegetable oil
½ tsp. salt
1 No. 303 can small peas
1 can green beans
1 bunch celery, finely cut
1 green pepper, finely cut
1 sm. onion, grated
1 jar pimentos, chopped

Mix sugar, vinegar, oil, salt and ⅓ cup water together. Drain peas and beans; combine vegetables in salad bowl. Pour dressing over vegetables; cover. Refrigerate until ready to serve. Yield: 16 servings.

Clara E. Ander, Pipestone H. S.
Pipestone, Minnesota

CALICO SALAD

2 cans Shoe Peg white corn, drained
½ c. chopped pimento
½ c. chopped green pepper
½ c. chopped onion
1 stalk celery, chopped
½ c. vinegar
½ c. sugar
½ c. salad oil
1 tsp. salt
1 tsp. pepper

Combine corn, pimento, green pepper, onion and celery; mix well. Combine vinegar, sugar, oil, salt

and pepper. Pour over corn mixture. Toss to blend. Refrigerate overnight. Toss and drain to serve. Yield: 6 servings.

Aillene Roberson, Turner Jr. H. S.
Carthage, Texas

CONFETTI SALAD

1 No. 2 can whole kernel corn, drained
1 pimento, chopped
1 sm. onion, chopped
1 sm. green pepper, chopped
1 sm. cucumber, chopped
½ c. French dressing

Combine all ingredients; toss to mix well. Serve in lettuce cups. Mayonnaise may be substituted for French dressing and the salad used for stuffing tomatoes, if desired. Yield: 4 servings.

Mrs. Judy Brumley, Kyle H. S.
Kyle, Texas

SHOE PEG CORN SALAD

1 can tiny peas, drained
1 can Shoe Peg corn, drained
1 bunch green onions, chopped
1 bell pepper, chopped
1 lg. jar chopped pimentos
1 c. oil
1 c. sugar
1 c. vinegar
1 tsp. salt
1 tsp. pepper

Combine first 5 ingredients; mix well. Combine remaining ingredients in a saucepan. Bring to a boil. Pour over corn mixture; mix well. Refrigerate overnight. Drain before serving.

Renee Rogers Weeks, Mineola H. S.
Mineola, Texas

COOL-AS-A-CUCUMBER SALAD

1 pkg. unflavored gelatin
½ tsp. salt
3 c. cream-style cottage cheese
1 8-oz. package cream cheese, softened
1 med. cucumber, pared
⅔ c. finely chopped celery
½ sm. onion, finely grated
⅓ c. chopped nuts
½ c. mayonnaise

Soften gelatin in ½ cup water; add salt. Stir over low heat until gelatin dissolves. Combine cheeses; beat until blended. Stir in gelatin. Remove seeds and grate cucumber. Stir cucumber and remaining ingredients into cheese mixture. Pour into 6-cup ring mold. Chill until firm. Yield: 8-10 servings.

Mrs. Billy Marks, Bodenham, H. S.
Pulaski, Tennessee

CUCUMBER ASPIC

2 pkg. unflavored gelatin
½ c. sugar
¼ c. vinegar
1 c. grated cucumber
1 c. crushed pineapple
Pinch of salt
Green food coloring

Soften gelatin in ¾ cup cold water; dissolve in ½ cup boiling water. Add sugar, vinegar, cucumber, pineapple and salt; stir until combined. Add food coloring; mix well. Chill until firm. Yield: 4 servings.

Mrs. Margaret M. Lee, Briarcliff H. S.
Atlanta, Georgia

CUCUMBERS IN SOUR CREAM

1 med. cucumber, sliced
1 tsp. salt
3 tbsp. sour cream
1 tsp. vinegar
1 tsp. sugar
¼ tsp. dillweed

Sprinkle cucumber with salt; cover with water to crisp. Combine sour cream, vinegar, sugar and dillweed. Drain cucumber; toss with sour cream dressing. Yield: 3 servings.

Teresa Bauman, Central Jr. H. S.
Alexandria, Minnesota

DUNCAN'S CUCUMBER SALAD

1 sm. package lime Jell-O
1 c. cottage cheese
2 tbsp. chopped pecans
1 c. Hellmann's mayonnaise
1 sm. cucumber, peeled and finely chopped
2 tbsp. finely chopped onion

Dissolve Jell-O in ½ cup boiling water. Cool. Add cottage cheese and pecans. Chill until partially set. Fold in mayonnaise, cucumber and onion. Chill until set. Yield: 6 servings.

Milton Curtis Starnes, Hendersonville H. S.
Hendersonville, Tennessee

FAVORITE CUCUMBER SALAD

1 pkg. lime gelatin
1 tsp. salt
2 tsp. vinegar
1 tsp. onion juice
1 c. sour cream
¼ c. mayonnaise
1 cucumber, grated

Dissolve gelatin in 1 cup boiling water. Add salt; let cool. Stir in remaining ingredients; blend well. Turn into ring mold. Chill until firm. Yield: 6 servings.

Dorothy B. Gifford, Sepulveda Jr. H. S.
Sepulveda, California

TOSSED CUCUMBER SALAD

¾ bottle Italian dressing
⅔ c. milk
⅔ c. sugar
1 pt. mayonnaise
Garlic salt to taste
4 lg. cucumbers, sliced
2 lg. tomatoes, cubed
1 pkg. Swiss cheese, diced
2 No. 303 cans mixed carrots and peas, drained
1 lg. onion, chopped

Combine Italian dressing and milk in saucepan; add sugar. Cook over low heat until sugar is dissolved, stirring constantly. Let cool. Add mayonnaise and garlic salt; mix well. Place remaining ingredients in salad bowl. Pour dressing over cucumber mixture; toss to mix well. Yield: 8 servings.

Mrs. Ella Jo Adams, Allen Sr. H. S.
Allen, Texas

ITALIAN ANTIPASTO SALAD

1 15-oz. jar artichokes in oil
1 8-oz. jar roasted red peppers in oil
1 8-oz. jar marinated mushrooms in oil
1 sm. jar Greek peppers, drained
1 15-oz. can black pitted olives, drained
1 15-oz. jar green olives, drained
1 c. salad oil
1 c. vinegar
1 c. sliced carrots
1 c. sliced celery
1 c. cauliflower, broken in sm. pieces

Combine all ingredients; mix well. Place in large container, tightly sealed. Marinate for 2 days before serving. Use as appetizer or salad. Yield: ½ gallon.

Sally Insko, Father Ryan H. S.
Nashville, Tennessee

ITALIAN MUSHROOM SALAD

⅓ c. wine vinegar
3 tbsp. olive oil
1 clove of garlic, minced
½ tsp. salt
¼ tsp. celery salt
¼ tsp. pepper
1 10-oz. package frozen baby lima beans
8 fresh mushrooms, sliced
1 lg. onion, chopped
1 tbsp. chopped fresh parsley
½ tsp. oregano

Combine vinegar, oil, garlic, salt, celery salt and pepper; blend well. Cook lima beans according to package directions; rinse with cold water. Drain well. Combine all ingredients; chill for 1 to 2 hours before serving. Yield: 4 servings.

Pauline Gist, North Salinas H. S.
Salinas, California

CAESAR SALAD

¼ c. salad oil
1 clove of garlic, crushed
1 sm. head lettuce
3 to 4 endive leaves
¼ c. Parmesan cheese
1 tsp. Worcestershire sauce
¼ tsp. lemon juice
1 egg, beaten
½ tsp. salt
¼ tsp. pepper
1 c. Salad Crispins, American-Style

Combine oil and garlic; let stand for 30 minutes. Tear lettuce and endive into pieces in salad bowl; add cheese. Mix garlic-oil mixture, Worcestershire sauce, and lemon juice. Add to lettuce and cheese. Add egg. Toss until egg is mixed well. Just before serving, add salt, pepper, and Salad Crispins. Toss well. Yield: 8 servings.

Gloria Jean Byrd, Vigor H. S.
Prichard, Alabama

CAESAR SALAD DELUXE

1 clove of garlic, mashed
½ c. salad oil
½ head lettuce
1 bunch curly endive
3 to 4 tomatoes, diced
1 c. croutons
1 2-oz. can anchovy fillets
1 egg, beaten
¼ c. lemon juice
1 tsp. Worcestershire sauce

½ c. grated Parmesan cheese
¼ c. finely crumbled bleu cheese
½ tsp. pepper
½ tsp. salt

Combine garlic and salad oil; let stand. Combine head lettuce, endive, tomatoes, croutons and anchovies in salad bowl. Strain oil; pour over lettuce mixture. Combine remaining ingredients; beat well. Pour over salad; toss lightly. Serve immediately. Yield: 6 servings.

Marie Jaspers, Pomeroy H. S.
Pomeroy, Washington

JOANNE'S CAESAR SALAD

¼ c. vinegar
¾ c. oil
2 cloves of garlic, crushed
1 tbsp. Worcestershire sauce
1 head iceberg lettuce
1 head romaine
Croutons
1 egg
1 can anchovies, chopped
Parmesan cheese

Combine vinegar, ⅛ cup water and oil in jar with lid. Shake well. Add garlic and Worcestershire sauce; shake well. Allow flavors to blend for 1 to 2 hours. Break lettuce and romaine into bite-sized pieces. Chill. Toast croutons in a medium oven until crisp. Place crisp greens in a wooden salad bowl. Add half the dressing; toss lightly. Add egg; toss well. Add anchovies and remaining dressing if desired; toss well. Sprinkle liberally with Parmesan cheese and croutons. Serve on chilled salad plates. Yield: 6-8 servings.

Joanne K. Mailander, Kings Mills Middle Sch.
Kings Mills, Ohio

CHEF'S SALAD

8 c. torn mixed greens
1 c. diced celery
1 c. julienne-cut cooked ham
2 hard-cooked eggs, finely chopped
2 tbsp. minced parsley
4 tomatoes, cut in wedges
1 c. garlic or French dressing

Chill all ingredients. Place greens, celery, ham, eggs, parsley and tomato wedges in salad bowl; toss to combine. Add dressing; toss again. Yield: 12 servings.

Myrtle Stevens, Gracemont H. S.
Gracemont, Oklahoma

CRISP SUMMER SALAD

1 head lettuce
2 c. spinach leaves
24 carrot curls
2 tomatoes, cut up
4 green onions, cut up
1 green pepper, cut up
Italian or oil-vinegar dressing

Tear lettuce and spinach into small pieces in a bowl. Combine all ingredients except dressing; mix well. Toss with dressing. Yield: 6 servings.

Patricia Crabtree, Bradley Central H. S.
Cleveland, Tennessee

DAY-OLD GREEN SALAD

1 lg. head lettuce
½ c. celery, chopped fine
½ c. green onions, chopped
½ c. bell pepper, chopped
1 pkg. frozen green peas, cooked and drained
1 pt. mayonnaise
3 tsp. sugar
Grated cheese
Bacon Bits or crumbled bacon

Line a 9 × 13-inch casserole with half the lettuce. Combine next 4 ingredients. Spread over lettuce. Top with remaining chopped lettuce. Combine mayonnaise and sugar. Spread mayonnaise mixture on top and around edges of casserole to seal. Sprinkle with grated cheese and Bacon Bits. Refrigerate overnight. Yield: 6-8 servings.

Mary Dickey Gill, West Lincoln H. S.
Brookhaven, Mississippi

TOSSED SALAD WITH BLEU CHEESE DRESSING

2 c. coarsely torn lettuce
1½ c. coarsely chopped cabbage
¾ c. coarsely torn watercress
¾ c. coarsely torn fresh spinach
½ c. chopped chives
2 tbsp. chopped anchovies
2 tbsp. crumbled bleu cheese
⅓ c. bleu cheese salad dressing

Combine all ingredients; toss lightly. Yield: 8 servings.

Barbara P. Russell, Rule H. S.
Knoxville, Tennessee

CRISPY SEVEN-LAYER SALAD

½ head lettuce, chopped fine
3 green onions, chopped fine
3 stalks celery, chopped fine
¼ green pepper, chopped fine
1 pkg. frozen green peas, thawed slightly
1½ c. mayonnaise
3 tsp. sugar
½ c. Parmesan cheese
5 or 6 slices bacon, fried and crumbled

Layer ingredients in order listed; do not toss. Refrigerate overnight. Serve, spooning from the bottom upwards.

Annette Snider, Whitewright H. S.
Whitewright, Texas

CRUNCHY SEVEN-LAYER SALAD

1 head lettuce
4 stalks celery, chopped
1 bell pepper, chopped
1 med. onion, sliced thin
1 sm. can green peas, drained
1 can water chestnuts, drained and sliced
1½ c. Miracle Whip salad dressing
1 tbsp. sugar
Grated cheese
Bacon Bits

Layer salad ingredients in order listed. Let marinate for 24 hours. Yield: 15-20 servings.

Joan Moore, Central H. S.
Newnan, Georgia

EIGHT-HOUR LAYERED SALAD

1 head lettuce, chopped
1 c. chopped celery
1 green pepper, chopped
1 green onion, chopped
1 pkg. frozen green peas, cooked and drained
1 pt. mayonnaise
2 tsp. sugar
1 c. Parmesan cheese
6 or 7 bacon strips, cooked and crumbled

Layer all ingredients in order listed. Let stand at least 8 hours before serving.

Mary George Elliott, Walnut H. S.
Walnut, Mississippi

JEANNIE'S SEVEN-LAYER SALAD

½ to ¾ lg. head lettuce
½ c. each chopped green pepper, celery, onion
1 10-oz. can peas
1 c. sour cream
1 c. mayonnaise
2 tbsp. sugar
4 to 6-oz. shredded cheese
8 strips crisp-fried bacon, crumbled

Shred lettuce into large bowl. Layer green pepper, celery, onion and peas over lettuce. Combine sour cream and mayonnaise; mix well. Spread over vegetables. Sprinkle sugar over sour cream mixture. Top with cheese and bacon. Cover. Refrigerate for several hours or overnight. Yield: 8 servings.

Jeannie Kenney, Whitthorne Jr. H. S.
Columbia, Tennessee

LAYERED LETTUCE TOSS

1 head lettuce, torn up
1 pkg. frozen English peas
1 can sliced water chestnuts
1 onion, sliced
Miracle Whip salad dressing to taste
1 tbsp. sugar
Parmesan cheese to taste

Layer first 4 ingredients in bowl. Toss. Add Miracle Whip and sugar. Sprinkle cheese on top. Chill for several hours before serving.

Linda Simmons, Hamilton H. S.
Hamilton, Texas

LETTUCE LAYER SALAD

1 head lettuce
1 c. diced celery
4 hard-cooked eggs, diced
1 10-oz. package frozen peas, uncooked
½ c diced green pepper (opt.)
1 med. sweet onion, diced
2 c. mayonnaise
2 tbsp. sugar
4 oz. Cheddar cheese, grated
8 bacon strips, fried and crushed

Tear lettuce into bite-sized pieces into a 9 x 12-inch glass dish. Layer next 5 ingredients in order listed. Spread mayonnaise over all evenly. Sprinkle sugar over mayonnaise. Garnish with cheese and bacon. Chill for 8 to 12 hours.

Mrs. Richard Pope, Upper Scioto Valley Sch.
McGuffey, Ohio

MIRACLE LAYERED SALAD

1 med. head lettuce
1 c. chopped green onions and tops
1 can water chestnuts, sliced
1 10 or 15-oz. package frozen peas, thawed
1 c. mayonnaise
1 c. Miracle Whip salad dressing
1 tsp. sugar
½ c. Parmesan cheese
4 hard-cooked eggs, quartered
16 cherry tomatoes

Tear lettuce into bite-sized pieces in 9 x 15-inch baking dish. Layer green onions, water chestnuts and uncooked peas over lettuce. Mix mayonnaise and Miracle Whip thoroughly. Frost the salad. Sprinkle sugar over all. Cover. Refrigerate overnight. Sprinkle Parmesan cheese over top. Garnish with eggs and cherry tomatoes. Will keep refrigerated for 3 days.

Mollie S. Olson, McClintock H. S.
Tempe, Arizona

OVERNIGHT LAYERED SALAD

1 pkg. frozen peas
1 head lettuce
1 med. red or green onion, sliced
½ to 1 pound bacon, fried and crumbled
1 can water chestnuts, sliced
2 tbsp. sugar
2 c. Miracle Whip salad dressing
Grated cheese

Place peas in hot water to thaw slightly; drain well. Break up lettuce; place in a 9 x 13-inch container. Place onion on top. Layer bacon over onion. Place water chestnuts on top. Top with peas. Add sugar to salad dressing; mix well. Spread dressing over all; seal edges. Sprinkle top with grated cheese; cover. Refrigerate several hours or overnight.

Carol Ann Rush, Hillside Jr. H. S.
Seven Hills, Ohio

NINE-LAYER SALAD

1 head lettuce, shredded
1 sweet pepper, chopped
1 onion, chopped
1 c. chopped celery
1 med. can green peas, drained
¾ c. mayonnaise
½ c. sour cream
1 pkg. Good Seasons Italian dressing mix
1 c. grated Cheddar cheese
6 slices crisp bacon, crumbled

Layer lettuce, sweet pepper, onion, celery and peas in air-tight container. Combine mayonnaise and sour cream; mix well. Spread over vegetables. Sprinkle with dry dressing mix and cheese. Top with crumbled bacon. Cover. Refrigerate until ready to use.

Wanda James Hastings, East Rutherford H. S.
Forest City, North Carolina

EASY TOSSED SALAD

1 pkg. frozen English peas
1 lg. head lettuce
1 med. purple onion, sliced into rings
2 or 3 stalks celery, chopped
1 qt. mayonnaise
1 can American-style croutons
Parmesan cheese

Cook peas according to package directions; drain. Tear lettuce into small pieces. Toss lettuce, peas, onion and celery together. Place in 9 x 13-inch dish. Spread mayonnaise over top of salad. Sprinkle croutons over mayonnaise. Top with Parmesan cheese. Yield: 9 servings.

Lynne Otwell, Beauregard H. S.
Opelika, Alabama

SALAD NICOISE

2 heads romaine
3 c. sliced boiled potatoes
3 tbsp. chopped fresh mint leaves
½ c. chopped watercress
3 tbsp. finely chopped parsley
3 tbsp. finely chopped scallions
1 tsp. salt
½ tsp. freshly ground pepper
½ c. olive oil
¼ c. wine vinegar
2 tbsp. lemon juice
2 cans flat anchovy fillets with oil
1 or 2 sweet Italian onions, sliced in rings
2 green peppers, sliced into rings
½ c. chopped black olives
24 sm. round tomatoes, halved
4 hard-cooked eggs, sliced

Break up romaine into 2-inch pieces; drain well. Refrigerate while preparing salad. Place next 11 ingredients in a large bowl; toss together. Add romaine, onion, peppers and black olives; toss again. Adjust seasoning to taste. Garnish with tomato halves and hard-cooked egg slices.

Vivien Swant, Sam Houston H. S.
Lake Charles, Louisiana

TABASCO TOSSED SALAD

12 cherry tomatoes or 3 tomatoes
Tabasco French Dressing
1 green pepper
1½ qt. assorted salad greens

Remove stems from tomatoes; cut in half or in wedges. Cover with Tabasco French Dressing. Marinate for at least 1 hour. Cut green pepper into strips. Drain tomatoes. Arrange with salad greens and green pepper in large salad bowl. Serve with Tabasco French Dressing. Yield: 6-8 servings.

Tabasco French Dressing

1 tsp. salt
1 tsp. sugar
1 tsp. dry mustard
1 tsp. paprika
1 c. salad oil
½ tsp. Tabasco
1 c. vinegar

Mix dry ingredients thoroughly. Add oil and Tabasco; stir until well blended. Add vinegar; beat or shake well. Dressing may be stored in refrigerator. Yield: 2 cups.

Photograph for this recipe on page 51.

TOSSED SALAD SUPREME

1 pkg. frozen green peas
1 head lettuce, broken into bite-sized pieces
1 c. cauliflower flowerets, broken into small pieces
½ c. thinly sliced radishes
½ c. thinly sliced cucumber
½ c. thinly sliced green onions
½ c. finely chopped celery
1 green pepper, chopped fine
8 oz. Swiss cheese, grated
1 c. Miracle Whip salad dressing
6 to 8 slices bacon, cooked and crumbled

Chill cooked green peas. Layer lettuce, cauliflower, radishes, cucumber, onions, celery and green pepper in a large salad bowl. Layer green peas over raw vegetables. Spread Swiss cheese over peas. Spread Miracle Whip over cheese carefully. Sprinkle bacon over Miracle Whip. Chill for several hours before serving to blend flavors.

Eleanor Helton, Fayetteville Jr. H. S.
Fayetteville, Tennessee

THE UNTOSSED SALAD

½ fresh bunch spinach
1 tsp. sugar
1 hard-cooked egg, chopped
½ head lettuce
1 pkg. frozen peas, thawed and uncooked
1 red onion, sliced thin
1 lb. bacon fried crisp and crumbled
1 pt. Hellmann's mayonnaise
½ c. grated Swiss cheese
Tomato wedges
Parsley

Layer the first 7 ingredients in a salad bowl in the order listed. Do not stir. Spread mayonnaise over top; seal edges. Sprinkle cheese over mayonnaise. Garnish with tomatoes and parsley. Refrigerate for several hours. Keeps well for 2 days.

Martha Dunlap, Corsicana H. S.
Corsicana, Texas

TWENTY-FOUR HOUR SALAD

1 head lettuce, broken into sm. pieces
1 cauliflower, broken into sm. flowerets
1 lb. bacon or 1 bottle Baco's
1 red onion, sliced
2 c. mayonnaise
3 tbsp. sugar
⅓ c. Parmesan cheese
1 box seasoned croutons
1 bottle Salad Delite

Layer first 4 ingredients in order listed. Combine the next 3 ingredients; mix well. Pour over lettuce mixture. Refrigerate overnight in sealed container. Add croutons and Salad Delight just before serving. Toss well. Yield: 10-12 servings.

Ramona Lawton, Flat Rock Jr. H. S.
Flat Rock, North Carolina

TWENTY-FOUR HOUR SALAD SUPREME

3 c. torn romaine
Salt and pepper to taste
Sugar to taste
1½ c. shredded Swiss cheese
4 hard-cooked eggs, sliced
½ lb. bacon, cooked, crumbled
3 c. torn leaf lettuce
1 10-oz. package frozen peas, thawed
¾ c. mayonnaise or salad dressing
2 tbsp. sliced green onions with tops

Place romaine in bottom of large bowl; sprinkle with salt, pepper and sugar. Top with 1 cup cheese. Layer eggs over cheese, standing some slices on edge, if desired. Sprinkle generously with salt. Layer in order listed half the bacon, leaf lettuce, and peas. Spread mayonnaise over top, sealing to edge of bowl; cover. Chill for 24 hours or overnight. Garnish with remaining cheese, remaining bacon and green onions. Toss before serving. Yield: 10-12 servings.

Linda Freiman, Alief Hastings H. S.
Alief, Texas

WATERCRESS A LA DENNIS

2 eggs, beaten
2 c. salad oil
2 tbsp. prepared horseradish
¼ c. catsup
¼ lg. onion, grated
1 tbsp. salt
⅓ c. vinegar
2 tbsp. paprika
Dash of pepper
2 tbsp. Worcestershire sauce
Dash of red pepper
1 slice bacon per serving
Watercress

Combine all ingredients except bacon and watercress for dressing; mix well. Fry bacon until crisp; drain and crumble. Combine watercress and bacon in salad bowl; toss with dressing.

Mrs. J. D. Wigley, Buckhorn H. S.
Huntsville, Alabama

WILTED LETTUCE SALAD

5 slices bacon
1 head lettuce, torn into bite-sized pieces
2 green onions, sliced
½ tsp. salt
¼ tsp. pepper
1 tbsp. sugar
¼ c. cider vinegar

Fry bacon until crisp; drain on paper towel, reserving 2 tablespoons drippings. Combine lettuce and onions in large serving bowl. Combine reserved bacon drippings with remaining ingredients and 2 tablespoons water. Heat just to boiling point. Pour over lettuce; toss lightly. Garnish with crumbled bacon. Serve immediately. Yield: 8 servings.

Cindy Knudson, Morgan ISD
Morgan, Texas

MARINATED VEGETABLE SALAD

1 10¾-oz. can chicken broth
5 med. carrots, sliced
3 c. cauliflowerets
2 sm. zucchini, sliced
2 c. sliced mushrooms
½ c. wine vinegar
1 6-oz. env. Italian dressing mix

Bring chicken broth to a boil in a saucepan. Add carrots. Let simmer for 2 minutes. Cool. Pour into serving bowl. Stir in remaining ingredients; mix well. Chill for at least 4 hours. Yield: 6 servings.

Sharon Whiteard, Hackneyville Sch.
Alexander City, Alabama

MADGE'S PEA SALAD

¾ head lettuce, broken up
Diced celery
Diced onion or onion flakes
2 c. (about) Miracle Whip salad dressing, thined with milk
Dash of garlic salt or powder
Durkee's Salad Seasoning with cheese
1 lb. bacon, fried and crumbled
1 pkg. frozen peas, thawed and drained
Grated Parmesan cheese.

Place lettuce in an 8 x 12-inch baking dish. Layer remaining ingredients in order listed. Refrigerate for several hours or overnight before serving. Will keep several days, if refrigerated. Yield: 10-12 servings.

Madge Lugibihl, Carey H. S.
Carey, Ohio

PEAS AND CHEESE SALAD

6 tbsp. mayonnaise
1 tbsp. Salad Supreme
1 tsp. minced onion
1 10-oz. package frozen peas
1 c. American cheese strips
1 tbsp. bacon bits

Combine mayonnaise, Salad Supreme and minced onion in a bowl. Break frozen peas apart. Add peas and cheese to mayonnaise mixture. Cover tightly. Refrigerate overnight. Stir in bacon bits before serving. Serve on lettuce leaf. Yield: 4-6 servings.

Janice Lampley, Dickson Jr. H. S.
Dickson, Tennessee

EASY ENGLISH PEA SALAD

1 1-lb. can English peas, chilled
½ c. chopped sweet pickles
¼ c. chopped pecans
2 hard-cooked eggs, chopped
Mayonnaise
Salt to taste

Drain peas and pickles; place in salad bowl. Add pecans and eggs; toss with enough mayonnaise to coat evenly. Season with salt. Serve on lettuce. Yield: 4 servings.

Mrs. J. H. Hellums, South Panola H. S.
Batesville, Mississippi

PEANUT SURPRISE

1 10-oz. package frozen peas
½ c. sour cream
½ c. mayonnaise
1 c. red skinned peanuts
1 c. diced celery

Combine all ingredients; mix well. Chill for 12 hours before serving. Yield: 8 servings.

Mrs. Thelma Schmid, Struthers H. S.
Struthers, Ohio

CREAMY POTATO SALAD

7 c. sliced cooked potatoes
⅓ c. chopped chives, (opt.)
1 tsp. salt
⅛ tsp. pepper
1 tbsp. grated onion
1 c. garlic salad dressing
½ c. chopped celery
½ c. diced cucumber
½ c. sour cream
½ c. mayonnaise

Combine warm potatoes, chives, salt, pepper, onion and ½ cup garlic salad dressing. Toss to mix well. Chill thoroughly. Combine celery, cucumber, sour cream and mayonnaise; stir in remaining garlic salad dressing. Chill thoroughly. Combine mayonnaise and potato mixtures; mix well. Yield: 8 servings.

Mrs. Jerrard Gould, Seymour Jr. H. S.
Seymour, Connecticut

DELICIOUS POTATO SALAD

8 potatoes, boiled
1 sm. can pimentos
1 lg. onion, minced
8 hard-cooked eggs, chopped
3 sweet pickles, chopped
1 c. salad dressing
½ c. (heaping) sugar
1 tbsp. prepared mustard
1 tsp. celery seed
Salt and pepper to taste

Peel and dice potatoes. Drain pimentos; reserve juice. Chop pimentos. Place potatoes, onion, eggs, pickles and pimentos in salad bowl. Combine reserved juice and remaining ingredients; mix well. Pour over potato mixture; toss to coat evenly. Chill for several hours before serving. Yield: 10-12 servings.

Janet Oyler, Glasco H.S.
Glasco, Kansas

FAMILY-FAVORITE POTATO SALAD

6 cooked potatoes, diced
¼ c. chopped celery
¼ c. chopped onion
¼ c. chopped sweet pickles
2 hard-cooked eggs, chopped
1 tbsp. flour
2 tbsp. sugar
1 tbsp. dry mustard
1 egg, beaten
¼ c. vinegar
2 tsp. celery seed

Combine first 5 ingredients in salad bowl. Mix flour, sugar, mustard and egg together in saucepan. Add vinegar, celery seed and ¾ cup water. Cook over medium heat until thickened, stirring constantly. Pour over potato mixture; toss to coat evenly. May serve hot or cold. Yield: 6 servings.

Harriet J. Harless, Logan Sr. H. S.
Logan, West Virginia

GERMAN POTATO SALAD

3 med. potatoes
3 slices bacon, diced
1 sm. onion, chopped
½ c. vinegar
½ c. stock or bouillon
1 tsp. salt
¼ tsp. pepper
1 tsp. sugar
2 to 3 tbsp. chopped pickle
2 to 3 tbsp. chopped bell pepper

2 tsp. pimento
1 egg yolk, beaten

Boil potatoes in jackets; let cool. Peel and slice or dice. Cook bacon until crisp. Remove bacon. Cook onion until transparent in bacon grease. Add next 7 ingredients; stir. Bring to a boil. Stir in egg yolk; Remove from heat. Pour over potatoes. Add bacon. Toss until potatoes are coated but do not break up potatoes. Serve hot or cold. Yield: 2-4 servings.

Dorothy Vacek, Corsicana H. S.
Corsicana, Texas

LINDA'S GERMAN POTATO SALAD

3 strips bacon
1 sm. onion, chopped
6 med. potatoes, cooked and diced
Diced green pepper
Diced celery
½ c. vinegar
¾ c. mayonnaise
Salt and pepper to taste
Paprika (opt.)

Fry bacon until crisp, drain about ½ the grease. Saute onion in bacon grease. Combine all ingredients except paprika; mix well. Sprinkle with paprika.

Linda McClure, Bartlett H. S.
Bartlett, Texas

HOT POTATO SALAD

5 slices bacon, diced
½ c. minced onion
¼ c. vinegar
3 tbsp. sugar
1½ tsp. salt
⅛ tsp. crushed oregano
¼ tsp. pepper
1 tsp. mustard
3 c. cooked, diced potatoes
½ c. diced celery
2 tbsp. chopped green pepper
2 hard-cooked eggs, chopped
½ c. grated cheese

Fry bacon until lightly browned. Add onion, vinegar, sugar, salt, oregano, pepper and mustard. Bring to a boil; boil for 2 minutes. Pour hot mixture over potatoes, bacon, celery, green pepper and hard-cooked eggs. Toss lightly. Turn into greased baking dish; top with cheese. Bake at 375° about 15 minutes or until cheese bubbles. Yield: 4-6 servings.

Mrs. Wilma F. Brown, Nacogdoches H. S.
Nacogdoches, Texas

HOT VIENNA'D POTATO SALAD

¾ c. mayonnaise
¼ c. finely chopped onion
½ tsp. salt
¾ c. finely chopped dill pickles
2 4-oz. cans Vienna sausage, sliced
4 c. cubed cooked potatoes

Heat mayonnaise, onion, salt and dill pickles in skillet or saucepan. Add half the sausages and potatoes to mayonnaise mixture. Heat thoroughly, stirring occasionally with a fork. Panfry remaining Vienna sausages. Serve with hot potato salad.

Linda E. Baker, Grove City H. S.
Grove City, Ohio

QUICK AND EASY POTATO SALAD

4 potatoes
¾ c. salad dressing
1 tsp. salt
1 tbsp. minced onion
½ c. finely cut celery
2 hard-cooked eggs, chopped

Cook potatoes in jackets until tender; peel and dice. Add remaining ingredients; toss together. Chill for 3 hours before serving. Yield: 4 servings.

Mrs. Nancy King, Chesterfield H. S.
Chesterfield, South Carolina

TOASTED ALMOND-POTATO SALAD

4 c. cubed boiled potatoes
2 tbsp. minced onion
2 tbsp. minced pimento
1 c. diced celery
½ c. chopped sweet cucumber pickles
1 c. toasted slivered almonds
Salt and pepper to taste
Salad dressing to taste

Combine all ingredients; toss carefully with a fork. Chill until ready to serve. Yield: 8 servings.

Mrs. Norma A. Piboin, Madisonville H. S.
Madisonville, Texas

CRUNCHY SPINACH SALAD

1 lb. fresh spinach
½ can bean sprouts
1 can water chestnuts, sliced
Red onion rings
3 hard-cooked eggs, chopped
½ c. salad oil
½ c. vinegar
3 tbsp. catsup

¼ c. sugar
1 tsp. salt
5 slices bacon, cooked and crumbled

Tear spinach leaves into bowl. Add next 4 ingredients; chill. Combine next 5 ingredients in a covered cruet; shake well. Toss dressing and salad about 30 minutes before serving. Garnish with bacon at serving time. Yield: 4-8 servings.

Karen L. McKeon, Berea H. S.
Berea, Ohio

SPINACH-LETTUCE-BACON SALAD

6 strips bacon, diced
4 c. spinach, torn
2 c. lettuce, torn
2 hard-cooked eggs, finely chopped
⅓ c. salad dressing

Fry bacon until crisp; drain. Combine spinach, lettuce, bacon and eggs. Add salad dressing; toss lightly. Yield: 8 servings.

Marilyn Bersie, Alexander Ramsey Sr. H. S.
St. Paul, Minnesota

FRESH SPINACH SALAD

1 lb. fresh spinach
4 hard-cooked eggs, chopped
8 slices bacon, fried
¼ c. chopped green onions
½ c. Italian salad dressing
Salt to taste

Remove large veins from spinach; tear into small pieces. Combine spinach, eggs and crumbled bacon. Add onions; toss lightly. Add salad dressing and salt; toss to mix evenly. Serve immediately.

Mrs. Jane Davis, South Park Jr., H. S.
Corpus Christi, Texas

SPINACH SALAD WITH HOT FRENCH DRESSING

½ lb. spinach, shredded
1 med. onion, finely chopped
¼ c. diced celery
6 to 8 radishes, chopped
4 hard-cooked eggs, chopped
½ tsp. salt
2 slices bacon
¼ c. vinegar
1 tbsp. sugar

Combine first 6 ingredients in salad bowl; chill until ready to serve. Fry bacon until crisp; drain well. Drain off all but ¼ cup bacon drippings. Add vinegar and sugar to bacon drippings; bring to a boil. Add crumbled bacon. Pour over salad; toss to mix evenly. Serve immediately. Yield: 8 servings.

Mary Martin, Cleburne H. S.
Cleburne, Texas

SPRING GARDEN SALAD

1¼ c. sugar
¾ c. oil
¾ c. vinegar
¼ tsp. pepper
1 tsp. salt
1 can Shoe Peg corn drained
1 can French-style greenbeans, drained
1 can peas, drained
1 c. chopped celery
1 c. chopped green pepper
2 bunches 8 green onions, chopped
1 4-oz. jar chopped pimentos

Combine sugar, oil, vingear, pepper and salt in a saucepan. Bring to a boil. Cool. Pour over vegetables; mix well. Chill overnight in a covered dish.

Sue Bode, Congress Jr. H. S.
Denton, Texas

TOMATO AND ONION SALAD

1 garlic clove, minced
1 tsp. salt
1 tsp. sugar
¼ tsp. pepper
2 tsp. prepared mustard
¼ c. olive oil or salad oil
2 tbsp. tarragon vinegar
6 firm tomatoes, sliced
1 onion, thinly sliced
Chopped parsley

Combine garlic and salt; mash with a spoon. Stir in sugar, pepper, mustard, oil and vinegar. Pour over tomato and onion slices; sprinkle with parsley. Chill thoroughly. Serve without dressing.

Mrs. Pat Ashbrook, Oldham County H. S.
LaGrange, Kentucky

TOMATO ASPIC

2½ c. tomatoes
1 slice onion
1 stalk celery, cut up
½ bay leaf
2 cloves
½ tsp. salt
3 drops of Tabasco sauce
1 pkg. unflavored gelatin

Combine all ingredients except gelatin in saucepan; cook until tomatoes are mushy. Remove cloves and bay leaf; puree tomato mixture in blender. Soften gelatin in ½ cup cold water. Pour tomato mixture into saucepan; bring to boiling point. Remove from heat. Add gelatin; stir until dissolved. Pour into mold; chill until firm.

Frances Bailey, State Department of Education
Little Rock, Arkansas

QUICK TOMATO SLAW

¼ c. salad dressing
1 tbsp. prepared mustard
2 c. coarsely shredded cabbage
1 c. diced tomatoes
¼ c. chopped green pepper
¼ c. sliced cucumber
1 tsp. salt

Combine salad dressing and mustard. Place remaining ingredients in salad bowl. Pour in dressing; toss carefully until well mixed. Chill for 30 minutes before serving. Yield: 6 servings.

Patsy K. Myers, Christian County H. S.
Hopkinsville, Kentucky

STUFFED TOMATO SALAD

6 firm tomatoes
Heart of 1 head lettuce, torn
1 stalk celery, chopped
1 sm. bottle stuffed olives, chopped
1 green pepper, chopped
¼ c. mayonnaise
French dressing

Cut off stem ends of tomatoes; scoop out insides. Combine tomato pulp, lettuce, celery, olives and green pepper. Mix in mayonnaise; spoon mixture into tomato cups. Top each tomato cup with French dressing.

Mrs. Lois Farrington, Mesick H. S.
Mesick, Michigan

SUMMER GARDEN SALAD

5 tomatoes
1 sm. white onion, thinly sliced
3 boiled potatoes, peeled and sliced
3 oregano leaves, minced or ¼ tsp. dried
    oregano
½ tsp. salt
½ tsp. pepper
½ green pepper, chopped
3 tbsp. salad oil

Peel tomatoes; cut into wedges. Combine all ingredients; toss gently until well coated. Chill until ready to serve.

Virginia Martell, Johnston City H. S.
Johnston City, Illinois

VEGETABLE SALAD VINAIGRETTE

Zucchini, thinly sliced
Whole kernel corn
Peas
French green beans
Carrots, thinly sliced
Cherry tomatoes, halved
Tabasco Vinaigrette Dressing

Prepare vegetables to make about 3 cups total. Arrange vegetables in separate dishes. Add Tabasco Vinaigrette Dressing to each dish. Marinate in refrigerator at least 2 hours. Drain. Arrange in serving dishes or in lettuce cups in salad bowl. Yield: 6 servings.

TABASCO VINAIGRETTE DRESSING

¾ c. olive oil
½ c. tarragon vinegar
¾ tsp. salt
¼ tsp. Tabasco
2 tsp. minced chives
2 tsp. minced fresh chervil or ⅛ tsp. dried chervil
2 tsp. capers
1 hard-cooked egg, chopped (opt.)

Combine all ingredients. Beat until well mixed. Yield: About 1⅓ cups.

Photograph for this recipe on page 51.

WISCONSIN SALAD

½ tsp. horseradish
½ tsp. salt
¼ tsp. pepper
½ c. sour cream
½ c. mayonnaise
7 hard-cooked eggs, chopped
½ lb. Swiss cheese
½ c. finely chopped green pepper
4 chilled tomatoes
Lettuce leaves

Combine horseradish, salt, pepper, sour cream and mayonnaise; stir carefully into eggs. Cut cheese into ½-inch cubes. Combine egg mixture, cheese and green pepper. Chill thoroughly. Peel tomatoes; cut into thick slices. Place 1 slice of tomato on lettuce leaf; cover with egg mixture. Top with tomato slice. Garnish with a sprig of parsley. French onion dip may be substituted for mayonnaise and sour cream, if desired. Yield: 4-6 servings.

Mrs. Vivian B. Barnes, Argyle H. S.
Argyle, Wisconsin

COLD BEEF SALAD

2 c. diced leftover roast beef
1 c. diced celery
1 c. diced, pared tart apple
¼ c. mayonnaise
1 tbsp. prepared mustard
½ tsp. salt

Mix beef, celery and apple together in salad bowl. Combine mayonnaise, mustard and salt; mix well. Add to beef mixture; toss lightly until well coated. Serve on crisp lettuce leaves, if desired. Yield: 5 servings.

Mrs. Elizabeth R. Whisnant, East Rutherford H. S.
Forest City, North Carolina

CORNED BEEF WITH MACARONI SALAD

1 4-oz. package macaroni rings
1 pkg. lemon gelatin
2 tbsp. vinegar
1 c. salad dressing
1 can corned beef, shredded
1½ c. finely diced celery
½ green pepper, finely chopped
1 tbsp. chopped onion
3 hard-cooked eggs, chopped

Cook macaroni according to package directions; let cool. Dissolve gelatin in 1½ cups boiling water. Stir in vinegar and salad dressing; chill until partially congealed. Stir in corned beef, celery, green pepper, onion and eggs; mix carefully. Pour into mold; chill until firm. Yield: 8 servings.

Mrs. Bonnie Shaw, Clarkfield Public School
Clarkfield, Minnesota

FAVORITE CORNED BEEF SALAD

1 3-oz. package lemon gelatin
1 c. mayonnaise
1 c. shredded corned beef
2 c. chopped celery
¾ c. chopped green pepper
½ onion, diced

Dissolve gelatin in 1 cup boiling water. Stir in mayonnaise; chill until partially congealed. Stir in remaining ingredients; pour into mold. Chill until firm. Serve on lettuce leaves, if desired. Yield: 4-6 servings.

Barbara Gaylor, Supervisor
Consumer and Homemaking Education
Michigan Department of Education
Lansing, Michigan

COOKOUT TACO SALAD

1½ lb. hamburger
1 15-oz. can kidney beans, drained
1 tsp. salt
1 head lettuce, broken into chunks
4 scallions, chopped
4 tomatoes, cut in chunks
8 oz. grated cheese
1 avocado, chopped
2 c. crushed taco chips
1 can tomato soup
¼ c. sugar
2 tbsp. green onions, sliced
2 tsp. prepared mustard
2 cloves
1 tsp. garlic powder
1¼ c. salad oil

Brown hamburger; drain. Add kidney beans and salt. Refrigerate. Toss hamburger mixture with lettuce, scallions, tomatoes, cheese and avocado in a large bowl. Add taco chips last. Toss well. Combine remaining ingredients in blender; blend well. Pour dressing over all at serving time. A great salad for cookout accompaniment.

Joy Ann Berto, Plymouth-Carver Intermediate Sch.
Plymouth, Massachusettes

GRANNY'S MEXICAN SALAD

1 lg. head lettuce, chopped
1 med. onion, chopped
1 can Mexican chili beans, drained and chilled
1 lb. longhorn cheese grated
2 tomatoes, chopped
1 10½-oz. package Fritos, crushed
1 8-oz. bottle Catalina French dressing

Combine lettuce, onion, chili beans and cheese. Add tomatoes and Fritos just before serving. Toss salad with dressing. Yield: 20-24 servings.

Mrs. Vivian Bailey, Eastbrook H. S.
Marion, Indiana

MAIN DISH MEXICAN SALAD

1 lb. ground round, browned
1 onion, chopped
1 green pepper, cut up
1 16-oz. can kidney beans, drained
1 head lettuce
2 tomatoes, cut up
½ lb. Cheddar cheese, grated
1 pkg. tortilla chips, broken
1 lg. avocado, cut up
1 7-oz. bottle Thousand Island dressing

Brown ground beef, onion and green pepper. Add kidney beans to hot meat mixture. Keep warm. Break lettuce into pieces into bowl. Add tomatoes, grated cheese, tortilla chips and avocado pieces. Toss together well. Add meat mixture to lettuce mixture. Toss with Thousand Island dressing.

Ruth Nelson, Greenwood H. S.
Greenwood, Wisconsin

SHARON'S TACO SALAD

1 lb. ground beef
1 med. onion, chopped
¼ tsp. salt
1 15-oz. can kidney or chili beans
½ head lettuce, torn or shredded
2 c. crushed taco chips
2 med. tomatoes, cut in pieces
½ c. sliced green olives (opt.)
1 c. grated Cheddar cheese
1 bottle taco sauce

Brown beef with onion and salt; drain. Stir in beans; heat through. Layer half the lettuce, beef mixture, taco chips, tomatoes, olives and cheese in a large salad bowl. Repeat layers. Pour taco sauce on top. Salad is served while beef mixture is hot.

Sharon Hattersley, Turpin H. S.
Cincinnati, Ohio

HAM SALAD IN A MOLD

1 cucumber, peeled
1 pkg. unflavored gelatin
1½ c. hot tomato juice
1 tsp. lemon juice
½ tsp. salt
½ c. mayonnaise
1 c. chopped cooked ham
3 hard-cooked eggs, chopped
1 c. chopped celery
½ c. chopped bell pepper
1 tbsp. chopped onion

Soak cucumber in salted water to crisp. Soften gelatin in ¼ cup cold water; dissolve in tomato juice. Stir in lemon juice, salt and mayonnaise; mix well. Chill until partially congealed. Drain cucumber; chop enough cucumber to measure ½ cup. Combine ham, eggs, celery, cucumber, bell pepper and onion; fold in gelatin mixture. Pour into mold; chill until firm. Yield: 6 servings.

Daphne Smith, Winnsboro H. S.
Winnsboro, Texas

CRUNCHY BAKED HAM SALAD

3 c. diced cooked ham
1 c. diced celery
½ c. chopped stuffed green olives
2 hard-cooked eggs, diced
¼ c. chopped onion
1 tbsp. lemon juice
1 tbsp. prepared mustard
Dash of pepper
¾ c. mayonnaise or salad dressing
1 c. crushed potato chips

Combine all ingredients except potato chips; place in
8 x 2-inch round baking dish. Sprinkle with potato
chips. Bake in 400-degree oven for 20 to 25 minutes or
until heated through. Yield: 6 servings.

Ilene Ridgely, East Richland H. S.
Olney, Illinois

GEORGIA'S HAM SALAD

2 c. diced cooked ham
1 c. diced celery
2 hard-cooked eggs, chopped
¼ c. mayonnaise
1 tbsp. chopped sweet pickles
1 tbsp. catsup

Combine ham, celery and eggs in salad bowl. Add
mayonnaise, pickles and catsup; toss well. Place in
lettuce cups; chill. Serve with crackers. Yield: 4
servings.

Georgia Matthews, Oliver Springs H. S.
Oliver Springs, Tennessee

QUICK AND EASY HAM SALAD

1 lb. pressed ham, ground
½ c. ground sweet pickles
1 c. salad dressing
¼ c. sweet pickle juice
1 tbsp. onion juice

Combine all ingredients; mix well. Serve on lettuce.
May use as a sandwich spread, if desired. Yield: 4
servings.

Mrs. Nerine Kinsey, Gatesville H. S.
Gatesville, Texas

SUPER CHEF SALAD

1 head lettuce, torn
1 c. diced ham
½ c. dry packaged dressing
French dressing

Combine ingredients in order listed, tossing with
French dressing just before serving. Yield: 6 servings.

Catherine H. Maeder, Alva H. S.
Alva, Florida

LUNCHEON MEAT-POTATO SALAD

8 to 10 med. cooked potatoes, diced
3 hard-cooked eggs, diced
½ c. diced cheese
¼ c. diced onions
3 tbsp. diced green pepper
¼ c. diced pickles
1 tbsp. celery seed
1 can luncheon meat, diced
¾ c. (about) salad dressing
Salt and pepper to taste

Combine first 8 ingredients in salad bowl. Toss
carefully with salad dressing; season with salt and
pepper. Serve on lettuce; sprinkle with paprika, if
desired. Yield: 10-12 servings.

Mrs. Tommy Long, Allen County H. S.
Scottsville, Kentucky

AVOCADO-CHICKEN-APPLE SALAD

2 lg. apples, cubed
1 ripe avocado, cubed
2 tbsp. lemon juice
½ c. mayonnaise
¼ c. cream
1 tsp. minced onion
2 c. cubed cooked chicken
½ c. crumbled bleu cheese

Sprinkle apples and avocado with lemon juice.
Combine mayonnaise and cream; stir in onion. Toss
avocado, apples, chicken and cheese with cream
dressing. Serve on lettuce leaves.

Mrs. Katherine S. Hunter, Irving H. S.
Irving, Texas

BROILED CHICKEN SALAD

2 c. diced cooked chicken
1 ½ c. diced celery
¼ c. French dressing
½ c. mayonnaise
⅓ c. sour cream
¼ c. toasted slivered almonds
2 c. crushed potato chips
1 c. grated cheese

Marinate chicken and celery in French dressing for 1
hour. Add mayonnaise, sour cream and almonds.

Place in baking dish. Combine potato chips and cheese; sprinkle on top of salad. Place under broiler. Broil until cheese melts. Yield: 4 servings.

Mrs. Johnnie T. Broome, Blackshear H. S.
Blackshear, Georgia

CHICKEN-FRUIT SALAD

4 c. cooked diced chicken breasts
1½ c. diced celery
1 15-oz. can pineapple chunks, drained and cubed
1½ c. mayonnaise
1 c. chopped apples
1 c. chopped pecans

Combine all ingredients, mixing well. Chill for 2 hours before serving. Yield: 8-10 servings.

Mrs. Stanley Graham, George County H. S.
Lucedale, Mississippi

BUSY DAY CHICKEN SALAD

2 c. diced chicken
3 hard-cooked eggs, chopped
1 c. chopped celery
½ c. mayonnaise or salad dressing
½ tsp. salt

Combine chicken, eggs, celery, mayonnaise and salt in chilled bowl; mix well. Serve on lettuce leaf or endive; garnish with stuffed olives and pimento strips, if desired. Yield: 6-8 servings.

Mrs. Mary W. Hall, Mabelvale H. S.
Mabelvale, Arkansas

CHICKEN-ALMOND RING SALAD

1 env. unflavored gelatin
2 c. chicken broth or bouillon
½ tsp. salt
¼ tsp. pepper
1½ tsp. curry powder
1 c. sour cream
2 c. diced cooked chicken
1 sm. onion, finely chopped
¼ c. chopped green pepper
1 tbsp. chopped pimento
1 c. slivered almonds

Combine gelatin and broth; heat until gelatin is dissolved. Stir in salt, pepper, curry powder and sour cream; chill until partially congealed. Combine remaining ingredients; fold into gelatin mixture. Pour into greased 5-cup ring mold. Chill until firm.

Unmold on greens. Fill center with crushed Vegetable Thins, if desired. Yield: 6 servings.

Mrs. Ann Davis, Trumann H. S.
Trumann, Arkansas

CHICKEN CREAM DELIGHT

1 stewing chicken
1 carrot
1 stalk celery
½ onion
1 env. unflavored gelatin
1 tbsp. onion juice
1 tbsp. lemon juice
1 c. whipped cream
½ c. finely chopped celery
½ green pepper, finely chopped
¼ c. diced stuffed olives
2 tbsp. minced sweet pickles
Salt and pepper to taste

Stew chicken in salted water with carrot, celery stalk and onion until tender. Strain and reserve ¾ cup stock. Remove skin and bones from cool chicken; cut into bite-sized pieces. Soften gelatin in ¼ cup cold water; add reserved hot stock. Stir until gelatin is dissolved. Add onion juice and lemon juice; chill until partially congealed. Beat with rotary beater until frothy. Fold in chicken, whipped cream, chopped celery, green pepper, diced olives and pickles; season with salt and pepper. Rinse individual molds with cold water; spoon chicken mixture into molds. Chill until firm. Decorate with stuffed olive slices; serve with mayonnaise mixed with chopped pecans, if desired. Yield: 8 servings.

Mrs. Ruby C. Irvine, Coalton H. S.
Coalton, West Virginia

CHICKEN CURRY SALAD

1 pkg. chicken noodle soup mix
1 c. instant rice
1 c. chopped celery
2 tbsp. minced onion
1 c. chopped chicken
1 tsp. curry powder
1 tsp. salt
½ tsp. dry mustard
⅛ tsp. pepper
¾ c. crushed pineapple
¾ c. mayonnaise

Add soup mix and rice to 2 cups boiling water. Cover; simmer until water is absorbed. Stir to fluff rice. Cover; chill for 15 to 20 minutes. Combine rice with remaining ingredients; blend well. Cover; chill thoroughly. Yield: 6-8 servings.

Enid Hedrick, Bolsa Grande H. S.
Garden Grove, California

CHICKEN DELICIOUS

1 4-lb. chicken, cooked and boned
3 pkg. unflavored gelatin
1¼ c. hot chicken stock
1 c. salad dressing
1 tsp. Worcestershire sauce
1 tbsp. lemon juice
1 c. diced celery
3 hard-cooked eggs, diced
¾ c. diced stuffed olives

Cut chicken in pieces. Soften gelatin in ¼ cup cold water. Add hot chicken stock; stir until gelatin is dissolved. Add salad dressing, Worcestershire sauce and lemon juice; mix well. Chill until partially congealed. Mix in chicken and remaining ingredients; pour into large ring mold. Chill until firm.

Mrs. Edith Pollock, Kerens H. S.
Kerens, Texas

CHICKEN IN CHEESE SHELL

½ c. shredded American cheese
½ c. shortening
½ tsp. salt
1½ c. sifted flour
1½ c. diced cooked chicken
1 9-oz. can pineapple tidbits, drained
1 c. chopped walnuts
½ c. chopped celery
1 c. sour cream
⅔ c. salad dressing

Combine ⅓ cup cheese and shortening. Place salt and flour in mixing bowl; cut in shortening mixture until crumbly. Work in 4 tablespoons cold water or enough to hold pastry together. Roll out thin; place in 8-inch pie pan. Flute edge; prick shell generously. Bake in preheated 450-degree oven for 12 minutes or until browned. Let shell cool. Combine chicken, pineapple, walnuts and celery. Mix sour cream and salad dressing together; stir ⅔ cup sour cream mixture into chicken mixture. Spread in pie shell. Top with remaining sour cream mixture; sprinkle with remaining cheese. Chill until ready to serve. Yield: 6 servings.

Mrs. Blanche Ivanish, Malta H. S.
Malta, Montana

CHICKEN PARTY SALAD

2 c. chopped cold chicken
1 c. chopped celery
1 tbsp. lemon juice
Salt and pepper to taste
½ c. mayonnaise
1 c. halved white seedless grapes
1 c. drained crushed pineapple (opt.)

Combine chicken, celery, lemon juice, salt, pepper, mayonnaise, grapes and pineapple; mix thoroughly. Chill until ready to serve. Spoon into lettuce cups; garnish with olives, salted almonds and pickles, if desired. Yield: 6 servings.

Opal Carpenter, Mentone H. S.
Mentone, Indiana

CHICKEN RICE-A-RONI SALAD

1 pkg. chicken Rice-A-Roni
1 c. chopped fresh tomatoes
½ c. chopped green onion
½ c. chopped celery
2 tbsp. wine vinegar
2 tbsp. lemon juice
1 tbsp. sugar
1 c. boned, boiled chicken

Prepare Rice-A-Roni according to package directions. Cool. Add remaining ingredients. Pour into 2-quart bowl or baking dish. Chill for several hours. Serve on lettuce leaves with avocado halves, if desired. Yield: 4-6 servings.

Linda Reed, Tennyson Jr. H. S.
Waco, Texas

CHICKEN SALAD DELUXE

1⅓ c. instant rice
1½ tsp. salt
⅔ c. mayonnaise
⅓ c. French dressing
⅛ tsp. pepper
1½ c. diced cooked chicken
1 c. diced celery
1 c. diced orange sections, drained
½ c. coarsely chopped walnuts

Combine rice, ½ teaspoon salt and 1⅓ cups boiling water; mix just enough to moisten rice. Cover; remove from heat. Let stand for 5 minutes. Remove cover; cool to room temperature. Combine mayonnaise, French dressing, pepper and remaining 1 teaspoon salt; mix well. Combine chicken, celery, orange sections and walnuts; stir in mayonnaise mixture. Add rice; mix lightly. Chill for 1 hour before serving. One cup drained, diced pineapple or 1½ cups seeded grapes may be substituted for orange sections, if desired. Yield: 4-6 servings.

Murlene Oakley, Canton H. S.
Canton, Oklahoma

CHICKEN SALAD IN A HURRY

3 c. diced chicken
2 c. chopped celery
1 c. salad dressing
2 c. seedless white grapes
1 sm. can slivered almonds

Toss all ingredients together; serve in lettuce cups. Yield: 8 servings.

*Mrs. Nervetta C. Lawrence, Tates Creek Jr. H. S.
Lexington, Kentucky*

CHICKEN SALAD MELODY

1 10-oz. package frozen peas
1 c. diced celery
1 2-oz. jar cocktail onions
2 c. cooked chicken
1 c. mayonnaise
1 tbsp. lemon juice
1 tbsp. soy sauce
¼ tsp. garlic salt
1 c. chow mein noodles
½ c. slivered almonds
Tomatoes

Combine peas, celery, onion and chicken. Combine mayonnaise, lemon juice, soy sauce and garlic salt in a small bowl. Pour mayonnaise mixture over chicken mixture. Chill for at least 1 hour. Add chow mein noodles and almonds just before serving. Serve on tomato flowers.

*Katherine McIlquham, Chippewa Falls Sr. H. S.
Chippewa Falls, Wisconsin*

CHICKEN SALAD ON TOMATO SLICES

6 ½-inch thick slices tomato
¼ c. vinegar
½ tsp. salt
¼ tsp. pepper
1 pkg. unflavored gelatin
1½ c. seasoned chicken stock
3 tbsp. mayonnaise
2 tbsp. chopped green pepper
½ c. slivered almonds
2 tbsp. diced celery
1½ c. chopped cooked chicken

Marinate tomatoes in vinegar seasoned with salt and pepper. Soften gelatin in ¼ cup water for 5 minutes. Bring chicken stock to a boil. Add gelatin; stir until dissolved. Stir in mayonnaise; chill until partially congealed. Stir in remaining ingredients; pour into individual molds. Chill until firm. Unmold; serve on tomato slices. Yield: 6 servings.

*Johnie Sport, Dozier H. S.
Dozier, Alabama*

CHICKEN SALAD SUPREME

2 ½ c. diced cold cooked chicken
1 c. finely chopped celery
1 c. sliced white grapes
½ c. toasted slivered almonds
2 tbsp. minced parsley
1 tsp. salt
½ c. whipped cream
1 c. mayonnaise or salad dressing

Combine all ingredients; mix well. Serve on lettuce; garnish with stuffed olives and chicken slices, if desired. Yield: 8 servings.

*Mrs. Grover C. Dear, Whitehaven H. S.
Memphis, Tennessee*

CHICKEN-STUFFED ROLLS

⅔ c. chopped cooked chicken
¼ c. chopped celery
⅛ tsp. salt
Pepper to taste (opt.)
2 tbsp. chopped pickles
3 tbsp. mayonnaise
1 tbsp. chopped green pepper
1 hard-cooked egg, chopped
12 brown and serve rolls

Combine all ingredients except rolls; mix well. Hollow out rolls; stuff with salad mixture. Place rolls on baking sheet. Bake at 425 degrees until rolls are browned, and heated through. Yield: 4-6 servings

*Agnes Dervishian, Caruthers H. S.
Caruthers, California*

CURRIED CHICKEN AND GRAPE SALAD

3 c. diced cooked chicken
1½ c. thinly sliced celery
1 c. seedless green grapes
2 tbsp. lemon juice
1¼ tsp. salt
¼ tsp. freshly ground pepper
1½ tsp. curry powder
6 tbsp. mayonnaise

Combine all ingredients; toss lightly. Chill thoroughly. Serve on lettuce; garnish with toasted slivered almonds. Yield: 6 servings.

*Lois Pullen, State Department of Education
Baton Rouge, Louisiana*

CHILLED CHICKEN SALAD PIE

2 c. chopped cooked chicken
¾ c. shredded American cheese
½ c. diced celery
½ c. drained crushed pineapple
½ c. chopped pecans
½ tsp. paprika
½ tsp. salt
¾ c. mayonnaise
1 baked 9-in. pie shell
½ c. whipping cream, whipped

Combine chicken, cheese, celery, pineapple, pecans, paprika, salt and ½ cup mayonnaise; spread in pie shell. Fold whipped cream into remaining ¼ cup mayonnaise; spread over chicken mixture. Garnish with shredded carrots, if desired. Chill for 3 hours or overnight.

Mrs. Melba Smith, Grandview H. S.
Grandview, Texas

DOUBLE CHICKEN SALAD

1 pkg. lemon gelatin
1 can cream of chicken soup
½ c. chopped celery
¼ c. diced green pepper
2 tbsp. diced pimento
1 tsp. minced onion
1 c. finely cut cooked chicken

Dissolve gelatin in 1 cup boiling water. Stir in chicken soup. Chill until partially congealed. Add remaining ingredients; chill until firm. Serve on bed of lettuce; garnish with hard-boiled egg slices. Yield: 8-10 servings.

Mrs. Melvin Tavares, Kempton-Cabery H. S.
Kempton, Illinois

FAR WEST CHICKEN SALAD

1 can pears
1 tsp. red food coloring
1 can chicken
1 c. diced celery
½ c. chopped walnuts
¼ c. chopped green pepper
¼ tsp. salt
Dash of pepper
½ c. (about) salad dressing or mayonnaise

Drain pears; reserve juice. Combine reserved juice and food coloring. Add pears; let stand for 10 minutes. Combine chicken, celery, walnuts and green pepper. Add salt and pepper with enough salad dressing to moisten. Arrange pears and chicken salad on salad greens; serve with additional salad dressing and olives, if desired. Yield: 4 servings.

Laura Mae Pernice, H. B. Turner Jr. H. S.
Warren, Ohio

FAVORITE CHICKEN SALAD

1 c. chopped cooked chicken
1 c. chopped apple or drained pineapple tidbits
½ c. chopped celery
½ c. chopped olives or ¼ c. chopped pecans
3 tbsp. mayonnaise
3 tbsp. lemon juice

Combine all ingredients; mix lightly. Chill until ready to serve. Yield: 4 servings.

Mrs. Joyce Edmondson, Bowdon H. S.
Bowdon, Georgia

FROZEN CHICKEN SALAD

1½ c. diced cooked chicken
¾ c. drained crushed pineapple
¾ c. chopped pecans
1 c. whipping cream, whipped
1 c. mayonnaise

Toss chicken, pineapple and pecans together. Combine whipped cream and mayonnaise; fold into chicken mixture. Freeze until firm. Yield: 8 servings.

Myrtle Cummings, Buna H. S.
Buna, Texas

HOT CHICKEN SALAD ROYALE

2 c. diced cooked chicken
1½ c. chopped celery
¼ c. chopped almonds
5 tsp. minced onion
1 tsp. grated lemon rind
1 tbsp. lemon juice
Pepper
3 hard-cooked eggs, chopped (opt.)
½ c. chopped stuffed olives (opt.)
⅔ c. mayonnaise
Salt to taste
1 c. grated Cheddar cheese
1 c. crushed potato chips

Combine chicken, celery, almonds, onion, lemon rind, lemon juice, ⅛ teaspoon pepper, eggs and olives. Add mayonnaise; mix carefully. Season with salt and pepper. Divide into 4 individual baking dishes or 1 medium casserole. Sprinkle with cheese; top with potato chips. Place on baking sheet. Bake in

375-degree oven for 25 minutes or until cheese is bubbly. Yield: 4 servings.

Mrs. Ruth T. Hanegan, Hope H. S.
Hope, Arkansas

TASTY HOT CHICKEN SALAD

¾ c. mayonnaise
2 c. cooked cubed chicken
1 c. diced celery
2 tbsp. chopped onion
½ c. sliced almonds
1½ c. cooked rice
1 c. cream of chicken soup
1 tbsp. lemon juice
Salt and pepper to taste
2 c. crushed potato chips
3 hard-cooked eggs, chopped

Combine mayonnaise and ½ cup water in a mixing bowl. Add next 8 ingredients; mix well. Fold in 1½ cups potato chips and eggs. Place in a 2-quart casserole. Top with remaining potato chips. Bake at 400 degrees for 15 to 20 minutes. Frozen. May be baked for 15 minutes at 400 degrees then 10 minutes at 350 degrees. Yield: 6 servings.

Diane Swan, Gerard H. S.
Phoenix, Arizona

TERESA'S HOT CHICKEN SALAD

⅔ c. mayonnaise
2 tsp. lemon juice
1 tsp. salt
¼ tsp. celery seed
⅛ tsp. pepper
2 c. diced, cooked chicken
1 c. chopped celery
¼ c. blanched slivered almonds
¼ c. chopped sweet dill pickle
2 tsp. chopped onion
1 c. grated cheese
1 c. crushed potato chips

Mix mayonnaise, lemon juice, salt, celery seed and pepper. Mix chicken with celery, almonds, pickle and onion in a separate bowl. Toss with dressing. Place in a 6 x 10-inch baking dish. Sprinkle with cheese and potato chips. Bake at 350 degrees for 20 minutes. Yield: 5-6 servings.

Teresa Heatherly, Alief Hastings H. S.
Alief, Texas

JAN'S CHICKEN SALAD

2 tbsp. salad oil
2 tbsp. vinegar
2 tbsp. orange juice
½ tsp. salt
3 c. cooked chopped chicken or turkey
½ c. almonds
1 c. mandarin oranges, drained
1 9-oz. can pineapple tidbits, drained
1 c. diced celery
½ c. halved green grapes

Combine salad oil, vinegar, orange juice and salt. Pour mixture over chicken. Marinate for 1 hour. Toast almonds in a 350° oven for 5 to 10 minutes or until lightly browned. Drain chicken. Combine with remaining ingredients; mix well. Chill for several hours. Yield: 6-8 servings.

Jan Doepner, Tartan H. S.
St. Paul, Minnesota

JELLIED CHICKEN SALAD

2 env. unflavored gelatin
2 chicken bouillon cubes
2 tbsp. vinegar
½ tsp. salt
2 c. chopped cooked chicken
½ c. cooked peas
¼ c. sliced pimento
¼ c. chopped celery
2 tbsp. minced onions

Soften gelatin in ½ cup cold water for 5 minutes. Dissolve bouillon cubes in 2 cups boiling water. Stir in softened gelatin, mixing well until gelatin is dissolved. Add vinegar and salt. Chill until thick. Fold in chicken, peas, pimento, celery and onions. Pour into lightly oiled 8-inch square baking pan. Chill until set. Yield: 6 servings.

Mrs. Mary Jo Lyle, Gatewood Schools Inc.
Eatonton, Georgia

PRESSED PARTY CHICKEN SALAD

1 env. unflavored gelatin
2 c. hot chicken broth
Juice of 1 lemon
1 c. mayonnaise
1 tsp. salt
5 c. chopped cooked chicken
1½ c. chopped celery
6 hard-cooked eggs, chopped
1 c. pickle relish

Soften gelatin in ½ cup cold water. Add chicken broth; stir until gelatin is dissolved. Add lemon juice, mayonnaise, and salt; chill until partially congealed. Stir in remaining ingredients; pour into mold. Chill until firm. Yield: 24 servings.

Mrs. Rebecca McGaughy, Montevallo H. S.
Montevallo, Alabama

MACARONI-CHICKEN SALAD

½ lb. elbow macaroni
2 c. diced, cooked chicken
1 c. chopped celery
1 tbsp. grated onion
1 tsp. salt
½ c. mayonnaise
2 tbsp. chopped green pepper
1 tbsp. minced pimento

Cook macaroni in boiling, salted water until tender. Drain and chill. Add remaining ingredients; mix lightly. Chill. Serve on lettuce.

Sara Kiker, Northwest Whitfield H. S.
Tunnel Hill, Georgia

SOUR CREAM-CHICKEN MOUSSE

2 env. unflavored gelatin
4 chicken bouillon cubes
3 tbsp. lemon juice
1 tsp. dry mustard
2½ tsp. curry powder
1 tsp. onion salt
2 c. sour cream
3 c. diced cooked chicken
1 c. chopped celery
¼ c. chopped green pepper
½ c. roasted, chopped almonds

Soften gelatin in ½ cup cold water. Pour 2 cups boiling water over bouillon cubes; stir until dissolved. Add lemon juice, mustard, curry powder and onion salt. Pour bouillon mixture over gelatin; stir until gelatin is dissolved. Cool for 5 minutes. Stir in sour cream; mix well. Refrigerate until partially congealed. Add chicken, celery, green pepper and almonds; mix well. Chill until firm. Yield: 8 servings.

Evelyne Dealy, Meridian H. S.
Bellingham, Washington

SPECIAL CHICKEN SALAD

2 c. green beans
1 c. cubed chicken
2 hard-cooked eggs, chopped
⅔ c. sliced water chestnuts
⅓ c. chopped sweet pickles
¼ c. mayonnaise
1 tbsp. chopped onion
1 tsp. prepared mustard
1 tsp. sweet pickle juice
1 tbsp. pimento
1 tsp. salt

Combine beans, chicken, eggs, water chestnuts and pickles. Combine remaining ingredients in order listed; mix well. Toss dressing and salad ingredients together lightly. Chill at least 2 hours. Yield: 8 servings.

Georgia Waters Scott, Clarksville H. S.
Clarksville, Texas

BAKED LEFTOVER TURKEY SALAD

2 c. diced cooked turkey
2 c. diced celery
½ tsp. salt
1 tbsp. minced onion
½ c. chopped nuts
1 c. mayonnaise
2 tbsp. lemon juice
½ c. sliced stuffed olives
½ c. grated Cheddar cheese
1 c. finely crushed potato chips

Combine all ingredients except cheese and potato chips; spoon into buttered 1½-quart casserole. Combine cheese and potato chips; sprinkle over turkey mixture. Bake in 375-degree oven for 20 minutes or until heated through. Serve hot. Yield: 10 servings.

Mary Ella Ingram, Wagram H. S.
Wagram, North Carolina

HOLIDAY TURKEY-CRANBERRY SALAD

1½ c. turkey broth
3 pkg. unflavored gelatin
2 tbsp. lemon juice
¾ tsp. salt
¾ c. mayonnaise
1½ c. finely diced turkey
½ c. finely diced celery
1 1-lb. can jellied cranberry sauce

Heat 1 cup turkey broth. Soften 2 packages gelatin in ½ cup cold water. Add to hot broth; stir until dissolved. Add remaining broth, 1 tablespoon lemon juice and ½ teaspoon salt; let cool. Stir a small amount of gelatin mixture into mayonnaise until smooth; stir in remaining gelatin mixture. Chill until partially congealed. Fold in turkey and celery; pour into oiled oblong dish. Chill until firm. Mash cranberry sauce; add remaining 1 tablespoon lemon juice and remaining ¼ teaspoon salt. Soften remaining package gelatin in ¼ cup cold water; dissolve in ½ cup boiling water. Stir into cranberry sauce; mix well. Pour over turkey layer; chill until firm. Yield: 10 servings.

Mrs. Kelley Storey, Paris H. S.
Paris, Tennessee

HOT TURKEY SALAD

2 c. diced cooked turkey
1½ c. diced celery
1½ c. toasted slivered almonds
½ c. chopped ripe olives
2 tbsp. chopped pimento
¼ c. French dressing
½ c. mayonnaise
⅓ c. sour cream
2 tsp. minced onion
1½ c. crushed potato chips
½ c. grated cheese

Combine first 5 ingredients with dressing in 3-quart casserole. Let stand in refrigerator for 1 hour or overnight. Combine mayonnaise, sour cream and onion. Add to turkey mixture. Bake for 20 to 30 minutes at 375 degrees. Remove from oven. Top with potato chips and cheese. Bake for 5 minutes longer.

Mrs. Gladys Herring, Corsicana H. S.
Corsicana, Texas

INDIVIDUAL HOT TURKEY SALADS

3 c. cubed cooked turkey
1 c. cubed sharp cheese
1 c. chopped celery
½ c. slivered almonds
½ c. mayonnaise
Salt and pepper to taste
1 c. crushed potato chips

Combine all ingredients except potato chips; toss gently. Place in individual casseroles; sprinkle potato chips over top. Bake in 325-degree oven for 35 minutes or until heated through. Yield: 4 servings.

Mrs. Audrey Johnson, Kickapoo Area School
Viola, Wisconsin

TURKEY-ALMOND SALAD

2 c. cubed cooked turkey
1 c. chopped seeded red grapes
⅓ c. diced celery
½ c. toasted slivered almonds
Salad dressing

Combine turkey, grapes, celery and almonds. Add enough salad dressing to moisten; toss gently. Serve on lettuce. Yield: 6-8 servings.

Ila Rea, Dayton Joint H. S.
Dayton, Pennsylvania

TURKEY SALAD FOR A CROWD

1 14-lb. turkey
Salt
Celery, cut in lg. pieces
Quartered onions
Parsley to taste
2 c. whipped cream
1 qt. salad dressing
¼ c. vinegar
¼ c. sugar
2 qt. diced celery
2 qt. seedless green grapes
18 hard-cooked eggs, diced
2 c. toasted slivered almonds

Rinse and dry turkey; sprinkle cavity with salt. Stuff with celery pieces, quartered onions and a small amount of parsley. Place turkey in roaster; cover. Bake at 325 degrees until tender. Let turkey cool. Remove skin and bones; cut into bite-sized pieces. Combine whipped cream, salad dressing, vinegar and sugar for dressing; season with salt. Combine turkey, diced celery, grapes, eggs and almonds in large salad bowl. Add dressing; toss gently to mix well. Chill for several hours before serving. Yield: 50 servings.

Marie Strand, Stillwater Jr. H. S.
Stillwater, Minnesota

BAYLEY'S WEST INDIES SALAD

1 med. onion, finely chopped
1 lb. fresh lump crab meat
Salt and pepper to taste
½ c. salad oil
6 tbsp. cider vinegar

Place half the onion in salad bowl. Separate crab meat lumps; place on top of onion. Spread remaining onion over crab meat. Season with salt and pepper. Pour oil, then vinegar over onion; pour ½ cup ice water over top. Cover; refrigerate 12 hours. Toss lightly just before serving. Yield: 6 servings.

Grace Lunsford, Foley School
Foley, Alabama

CRAB MEAT SALAD

6 green onions, chopped
1 c. mayonnaise
1 tomato, chopped
½ green pepper, chopped
1 tbsp. lemon juice
2 hard-cooked eggs, chopped
2 6½-oz. cans white crab meat

Mix all ingredients together. Chill. Serve with assorted crackers. Yield: 6-12 servings.

Patsy Leeser, Montgomery County R-II H. S.
Montgomery City, Missouri

CRAB LOUIS

1 lg. head lettuce
3 c. chilled crab meat
2 lg. tomatoes, cut in wedges
2 hard-cooked eggs, cut in wedges
Salt to taste
Louis Dressing

Line 4 large plates with lettuce leaves. Shred remaining lettuce; arrange on leaves. Arrange crab meat on lettuce; circle with tomato wedges and egg wedges. Sprinkle with salt. Pour ¼ cup Louis Dressing over each salad. Garnish with paprika. Pass remaining dressing. Yield: 4 servings.

Louis Dressing
1 c. mayonnaise
¼ c. sour cream
¼ c. chili sauce
¼ c. chopped green onion
1 tsp. lemon juice
Salt to taste

Combine mayonnaise, sour cream, chili sauce, green onion and lemon juice; season with salt. Chill thoroughly. Yield: 2 cups dressing.

Betty Ann McCullough, Conneaut Lake Area H. S.
Conneaut Lake, Pennsylvania

CRAB SALAD IN ORANGE SHELLS

8 oranges
2 6½-oz. cans crab meat, flaked
1 c. minced celery
1 tsp. grated onion
½ c. mayonnaise

Cut off blossom end of each orange; cut rind in points. Scoop out segments. Dice enough segments to measure 1 cup. Combine orange segments and remaining ingredients; toss lightly. Heap crab salad in orange shells; chill thoroughly. Garnish with additional mayonnaise. Yield: 8 servings.

Mrs. Violet Horne, Forest Hills School
Marshville, North Carolina

CRAB SALAD RING

1 pkg. lemon gelatin
2 c. boiling tomato juice
2 tsp. lemon juice
1 c. mayonnaise
2 pkg. cream cheese, softened
1 c. diced celery
2 tsp. onion juice

Salt to taste
1 can crab, shrimp or tuna

Dissolve gelatin in tomato juice; stir in lemon juice. Chill until partially congealed. Add mayonnaise to cream cheese; beat until smooth. Add celery, onion juice, salt and crab; pour into ring mold. Chill until firm. May serve with coleslaw in center; garnish with hard-cooked eggs, if desired. Yield: 6 servings.

Mrs. F. A. Putney, Cumberland H. S.
Cumberland, Virginia

CRAB-STUFFED AVOCADO

Mayonnaise
Chili sauce
½ c. crab meat
Salt and pepper to taste
Lemon juice to taste
Shredded Lettuce
1 carrot, shredded
1 radish, shredded
1 avocado half

Combine equal parts of mayonnaise and chili sauce to make a dressing. Mix crab with dressing; season with salt, pepper and lemon juice. Combine shredded vegetables; place on salad plate. Place avocado on vegetables; fill with crab mixture. Top with additional mayonnaise and thin strips of tomato, if desired. Yield: 1 serving.

Shirley L. Andersen, Enterprise H. S.
Enterprise, Oregon

DELICIOUS CRAB SALAD

4 c. flaked crab meat
1½ c. diced celery
Juice of 1 lemon
1 sm. onion, minced
⅓ c. minced parsley
1½ c. mayonnaise

Combine all ingredients; mix gently. Serve in lettuce cups. Yield: 6 servings.

Owinta Powell, Mowat Sr. H. S.
Lynn Haven, Florida

DEVILED CRAB SALAD CAKES

1 6½-oz. can crab meat, flaked
½ c. diced celery
6 stuffed olives, chopped
2 hard-cooked eggs, chopped
½ tsp. Worcestershire sauce

½ tsp. salt
¼ tsp. pepper
½ tsp. paprika
½ c. medium white sauce
Cracker meal

Combine crab, celery, olives, eggs and seasonings; mix well. Add white sauce; chill thoroughly. Shape crab mixture into patties; roll in cracker meal. Fry in deep hot fat until golden brown. Yield: 6-8 servings.

Sister M. Daniel SS.C.M., Andrean H. S.
Gary, Indiana

EASY SEAFOOD SALAD BAKE

2 tbsp. minced green pepper
1 sm. onion, finely chopped
1 c. chopped celery
1 c. flaked crab meat
½ c. shrimp
2 hard-cooked eggs, chopped
¾ c. fine soft bread crumbs
½ c. mayonnaise
Pepper to taste
1 tsp. Worcestershire sauce

Toss green pepper, onion, celery, crab meat, shrimp, eggs and bread crumbs together. Season mayonnaise with pepper and Worcestershire sauce; combine with crab mixture. Place in greased baking shells or casserole; sprinkle with cracker crumbs or bread crumbs. Bake in 350-degree oven for 30 minutes or until heated through. Yield: 4 servings.

Barbara A. West, Cradock H. S.
Portsmouth, Virginia

HOT CRAB SALAD IN SHELLS

1 lb. crab meat
1 c. shrimp (opt.)
1 c. finely chopped celery
1 sm. bell pepper, chopped
1 sm. onion, chopped
½ c. mayonnaise
1 tsp. Worcestershire sauce
½ tsp. salt
Cayenne pepper to taste
2 tbsp. melted butter
1 c. bread crumbs

Combine first 9 ingredients; mix well. Place in buttered shells. Mix butter and bread crumbs together; sprinkle over crab mixture. Bake in 350-degree oven for 30 minutes or until heated through. Yield: 6-8 servings.

Mrs. Helen Scott, Haynesville H. S.
Haynesville, Louisiana

QUICK CRAB SALAD

1½ c. flaked crab meat
3 tbsp. French dressing
1 c. finely diced celery
Mayonnaise to taste

Combine crab and French dressing; let stand in refrigerator for 30 minutes. Drain off dressing. Add celery and mayonnaise; mix well. Serve on bed of lettuce. Yield: 4 servings.

Mrs. LaRue B. Fleming, Bogalusa Sr. H. S.
Bogalusa, Louisiana

SAUCY HOT CRAB SALAD

6 tbsp. butter
6 tbsp. flour
1 tsp. salt
⅛ tsp. pepper
2½ c. milk
1 lb. crab meat
6 hard-cooked eggs, chopped
1 c. slivered almonds
Buttered bread crumbs

Melt butter in saucepan. Add flour, salt and pepper; stir to make a smooth paste. Stir in milk; cook until smooth and thick, stirring constantly. Remove from heat. Stir in crab, eggs and almonds; spread in buttered 8-inch square pan. Cover generously with buttered bread crumbs. Bake in 375-degree oven for 20 minutes or until heated through. Do not let salad boil. Salad may be prepared ahead and refrigerated until ready to bake. Yield: 6-8 servings.

Mrs. Mina A. Qualley, Public Sch.
Breckenridge, Minnesota

SLICED CRAB SALAD

2 tsp. unflavored gelatin
½ c. mayonnaise
¼ c. catsup
1 tbsp. lemon juice
½ tsp. salt
1 tsp. Worcestershire sauce
1 c. flaked crab meat
1 egg white, beaten

Soften gelatin in 2 tablespoons cold water; dissolve over hot water. Combine gelatin, mayonnaise, catsup and seasonings. Stir in crab; fold in egg white. Place in ice cube tray; chill until firm. Cut in slices to serve. Yield: 6 servings.

Sue K. Sloan, Tascosa H. S.
Amarillo, Texas

TASTY CRAB SALAD

1 lb. crab meat
¾ c. chopped celery
¼ c. chopped green pepper
1 tbsp. minced onion
3 dashes of Worcestershire sauce
1 tsp. dry mustard
Salt and pepper to taste
Juice of ¼ lemon
Mayonnaise
Tomatoes, cut into eighths

Combine crab, celery, green pepper and onion; season with Worcestershire sauce, mustard, salt, pepper and lemon juice. Toss with enough mayonnaise to moisten ingredients. Arrange tomatoes on lettuce, if desired; serve crab salad over tomatoes. Yield: 6 servings.

Dorothy A. Foster, Mathews H. S.
Mathews, Virginia

HALIBUT WITH A FLAIR

1 tbsp. lemon juice
½ tsp. dry mustard
¼ c. mayonnaise
1 c. flaked cooked halibut
1 c. flaked crab meat
¾ c. finely diced celery
¼ c. minced sweet pickles, drained
Salt and pepper to taste

Combine lemon juice, mustard and mayonnaise; mix well. Mix halibut, crab, celery and pickles together. Toss lightly with mayonnaise dressing; season with salt and pepper. Yield: 4 servings.

Mrs. Lillian Wise, Rabun Gap Nacoochee H. S.
Rabun Gap, Georgia

CREAMY LOBSTER SALAD

1 can tomato soup
1 8-oz. package cheese food
2 env. unflavored gelatin
1 tsp. salt
1 c. mayonnaise
1 8-oz. can lobster, crab or shrimp
1 c. chopped celery
1 onion, grated
1 c. finely shredded green pepper

Combine soup and cheese in top of double boiler; cook over hot water until cheese is melted. Soften gelatin in ½ cup cold water; dissolve in hot soup mixture. Stir in salt and mayonnaise; chill until partially con-

gealed. Stir in remaining ingredients; pour into mold. Chill until firm. Yield: 8 servings.

Mrs. Dorothy Boen, Central H. S.
Muskogee, Oklahoma

ESTHER'S FLORIDA LOBSTER SALAD

1½ c. diced lobster
Lime juice
4 avocado halves
½ c. chopped celery
1 tsp. salt
¼ tsp. pepper
Mayonnaise or equal parts mayonnaise and
    sour cream
2 tbsp. capers (opt.)
Halved hard-cooked eggs
Pitted ripe olives

Combine lobster and ¼ cup lime juice; store in refrigerator to marinate. Sprinkle avocado halves with lime juice to prevent discoloration; chill in refrigerator. Combine celery, salt and pepper with enough mayonnaise to moisten salad. Add to lobster; toss lightly. Spoon salad into avocado halves; sprinkle capers over top. Serve salad with halved eggs and ripe olives. Yield: 4 servings.

Mrs. Esther Blaylock, Marathon H. S.
Marathon, Florida

LOBSTER AND CHICKEN SALAD SUPREME

1 cooked chicken breast
½ lb. lobster, diced
3 hard-cooked eggs
1 c. finely chopped celery
French dressing
1 c. mayonnaise
2 tbsp. chili sauce
1 tbsp. chopped chives
Salt to taste
½ c. whipped cream

Remove skin and bones from chicken breast; cut into strips. Combine chicken, lobster, chopped egg whites and celery in a small amount of French dressing; set aside to marinate for about 1 hour. Mash egg yolks. Add mayonnaise, chili sauce, chives and salt; mix well. Fold in whipped cream; let dressing chill thoroughly. Combine lobster mixture and dressing; toss lightly. Serve on lettuce, if desired. Yield 4-6 servings.

Margaret K. Shollenberger, Rice Ave. Union H. S.
Girard, Pennsylvania

LOBSTER LUNCHEON SALAD

4 c. cubed lobster
4 hard-cooked eggs, chopped
½ c. diced celery
¼ c. minced parsley
1 tsp. dry mustard
1 tsp. grated onion
1 tsp. Worcestershire sauce
½ tsp. salt
1 c. mayonnaise

Combine lobster, eggs, celery and parsley; add mustard, onion, Worcestershire sauce and salt. Add mayonnaise; toss gently until well mixed. Serve on lettuce, if desired. Yield: 6 servings.

*Mrs. Emily Porter, Savoy H. S.
Savoy, Texas*

LOBSTER MOUSSE

1 pkg. unflavored gelatin
¾ c. minced celery
1½ c. lobster
⅔ c. minced apple
¾ c. mayonnaise
3 tbsp. lemon juice
Salt to taste
Paprika to taste
⅓ c. whipped cream

Soften gelatin in ¼ cup cold water. Dissolve over boiling water. Combine celery, lobster, apple, mayonnaise and lemon juice in mixer bowl; season with salt and paprika. Add gelatin; beat until mixture is well mixed. Fold in whipped cream; spread in wet mold. Chill until firm. Unmold onto serving platter; garnish with watercress and marinated cucumbers, if desired. Yield: 6 servings.

*Gloria Shelton, Clarksville H. S.
Clarksville, Tennessee*

MOLDED SEAFOOD SALAD

2 3-oz. packages lemon Jell-O
1 can cream of shrimp soup
3 3-oz. packages cream cheese, softened
1 c. mayonnaise
1½ c. minced celery
1 tsp. minced onion
1 can crab meat *or* lobster

Dissolve Jell-O in 1 cup boiling water; add 1 cup cold water. Add shrimp soup to cream cheese a small amount at a time; blend until smooth. Add Jell-O to soup mixture; blend well. Cool. Add remaining ingredients. Pour into 9 x 13-inch pan or baking dish.

Chill. Cut in squares. Serve on a lettuce leaf. Yield: 9-12 servings.

*Darlene Caldwell, John Muir Middle Sch.
Wausau, Wisconsin*

BROWNSVILLE OYSTER SALAD

2 No. 1 can oysters
1 med. can pimentos
8 hard-cooked eggs
4 sour pickles
¼ c. margarine, melted
30 soda crackers, crushed
Salt and vinegar to taste

Drain oysters; reserve liquid. Put oysters, pimentos, eggs and pickles through meat grinder; combine in salad bowl. Stir in margarine and cracker crumbs; season with salt and vinegar. Moisten salad with reserved liquid, if needed. Chill thoroughly. Yield: 12 servings.

*Mrs. Joyzelle Sauls, Brownsville H. S.
Brownsville, Texas*

BANANA-SALMON SALAD

3 ripe bananas, chopped
½ c. crushed pineapple
1½ c. flaked canned salmon
¼ c. diced celery
½ tsp. salt
1 tbsp. chopped sweet pickles
Mayonnaise

Combine bananas and pineapple; add salmon. Fold in remaining ingredients with enough mayonnaise to moisten. Garnish with lettuce and lemon slices, if desired. Yield: 4-5 servings.

*Mrs. Margaret Rettke, Mason County Central H. S.
Scottville, Michigan*

BUSY DAY SALMON SALAD

1 1-lb. can salmon, drained and flaked
½ c. diced celery
½ c. chopped sweet pickles
2 tbsp. chopped green pepper
½ tsp. salt
1 tbsp. lemon juice
⅓ c. mayonnaise

Remove skin and bones from salmon. Combine all ingredients; toss carefully. Chill until ready to serve. Yield: 4 servings.

*Mrs. Hazel M. Brown, McAdoo H. S.
McAdoo, Texas*

FAVORITE SALMON-MACARONI SALAD

1 1-lb. can salmon, drained and flaked
½ c. chopped celery
½ c. minced sweet pickles
2 tbsp. chopped green pepper
2 c. cooked macaroni
1 tsp. salt
1 tbsp. lemon juice
⅓ c. boiled dressing

Combine all ingredients in salad bowl. Cover; place in refrigerator until thoroughly chilled and ready to serve. Yield: 8 servings.

Virginia Dale Rawls. Pearl River Jr. H. S.
Pearl River, Louisiana

LOMI LOMI

1 1-lb. can red salmon, flaked
1 lg. onion, minced
2 lg. ripe tomatoes, cubed

Combine salmon and onion in salad bowl. Add tomatoes; toss gently. Chill until ready to serve. Yield: 6 servings.

Mrs. Betty Kirk Thomas, J. I. Carter Jr. H. S.
Arlington, Texas

MAKE-AHEAD SALMON-MACARONI SALAD

1 can salmon, drained
1 med. cucumber, diced
1 tsp. grated onion
1 tbsp. chopped parsley
2 c. cooked macaroni
1 c. mayonnaise
Salt and pepper to taste

Combine all ingredients in salad bowl; toss gently. Cover; refrigerate until thoroughly chilled and ready to serve. Yield: 8 servings.

Mrs. Betty C. Coles, Bowling Green H. S.
Bowling Green, Kentucky

REAL COOL FISH

2 1-lb. cans salmon, tuna or mackerel
1 8-oz. package cream cheese, softened
½ c. butter, softened
2 tbsp. lemon juice
Few drops of Tabasco sauce

1 c. chopped celery
1 c. chopped green pepper
2 tbsp. grated onion
3 c. (about) chopped hard-cooked eggs
Pimento strips
1 stuffed olive

Drain salmon, remove bones. Combine cream cheese and butter; mix well. Mix in lemon juice and Tabasco sauce; stir in celery, green pepper and onion. Add salmon and eggs; toss gently until well mixed. Pack salad into 6-cup fish mold; chill for 2 to 3 hours. Loosen salad from edge of mold, using sharp knife; invert onto serving plate. Place hot cloth over top to unmold. Decorate fish with thin pimento strips for scales and tail stripes; use olive for eyes. May add smiling mouth cut from green pepper, if desired. Yield: 6 servings.

Sally Marnen, Moon H. S.
Caraopolis, Pennsylvania

SALMON PARTY MOLD

2 egg yolks
1 tsp. salt
1 tbsp. prepared mustard
¼ tbsp. paprika
1½ tbsp. melted butter
¾ c. milk
2½ tbsp. lemon juice
1½ env. unflavored gelatin
2 c. flaked red salmon
1 stuffed olive slice
Pimento strips

Combine egg yolks, salt, mustard and paprika in top of double boiler; beat slightly. Add butter, milk and lemon juice; cook over hot water until mixture thickens, stirring constantly. Soften gelatin in ¼ cup cold water. Add to egg mixture; stir until dissolved. Stir in salmon. Rinse fish mold with cold water. Pour about ½ cup salmon mixture in mold; turn mold to coat inside. Chill until firm. Place 1 olive slice in mold for eye; arrange pimento strips in mold for back and fins. Pour in remaining salmon mixture carefully; chill until firm. Place hot towel over inverted mold to remove salad. Garnish with lemon wedges sprinkled with paprika, if desired. Yield: 8 servings.

Mrs. Hannah Hoff Brown
Waco, Texas

SALMON SALAD LOAF

1 pkg. unflavored gelatin
⅓ c. lemon juice
1 1-lb. can salmon, flaked

1 c. chopped celery
½ tsp. salt
½ c. stuffed olives chopped
½ c. chopped pecans
1 c. mayonnaise

Soften gelatin in ½ cup cold water; dissolve over hot water. Mix all ingredients together lightly; pour into oiled 9 x 5 x 3-inch loaf pan. Chill until firm. Yield: 8 servings.

Mrs. Mary Louise Warren, Cedar Hill H. S.
Cedar Hill, Texas

SUPPER SALMON SALAD

1 pkg. lime or lemon gelatin
3 tbsp. vinegar
¼ tsp. salt
1 tsp. sugar
¼ tsp. dry mustard
½ c. mayonnaise
1 c. chopped celery
1 c. diced cucumber
1 tall can red salmon, flaked

Dissolve gelatin in 1¾ cups boiling water. Add vinegar, salt, sugar, mustard and mayonnaise. Chill until partially congealed. Add remaining ingredients; pour into wet molds. Chill until firm. Serve on lettuce; garnish with pimento, if desired. Yield: 8 servings.

Mrs. Ann Click McGaughy, Calera H. S.
Calera, Alabama

AVOCADO PONTCHARTRAIN WITH SHRIMP REMOULADE

¼ c. tarragon vinegar
2 tbsp. horseradish mustard
1 tbsp. catsup
1½ tsp. paprika
½ tsp. salt
¼ tsp. cayenne pepper
½ c. salad oil
¼ c. minced celery
¼ c. minced green onions and tops
2 lb. shrimp, cleaned and cooked
4 med. avocados, peeled and halved

Combine vinegar, mustard, catsup, paprika, salt and cayenne pepper; add oil slowly, beating constantly. Stir in celery and onions; pour sauce over shrimp. Marinate in refrigerator for 4 to 5 hours. Lift shrimp out of sauce; arrange 5 or 6 shrimp in each avocado half. May be served with cooked chilled asparagus spears, carrot strips and sliced hard-cooked eggs with additional Remoulade sauce or French dressing. Yield: 8 servings.

Mrs. Ruby Walker, Kate Griffin Jr. H. S.
Meridian, Mississippi

BRIGHT JEWEL SHRIMP SALAD

1 pkg. lemon gelatin
1 tsp. salt
¼ tsp. garlic salt
Dash of pepper
1 tbsp. vinegar
1 c. ½-inch pieces cooked shrimp
1 avocado, diced
1½ c. grapefruit sections
1 c. diced tomato
1 c. julienne-cut cheese (opt.)
½ c. sliced pitted ripe olives
¼ c. chopped green onions
3 qt. salad greens

Dissolve gelatin in 1 cup boiling water. Add seasonings, vinegar and ½ cup cold water; pour into 8-inch square pan. Chill until partially congealed. Add shrimp and avocado; chill until firm. Cut into 1-inch squares. Combine remaining ingredients; toss lightly. Arrange shrimp squares on top; serve with favorite salad dressing. Yield: 8 servings.

Mrs. Loretta Fowler Bennett
Edgar Allan Poe Intermediate School
Annandale, Virginia

BRUNCH SHRIMP SALAD

3 pkg. unflavored gelatin
2 tbsp. sugar
2 tbsp. vinegar
1 can tomato soup
1½ tsp. salt
1 sm. onion, grated
1 c. small English peas
1 lb. cooked cleaned shrimp
1 c. diced celery
1 sm. jar pimentos, chopped
1 bottle stuffed olives, chopped
1 c. finely chopped pecans

Soften gelatin in ½ cup cold water. Add 2 cups boiling water; stir until gelatin is dissolved. Stir in sugar, vinegar, soup and salt; mix well. Chill until partially congealed. Stir in remaining ingredients; pour into mold. Chill until firm. Yield: 6-8 servings.

Mrs. Lemoyne Graham, Lucedale H. S.
Lucedale, Mississippi

CHILLED SHRIMP SALAD

⅓ c. mayonnaise
¼ c. sour cream
¼ tsp. sugar
1 tbsp. chili sauce
1½ tsp. salt
2 tbsp. lemon juice
2 c. boiled cleaned shrimp
2 hard-cooked eggs, diced
1 c. julienne-cut celery
1 tbsp. chopped pimento
1 tbsp. chopped green pepper

Chill all ingredients. Combine mayonnaise, sour cream, sugar, chili sauce, salt and lemon juice; blend well. Drain shrimp; add to mayonnaise mixture. Add all remaining ingredients; toss lightly. Heap lightly into lettuce cups. Serve immediately. Yield: 6 servings.

Mrs. Tillie B. Jones, Tylertown H. S.
Tylertown, Mississippi

CREAMY AVOCADO-SHRIMP SALAD

1 pkg. unflavored gelatin
1 tbsp. lemon juice
1 3-oz. package cream cheese, softened
½ c. mayonnaise
¼ tsp. monosodium glutamate
½ tsp. grated onion
¼ tsp. Worcestershire sauce
1 c. finely chopped celery
1 can shrimp
1 avocado, mashed

Soften gelatin in lemon juice; place over hot water and stir until dissolved. Blend cream cheese, mayonnaise, monosodium glutamate, onion and Worcestershire sauce together; stir in gelatin. Fold in remaining ingredients; pour into oiled mold. Chill until firm. Yield: 8 servings.

Mrs. Elizabeth T. Carlton, Morgantown School
Natchez, Mississippi

CURRIED SHRIMP AND TUNA SALAD

1 c. cleaned cooked shrimp
1 7-oz. can solid pack tuna, drained
½ c. chopped celery
¼ c. chopped ripe or stuffed olives
½ c. mayonnaise
1 tsp. curry powder
2 tbsp. lemon juice
3 c. cold cooked rice
2 to 3 tbsp. French dressing
½ c. snipped parsley

Chill shrimp and tuna. Mix celery and olives together. Combine mayonnaise, curry powder and lemon juice. Stir shrimp mixture, celery mixture and curried mayonnaise together. Toss rice with French dressing and parsley; spoon onto serving platter. Spoon shrimp salad over rice. Yield: 6 servings.

Mrs. Esther Sigmund, L. J. Christen Jr. H. S.
Laredo, Texas

CURRIED SHRIMP SALAD WITH RICE

1⅓ c. instant rice
½ tsp. salt
¾ c. mayonnaise
1½ tsp. lemon juice
¾ tsp. curry powder
1 tbsp. grated onion
1 c. diced cooked shrimp
1 c. chopped celery

Combine rice, salt and 1⅓ cups boiling water in saucepan; stir until rice is moistened. Cover; remove from heat. Let stand for 5 minutes. Uncover; let cool until rice reaches room temperature. Combine mayonnaise, lemon juice, curry powder and onion; mix well. Combine shrimp and celery; stir in mayonnaise mixture. Add rice; mix lightly. Chill for at least 1 hour before serving. Yield: 4-5 servings.

Linda R. Kelley, Sumner Jr. H. S.
Sumner, Washington

DELICIOUS SHRIMP SALAD

2 c. cooked shrimp
¾ c. chopped celery
½ c. slivered almonds
12 stuffed olives, sliced
6 sweet gherkins, sliced
¼ c. French dressing
Mayonnaise

Combine all ingredients except mayonnaise. Cover; chill thoroughly. Mix desired amount of mayonnaise with salad; serve on crisp lettuce. Yield: 6 servings.

Nelda Bishop, Woodland H. S.
Woodland, Alabama

EASY SHRIMP SALAD WITH AVOCADO

1 pkg. unflavored gelatin
1 tsp. salt
2 tbsp. lemon juice
Dash of Tabasco sauce
¼ tsp. grated onion
1 c. sieved avocado
½ c. sour cream

1 c. cooked shrimp
1 c. chopped celery

Soften gelatin in ¼ cup cold water; dissolve in ¾ cup hot water. Blend in seasonings and onion; chill until partially congealed. Add avocado and sour cream; fold in shrimp and celery. Pour into mold; chill until firm. Garnish with whole shrimp. Yield: 6 servings.

Mrs. Jabie Effinger, Burleson H. S.
Burleson, Texas

EL PASO AVOCADO-SHRIMP SALAD

1 10-oz. package frozen shrimp
2 stalks celery, chopped
½ sweet red pepper, chopped
2 hard-cooked eggs, chopped
½ c. mayonnaise
1 head lettuce
2 avocados, peeled and halved
Juice of 1 lemon

Thaw shrimp; remove shells and back veins. Place in boiling water; cook for about 5 minutes or until pink. Chop shrimp; add celery, sweet pepper, eggs and mayonnaise. Toss to mix well. Make nests of lettuce on 4 salad plates. Dip avocado halves in lemon juice to prevent discoloration; place in lettuce nests. Mound shrimp mixture in avocados. Garnish with pitted ripe olives, tomato wedges and parsley. Yield: 4 servings.

Mrs. Eileen Blake, Jefferson H. S.
El Paso, Texas

GEORGIA SHRIMP SALAD

1 sm. package cream cheese, softened
⅓ c. mayonnaise
½ c. catsup
½ c. chopped pecans
2 tbsp. chopped onion
1½ lb. cooked shrimp, cleaned
2 cans frozen grapefruit sections, thawed
Lettuce cups

Combine cheese and mayonnaise. Add catsup, pecans and onion; mix thoroughly. Stir in shrimp. Drain grapefruit sections. Place grapefruit sections in lettuce cups; spoon shrimp mixture over grapefruit. Yield: 4 servings.

Mrs. Malcom D. Cameron, Snook H. S.
Snook, Texas

HOT SEAFOOD SALAD

1 10-oz. can shrimp soup
¼ c. milk
1 c. process cheese spread
1 7-oz. can chunk tuna
1 c. chopped celery
¼ c. chopped onion
¼ c. chopped green pepper

Combine soup and milk in saucepan. Stir in remaining ingredients; cook over low heat until heated through and vegetables are crisp, tender. Serve hot in patty shells or on toast points. Yield: 4-5 servings.

Mrs. Martha Bagwell, West Memphis H. S.
West Memphis, Arkansas

LUNCHEON SHRIMP SALAD

1½ pkg. unflavored gelatin
1 can tomato soup
3 sm. packages cream cheese, softened
1 c. mayonnaise
3 cans sm. shrimp, drained
¾ c. chopped scallions
¾ c. finely chopped celery

Dissolve gelatin in ¼ cup water. Heat soup on low temperature in a saucepan. Add gelatin. Stir cream cheese into soup until all ingredients are blended well. Add mayonnaise; stir well. Add shrimp, scallions and celery; mix well. Pour into 1-quart mold. Chill overnight. Serve on lettuce leaf. Yield: 16 servings.

Donna B. Warren, Center H. S.
Center, Texas

NEW ORLEANS SHRIMP SALAD

1 c. cold cooked rice
1 c. diced cooked shrimp
¾ tsp. salt
1 tbsp. lemon juice
¼ c. slivered green pepper
1 tbsp. minced onion
1 tbsp. chopped olives
¾ c. diced fresh cauliflower
2 tbsp. French dressing
Dash of pepper
⅓ c. mayonnaise

Toss all ingredients together; chill thoroughly. Serve on lettuce. Yield: 4 servings.

Mrs. Richard A. Dearing, Christiansburg H. S.
Christiansburg, Virginia

PARTY SHRIMP MOLD

1 can tomato soup
3 3-oz. packages cream cheese, softened
2 pkg. unflavored gelatin
½ c. minced bell pepper
½ c. minced onion
½ c. minced celery
2 lb. boiled fresh shrimp, cleaned
1 c. mayonnaise
1 stuffed olive

Heat soup and cream cheese in saucepan; stir until smooth. Soften gelatin in ½ cup cold water. Add to soup mixture; stir until gelatin is dissolved. Chill until partially congealed. Stir in remaining ingredients except olive. Cut olive in half; place halves, cut side down, in eyes of oiled fish mold. Pour shrimp mixture carefully into mold; chill until firm. Place hot cloth over bottom of mold until salad is loosened; unmold onto serving plate. Yield: 10 servings.

Tina Butler, Brantley H. S.
Brantley, Alabama

PINEAPPLE-SHRIMP OUTRIGGERS

1 lb. fresh shrimp
1 tbsp. seafood seasoning
1 tbsp. salt
¼ c. vinegar
1 ripe pineapple
French dressing

Combine shrimp, seafood seasoning, salt, vinegar and ¼ cup water in saucepan; cover. Bring to a boil. Simmer until shrimp has turned pink and is done. Remove shells; devein shrimp. Let cool. Cut pineapple and frond in half; hollow out, leaving shells about ¼-inch thick for outriggers. Remove core; dice pineapple. Combine pineapple and shrimp with enough French dressing to coat evenly. Let marinate to blend flavors. Pile shrimp mixture into pineapple outriggers, garnish with fresh flowers, if desired. Yield: 4-6 servings.

Mrs. Rose Marie Staley, Francis Scott Key H. S.
Union Bridge, Maryland

SATURDAY LUNCH SALAD

2 c. diced cooked potatoes
2 c. chopped, deveined cooked shrimp
½ c. finely shredded carrot
¼ c. grated onion
¾ c. diced tart apple
¾ c. mayonnaise
1 tsp. salt
½ tsp. pepper
2 tbsp. prepared mustard
1 tbsp. lemon juice

Combine all ingredients in order listed; chill until ready to serve. Yield: 6 servings.

Mrs. Enid Beazley, Princess Anne H. S.
Virginia Beach, Virginia

RICE AND SHRIMP SALAD

1 c. boiled shrimp
1 c. diced celery
3 c. cold cooked rice
6 hard-cooked eggs, chopped
1 c. diced sweet or sour pickles
1 c. finely chopped stuffed olives
Salt and pepper to taste
Salad dressing

Combine all ingredients. Garnish with additional hard-cooked eggs. Yield: 6-8 servings.

June Wright Curtis, Hamshire-Fannett H. S.
Hamshire, Texas

SHRIMP ASPIC

1 pkg. gelatin
1 can tomato soup
2 3-oz. packages cream cheese, softened
½ c. mayonnaise
1 tsp. minced onion
½ tsp. salt
1 c. chopped celery
3 c. mashed shrimp

Soften gelatin in ½ cup cold water. Combine soup, cream cheese and gelatin in saucepan; heat until cheese is melted, stirring frequently. Stir in mayonnaise, onion and salt; chill until partially congealed. Stir in celery and shrimp; place in mold. Chill until firm. Serve on lettuce. Yield: 6-8 servings.

Elizabeth Curry, Marianna H. S.
Marianna, Florida

SHRIMP CREME

1 pkg. lemon gelatin
1 sm. can shrimp
1 c. diced celery
½ c. chopped walnuts
½ tsp. grated onion
Juice of ½ lemon
1 c. salad dressing

Dissolve gelatin in 1⅓ cups boiling water. Chill until partially congealed. Beat with rotary beater until doubled in bulk. Stir in remaining ingredients; pour into oiled mold. Chill until firm. Yield: 8-10 servings.

Mrs. Doris Smith, Dayton H. S.
Dayton, Washington

SHRIMP-MACARONI SALAD

1 lb. shelled shrimp, cooked and chopped
1½ c. macaroni shells, cooked and drained
1 c. cubed American Cheese
½ c. chopped celery
¼ c. chopped green pepper
2 tbsp. chopped onion
½ c. mayonnaise
½ c. sour cream
3 tbsp. vinegar
¾ tsp. salt
Dash of hot pepper sauce

Toss together shrimp, macaroni, cheese, celery, green pepper and onion. Blend remaining ingredients. Toss with shrimp mixture; cover. Chill. Stir salad before serving. Serve on lettuce; top with green pepper rings. Yield: 4-6 servings.

Martha Johnson, Soddy-Daisy H. S.
Soddy, Tennessee

SHRIMP SALAD DELUXE

1 pkg. lemon Jell-O
1 tbsp. onion juice
½ tsp. salt
½ c. Miracle Whip salad dressing
½ c. heavy cream, whipped
3 hard-cooked eggs, chopped
½ lb. American Cheese, grated
1 tbsp. chopped green pepper
¾ c. finely cut celery
1 can shrimp, cut up

Combine Jell-O, 1 cup boiling water, onion juice and salt. Chill slightly. Add Miracle Whip and cream; mix well. Add eggs, cheese, green pepper, celery and shrimp; mix well. Chill overnight.

Merle C. Parr, Hutcheson Jr. H. S.
Arlington, Texas

SHRIMP SALAD FOR A KING

2 lb. boiled, cleaned, chopped shrimp
1 c. diced celery
½ c. chopped olives
½ c. chopped pickles
¼ c. chopped green pepper
¼ c. chopped pimento
1 c. mayonnaise
Salt and pepper to taste

Combine shrimp, celery, olives, pickles, green pepper and pimento; mix well. Add mayonnaise, salt and pepper; toss lightly to coat all ingredients. Chill for 1 hour. Serve in lettuce cups. Yield: 8 servings.

Mrs. Jilma Vidaurri, King H. S.
Kingsville, Texas

SHRIMP SALAD LOUIS

1 c. mayonnaise
¼ c. French dressing
¼ c. catsup or chili sauce
1 tsp. horseradish
1 tsp. Worcestershire sauce
1½ tsp. salt
½ tsp. Tabasco
1 lb. cleaned and cooked shrimp
Shredded lettuce

Combine mayonnaise, French dressing, catsup, horseradish, Worcestershire sauce, salt and Tabasco; mix well. Arrange shrimp on shredded lettuce in salad bowl. Serve with mayonnaise dressing. Yield: 4 servings.

Photograph for this recipe on page 51.

SMOOTH SHRIMP SALAD

2 pkg. unflavored gelatin
1 can cream of celery soup
3 3-oz. packages cream cheese
½ c. ground green pepper
½ c. ground onion
1 tall can shrimp, ground
1 c. mayonnaise

Soften gelatin in ½ cup cold water. Heat soup; add gelatin and cream cheese. Stir until cheese is melted. Combine all ingredients; pour into mold. Chill until firm. Shrimp may be omitted and remaining salad mixture congealed in ring mold, if desired. Serve with center filled with boiled shrimp. Yield: 10 servings.

Mrs. Willa Mae Scroggs, Sylva-Webster H. S.
Sylva, North Carolina

SOUTHERN SHRIMP SALAD

1 lb. cold cooked shrimp
1 c. cold cooked rice
½ sm. onion, chopped
2 stalks celery, chopped
1 green pepper, cut in thin strips
2 hard-cooked eggs, chopped
1 sm. pimento, chopped (opt.)
2 tbsp. French dressing
⅓ c. mayonnaise
Salt and pepper to taste

Mix all ingredients together. Season to taste. Serve cold on a bed of salad greens. Yield: 6 servings.

Earleen F. Williams, Williston H. S.
Williston, Florida

SYLVIA'S SHRIMP SALAD

3 c. small shrimp
3 hard-cooked eggs, chopped
¾ c. chopped celery
3 tbsp. capers
½ c. mayonnaise
1 tbsp. lemon juice
Salt and pepper to taste

Mix all ingredients together. Chill. Serve in lettuce cups. Garnish with sliced tomatoes and additional sliced hard-cooked eggs. Sprinkle top with paprika, if desired. Yield: 4 servings.

Sylvia M. Wilson,
Southwest Complex–Ballard A Sch.
Macon, Georgia

TOMATO-SHRIMP SUPPER SALAD

2 env. unflavored gelatin
2 1-lb. cans stewed tomatoes
2 tbsp. vinegar
1 tbsp. horseradish
½ tsp. salt
1 4½-oz. can med. shrimp, deveined

Soften gelatin in ½ cup cold water. Combine tomatoes, vinegar, horseradish and salt; heat to boiling point. Add gelatin; stir until dissolved. Chill until partially congealed. Arrange shrimp around bottom of ring mold; pour in tomato mixture. Chill until firm. Unmold on salad greens; fill center with peas, if desired. Garnish with cucumber slices. Yield: 6-8 servings.

Mary Jane Bertrand, Blackfoot H. S.
Blackfoot, Idaho

WEDDING SUPPER SALAD

1 6-oz. package lemon gelatin
¼ c. lemon juice
½ tsp. salt
1 c. mayonnaise
½ c. (or more) sm. deveined shrimp
1 bunch red radishes, sliced
1 sm. sweet onion, minced
½ c. sliced stuffed green olives
1 c. diced white celery

Dissolve gelatin in 2 cups boiling water; add 1½ cups ice water, lemon juice and salt. Stir in mayonnaise; chill until partially congealed. Beat with rotary beater until frothy. Fold in shrimp, radishes, onion, olives and celery. Pour into ring mold or individual molds; chill until firm. Serve on lettuce. Top with

mayonnaise and garnish with radish roses, if desired. Yield: 20 servings.

Mrs. Gladys B. Phillips, Post Falls H. S.
Post Falls, Idaho

AMERICAN NICOISE SALAD

1 sm. head lettuce, shredded
2 7-oz. cans solid pack tuna, drained
1 c. sliced cooked potatoes
1 c. cooked snap beans
3 hard-cooked eggs, quartered
3 sm. tomatoes, quartered
1 sm. red onion, thinly sliced
12 pitted ripe olives
¾ tsp. salt
Dash of paprika
½ tsp. monosodium glutamate
⅓ c. lemon juice or vinegar
⅔ c. salad oil

Place lettuce in large shallow bowl. Pile large chunks of tuna in center of bowl; surround with ring of potatoes and ring of beans. Alternate egg quarters and tomato quarters around beans. Separate onion slices into rings. Garnish salad with onion slices and olives. Cover tightly with plastic wrap; refrigerate until ready to serve. Add salt, paprika and monosodium glutamate to lemon juice; stir with fork until dissolved. Add oil; beat with fork until blended. Pour dressing over salad; serve immediately. Yield: 6 servings.

Mrs. Irene Wells, Grant County Rural H. S.
Ulysses, Kansas

FAVORITE TUNA SALAD

1 can tomato soup
3 pkg. cream cheese or 1 pkg. cream cheese
    and 1 c. sour cream
2 env. unflavored gelatin
1 c. salad dressing
1 can tuna, drained
1 c. chopped celery
1 tbsp. chopped green pepper
1 tbsp. chopped onion

Combine tomato soup and cream cheese in saucepan; heat until cheese is melted, stirring constantly. Soften gelatin in ½ cup cold water; stir into tomato soup mixture until melted. Stir in salad dressing; chill until partially congealed. Stir in remaining ingredients; pour into mold. Chill for several hours or overnight. Yield: 8 servings.

Yvonne McCoy, Paul H. Pewitt Sch.
Omaha-Naples, Texas

TUNA GARDEN LOAF

2 pkg. unflavored gelatin
1 can cream of celery soup
¼ c. lemon juice
1 tbsp. prepared mustard
1 tsp. salt
1 c. mayonnaise
⅛ tsp. pepper
2 7-oz. cans tuna, drained
1 c. chopped celery
½ c. grated cucumber
¼ c. chopped green pepper

Soften gelatin in ½ cup cold water. Heat soup just to boiling point. Add gelatin to soup; stir to dissolve. Stir in lemon juice, mustard, salt, mayonnaise and pepper. Chill until partially congealed. Fold in tuna, celery, cucumber and green pepper; pour into 8½ x 4½ x 2½-inch loaf pan. Chill until firm. Yield: 8 servings.

Mary Elizabeth Ball, Kentwood H. S.
Grand Rapids, Michigan

TUNA-MACARONI SALAD

1 6-oz. package shell macaroni
1 c. cubed Cheddar cheese
1 7-oz. can tuna, drained
¾ c. sliced sweet pickles
⅓ c. minced onion
1 c. salad dressing
¾ tsp. salt
¼ tsp. pepper
2 cloves of garlic, crushed

Cook macaroni, according to package directions. Combine macaroni, cheese, tuna, pickles and onion in large bowl. Combine salad dressing, salt, pepper and garlic; mix well. Pour over macaroni mixture. Toss to coat; cover. Chill at least 3 hours before serving.

Debbie Jackson, Pine Tree H. S.
Longview, Texas

TUNA-MACARONI SALAD DELUXE

1 8-oz. package elbow macaroni
1 sm. onion, chopped
½ c. chopped celery
1 6½-oz. can tuna, drained and flaked
1 17-oz. can early peas, drained
Dash of garlic salt
Salt and pepper to taste
1 c. mayonnaise
2 tbsp. prepared mustard
2 tbsp. sugar
1 tbsp. white vinegar

2 or 3 hard-cooked eggs, halved
Paprika

Cook macaroni according to package directions. Drain, rinse and cool. Add onion, celery, tuna, peas and garlic salt to cooled macaroni; mix well. Season with salt and pepper. Blend mayonnaise, prepared mustard, sugar and vinegar in a small bowl. Pour over macaroni-tuna mixture. Toss lightly until coated. Garnish with eggs. Sprinkle with paprika. Yield: 12 servings.

Rosemary T. Baur, Hambrick Jr. H. S.
Houston, Texas

TUNA MEAL-IN-ONE

½ head lettuce, torn
1 9¼-oz. can flaked tuna
3 cooked potatoes, diced
1 No. 303 can peas, drained
½ c. chopped celery
½ med. onion, chopped
2 sweet pickles, chopped
Salt to taste
Salad dressing or mayonnaise

Reserve half the lettuce. Combine remaining lettuce with remaining ingredients; toss lightly. Chill thoroughly. Serve on reserved lettuce. Yield: 6 servings.

Mrs. Margaret C. Hoffman, Victory Joint School
Harrisville, Pennsylvania

TUNA MOUSSE

1 pkg. unflavored gelatin
¼ c. pickle juice
¼ c. mayonnaise
¼ tsp. salt
⅛ tsp. pepper
1 7-oz. can flaked tuna, drained
1 c. chopped celery
2 hard-cooked eggs, chopped
8 stuffed olives, sliced
8 sweet pickles, chopped
1 tbsp. minced onion

Soften gelatin in ¼ cup cold water. Add pickle juice and softened gelatin to ½ cup hot water; heat until dissolved. Stir in mayonnaise, salt and pepper; chill until partially congealed. Add remaining ingredients; mix thoroughly. Pour into greased mold. Refrigerate until firm. Yield: 6 servings.

Letha Pearl Simpson, Sterling H. S.
Sterling, Kansas

TUNA SALAD LUAU

¾ c. mayonnaise
¾ tsp. curry powder
1 tbsp. parsley flakes
1 13-oz. can tuna, drained
1 c. drained pineapple chunks
1 c. chopped celery
½ c. chopped walnuts

Combine first 3 ingredients for curried mayonnaise; chill until ready to use. Combine remaining ingredients; fold in curried mayonnaise. Serve on lettuce leaves; garnish with walnut halves. Yield: 8 servings.

Mrs. Donald Young, Greenwood H. S.
Greenwood, Arkansas

TUNA SALAD RING

1 pkg. unflavored gelatin
¾ c. mayonnaise
½ tsp. paprika
1 tsp. vinegar
1 tbsp. lemon juice
Salt and pepper to taste
1 7-oz. can tuna, drained
1 c. diced celery
3 tbsp. chopped sweet pickles
3 tbsp. chopped stuffed olives
2 tbsp. chopped parsley

Soften gelatin in ¼ cup cold water. Dissolve in ½ cup boiling water. Stir in mayonnaise, paprika, vinegar, lemon juice, salt and pepper; chill until partially congealed. Mix remaining ingredients together; stir in gelatin mixture. Pour into 9-inch ring mold. Chill until firm. May be used as a sandwich filling omitting gelatin and water and adding more mayonnaise or pickle juice. Yield: 6-8 servings.

Mrs. Jack Searcy, Lewisville H. S.
Lewisville, Arkansas

TUNA SHOESTRING SALAD

1 c. mayonnaise
1 tbsp. prepared mustard
¾ c. milk
Dash of Tabasco sauce
2 7-oz. cans tuna, drained
1½ c. diced celery
2 4½-oz. cans shoestring potatoes

Combine mayonnaise, mustard, milk and Tabasco sauce. Add tuna and celery; chill until ready to serve.

Add shoestring potatoes; mix until moistened. Serve on lettuce leaf. Yield: 8 servings.

Myrna E. Erickson, Cooperstown H. S.
Cooperstown, North Dakota

TUNA TANGS

1 env. unflavored gelatin
¾ c. cooked dressing or mayonnaise
½ tsp. salt
¼ tsp. paprika
1 tbsp. vinegar
1 can tuna, drained
½ c. chopped celery
¼ c. chopped cucumber or pickles
½ c. finely chopped green peppers
3 tbsp. chopped stuffed olives

Soften gelatin in ¼ cup cold water; dissolve over hot water. Cool slightly. Fold in dressing, salt, paprika and vinegar; chill until partially congealed. Combine remaining ingredients; add to gelatin mixture. Chill until firm. Yield: 6 servings.

Lucy Justine Davis, Sinton H. S.
Sinton, Texas

TUNA-APPLE MOUSSE

1 3-oz. package lemon-lime or lime flavored
  gelatin
¼ tsp. salt
Pepper
⅔ c. evaporated milk
1 tbsp. chopped chives or green onions
1 7-oz. can tuna, drained
1 c. chopped apples
½ c. dark olives, pitted and sliced
2 tbsp. chopped chives or green onions
Salad greens
1 apple, sliced

Place gelatin in a medium-sized mixing bowl. Add 1 cup boiling water, salt and pepper; stir until gelatin is dissolved. Chill until syrupy. Chill evaporated milk in ice cube tray until partially frozen. Whip evaporated milk until stiff peaks form. Add lemon juice to milk; blend. Add tuna, apples, olives and chives to partially-set gelatin. Fold tuna-gelatin mixture into whipped evaporated milk. Turn into 8-inch square pan or fish-shaped mold. Chill until set. Cut salad in half one way and thirds the other way. Lift pieces out with spatula; place on salad greens on individual plates. Ring each serving with thin apple slices and a few olive slices. Yield: 6 servings.

Photograph for this recipe on page 79.

TUNA VEGETABLE SALAD LOAF

1 env. unflavored gelatin
⅔ c. mayonnaise
2 tsp. prepared mustard
2 tbsp. lemon juice
1 tsp. salt
1 7-oz. can tuna, drained
¾ c. minced celery
½ c. cooked peas
2 tbsp. minced pimento
1 hard-cooked egg, chopped

Soften gelatin in ¼ cup cold water; dissolve in ¼ cup hot water. Combine mayonnaise, mustard, lemon juice and salt. Add dissolved gelatin; chill until partially congealed. Mix tuna, celery, peas, pimento and egg together; combine with gelatin mixture. Pour into loaf pan; chill until firm. Yield: 8 servings.

Mrs. Robbie Hanks, Ysleta H.S.
El Paso, Texas

TUNA VEGETABLE TOSS

1 6½-oz. can tuna, flaked
1 c. drained cooked peas
1 c. coarsley diced celery
3 hard-cooked eggs, sliced
½ c. quartered ripe olives (opt.)
1 c. drained cooked macaroni
½ c. salad dressing
3 tbsp. lemon juice
Dash of thyme
Salt and pepper to taste

Combine tuna, peas, celery, eggs, olives and macaroni. Blend salad dressing with lemon juice and seasonings. Drizzle dressing over salad ingredients; toss lightly. Chill thoroughly before serving. Yield: 6-8 servings.

Ruth Wiman, Roscoe H.S.
Roscoe, Texas

TUNA WALDORF WITH POPPY SEED DRESSING

⅔ c. vinegar
½ c. sugar
2 tsp. dry mustard
2 tsp. salt
1 tsp. onion juice
1 c. salad oil
1½ tbsp. poppy seed
2 7-oz. cans tuna, drained and chopped
1 c. diced unpeeled apples
½ c. chopped celery
¼ c. chopped nuts
½ c. mayonnaise or salad dressing
3 avocados, halved

Combine ½ cup vinegar, sugar, mustard, salt and onion juice; beat well. Add remaining vinegar and salad oil slowly, beating continuously until mixture thickens. Add poppy seed. Set poppy seed dressing aside. Combine tuna, apples, celery, nuts and mayonnaise; mix well. Fill avocado halves with tuna salad; serve with poppy seed dressing. Yield: 6 servings.

Mrs. Suanne Lett Black, Sidney Lanier H.S.
Montgomery, Alabama

WESTERN TUNA TOSS

1 7-oz. can chuck tuna, drained
¼ c. wine vinegar
½ tsp. crushed vasil leaves
Dash of coarsely ground pepper
Dash of salt
1 sm. head lettuce, torn
2 med. tomatoes, cut in wedges
1 sm. onion, thinly sliced

Combine tuna, vinegar, basil leaves, pepper and salt. Add lettuce, tomato and onion; toss lightly. Serve immediately. Yield: 4 servings.

Ouida Capps, Nichols Jr. H.S.
Arlington, Texas

HOT SEAFOOD SALAD

1 7½-oz. can crab meat
1 5-oz. can med. shrimp
¾ c. diced celery
1 sm. onion, diced
1 5-oz. can water chestnuts
1 sm. can sliced mushrooms
½ tsp. Tabasco sauce
2 hard-cooked eggs
2 tbsp. lemon juice
1 tsp. Accent
1 tsp. salt
¼ tsp. dry mustard
1 tsp. Worcestershire sauce
1 c. mayonnaise
10 Ritz crackers

Mix all ingredients, except Ritz crackers, adding mayonnaise last. Place in 1½-quart baking dish. Crush Ritz crackers; sprinkle on top. Bake for 25 to 30 minutes at 350 degrees. Yield: 6 servings.

Mrs. Carol Erickson, North Jr. H.S.
Hopkins, Minnesota

HOT SEAFOOD SALAD

1 can crab meat
2 cans shrimp

1 lge. can mushrooms
4 hard-cooked eggs, diced
¼ c. chopped green pepper
1 med. onion, chopped
2 cans water chestnuts, sliced thin
2 cans cream of chicken soup
2 tbsp. Worcestershire sauce
1 tsp. salt
Buttered crumbs
Toasted almonds

Mix all ingredients except crumbs and almonds together. Just before putting in oven cover with crumbs. Bake at 350 degrees for 20 to 30 minutes. Top with toasted almonds. Yield: 6 servings.

Mrs. Beverly Witt, Williston H.S.
Williston, North Dakota

SEAFOOD POTPOURRI

1 6½ or 7-oz. can tuna
1 6½-oz. can crab meat
1 5-oz. can shrimp
2 tbsp. French dressing
1 c. diced cucumbers
2 tbsp. chopped radishes
1 tbsp. capers
2 tbsp. lemon juice
½ c. mayonnaise
Salt, pepper and paprika to taste

Flake tuna and crab meat. Devein shrimp; mix with tuna and crab meat. Add French dressing; chill 15 minutes. Add remaining ingredients; toss lightly. Serve in crisp lettuce cups. Yield: 6 servings.

Linda Gail Pack, Pisgah H.S.
Cantos, North Carolina

MACARONI-SEAFOOD SALAD

Garlic
½ lb. cooked shell macaroni
1 lb. boiled shrimp
1 can white crab meat
1 clove garlic
12 olives, finely chopped
½ c. finely chopped parsley
Mayonnaise
Lettuce leaves

Chill all ingredients thoroughly. Rub well-chilled bowl generously with garlic. Cut shrimp into pieces. Mix all remaining ingredients except mayonnaise and lettuce. Add mayonnaise; toss lightly. Serve cold on lettuce. Yield: 6 servings.

Mrs. Catherine R. Trotter, Independence H.S.
Independence, Louisiana

RICE AND TURKEY SALAD

1½ c. cookied rice, chilled
1½ c. diced turkey or chicken
1 c. English peas
1 c. shredded carrots
½ c. French dressing
¼ c. chili sauce (opt.)
¼ tsp. curry powder
½ tsp. salt

Place rice, turkey, peas and carrots in salad bowl; toss lightly. Combine French dressing, chili sauce, curry powder and salt; mix well. Pour over rice mixture; toss lightly. Yield: 6 servings.

Mrs. Harriet Krause, Pasadena H.S.
Pasadena, Texas

DELICIOUS RICE SALAD

½ c. salad dressing
1 tbsp. prepared mustard
1 tbsp. pickle juice
2 c. cooked rice
4 hard-cooked eggs, chopped
4 sweet pickles, chopped
¼ c. celery, diced
¼ c. diced green pepper
1 tbsp. minced onion
½ c. chopped pecans (opt.)
1 tsp. salt
½ tsp. pepper

Mix salad dressing, mustard and pickle juice together. Combine remaining ingredients in salad bowl. Add dressing mixture; toss lightly. Chill until ready to serve. Yield: 8 servings.

Mrs. Dorothy Weikal Bickerstaff, Marianna H.S.
Marianna, Arkansas

KOREAN SALAD

1½ c. cooked rice
2 tbsp. vegetable oil
1 tbsp. vinegar
1 tsp. salt
1 tsp. curry
1 16-oz. can English peas
1 c. chopped celery
¼ c. chopped onion
3 hard-cooked eggs, chopped
¼ c. chopped almonds
½ c. mayonnaise

Combine first 5 ingredients while rice is warm. Chill at least 3 hours. Add remaining ingredients. Chill until ready to serve. Yield: 6-8 servings.

Carolyn H. Whitehurst, Pike County Middle Sch.
Concord, Georgia

CURRIED RICE SALAD

1 c. long grain rice
Salt
1 pkg. frozen green peas
3 chicken bouillon cubes
¼ c. finely chopped green onion
½ tsp. white pepper
¾ tsp. curry powder
½ c. plus 3 tbsp. Italian dressing
1 c. finely chopped celery
½ c. mayonnaise

Cook rice in 2½ cups water, using salt as directed on the package. Cook green peas in ¼ cup water. Drain and reserve liquid. Combine reserved liquid with chicken bouillon cubes. Add peas, rice, green onion, white pepper, curry powder and 3 tablespoons Italian dressing. Stir lightly with a fork. Refrigerate overnight. Add celery, mayonnaise and remaining ½ cup Italian dressing. Just before serving toss lightly. Yield: 8-10 servings.

Deana Koonsman, Arlington H. S.
Arlington, Texas

MAIN DISH RICE AND HAM SALAD

1 ⅓ c. instant rice
1½ tbsp. dry mustard
1½ tbsp. sugar
1½ tbsp. wine vinegar
¼ c. vegetable oil
½ c. chopped green pepper
1 c. diced cooked ham
½ c. cooked peas
Chopped parsley

Cook rice according to package directions. Combine mustard, 2 tablespoons cold water, sugar and vinegar; add oil gradually, beating constantly. Stir lightly into warm rice; let cool. Add green pepper, ham and peas; toss lightly. Sprinkle with chopped parsley. Serve on salad greens, if desired. Yield: 4-6 servings.

Mrs. Jean Jordan, Spurger H. S.
Spurger, Texas

CRUNCHY ORIENTAL SALAD

1 can La Choy fried rice
1 bunch green onions, chopped
½ c. chopped celery
1 can water chestnuts, chopped
1 c. chopped green pepper
1 c. chopped cucumber
6 radishes, chopped
1 bottle Italian dressing
1 can bean sprouts

Heat rice according to directions. Cool. Add next 6 ingredients; mix well. Add dressing, stirring well. Marinate overnight in refrigerator. Rinse bean sprouts in water. Crisp in water overnight. Add to rice salad just before serving.

Mrs. ElRuth B. McCullough, Nacogdoches H. S.
Nacogdoches, Texas

ORIENTAL SALAD

1 lb. bean sprouts
1¼ c. cooked rice
1 c. thinly sliced celery
2 tbsp. chopped green pepper
2 sm. carrots, finely grated
3 green onions and tops, sliced
½ c. toasted slivered almonds
2 c. diced cooked chicken or pork
Salt and pepper to taste
Juice of ½ lemon
¾ c. French dressing
Soy sauce to taste

Cook bean sprouts in small amount of salted water for about 3 minutes or until crisp tender. Drain and cool. Combine bean sprouts, rice, celery, green pepper, carrots, onions, almonds and chicken; chill thoroughly. Season with salt, pepper and lemon juice. Add French dressing; toss lightly. Sprinkle with soy sauce; serve immediately. Yield: 6 servings.

Mrs. Luisa Pitchford, Los Banos Elementary Sch.
Los Banos, California

SEAFOOD RICE RING

1½ c. rice
1 c. cooked whole shrimp
1 c. crab
3 tbsp. lemon juice
¼ c. chopped green onions
¼ c. chopped green pepper
½ c. sliced stuffed olives
1 c. salad dressing
½ c. chili sauce
½ tsp. dry mustard
¼ tsp. pepper
¼ tsp. garlic salt
1 tsp. salt
1 tsp. Worcestershire sauce
1 tbsp. vinegar (opt.)

Cook rice according to package directions; let cool. Sprinkle shrimp and crab with lemon juice; toss with rice. Add onions, green pepper and olives. Combine remaining ingredients; add to rice mixture. Pack into 1¾-quart ring mold. Chill for several hours or overnight before serving. Yield: 8-12 servings.

Mrs. Ireta Lyngstad, Coeur d'Alene Jr. H. S.
Coeur d'Alene, Idaho

HOT MACARONI SALAD WITH BACON

4 oz. elbow macaroni
4 strips bacon, cut in ½-in. pieces
½ c. diced celery
¼ c. chopped green pepper
¾ c. chopped cucumber pickles
¼ c. chopped onion
2 tbsp. chili sauce
½ tsp. Worcestershire sauce
1 tsp. salt
⅛ tsp. pepper
1 tsp. sugar
¼ c. mayonnaise

Cook macaroni in boiling salted water for about 12 minutes; rinse and drain. Cook bacon bits until crisp; drain well. Fold all ingredients into macaroni; place in top of double boiler. Heat through. Serve hot. Yield: 8 servings.

Mrs. Mary C. Williamson, Hallsboro School
Hallsboro, North Carolina

HOT MACARONI-TUNA TOSS

1 c. elbow macaroni
¼ c. Italian dressing
1 tsp. celery seed
¾ tsp. dry mustard
½ tsp. salt
Dash of pepper
1 6½-oz. can tuna drained
½ c. diced celery
½ c. diced green pepper
3 tbsp. salad dressing

Cook macaroni according to package directions; rinse and drain. Combine Italian dressing and seasonings in saucepan; bring to boiling point. Add macaroni, tuna, celery and green pepper. Toss lightly; heat through, stirring frequently. Stir in salad dressing; serve immediately. Top with green pepper rings, if desired. Yield: 6 servings.

Mrs. Sarah Strange Martin, Memorial Jr. H. S.
Tampa, Florida

MACARONI AND HAM SALAD

2 c. macaroni
1 c. diced ham or cheese
1 sm. onion, chopped
Salt and pepper to taste
Mayonnaise or salad dressing

Cook macaroni according to package directions; drain and cool. Combine all ingredients, adding enough mayonnaise to moisten as desired. Yield: 4 servings.

Phyllis Rae Horner, Severna Park H. S.
Severna Park, Maryland

MACARONI BUFFET SALAD

1 12-oz. package shell macaroni
1 tbsp. seasoned salt
1 tsp. salt
2 lg. onions, chopped
8 hard-cooked eggs, sliced
2 c. chopped celery
½ c. sliced pimentos
1 c. sliced green pepper
2 No. 2½ cans English peas, drained
1½ c. mayonnaise

Cook macaroni in salted water until tender. Drain; blanch with cold water and drain again. Add seasoned salt, salt, onions, eggs, celery, pimentos and green pepper; toss lightly. Add English peas; toss lightly. Mix in mayonnaise gently; chill for several hours before serving. Garnish as desired. Yield: 12 servings.

Mrs. Oleta M. Smith, O'Donnell H. S.
O'Donnell, Texas

MACA-SALMON SALAD

2 c. macaroni
1 c. diced cheese
1 c. diced sweet pickles
1 c. diced celery
¼ c. diced pimento
¼ c. minced green pepper
¼ c. minced onion
4 c. drained, flaked canned salmon
2 c. mayonnaise
2 tbsp. prepared mustard
6 tbsp. vinegar
2 heads lettuce

Cook macaroni according to package directions; rinse and drain. Add cheese; toss until well mixed. Let cool. Add pickles, celery, pimento, green pepper, onion and salmon. Combine mayonnaise, mustard and vinegar. Pour over salad; toss gently. Chill thoroughly. Line large bowls or chop plates with outer leaves of lettuce. Tear remaining lettuce. Add to salad; toss lightly. Serve salad in prepared bowls. Yield: 14 servings.

Mrs. Ellen D. Feagan, Las Cruces H. S.
Las Cruces, New Mexico

MACARONI POTPOURRI

3 c. drained cooked macaroni
¾ c. chopped ham
¾ c. chopped chicken
¼ c. diced celery
¼ c. minced onion
¼ c. chopped green pepper
1 pimento, chopped
½ c. mayonnaise
Salt and pepper to taste
2 hard-cooked eggs, chopped

Combine all ingredients except eggs; mix well. Garnish with chopped eggs when ready to serve. Yield: 6-8 servings.

Judy Lennon, Achille H. S.
Achille, Oklahoma

MACARONI-SHRIMP SALAD

2 c. macaroni
1 c. finely chopped celery
1 can shrimp, drained
2 hard-cooked eggs, finely chopped
¼ c. chopped pimento
¼ tsp. paprika
½ tsp. salt
1 c. mayonnaise
¼ c. French dressing

Cook macaroni according to package directions; drain and cool. Add celery, shrimp, eggs, pimento, paprika and salt. Combine mayonnaise and French dressing. Add to macaroni mixture; toss lightly.

Mrs. Sharon Nelson, Karlstad H. S.
Karlstad, Minnesota

CHARLIE'S MACARONI SALAD

8 oz. elbow macaroni
1 tsp. Worcestershire sauce
⅓ c. mayonnaise
¼ c. horseradish mustard
Dash of salt and pepper
½ c. chopped celery
1 sm. onion, minced
4 hard-cooked eggs, sliced
1 c. cooked cubed ham

Cook macaroni in salted water; drain. Add Worcestershire sauce, mayonnaise, horseradish mustard, salt and pepper to hot macaroni. Mix thoroughly. Add

celery, onion, 3 eggs and ham. Garnish salad with 1 sliced egg. Serve warm or chilled. Yield: 8 servings.

Charmaine K. Baker, Buckeye H. S.
Medina, Ohio

MY MOTHER'S MACARONI SALAD

2 tbsp. salad dressing or mayonnaise
1 to 3 tbsp. vinegar
½ tsp. prepared mustard
2 tsp. sugar
Salt to taste
1½ c. macaroni
2 stalks celery, chopped or ½ tsp. celery seed
1 green pepper, chopped
1 cucumber, chopped
½ med. onion, chopped
2 med. tomatoes, chopped
1 carrot, chopped

Combine first 5 ingredients for dressing; mix well. Set aside. Cook macaroni in salted water until tender; rinse and drain. Combine vegetables and warm macaroni. Add dressing; toss gently. Let stand to marinate for at least 1 hour before serving. Yield: 10 servings.

Mrs. Eileen Skaggs, Alderson H. S.
Alderson, West Virginia

RUTH'S MAIN DISH MACARONI SALAD

4 oz. elbow macaroni
1 c. chopped cooked chicken, turkey or tuna
2 hard-cooked eggs, diced
½ c. drained crushed pineapple
¼ c. sliced radishes
¼ c. chopped nuts
1 tbsp. chopped onion
⅓ c. mayonnaise
1½ tbsp. pineapple juice
¼ tsp. celery seed
¼ tsp. salt
Dash of pepper

Cook macaroni according to package directions; drain well. Combine chicken, eggs, pineapple, radishes, nuts and onion. Add macaroni, toss lightly. Combine mayonnaise and pineapple juice; mix until smooth. Stir in celery seed, salt and pepper. Pour over macaroni salad; toss carefully until well blended. Chill thoroughly. Serve on salad greens. Yield: 4 servings.

Mrs. Ruth A. Blomgren, Eastern Jr. H. S.
Silver Spring, Maryland

TABASCO-MACARONI SALAD

3 tbsp. butter or margarine
2 tbsp. flour
2 tsp. salt
1 tsp. dry mustard
1 tbsp. sugar
½ tsp. paprika
1¼ c. milk
2 egg yolks
¾ tsp. Tabasco, divided
⅓ c. cider vinegar
⅛ tsp (each) onion and garlic powder
2 c. macaroni
1 green pepper, cut into strips
1 4-oz. can pimento, diced
½ c. sliced scallions

Melt butter in saucepan. Stir in flour, salt, dry mustard, sugar and paprika. Add 1 cup milk. Stir to medium thickness. Mix remaining ¼ cup milk with egg yolks and ½ teaspoon Tabasco. Stir into hot mixture. Add cider vinegar, onion and garlic powder. Cook, stirring, until thickened; cool. Cook macaroni according to package directions, adding remaining ¼ teaspoon Tabasco to cooking water. Drain and cool. Combine macaroni, green pepper, pimento and scallions. Toss lightly. Serve with cooked dressing. Yield: 6 servings.

Photograph for this recipe on page 51

TUNA-CHEESE MACARONI SALAD

1 8-oz. package macaroni, cooked
1 6½-oz. can tuna, drained
1 c. cubed Cheddar cheese
½ c. chopped sweet pickles
¼ c. minced onion
½ c. mayonnaise
2 tbsp. prepared mustard
1 tbsp. sugar
1 No. 303 can peas, drained
Salt to taste

Rinse macaroni; drain well. Combine macaroni, tuna, cheese, pickles and onion in salad bowl. Mix mayonnaise, mustard and sugar together. Add to macaroni mixture; toss gently. Add peas; season with salt. Mix gently. Yield: 6 servings.

*Mrs. Robert Berkner, Lamberton Community School
Lamberton, Minnesota*

GEORGE RECTOR'S SPAGHETTI-CHICKEN SALAD

½ lb. elbow spaghetti
2 c. diced cooked chicken
1 c. chopped celery
2 tbsp. chopped green pepper
1 tbsp. minced sweet red pepper or pimento
1 tbsp. grated onion
½ c. mayonnaise or salad dressing
1 tsp. salt

Cook spaghetti until tender; drain and chill. Add all remaining ingredients; mix lightly. Serve on watercress or lettuce. May top with sieved hard-cooked eggs if desired. Yield: 6 servings.

*Mrs. K. E. Sharp, Houston Jr. H. S.
Borger, Texas*

SPAGHETTI AND TOMATO SALAD

1 c. elbow spaghetti
1 can chicken, turkey or tuna
1 c. diced celery
2 tsp. grated onion
¼ tsp. salt
Freshly ground pepper to taste
½ c. mayonnaise or Cheddar cheese soup
5 tomatoes, peeled

Cook spaghetti according to package directions; let cool. Combine chicken, celery, onion, salt, pepper, mayonnaise and spaghetti. Cut tomatoes into 4 or 8 sections from blossom end almost to stem end. Place tomato flowers on lettuce, if desired; fill tomatoes with spaghetti salad. Yield: 5 servings.

*Mrs. Gloria Hixson, Scranton H. S.
Scranton, Arkansas*

SPAGHETTI-BEAN SALAD

1 16-oz. package spaghetti
2 cans kidney beans
1 sm. head cabbage, shredded
1 sm. onion, minced
1 stalk celery, minced
3 eggs, beaten
1⅛ c. sugar
1 sm. jar prepared mustard
3 tbsp. butter

Cook spaghetti according to package directions; let cool. Rinse and drain kidney beans. Combine spaghetti, cabbage, onion, celery and beans; toss lightly. Combine remaining ingredients in saucepan; cook until slightly thickened, stirring constantly. Let cool. Pour over spaghetti salad; toss lightly. Yield: 12 servings.

*Mrs. Margaret P. Samson,
Western Wayne Jointure Sch.
Lake Ariel, Pennsylvania*

MAKING YOUR OWN DRESSINGS

Bottled dressings are very convenient for today's busy homemaker. But it takes so little time to create your own dressing, you should give it a try.

A light French dressing—oil, vinegar or lemon juice and seasonings—is the undisputed queen of dressings, appropriate on any salad. Mayonnaise, whipped or sour cream, and cooked dressing are all excellent and can be used in any way your taste dictates.

Never be afraid to experiment when making dressings. Vary the seasonings according to the ingredients, and who knows—you may create something very new and special.

Basic Ingredients

To make good dressings, you need certain staples. Oil and vinegar go in almost all dressings. The seasonings you choose depend on the flavor you want to achieve. Always use only the freshest ingredients.

Oil

Some people insist on fruity Italian oil; others prefer the more delicate French type. Olive oil is used widely, but a good vegetable oil has more food value.

Vegetable oils are made from corn, cotton seed, peanuts and soy beans. Regardless of the type oil you choose, top quality is essential.

Vinegar

"Use a little at a time" is your guide for vinegar. Strength in vinegars differs so much you just have to try a little, then a little more, until you get exactly the flavor you want. Old-fashioned cider vinegar has a mild, sweet taste. For distinctiveness in dressings, use tarragon, wine, pear, garlic or other specially seasoned vinegars.

Seasonings

Regular table salt is fine for dressings; it won't cake. Freshly-ground black pepper is the best choice. Use dried or fresh herbs sparingly. A little goes a long way.

Garlic, too, has a habit of making itself well known if you use too much. Go lightly on it, whether you use fresh garlic, powdered dry garlic or garlic salt. Many salad-makers merely rub the salad bowl with a garlic clove.

Other Salad Standbys

A variety of seasonings should be kept on hand in small amounts to add interest to every type of salad. Essential are celery salt, onion salt, minced onion and onion juice.

Adding distinctive flavor to both salads and dressings are horseradish, pickle relish, and caraway, sesame, celery and mustard seeds. Don't overlook fresh and dried herbs like sage, mint, basil, chives, oregano, marjoram, dill, thyme. Use a sharp steak sauce or red pepper sauce for zest.

Crunchy nuts and raisins give a pleasing texture and taste contrast to meat, fish and fruit salads and aspics.

DILLY AVOCADO DRESSING

1 med. avocado, peeled and sliced
⅓ c. salad oil
1 tbsp. sugar
¼ c. lemon juice
½ tsp. salt
1 tsp. dillseed

Combine all ingredients in blender container; blend for 2 minutes. Add ½ cup cold water; blend to mix well. Add more water if dressing is too thick. Keep refrigerated. Serve on mixed fruit salads. Yield: 2 cups.

Mrs. E. Howard, Kent-Meridian Sr. H. S.
Kent, Washington

GREEN GODDESS SALAD DRESSING

½ can anchovy fillets
½ med. avocado
1 c. sour cream
2 tbsp. chopped parsley
Salt and freshly ground pepper to taste

Mash anchovies and avocado. Add remaining ingredients; mix well. More anchovies may be added, if desired.

Nita P. Lowery, South Mountain H. S.
Phoenix, Arizona

BLEU CHEESE DRESSING

1½ c. salad oil
¼ c. vinegar
¼ c. lemon juice
½ c. crumbled bleu cheese
⅛ tsp. Worcestershire sauce
Dash of Tabasco sauce
⅛ tsp. coarsely ground pepper
Dash of cayenne pepper
¼ tsp. ground celery seed
¼ tsp. dry mustard
1 tsp. paprika
1 tsp. garlic salt
½ tsp. salt
1 tsp. onion salt

Combine all ingredients and ¼ cup water in quart jar; stir to moisten dry ingredients. Cover tightly; shake jar vigorously to mix well. Store in refrigerator. Shake well before using. Yield: 2¾ cups.

Mrs. C. A. Fricke, Glendale H. S.
Glendale, Oregon

BUTTERMILK SPECIAL SALAD DRESSING

2 c. salad dressing
1 c. buttermilk

¼ c. catsup
¼ c. sugar
½ tsp. salt
1 tsp. paprika
2 tsp. vinegar
1 garlic clove, mashed

Combine all ingredients in quart jar; cover. Shake until thoroughly mixed. Keep refrigerated. Yield: 3 cups.

Mrs. Charles W. Parton, Estacado Jr. H. S.
Plainview, Texas

CELERY SEED DRESSING

½ c. sugar
1 tsp. dry mustard
1 tsp. salt
1 tsp. (or more) grated onion
⅓ c. vinegar
1 c. salad oil
1 tbsp. celery seed
1 tsp. paprika

Combine sugar, mustard, salt and onion. Add vinegar and oil alternately, a small amount at a time, beginning with vinegar. Beat well. Stir in celery seed and paprika. Store, covered, in refrigerator. Serve on fruit or fresh vegetable salads.

Bonnie Moore, Wiley H. S.
Wiley, Colorado

CRIMSON CELERY SEED DRESSING

1 c. sugar
½ c. vinegar
½ c. oil
½ tsp. celery seed
½ tsp. paprika

Combine all ingredients; mix well. Refrigerate for several hours. Serve over fruit. Yield: 1½ cups.

Wanda A. Gerard, Superior Sr. H, S.
Superior, Wisconsin

MARY'S CELERY SEED DRESSING

⅔ c. sugar
1 tsp. dry mustard
1 tsp. celery seed
¼ tsp. salt
⅓ c. honey
⅓ c. vinegar
1 tbsp. lemon juice
1 tsp. grated onion
1 c. salad oil

Mix first 4 ingredients. Blend in honey, vinegar, lemon juice and onion. Add oil in slow stream, beating constantly with electric mixer until thick.

Mrs. Mary Gregg, Vanguard Vocational Center
Fremont, Ohio

COLESLAW DRESSING

5 tbsp. vinegar
½ c. sugar
1 tsp. dry mustard
1 tsp. salt
1 tbsp. grated onion
1 c. salad oil
1 tsp. celery seed

Combine 2 tablespoons vinegar with the next 4 ingredients; mix well. Add salad oil, beating constantly. Add 3 tablespoons vinegar and celery seed; mix well. Continue beating until very thick.

Muriel Erickson, Bayfield H. S.
Bayfield, Wisconsin

CREAM CHEESE DRESSING

1 8-oz. package cream cheese, softened
⅛ tsp. salt
1 tbsp. lemon juice
2 to 3 tbsp. mayonnaise

Beat cream cheese with electric mixer. Add remaining ingredients; mix well. Serve on fruit salads or head lettuce. Yield: 6 servings.

Mrs. Deanna Patin Roy, Fifth Ward H. S.
Marksville, Louisiana

CREAMY FRUIT DRESSING

4 egg yolks, beaten
4 tbsp. sugar
1 tbsp. butter
4 tbsp. vinegar
½ tsp. salt
12 marshmallows
1 carton whipping cream, whipped
1 c. chopped pecans

Combine first 5 ingredients in a saucepan. Cook over low heat until mixture begins to heat. Add marshmallows. Stir constantly with wire whisk until mixture is smooth and thick. Set aside to cool. Add whipped cream to cooled mixture. Fold in pecans.

Serve as dressing for pear salad. Garnish with mint leaves or maraschino cherries.

Rebecca Jones Milan H. S.
Milan, Tennessee

FAVORITE FRENCH DRESSING

1 c. salad oil
⅔ c. catsup
¼ c. sugar
Juice of 1 to 2 lemons
1 tsp. Worcestershire sauce
1 tsp. dry mustard
1 tsp. paprika
1 tsp. salt
½ c. vinegar
1 clove of garlic

Mix all ingredients except vinegar and garlic with rotary beater. Stir in vinegar; add garlic. Shake before using. Yield: 32 servings.

Mrs. Lenda B. Edwards, Bennettsville H. S.
Bennettsville, South Carolina

LAURA'S FRENCH DRESSING

½ c. salad oil
½ tsp. salt
½ tsp. dry mustard
1 clove of garlic, pressed
2 tbsp. vinegar
½ tsp. paprika
Pinch of sugar

Place all ingredients in jar with a lid. Shake well to mix. Chill for several hours before serving.

Laura E. Hall, Glascock Consolidated Sch.
Gibson, Georgia

MILD FRENCH DRESSING

3 tbsp. sugar
3 tbsp. catsup
1 tsp. salt
½ tsp. dry mustard
¼ c. evaporated milk
½ c. salad oil
3 tbsp. vinegar

Combine all ingredients except vinegar; beat until well blended. Add vinegar; beat thoroughly. Yield: 1¼ cups.

Mrs. Margaret W. Lyles, Westminster H. S.
Westminster, South Carolina

TASTY FRENCH DRESSING

1 tbsp. sugar
1 tsp. salt
1 tsp. dry mustard
1 tsp. paprika
1 10½-oz. can tomato soup
1 c. vinegar
1 tbsp. Worcestershire sauce
1 c. salad oil
1 clove of garlic, grated
1 sm. onion, grated

Combine all ingredients in quart jar or bottle; cover. Shake thoroughly before using. Yield: 1 quart.

Mrs. Luana Hutchings, Moapa Valley H. S.
Overton, Nevada

FRUIT SALAD DRESSING

2 eggs, beaten
1 c. sugar
Juice of 1 lemon
½ c. pineapple juice
½ c. whipping cream, whipped

Combine eggs, sugar, lemon juice and pineapple juice in saucepan. Cook over low heat until thickened, stirring constantly. Let cool. Fold in whipped cream.

Mrs. Lula S. Patrick, Monticello H. S.
Monticello, Kentucky

ITALIAN SALAD DRESSING

¼ c. olive oil
2 tbsp. lemon juice
1 tsp. grated lemon rind
Salt to taste
½ tsp. oregano or thyme
1 clove of garlic, minced
1 tbsp. grated Parmesan cheese
½ tsp. freshly ground pepper

Combine all ingredients; mix well. Keep refrigerated. Shake before using. Yield: 6 servings.

Angela D'Gerolamo, Riverdale H. S.
New Orleans, Louisiana

LOW-CALORIE DRESSING

1 c. cottage cheese
1 10½-oz. can tomato soup
1 tbsp. India relish or sweet pickle relish
1 tbsp. lemon juice
Grated rind of 1 lemon (opt.)

Combine all ingredients; mix well. Chill thoroughly. Stir well before using. Serve over crisp salad greens. Yield: 2 cups/25 calories per 2 tablespoons.

Charlyene Deck, Exeter Union H. S.
Exeter, California

COOKED MAYONNAISE

¼ tsp. butter or margarine
2 tbsp. flour
½ tsp. dry mustard
½ tsp. salt
Dash of paprika
1 egg yolk, well beaten
1 tbsp. lemon juice or vinegar
½ c. salad oil

Melt butter in saucepan. Stir in flour to make a smooth paste. Add ½ cup hot water; cook until thick and clear, stirring constantly. Combine remaining ingredients in mixing bowl. Add hot sauce slowly, beating rapidly with electric beater. Yield: 1 cup.

Joyce Gandy Garrison, Chesnee H. S.
Chesnee, South Carolina

LOW-CHOLESTEROL MAYONNAISE

¼ tsp. paprika
Dash of cayenne pepper
1 tsp. salt
½ tsp. dry mustard
2 egg yolks at room temperature
2 tbsp. vinegar
2 c. Wesson oil
2 to 3 tbsp. lemon juice

Combine first 4 ingredients in mixer bowl; blend in egg yolks. Add vinegar; mix well. Add ¼ cup oil, 1 teaspoon at a time, beating at high speed of electric mixer. Add 1¼ cups oil in increasing amounts. Mix in remaining ½ cup oil alternately with lemon juice. Beat in 1 tablespoon hot water to lessen oily appearance. Yield: 1 pint.

Barbara Waybourn, Patton Springs H. S.
Afton, Texas

ONE-MINUTE MAYONNAISE

1 c. Wesson oil
1 tbsp. vinegar
1 tbsp. lemon juice
1 egg
½ tsp. salt
⅛ tsp. paprika
¼ tsp. dry mustard
Dash of cayenne pepper

Pour ¼ cup oil into blender container; add remaining ingredients. Cover; blend for 5 seconds. Remove cover while blender is processing; add remaining oil slowly in a fine stream. Turn off blender immediately after oil has been added. Store, covered, in refrigerator. Yield: 1½ cups.

Josephine L. Grissette, Robert E. Lee H. S.
Montgomery, Alabama

POPPY SEED DRESSING

¼ c. sugar
1 tsp. salt
1 tsp. dry mustard
1 tsp. onion juice
¼ c. cider vinegar
1 c. salad oil
2 tbsp. poppy seed

Combine sugar, salt, mustard and onion juice; stir in vinegar slowly, beating constantly. Add oil and poppy seed. Let stand at room temperature.

Mrs. Brenda S. Pitts, St. Matthews H. S.
St. Matthews, South Carolina

QUICK SALAD DRESSING

½ c. catsup
½ c. mayonnaise
½ c. finely chopped sweet pickles

Blend catsup and mayonnaise in small container; add chopped pickles. Chill thoroughly. Serve over green vegetable salads. Yield: 1¼ cups.

Mrs. Yvonne T. Napp, Choctaw County H. S.
Butler, Alabama

CLASSIC ROQUEFORT DRESSING

½ lb. Roquefort cheese
3 hard-cooked eggs
1 tsp. minced onion
1 clove of garlic, minced (opt.)
1 tsp. sugar
¼ c. vinegar
1 tsp. Worcestershire sauce
2 c. salad oil

Make a paste of cheese, egg yolks, onion and garlic using a fork. Add sugar, vinegar and Worcestershire sauce. Add chopped egg whites and salad oil; mix thoroughly. Serve over head lettuce or mixed vegetable salads. Will keep indefinitely if refrigerated. Yield: 10 servings.

Mrs. Isabel M. Booher, East Jr. H. S.
Nashville, Tennessee

ROQUEFORT-SOUR CREAM DRESSING

2 c. mayonnaise
1½ c. sour cream
½ tbsp. lemon juice
1½ tbsp. vinegar
½ tbsp. salt
½ tbsp. Worcestershire sauce
1 tsp. onion juice
¼ tsp. pepper
1 tsp. garlic powder
Dash of Tabasco sauce
2 lg. packages Roquefort cheese, crumbled

Combine all ingredients in mixer bowl; beat with electric mixer until well blended. Store in covered container in refrigerator. Yield: 4 cups.

Mrs. Garnet C. Jackson, Indio H. S.
Indio, California

RUBY RED DRESSING

½ c. currant jelly
¼ c. vegetable oil
2 tbsp. lemon juice
Dash of salt
Few drops of onion juice

Stir jelly with fork until smooth. Add remaining ingredients; beat until smooth. Serve on citrus fruits. Yield: ¾ cup.

Agnes Falkowski, Southern Door H. S.
Brussels, Wisconsin

DELICIOUS RUSSIAN DRESSING

1 c. sugar
Juice of 2 lemons
2 c. salad oil
1 c. catsup
2 tsp. Worcestershire sauce
2 tbsp. grated onion
1 tsp. celery salt
1 tsp. paprika
Pinch of red pepper

Combine sugar and 1 cup water in saucepan. Bring to a boil; boil until syrupy. Let cool. Add remaining ingredients; mix well. Chill until ready to use.

Carol Van Sickle, Wells Public Schools
Wells, Minnesota

QUICK RUSSIAN DRESSING

½ c. mayonnaise
¼ c. chili sauce
½ tsp. lemon juice

Combine ingredients; mix well. Chill until ready to use. Yield: 4 servings.

Mrs. DeLaura Jones, Warwick H. S.
Newport News, Virginia

SHRIMP LOUIS SALAD DRESSING

2 c. mayonnaise
½ c. chili sauce
¼ tsp. Accent
2 tsp. sugar
Dash of white pepper
Juice of 1 lemon
⅓ c. India relish
2 hard-boiled eggs, chopped

Mix all ingredients together; chill well. Serve over green salad, lettuce and tomato salad or boiled shrimp.

Mrs. May Campbell, Orangefield H. S.
Orangefield, Texas

QUICK THOUSAND ISLAND DRESSING

1 c. salad dressing or mayonnaise
¼ c. catsup
1 tsp. prepared mustard
1 tbsp. chopped onion
2 tbsp. vinegar

Combine all ingredients; let stand for at least 1 hour before serving. Yield: 8 servings.

Louise Ferguson, Violet Hill H. S.
Violet Hill, Arkansas

RICH THOUSAND ISLAND DRESSING

1 egg yolk
1 tsp. dry mustard
1 tsp. confectioners' sugar
½ tsp. salt
Dash of cayenne pepper
1 c. salad oil
1 tbsp. lemon juice or vinegar
¼ c. chili sauce
¼ c. chopped stuffed olives

1 tbsp. chopped chives
1 hard-cooked egg, chopped
½ tsp. paprika

Beat egg yolk, mustard, sugar, salt and cayenne pepper together. Add ⅓ of the oil, a drop at a time, beating constantly. Add remaining oil more quickly, thinning mixture occasionally with lemon juice. Stir in remaining ingredients; mix well. Chill in refrigerator. Yield: 2¾ cups.

Virginia Boxley, Berryville School
Berryville, Arkansas

TASTY THOUSAND ISLAND DRESSING

1 qt. mayonnaise
1 12-oz. bottle chili sauce
½ onion, grated
2 hard-boiled eggs, grated or finely chopped
1 sm. jar pimento, diced
1 tbsp. sweet relish

Combine all ingredients; mix well. Store in a tightly sealed container in refrigerator.

Mrs. Judith P. Eubank, Giles County H. S.
Pulaski, Tennessee

TANGY SALAD DRESSING

½ c. salad oil
¼ c. vinegar
2 tbsp. sugar
1 tbsp. onion, chopped
½ c. tomato soup

Combine all ingredients; shake well. Cover and refrigerate. Shake before using. Yield: 12 servings.

Mary Joe Whitefield, Lebanon H.S
Lebanon, Tennessee

TARTAR SAUCE SALAD DRESSING

1 pt. Miracle Whip salad dressing
½ c. chopped stuffed olives
½ c. sweet cucumber pickles
½ c. chopped onions
¼ c. thick cream

Combine all ingredients in large mixing bowl; chill. Serve over tossed green salad, sliced cucumbers or fish. Yield: 35-40 servings.

Mrs. Floyd Craig, Divide H.S.
Nolan, Texas

TOSSED SALAD DRESSING

1 c. sugar
½ c. chili sauce
½ c. catsup
½ c. vinegar
1 c. oil
2 or 3 cloves of garlic, minced
1 tsp. salt
½ tsp. pepper

Measure all ingredients into wide mouthed jar; shake well. Chill 5 to 6 hours. Shake well before serving. Yield: 1½ pints.

Mrs. Mary Weaver, Schwenksville Union Sch.
Schwenksville, Pennsylvania

WHITE RIVER

3 eggs
1 qt. Wesson oil
1 qt. buttermilk
5 to 6 tbsp. dry mustard
2 to 4 tbsp. garlic salt
1 tsp. salt

Place eggs in blender; beat until creamy. Add remaining ingredients; blend until creamy. Store in covered container in refrigerator. Yield: 2 quarts.

Ann Good, Inola H.S.
Inola, Oklahoma

OLD-FASHIONED WALDORF DRESSING

1 c. salad dressing
½ c. sugar
¼ c. vinegar

Mix all ingredients until well blended. Set in refrigerator for several days. Will keep, refrigerated, for long period of time. Good served on fruit salad, cabbage slaw or any kind of salad. Yield: 1 pint.

Mrs. Robbie White, Paris Sr. H.S.
Paris, Texas

WALDORF SALAD DRESSING

1 egg
¼ tsp. pepper
¼ tsp. mustard
¼ tsp. turmeric
1 tsp. salt
¼ c. vinegar
Sugar

Beat egg until well mixed. Add remaining ingredients with enough sugar to make one cup of mixture. Cook until dressing begins to thicken. Delicious with any fruit salad or mixed with mayonnaise on cabbage salad. Yield: 1 cup.

Mary J. Strand, Sr. H.S.
Jamestown, New York

YOGURT DRESSING

1 c. yogurt
1 tbsp. lemon juice
1 tbsp. minced onion
2 tsp. sugar
¼ tsp. salt
Dash of cayenne pepper
Dash of cumin powder

Mix all ingredients thoroughly. Serve on Rice Krispies, smoked fish or green salad. Yield: 4 servings.

Mrs. H. Singh, Revelstoke Secondary Sch.
Revelstoke, British Columbia, Canada

ZIPPY DRESSING

1 c. salad dressing
⅓ c. chili sauce
¼ tsp. salt
1 tsp. lemon juice
1 tsp. horseradish
1 sm. onion, chopped fine
1 sm. cucumber, chopped fine

Mix all ingredients; let stand 5 to 6 hours before serving. Yield: 1½ cups.

May Lohmann, Miami H.S.
Miami, Oklahoma

HONEY-LIME DRESSING

1 6-oz. can frozen limeade concentrate
¾ c. salad oil
½ c. honey
¼ tsp. salt
2 tsp. celery seed

Combine limeade concentrate, salad oil, honey and salt in blender container; blend a few seconds. Stir in celery seed. Mixture may be beaten or shaken to mix. Serve over fresh or canned fruit salad. Yield: 2 cups.

Photograph for this recipe on page 87.

Vegetables From A to Z

There's more to the ABC's of vegetable cookery than *A* touch of salt, *B*oiling water, and the *C*ook. Like so many of the good things in life, creative vegetable cookery can be both fun and rewarding—especially when approached with a flair for flavor and imagination.

The flair in creative vegetable cookery is in learning new and unusual flavor combinations as well as the variations on old favorites. Take advantage of the fact that the natural variety of vegetables allows the cook to choose not only the taste she needs to balance a meal, but also the color and design that will look particularly appealing with other foods on the menu.

Consider new ways to serve your favorite vegetables—ways that will also make new vegetables more appealing. Bake your best meat loaf mixture in cabbage rolls, scooped-out green peppers, or hollowed-out onions. Also, learn the ancient Oriental art of stir-frying vegetables. Your whole family will love the crisp, refreshing results, and you will love the color and nutrition it adds to mealtime.

The flavor of most vegetables is delicate, yet definite, which calls for careful attention from the cook when it comes to seasonings and sauces. The subtle blend of an herb-lemon sauce is the perfect way to perk up string beans, zucchini, mushrooms, asparagus, and other tender, succulent vegetables. Cheese sauces are an excellent "toss together" for steamed cauliflower, broccoli, or cabbage. And, don't forget the use of a variety of flavorful garnishes and toppings for just a touch of flavor—sour cream, grated cheeses, cream cheese, chopped nuts, crispy bits of bacon, bottled hot or savory sauces, and herb butters.

From A to Z, the art of vegetable cookery never loses its excitement and appeal. And, the more imaginative you become in presenting delicious vegetables to your family, they may never be satisfied with plain butter and salt on their vegetables again. But, don't worry! The following collection of Home Economics Teachers recipes will give you as many ways to prepare vegetables as you will ever need!

Vegetable Cookery Chart

VEGETABLE	AMOUNT TO BUY	NO. OF SERVINGS	WAYS TO PREPARE	Cooking Time After Water Boils FRESH	FROZEN
ARTICHOKES (April-May)	Fresh— 1 artichoke	1	Simmered in water	Until Tender	
ASPARAGUS (Mid-February)	Fresh—1 lb. Frozen—10-oz. package	2	Boiled, Steamed, Baked	10-20 minutes (whole spears)	5-10 minutes
BEANS, Green (June-Aug)	Fresh-1 lb. Frozen—12-oz. package	4-6	Steamed Baked Simmered	12-16 minutes	12-20 minutes
BEETS (Year-Round)	(Fresh—1 lb. Canned—12-oz. can	3 to 4 3 to 4	Boiled Baked	30-45 (young) 45-90 (older) minutes	
BROCCOLI (Year-Round)	Fresh-1 lb. Frozen—10-oz. package	3 to 4 2 to 3	Boiled, Baked, Raw flowerets	10-15 minutes (stalks cut)	8-15 minutes
BRUSSELS SPROUTS (October-December)	Fresh—1 lb. Frozen—10-oz. package	3 to 4 3 to 4	Baked Boiled Stuffed	15-20 minutes	10-15 minutes
CABBAGE (Year-Round)	Fresh—1 lb.	3 to 4	Pan stirred Baked Steamed Braised, Raw	3-10 (shredded) 10-15 (wedges)	
CARROTS (Year-Round)	Fresh—1 lb. Canned—16 or 17-oz. can	3 to 4 3 to 4	Steamed Braised Raw	15-20 (young, whole) 20-30 (older, whole) minutes	5-10 (sliced) minutes
CAULIFLOWER (September-January)	Fresh—1 med. head	4	Steamed Boiled Raw in salads	8-15 (pieces) 15-25 (whole) minutes	5-8 (pieces) minutes
COLLARDS (December-March)	Fresh—1 lb. Frozen—10-oz. package Canned—16 or 17-oz. can	4 to 3 2 to 3 2 to 3	Boiled	15-20 minutes	
CORN (May-September)	Fresh—1 ear Frozen-10-oz. package Canned—12-oz. can	1 2 to 3 Steamed 3 to 4	Baked Boiled	5-15 minutes (on the cob)	3-5 minutes
EGGPLANT (Late Summer)	Fresh—1 med. eggplant	4	Baked Boiled, Fried Mashed	10-12 minutes	
LIMA BEANS (July-November)	Fresh—1 lb. (in pod) Frozen—10-oz. Package Canned—16 or 17-oz. can	1 to 2 3 to 4 3 to 4	Boiled Dried In soups	25-30 minutes	10-18 minutes

VEGETABLE	AMOUNT TO BUY	NO. OF SERVINGS	WAYS TO PREPARE	Cooking Time After Water Boils FRESH	FROZEN
OKRA (June-October)	Fresh—1 lb. Frozen—10-oz. package Canned—16 or 17-oz. can	4 3 to 4 3 to 4	Boiled Fried	10-15 minutes	8-15 minutes
ONIONS, dry (Year-Round)	Fresh—1 lb.	6 to 8	Baked Boiled Fried Sauteed	15-30 minutes	
ONIONS, fresh	1 bunch	3	In fresh salads		
PARSNIPS (Year-Round, Late Winter)	Fresh—1 lb.	2 to 3	Baked Braised In stews Steamed	20-40 (whole) 8-15 (quarters) minutes	
PEAS (March-June)	Fresh—1 lb. (in pod) Frozen—10-oz. package Canned—16 or 17-oz. can	1 to 2 3 to 4 3 to 4	Baked Boiled	12-16 minutes	5-15 minutes
PEPPERS (red and green) (Late Summer)	Fresh—1/2 pepper	1	Chopped Stuffed Diced		
POTATOES, white (Year-Round)	Fresh—1 lb.	2 to 3	Baked Boiled Stuffed Mashed Fried, Steamed	25-40 (whole) 20-25 (quarters) minutes	
SPINACH (March-June)	Fresh—1 lb. Frozen—10-oz. package Canned—15-oz. can	2 to 3 2 to 3	Boiled Creamed Steamed	3-10 minutes	5-14 minutes
SQUASH, summer (Summer Months)	Fresh—1 lb. Frozen—10-oz. package Canned—16 or 17-oz. can	2 to 3 2 to 3 3 to 4	Baked Boiled Fried	8-15 minutes	10-12 minutes
SQUASH, winter (Fall and Winter)	Fresh—1 lb.	2 to 3	Baked Mashed Steamed	15-20 (cut up) minutes	
SWEET POTATOES (Year-Round)	Fresh—1 lb. Canned—16 or 17-oz. can	2 to 3 3 to 4	Baked Boiled Glazed	35-55 (whole) minutes	
TURNIPS AND RUTABAGAS (Year-Round)	Fresh—1 lb.	2	Baked Boiled Mashed	20-30 (whole) 10-20 (cut up) minutes	

ARTICHOKE HEARTS AND PECANS

2 No. 2 cans artichoke hearts, drained
1 c. half and half
2 tbsp. butter
2 tbsp. flour
Salt and pepper to taste
Tabasco sauce to taste
½ c. broken pecans
¼ c. bread crumbs
2 tbsp. grated Parmesan cheese

Place artichoke hearts in small casserole. Combine half and half, butter and flour in saucepan; cook until thickened, stirring constantly. Season with salt, pepper and Tabasco sauce. Pour sauce over artichoke hearts; add pecans. Sprinkle with bread crumbs and cheese. Bake at 300 degrees until bubbly. Yield: 6 servings.

Selma Sailors, Diller Community Sch.
Diller, Nebraska

ARTICHOKE HEARTS IN LEMON BUTTER

½ c. minced onion
½ clove of garlic, crushed
2 tbsp. butter
¾ c. chicken broth
2 15-oz. cans artichoke hearts, drained
3 tbsp. lemon juice
1½ tsp. salt
1 tsp. oregano
¼ tsp. grated lemon rind

Saute onion and garlic in butter until transparent. Add broth and artichoke hearts; season with lemon juice, salt, oregano and lemon rind. Simmer for 10 minutes or until artichokes are heated through. Yield: 6-8 servings.

Florence B. Fisackerly, Inverness H. S.
Inverness, Mississippi

ARTICHOKES AND SPINACH WITH HOLLANDAISE SAUCE

2 pkg. frozen spinach
1 1-lb. can artichoke hearts
2 egg yolks
3 tbsp. lemon juice
½ c. butter

Cook spinach according to package directions; drain well. Drain artichoke hearts; place in buttered baking dish. Place spinach over each artichoke heart. Mix egg yolks and lemon juice together in top of double boiler; place over hot water to heat slowly. Add half the butter; cook and stir until butter is melted. Add remaining butter, 1 tablespoon at a time; cook until thickened, stirring constantly. Pour sauce over spinach. Bake at 250 degrees until heated through. Yield: 6-8 servings.

Mrs. Richard E. Boquist, Albrook H. S.
Saginaw, Minnesota

ARTICHOKES WITH SHRIMP STUFFING

2 artichokes, cleaned
½ lemon, sliced
½ tsp. tarragon
¼ tsp. celery seed
1½ c. sour cream
½ tsp. horseradish
⅛ tsp. curry powder
⅛ tsp. salt
⅛ tsp. white pepper
½ lb. shrimp, cleaned
1 tbsp. crab boil

Place artichokes, lemon, tarragon and celery seed in large saucepan. Bring to a boil; cook until tender. Drain and cool slightly. Mix next 5 ingredients for sauce; set aside. Boil shrimp with crab boil in separate pan until firm and pink. Drain; cut each shrimp into bite-sized pieces. Combine shrimp with sauce; mix well. Pull open artichokes carefully. Clean inside. Spoon filling into center. Chill for several hours before serving. Yield: 2 servings.

Leesa K. Sulgrove, Shea Middle Sch.
Phoenix, Arizona

ASPARAGUS AND ALMONDS IN CHEESE SAUCE

2 tbsp. butter
2 tbsp. flour
½ tsp. salt
⅛ tsp. pepper
¼ tsp. dry mustard
1 c. milk
½ c. shredded sharp American cheese
2 c. drained cooked asparagus
½ c. chopped blanched almonds

Melt butter in saucepan; blend in flour to make a smooth paste. Stir in salt, pepper and mustard. Add milk; cook until thickened, stirring constantly. Remove from heat; stir in cheese until melted. Place asparagus in shallow casserole. Pour cheese sauce over asparagus; sprinkle with almonds. Bake at 350 degrees for 20 minutes or until bubbly. Yield: 4 servings.

Mrs. Patsy Lynch, Copper Basin H. S.
Copperhill, Tennessee

ASPARAGUS AU PRINTEMPS

1 lb. fresh asparagus
2 tbsp. butter
1 tsp. Spice Islands chicken seasoned stock base
1 tsp. Spice Islands Mei Yen seasoning
¼ tsp. grated lemon rind
¼ tsp. sweet basil
1 tsp. cornstarch
2 lg. ripe tomatoes, coarsely chopped

Cut tough ends from asparagus; steam asparagus for 15 minutes or until just tender. Melt butter in small skillet; blend in chicken stock base, Mei Yen seasoning, lemon rind and sweet basil. Blend cornstarch with ½ cup water; add to butter mixture. Cook until thick, stirring constantly. Add tomatoes to sauce; cook for 2 to 3 minutes longer. Turn asparagus out onto heated serving dish; spoon sauce over asparagus. Yield: 4 servings.

Mrs. Elvira Schmidt, Frederic H. S.
Frederic, Wisconsin

ASPARAGUS-CHESTNUT BAKE

1 15-oz. can asparagus, drained
1 17-oz. can peas, drained
1 6-oz. can water chestnuts, sliced
Salt to taste
1 10¾-oz. can mushroom soup
¾ c. grated American cheese
2 to 3 slices white bread
2 to 3 tbsp. melted butter

Layer vegetables and water chestnuts in order listed in a buttered casserole. Season to taste. Spread soup over top. Sprinkle with grated cheese. Cut bread into 1 x 3-inch strips. Saturate with melted butter. Place bread over casserole. Bake, uncovered at 350 degrees for 30 to 40 minutes or until brown and bubbly. Yield: 8 servings.

Carolyn Hartman, Killeen H. S.
Killeen, Texas

ASPARAGUS-ENGLISH PEA CASSEROLE

1 20-oz. can asparagus
2 tbsp. margarine
2 tbsp. all-purpose flour
Milk
7 oz. New York sharp Cheddar cheese, grated
1 ⅝-oz. package corn flakes
2 hard-cooked eggs, chopped
1 3-oz. can sliced mushrooms
1 8½-oz. can tiny peas
1 2-oz. jar pimentos

Drain asparagus, reserving liquid. Melt margarine in a saucepan over low heat. Add flour; blend in with wire whisk. Add enough milk to liquid to measure 1 cup. Warm slowly in separate saucepan. Add to flour; stir slowly. Bring sauce to boiling point. Add ¼ of the grated cheese. Butter a 1½-quart casserole. Cover the bottom of casserole with ½ of the corn flakes. Layer the asparagus, eggs, sliced mushrooms, peas, pimentos. Add half the cream sauce; top with half the cheese. Repeat layers, ending with cheese. Sprinkle with remaining corn flakes. Bake in preheated 350-degree oven for 20 to 25 minutes. Yield: 8 to 10 servings.

Mrs. Teresa V. Stephens, R. S. Central H. S.
Rutherfordton, North Carolina

CONNIE'S ASPARAGUS CASSEROLE

1 10-oz. package frozen English peas
1 10-oz. can asparagus
1 sm. can sliced mushrooms
Butter
1½ tbsp. flour
½ c. milk
⅔ c. grated Velveeta cheese
¼ tsp. salt
⅛ tsp. pepper
1 c. cracker crumbs

Cook peas according to package directions. Drain, reserving liquid. Drain asparagus and mushrooms, reserving liquids. Mix liquids in a saucepan; boil until reduced to measure ½ cup. Melt 2 tablespoons butter in a saucepan; stir in flour slowly. Add milk and vegetable liquid. Cook, stirring constantly, until mixture is thickened. Add the cheese, salt, and pepper; stir until cheese is melted. Remove from heat. Place peas, asparagus and mushrooms in a casserole. Cover with cheese sauce; mix gently. Top with cracker crumbs; dot generously with butter. Bake for 20 minutes at 325 degrees or until lightly browned.

Connie Middleton, Northwest Whitfield County H. S.
Tunnel Hill, Georgia

ASPARAGUS-PEANUT CASSEROLE

1 can asparagus, drained
1 can cream of mushroom soup
½ c. peanuts
1 c. grated cheese
Dash of salt and pepper
¼ c. butter

Place asparagus, soup, peanuts and cheese in layers in casserole, seasoning each layer with salt and pepper. Dot with butter. Bake at 350 degrees for 30 minutes or until heated through.

Martha Ann Horn, Mowat Jr. H. S.
Lynn Haven, Florida

ASPARAGUS SOUFFLE

3 tbsp. butter
3 tbsp. flour
1 c. milk
4 eggs, separated
2½ c. diced cooked asparagus
¾ tsp. salt

Melt butter in saucepan; stir in flour to make a smooth paste. Add milk gradually; cook slowly until thickened, stirring constantly. Beat egg yolks until thick and lemon colored; stir in asparagus and salt. Stir in white sauce; mix gently. Beat egg whites until stiff; fold into asparagus mixture. Pour into greased casserole; place casserole in pan of hot water. Bake at 325 degrees for 45 minutes or until firm. Yield: 6 servings.

Judi Rea, Baker H. S.
Baker, Montana

COMPANY ASPARAGUS

2 cans asparagus
3 tbsp. margarine
3½ tbsp. instant flour
1 tsp. salt
1½ c. grated cheese
1 can water chestnuts, sliced
2 tbsp. minced pimento
Cracker crumbs

Drain asparagus, reserving liquid. Melt margarine in saucepan. Stir in flour and salt. Add reserved liquid, stirring constantly. Bring to a boil. Cook until thick. Add grated cheese; mix well. Layer asparagus, water chestnuts and pimento in a baking dish. Pour cheese sauce over asparagus. Top with crushed cracker crumbs. Bake in 325-degree oven until sauce bubbles.

Myrtle D. Brookshire, Johnson County H. S.
Mountain City, Tennessee

DEVILED ASPARAGUS

1 can cream of mushroom soup
1 tbsp. onion juice
1 tsp. Worcestershire sauce
1 tsp. Tabasco sauce
1 tbsp. chopped green pepper
1 tbsp. chopped pimento
1 can cut asparagus, drained
½ box Ritz cheese crackers, crushed
¼ c. melted butter
Toasted almonds

Combine soup, onion juice, Worcestershire sauce, Tabasco sauce, green pepper and pimento; pour into buttered casserole. Add asparagus. Mix crumbs with butter; sprinkle over asparagus. Garnish with almonds. Bake at 350 degrees for 15 to 20 minutes or until heated through.

Mrs. Frances E. Poole, Mary Persons H. S.
Forsyth, Georgia

FRENCH-FRIED ASPARAGUS

1 lg. can asparagus tips
2 eggs
2 tbsp. cream
½ tsp. salt
½ tsp. pepper
1 tsp. monosodium glutamate
1 c. fine cracker crumbs

Drain asparagus tips well on paper toweling. Beat eggs, cream, salt, pepper and monosodium glutamate together. Dip asparagus tips in egg mixture; roll carefully in cracker crumbs. Fry in hot deep fat until golden brown; drain on paper toweling. Serve immediately.

Jane Ann Leach, Clear Creek H. S.
League City, Texas

GOLDENROD ASPARAGUS

1 No. 1 can asparagus and juice
3 hard-cooked eggs
12 stuffed olives
2 c. medium white sauce
Buttered toast

Heat asparagus in juice. Chop egg whites and olives; stir into white sauce. Remove asparagus from juice. Arrange hot asparagus on toast; cover with sauce. Garnish with sieved egg yolks.

Mrs. Ethel G. Burns, Chinook H. S.
Chinook, Montana

SCALLOPED ASPARAGUS

2 cans asparagus, drained
1 2¼-oz. package slivered almonds
1 c. grated Cracker Barrel cheese
1 can asparagus soup
15 to 18 Ritz crackers, crushed

Place asparagus in baking dish. Mix in almonds and cheese; stir in soup. Top with cracker crumbs. Bake at 350 degrees for 15 to 20 minutes or until crackers are brown. Yield: 8-10 servings.

Naomi M. Vaught, Manatee H. S.
Bradenton, Florida

SUNDAY ASPARAGUS

1 1-lb. can green asparagus spears, drained
1 box frozen green peas, thawed
1 7-oz. can mushrooms, drained
2 hard-cooked eggs, chopped
1 tsp. salt
2 tbsp. butter
1 c. flour
1 c. milk
1 tbsp. grated Parmesan cheese

Combine vegetables, eggs and salt in greased 1½-quart casserole. Melt butter in saucepan; blend in flour to make a smooth paste. Add milk gradually; cook until thickened, stirring constantly. Stir in cheese; pour sauce over vegetables. Bake at 350 degrees for 20 minutes or until bubbly. Yield: 6 servings.

Roberta Crafton, Shepherdsville H. S.
Shepherdsville, Kentucky

ASPARAGUS PARMESAN

2 14-oz. cans asparagus spears
2 green onions, chopped
¼ c. butter or margarine
1 tbsp. flour
½ tsp. salt
Dash of pepper
½ c. half and half
2 tbsp. diced pimento
½ c. grated Parmesan cheese

Drain asparagus; reserve liquid. Saute onions in butter until transparent. Stir in flour, salt and pepper to make a paste. Add ½ cup reserved asparagus liquid and half and half; cook until thick, stirring constantly. Stir in pimento. Arrange asparagus spears in shallow baking dish; pour sauce over top. Sprinkle with cheese. Bake at 400 degrees for 20 minutes or until asparagus is heated through and cheese is lightly browned. Yield: 6-8 servings.

Mrs. Eleanor V. Puckett, North Mecklenburg Sch.
Huntersville, North Carolina

SWEET-SOUR ASPARAGUS

1 pkg. frozen asparagus, cooked
½ c. sugar
½ c. vinegar
2 tbsp. salad oil
1 tsp. monosodium glutamate
Salt and pepper to taste

Place asparagus in serving dish. Combine ¼ cup water and remaining ingredients in saucepan; bring to a boil. Pour over asparagus. Cool thoroughly; serve cold.

Mrs. B. A. Woods, Kirbyville H. S.
Kirbyville, Texas

BEAN MEDLEY

1 c. mayonaise or salad dressing
2 hard-cooked eggs, chopped
3 tbsp. lemon juice
2 tbsp. minced onion
1 tsp. Worcestershire sauce
1 tsp. prepared mustard
¼ tsp. garlic salt
Dash of hot pepper sauce
1 9-oz. package frozen French-style green beans
1 10-oz. package frozen peas
1 10-oz. package frozen baby limas

Mix all ingredients except vegetables. Heat over low heat stirring until hot. Cook vegetables according to package directions; drain. Pour sauce over vegetables; mix thoroughly. Serve hot. Yield: 10 servings.

Mrs. John Anna Hunt, Polk County H. S.
Benton, Tennessee

BOSTON-BAKED BEANS

2 c. pea beans
¼ lb. salt pork
1 onion
1 tsp. salt
½ c. light molasses
½ tsp. dry mustard
1 tbsp. sugar

Place beans in kettle; cover with cold water. Let soak overnight. Drain beans; cover with fresh water. Bring to a boil. Reduce heat; simmer until skins burst. Drain beans; reserve stock. Scald pork. Cut one ¼-inch slice from pork; place in 2-quart bean pot. Make 1 inch deep cuts at ½ inch intervals in rind of remaining pork. Place onion and beans in pot; bury pork in beans, leaving rind exposed. Bring reserved stock to boiling point. Combine 1 cup stock and remaining ingredients; pour over beans. Pour in enough additional stock to cover beans; cover bean pot. Bake at 300 degrees for 6 to 7 hours or until done, adding stock if needed. Uncover; bake for 1 hour longer or until rind is crisp.

Azalee S. Bowlin, Dacusville H. S.
Greenville, South Carolina

BEANS WITH WATER CHESTNUTS

1 can French-style green beans
1 can butterbeans
1 can green peas
1 can water chestnuts, sliced
1 onion, chopped
Worcestershire sauce to taste
1 c. mayonnaise
1 can fried onions rings

Drain beans, peas and water chestnuts well. Toss with onion. Add Worcestershire sauce and mayonnaise; mix well. Bake at 350 degrees for 20 minutes. Add onion rings; bake for 10 minutes longer.

Jeri O'Quinn, Jones County H. S.
Gray, Georgia

EASY BAKED BEANS

4 slices bacon
½ c. chopped onion
2 1-lb. cans pork and beans with tomato sauce
3 tbsp. brown sugar
1 tbsp. molasses (opt.)
1 tbsp. Worcestershire sauce
1 tsp. mustard

Fry bacon until crisp; drain on paper toweling. Pour off all but 2 tablespoons bacon drippings. Saute onion in bacon drippings until transparent. Crumble bacon. Combine bacon, onion and remaining ingredients; pour into 1½ quart bean pot. Bake at 350 degrees for 2 hours or until done. Yield: 6 servings.

Mrs. Sally Hildebrand, Enumclaw H. S.
Enumclaw, Washington

BAKED GREEN BEANS AND MUSHROOMS

2 ½ c. fresh white bread cubes
½ c. melted butter or margarine
4 3-oz. cans sliced mushrooms, drained
3 15½-oz. cans cut green beans, drained
¼ tsp. salt
⅛ tsp. pepper
2 tsp. chopped onion
2 cans cream of mushroom soup
1 c. milk
½ c. toasted sliced almonds

Toss bread cubes with butter; place half the cubes in greased 13 x 9 x 2-inch casserole. Add mushrooms and beans; sprinkle with salt, pepper and onion. Combine soup and milk; pour over beans. Sprinkle with remaining bread cubes and almonds. Bake at

400 degrees for 30 minutes or until done. Yield: 12 servings.

Mrs. Freddie Morrison, Marshall H. S.
Marshall, Texas

CAROL'S GREEN BEAN CASSEROLE

2 14½-oz. cans green beans, drained
1 can bean sprouts, drained
1 to 2 sm. cans mushrooms, drained
1 can cream of mushroom soup
¼ tsp. onion powder
1 can French-fried onion rings

Mix together drained vegetables, soup and onion powder. Pour into buttered 1½-quart casserole. Bake at 350 degrees for 30 minutes. Top with onion rings. Bake 15 minutes or until onion rings are browned. Yield: 6 servings

Mrs. Carol J. Swank, Franklin Heights H. S.
Columbus, Ohio

CREOLE GREEN BEANS

3 slices bacon
¼ c. chopped onion
¼ c. chopped celery
¼ c. chopped green pepper
1 No. 2 can tomatoes
2 tsp. salt
1 tsp. pepper
1 No. 303 can whole green beans, drained

Fry bacon until crisp; drain. Saute onion, celery and green pepper in bacon drippings. Add tomatoes, salt and pepper; simmer for 5 minutes. Stir in green beans; simmer for 5 minutes. Pour into serving bowl; sprinkle with crumbled bacon. Yield: 6 servings.

Mrs. Joanne Snider, Dimmitt H. S.
Dimmitt, Texas

CHEESY ITALIAN GREEN BEANS

1 env. instant broth
1 pkg. frozen Italian green beans
3 med. tomatoes, peeled and sliced
1 tsp. instant minced onion
½ tsp. salt
1 tsp. leaf oregano, crumbled
2 oz. mozzarella cheese, grated

Dissolve instant broth in ½ cup boiling water in medium saucepan. Add green beans. Cook for 3 minutes. Pour into baking dish. Top with tomato slices, minced onion, salt, oregano and cheese. Bake at 325 degrees for 30 minutes. Yield: 6 servings.

Mrs. Billie Ruth Daniel, Frost H. S.
Frost, Texas

DELUXE GREEN BEAN CASSEROLE

2 4-oz. cans mushrooms, drained
1 med. onion, chopped
½ c. margarine
2 c. medium white sauce
¾ lb. sharp Cheddar cheese, grated
½ tsp. soy sauce
½ tsp. Tabasco sauce
1 tsp. salt
½ tsp. pepper
1 tsp. monosodium glutamate
3 pkg. frozen French-style beans
1 5-oz. can water chestnuts, sliced
½ c. slivered almonds

Saute mushrooms and onion in margarine; add remaining ingredients except beans, water chestnuts and almonds. Simmer until cheese has melted, stirring frequently. Prepare beans according to package directions; combine with cheese mixture and water chestnuts. Pour into casserole; sprinkle with almonds. Bake at 350 degrees for about 20 minutes or until brown. Yield: 6-8 servings.

Mrs. Betty Bray, Chalmette H. S.
Chalmette, Louisiana

DILLED GREEN BEANS

1 med. onion, chopped
2 tbsp. butter
1 lb. green beans, cut
1 tsp. salt
1 tsp. dillseed
2 tbsp. instant flour
⅛ tsp. pepper
1 c. light cream

Saute onion in butter until transparent; stir in beans, salt, dillseed and 1 cup water. Cook, covered, for 20 minutes or until beans are tender. Do not drain. Combine flour, pepper and cream; stir into beans. Cook until thickened, stirring constantly. Yield: 4 servings.

Mrs. Frances W. Utley, Lyon County H. S.
Eddyville, Kentucky

GREEN BEANS BEARNAISE

6 pkg. frozen French-style green beans
¾ c. melted butter or margarine
3 6-oz. cans evaporated milk

3 tbsp. vinegar
1½ tsp. salt
½ tsp. thyme
½ tsp. tarragon
1½ tsp. chopped parsley
1 tbsp. grated onion
9 egg yolks, slightly beaten
1½ beef bouillon cubes

Cook green beans according to package directions; drain. Pour butter into top of double boiler; place over hot water. Stir in milk, vinegar, salt, thyme, tarragon, parsley and onion. Stir constantly until smooth. Add 1 tablespoon boiling water and beat with rotary beater if mixture should start to curdle. Pour half the hot sauce into egg yolks, stirring constantly; return to remaining mixture in double boiler. Add bouillon cubes; cook until thick, stirring frequently. Serve over hot beans. Yield: 24 servings.

Mrs. Mary Kraner, Fairfield Union H. S.
Lancaster, Ohio

GREEN BEANS GOLDENROD

2 10-oz. packages frozen green beans
2 hard-cooked eggs
2 tsp. margarine
2 tsp. flour
¼ tsp. salt
⅛ tsp. pepper
½ c. milk
½ c. salad dressing or mayonnaise

Cook green beans according to package directions; drain. Chop egg whites; put egg yolks through sieve. Melt margarine in small saucepan. Blend in flour, salt and pepper. Remove from heat; stir in milk gradually. Cook over medium heat until thickened, stirring constantly. Stir in chopped egg whites. Remove white sauce from heat. Stir in salad dressing. Place beans in serving dish. Spoon sauce over beans; sprinkle with sieved egg yolks. Yield: 6-8 servings.

Dr. *Leanne Hearne, Middle Tennessee State University*
Murfreesboro, Tennessee

PIZZARINO GREEN BEANS

2 1-lb. cans green beans, drained
2 tbsp. cooking oil
2 tbsp. wine vinegar
2 tsp. oregano
½ tsp. garlic salt
½ c. sliced pitted ripe olives

Combine beans with remaining ingredients. Heat thoroughly, stirring gently. Yield: 6-8 servings.

Mrs. Jane Fribley, Central Jr. H. S.
Anderson, Indiana

GREEN BEANS IN WINE SAUCE

1 med. onion, chopped
1 clove of garlic, minced
1 med. green pepper, chopped
1 tbsp. butter
1 sm. can tomato paste
⅔ c. Sauterne
1 can cut green beans
Salt and pepper to taste
1 c. pitted ripe olives

Saute onion, garlic and green pepper in butter until golden. Stir in tomato paste and Sauterne. Add beans; season with salt and pepper. Simmer for 25 minutes. Add olives; serve. Yield: 6 servings.

Agnes Lafleur, Lawtell H. S.
Lawtell, Louisiana

GREEN BEANS WITH HERB BUTTER

1 lb. green beans
¼ c. butter or margarine
¾ c. minced onions
1 clove of garlic, minced
¼ c. minced celery
2 tbsp. sesame seed
¼ tsp. rosemary
¼ tsp. dried basil
¾ tsp. salt
¼ c. snipped parsley

Wash and trim beans; cut crosswise into thin, diagonal slices. Cook beans, covered, in ½-inch boiling salted water for 15 minutes or until tender; drain. Melt butter in saucepan; add onions, garlic, celery and sesame seed. Saute for 5 minutes. Add remaining ingredients; simmer, covered, for 10 minutes. Toss well with beans. Yield: 4 servings.

Jo Anna Littrel, Columbus Community Sch.
Columbus Junction, Iowa

BEAN AND PEA CASSEROLE

1 pkg. frozen string beans
1 pkg. frozen lima beans
1 pkg. frozen English peas
1 c. sour cream
1 c. mayonnaise
1 c. grated Cheddar cheese
Paprika

Cook vegetables according to package directions; drain. Place vegetables in a casserole. Add sour cream and mayonnaise, mixing well. Top with grated cheese and paprika. Bake at 350 degrees for 20 to 30 minutes. Yield: 6-8 servings.

Jeanie Guilloud, Pottsboro H. S.
Pottsboro, Texas

GREEN BEANS ITALIAN

1 15-oz. can tomato sauce
2 1-lb. can green beans, drained
1 tbsp. instant minced onion
2 tsp. sugar
¼ tsp. Worcestershire sauce
¼ tsp. oregano
4 oz. mozzarella cheese, shredded

Combine all ingredients except ½ of the mozzarella. Place in baking dish. Top with remaining cheese. Bake at 350 degrees for 30 minutes. Yield: 6-8 servings.

Mrs. Deborah J. Crook,
Upper Scioto Valley Local Sch.
McGuffey, Ohio

MIXED BEAN CASSEROLE

Juice of 1 lemon
1 tbsp. Worcestershire sauce
1 tsp. dry mustard
1¼ c. mayonnaise
1 can French-style green beans, drained
1 can baby limas
1 can White Acre peas or small field peas
1 can water chestnuts, drained and sliced
1 med. purple onion, sliced into rings
Buttered bread crumbs

Combine first 4 ingredients. Place vegetables in a casserole. Pour mayonnaise mixture over vegetables; mix well. Top with bread crumbs. Bake at 350 degrees for 20 minutes.

Mrs. Pam Odom Chastain, Gresham Jr. H. S.
Birmingham, Alabama

SCALLOPED GREEN BEANS

1 10-oz. box frozen green beans, thawed
1 sm. onion, sliced
2 hard-cooked eggs, sliced
⅓ c. grated cheese
½ c. broken cashews
1 can cream of chicken soup
½ soup can milk
Buttered bread crumbs

Combine all ingredients except buttered crumbs in greased casserole; mix well. Top with buttered crumbs. Bake at 325 degrees for 45 minutes or until bubbly. Yield: 6-8 servings.

Mrs. Ella Mae Korthals, Huron Jr. H. S.
Huron, South Dakota

SOUTHERN GREEN BEANS

3 c. frozen green beans
6 slices bacon
1 med. onion, chopped
3 tsp. seasoned salt
Parmesan cheese

Cover beans with water. Bring to a boil. Fry bacon until crisp. Crumble bacon. Combine onion, bacon and seasoned salt; add to green beans. Simmer for 15 to 20 minutes. Sprinkle with Parmesan Cheese. Serve hot.

Cynthia Berend Mt. Vernon H. S.
Mt. Vernon, Texas

SPANISH GREEN BEANS

2 strips bacon, chopped
¼ c. chopped onion
2 tbsp. chopped green pepper
1 tbsp. flour
2 c. drained canned tomatoes
1 c. drained canned green beans
Salt and pepper to taste

Saute bacon, onion and green pepper in heavy skillet until bacon is crisp. Stir in flour to make a paste; stir in tomatoes to mix well. Add green beans; season with salt and pepper. Place in casserole; cover. Bake at 350 degrees for 30 minutes or until bubbly.

Mrs. Marilynn Collins, Bridgeport H. S.
Bridgeport, Texas

STIR-FRIED GREEN BEANS

4 strips bacon
8 oz. mushrooms, fresh or canned
1 lb. fresh green beans or 10 oz. whole frozen green beans

Fry bacon in skillet. Set aside. Reserve 2 to 3 tablespoons bacon drippings. Add mushrooms; cook until tender over medium heat. Remove mushrooms. Add green beans. Cook until tender over medium heat. Add mushrooms and bacon.

Jane Hawkins, No. Union H. S.
Richwood, Ohio

SUMMER BEANS

1 c. sliced onions
½ c. sliced green pepper
¼ c. olive oil
1½ lb. prepared fresh green beans
1 tbsp. brown sugar
½ c. lemon juice
2 c. diced peeled tomatoes
1 tsp. salt
Pinch of savory salt (opt.)

Saute onions and green pepper in olive oil until lightly browned. Add beans, brown sugar, lemon juice and tomatoes; stir in seasonings. Simmer, covered, for 30 to 35 minutes. Chill thoroughly; serve cold.

Mrs. Nerine Cavins, Ringling H. S.
Ringling, Oklahoma

TOASTED GREEN BEANS

2 cans green beans
¼ c. chopped onion
¼ c. butter
¼ c. flour
1 tsp. salt
2 c. milk
1 c. crushed corn flakes
½ c. grated Swiss cheese

Heat beans thoroughly; drain well. Saute onion in butter until golden. Stir in flour and salt to make a paste. Add milk; cook until sauce is smooth and thick, stirring constantly. Mix sauce and beans together; place in casserole. Sprinkle corn flake crumbs and cheese over top. Bake at 375 degrees until bubbly and cheese has melted.

Mrs. Bessie Earle Halliday, Galena Park H. S.
Galena Park, Texas

COPENHAGEN LIMAS

1 10-oz. package frozen lima beans
¼ c. milk
¼ c. crumbled bleu cheese
¼ c. fine dry bread crumbs
1 tbsp. melted butter

Cook lima beans in unsalted water according to package directions. Heat milk with cheese, stirring until cheese melts. Add beans. Combine bread crumbs and butter in small frying pan; stir over medium heat until golden brown. Pour beans into serving bowl; sprinkle crumbs over top.

Mrs. Ralph E. Smith, Garrett H. S.
Garrett, Indiana

CREAMED LIMAS

1 onion, sliced
6 stalks celery, chopped
½ c. butter
1 to 2 tbsp. flour
½ c. half and half
1 jar pimentos, drained and chopped
1 sm. can mushrooms, drained
¼ tsp. nutmeg
2 pkg. frozen lima beans, cooked

Saute onion and celery in butter. Stir in flour to make a paste. Add half and half gradually; cook until thick, stirring constantly. Add remaining ingredients; heat through, stirring frequently. Yield: 8 servings.

Mrs. Mary R. Archer, Woodbourne Jr. H. S.
Baltimore, Maryland

BAKED LIMA BEANS
WITH TOMATO SAUCE

1 ½ c. dried lima beans
4 slices bacon, cut into 1-in. pieces
⅓ c. minced celery
½ c. minced onion
¼ c. diced green pepper
1 clove of garlic, minced
2 tbsp. flour
1½ c. canned tomatoes
2 tsp. salt
⅛ tsp. pepper
2 tbsp. sugar

Soak beans overnight in 3 cups cold water in large saucepan. Add 2 cups cold water; cover. Bring to a boil. Simmer for 30 minutes or until tender; drain. Place in 1½-quart casserole. Fry bacon until crisp. Add celery, onion, green pepper and garlic; cook until vegetables are golden. Stir in flour, tomatoes, salt, pepper and sugar; cook until thickened, stirring constantly. Pour sauce over beans. Bake, covered, at 300 degrees for 1 hour or until done. Yield: 4 servings.

Mrs. Elizabeth Lehew, Coloma Community Schs.
Coloma, Michigan

LIMA BEANS AND MUSHROOMS

1 8-oz. box fresh mushrooms, sliced
1½ tbsp. butter or margarine
¾ c. sour cream
Dash of paprika
½ tsp. dried basil
Salt and pepper to taste
2 pkg. frozen lima beans

Saute mushrooms in butter for 5 minutes or until golden. Remove from heat; stir in sour cream and seasonings. Cook beans according to package directions; drain. Stir into mushroom mixture; cook over low heat for 2 to 3 minutes or until heated through, stirring frequently. Yield: 6-8 servings.

Louetta Greeno, Highlands H. S.
Fort Thomas, Kentucky

LIMAS IN PIQUANT SAUCE

4 c. lima beans
2 tsp. salt
¼ c. butter
¼ c. flour
¼ tsp. pepper
4 tsp. prepared mustard
1 c. milk
4 tsp. lemon juice
¼ c. diced pimento

Combine beans, 2 cups water and 1 teaspoon salt in saucepan; cook until tender. Drain well, reserving liquid. Add enough water to reserved liquid to measure 1 cup. Melt butter in saucepan; stir in flour, remaining 1 teaspoon salt, pepper and mustard to make a paste. Add bean liquid and milk; cook until smooth and thick, stirring constantly. Stir in lemon juice and pimento. Add beans; heat thoroughly. Yield: 8 servings.

Mrs. Gene Taresh, East Nicolaus, H. S.
East Nicolaus, California

PARTY BEAN CASSEROLE

1 No. 303 can lima beans
1 No. 303 can green beans
1 No. 303 can English peas
1 2-oz. jar pimentos, drained and chopped
1 med. onion, chopped
1 can cream of chicken soup
Salt and pepper to taste
2 tbsp. butter, melted
1 c. crushed garlic potato chips

Drain beans and peas; add pimentos, onion and soup. Season with salt, pepper and butter. Pour into casserole; top with crushed potato chips. Bake at 350 degrees for 30 minutes or until done.

Mrs. Pat Duncan, Haltom Jr. H.S.
Ft. Worth, Texas

PORTUGUESE BEANS

1 lb. dried pinto beans
1 sm. ham hock or ham shank
4 slices bacon, chopped
1 lg. onion, chopped
1 tsp. salt
½ tsp. pepper
1 tsp. ground allspice
1 tsp. cumin

Place beans and ham hock in large kettle; cover with water. Bring to a boil. Reduce heat; simmer, covered, for about 3 hours and 30 minutes or until beans are tender, stirring occasionally and adding water if needed. Remove ham hock. Cut ham from bone; discard fat and bone. Fry bacon until crisp; remove from pan. Pour off half the drippings. Saute onion in remaining drippings until transparent. Stir bacon, onion and seasonings into beans; add ham slivers. Let stand for 10 minutes to blend flavors. Yield: 8 servings.

Mrs. Lillian M. Whittemore, Ursuline H. S.
Santa Rosa, California

PRESSURE-COOKED BEANS

2 c. dried navy beans
⅓ lb. salt pork, diced
3 tbsp. brown sugar
3 tbsp. molasses
2 tsp. salt
½ tsp. mustard
1 med. onion, diced
2 tbsp. catsup

Soak beans in water to cover overnight; drain well. Sear pork in 4-quart pressure cooker; add beans and remaining ingredients. Pour in enough water to cover beans. Cook at 15 pounds pressure for 40 minutes. Yield: 6 servings.

Mrs. Louis N. Neumeyer, Karnack H. S.
Karnack, Texas

SWEDISH BROWN BEANS

2 c. dried brown beans
¼ c. butter
3 tbsp. vinegar
¼ c. (packed) brown sugar
Salt to taste
½ tsp. ground nutmeg

Place beans in kettle; cover with water. Bring to a boil. Reduce heat; simmer until beans are tender, adding water as needed. Stir remaining ingredients into beans; return to a boil. Remove from heat; serve

immediately. Garnish with lemon slices, if desired. Yield: 4-6 servings.

Mrs. Frances Miller, Springfield H. S.
Battle Creek, Michigan

CREAMED BEETS

2 tbsp. vinegar
2 tbsp. butter
Salt and pepper to taste
⅓ c. sour cream
12 sm. cooked or canned beets

Combine vinegar, butter, salt, pepper and 1 tablespoon water in saucepan; bring to boiling point. Stir in sour cream and beets. Cook over low heat until beets are heated through. Serve immediately. Yield: 6 servings.

Mrs. Dixie Black, Honey Grove H. S.
Honey Grove, Texas

DEVILED BEETS

3 tbsp. butter
2 tbsp. prepared mustard
½ tsp. salt
½ tsp. paprika
1 tbsp. honey or to taste
1 tsp. Worcestershire sauce
3 c. cubed canned or cooked beets

Combine all ingredients except beets in saucepan; bring to boiling point, stirring frequently. Add beets; simmer until heated through. Serve hot. Yield: 6-8 servings.

Mrs. Martha G. Akers, Auburn H. S.
Riner, Virginia

HARVARD BEETS

2 1-lb. cans diced beets
⅔ c. sugar
2 tbsp. cornstarch
½ c. white vinegar
¾ tsp. salt
¼ c. butter or margarine

Drain beets; reserve juice. Combine sugar and cornstarch in 3-quart saucepan; stir in ½ cup reserved beet juice, vinegar and salt. Bring to a boil, stirring constantly. Reduce heat; simmer for 2 minutes or until slightly thickened and clear. Add beets; simmer for 15 minutes. Add butter; return to a boil. Serve immediately. Yield: 8 servings.

Kathryn Sue Hurst, Clarksville H. S
Clarksville, Arkansas

ORANGE BEETS

1 tsp. grated orange rind
½ c. orange juice
2 tbsp. lemon juice
¼ c. sugar
1 tbsp. cornstarch
½ tsp. salt
2 tbsp. butter
3 c. drained, sliced, cooked beets

Heat orange rind and juices in top of double boiler. Combine sugar, cornstarch and salt; stir into juice mixture until dissolved. Cook until thickened and clear, stirring constantly. Add butter and beets; cook for 15 minutes or until heated through. Yield: 6 servings.

Mary Kate Stover, Benjamin Sch.
Benjamin, Texas

SWEET-SOUR BEETS WITH ORANGE MARMALADE

½ c. sugar
1 tbsp. cornstarch
½ tsp. salt
2 whole cloves
½ c. vinegar
3 c. cooked sliced beets
2 tbsp. margarine
3 tbsp. orange marmalade

Combine sugar, cornstarch, salt, cloves and vinegar in top of double boiler; cook until thickened, stirring constantly. Add beets; cook over hot water for 30 minutes, stirring occasionally. Stir in margarine and marmalade just before serving. Yield: 6 servings.

Mrs. Dorothy M. Hardin, Lebanon Community H. S.
Lebanon, Illinois

HAWAIIAN BEETS

2 No. 2 cans cut beets
1 No. 2 can pineapple chunks
3 tbsp. cornstarch ·
5 tbsp. sugar
2 tbsp. vinegar
½ tsp. salt
2 tbsp. butter

Drain beets and pineapple; reserve juices. Combine cornstarch, sugar, vinegar and reserved juices in saucepan; add salt. Cook until sauce is thickened and clear, stirring constantly. Fold in beets and pineapple; add butter. Heat through, stirring frequently. Serve immediately. Yield: 6-8 servings.

Catherine H. Meader, Alva H. S.
Alva, Florida

BROCCOLI A LA TEGGART

2 pkg. frozen broccoli spears
¼ c. butter
¼ c. flour
1 c. milk
½ c. chicken consomme
½ c. white wine
Salt and pepper to taste
1 can French-fried onion rings
½ c. slivered almonds
½ c. grated sharp cheese

Cook broccoli according to package directions; drain. Place in 1½-quart casserole. Melt butter in saucepan; blend in flour to make a smooth paste. Add milk and consomme; cook until thickened, stirring constantly. Remove from heat; stir in wine. Add salt and pepper. Pour over broccoli; top with onion rings. Sprinkle with almonds and cheese. Bake at 375 degrees for 30 minutes or until bubbly. Yield: 8-10 servings.

Mrs. Beatrice Carmichael,
Washington and Greene County Sch.
Washington, Pennsylvania

BROCCOLI AND BLEU CHEESE

3 pkg. frozen chopped broccoli, cooked
2 tbsp. margarine
2 tbsp. flour
½ tsp. salt
1 c. milk
1 3-oz. package cream cheese, softened
1 wedge bleu cheese
½ c. cheese cracker crumbs

Drain broccoli; place in casserole. Melt margarine in saucepan; blend in flour and salt to make a smooth paste. Add milk; cook until thick, stirring constantly. Add cheeses; stir until melted. Pour cheese sauce over broccoli; sprinkle with crumbs. Bake at 325 degrees for 20 minutes or until heated through. Yield: 6-8 servings.

Mrs. Irene Turner, George Washington Jr. H. S.
Tampa, Florida

BROCCOLI A LA CHRISTY

1 10¾-oz. can mushroom soup
2 10-oz. packages frozen chopped broccoli, thawed
1 c. chopped sweet onions
1 sm. jar pimentos
Salt and pepper to taste
1 c. cracker crumbs
1 stick butter, melted
2 c. grated Cheddar cheese

Mix soup, broccoli, onions, pimentos, salt and pepper. Place mixture in 1½-quart casserole. Sprinkle cracker crumbs over top. Drizzle butter over crumbs. Sprinkle cheese over all. Bake at 375 degrees for 1 hour.

Margaret H. Christy, Wildwood Middle Sch.
Wildwood, Florida

BROCCOLI-GREEN BEAN CASSEROLE

1 can French-style green beans
1 10-oz. package frozen broccoli, cooked
1 can mushroom soup
1 c. mayonnaise
1 c. grated sharp cheese
1 med onion, chopped
2 eggs, beaten
½ tsp. salt
¼ tsp. pepper
Cracker crumbs (opt.)

Arrange beans and broccoli in greased casserole. Mix next 7 ingredients together; pour mixture over vegetables. Cover with crushed cracker crumbs. Bake at 350 degrees about 20 to 25 minutes or until bubbly.

Joan W. Burson, Mt. Zion H. S.
Mt. Zion, Georgia

BROCCOLI-LIMA BEAN CASSEROLE

1 lg. package frozen chopped broccoli
1 lg. package frozen baby lima beans
1 c. sour cream
1 pkg. dry onion soup mix
1 can cream of mushroom soup
1 can water chestnuts, drained and sliced
3 c. Rice Krispies cereal
½ c. butter

Cook vegetables according to package directions until tender-crisp; drain well. Blend in sour cream. Mix together soups; add to vegetable mixture. Add water chestnuts. Mix ingredients thoroughly. Place in casserole. Brown cereal in butter in a skillet. Spread over vegetable mixture. Cover with foil. Bake at 350 degrees for 35 minutes.

Debby Snyder, Ross Middle Sch.
Hamilton, Ohio

BROCCOLI PUFF

3 10-oz. packages frozen broccoli or 1 lg.
   bunch fresh broccoli
1 can cream of mushroom soup
1 ½ c. grated Cheddar cheese

¼ c. milk
¼ c. salad dressing or mayonnaise
2 eggs, beaten
¼ c. fine bread crumbs or croutons
2 tbsp. butter

Cook broccoli until tender; drain. Place in a 9 x 13-inch baking dish. Stir together soup and cheese. Add milk, salad dressing and eggs; stir until smooth. Pour cheese mixture over broccoli. Combine crumbs and butter; sprinkle over top of cheese sauce. Bake at 350 degrees for 30 minutes, or until lightly browned.

Elaine Elnes, Tartan H. S.
St. Paul, Minnesota

BROCCOLI SOUFFLE WITH MUSHROOM SAUCE

1 10-oz. package chopped broccoli
2 tbsp. butter or margarine
2 tbsp. all-purpose flour
½ tsp. salt
½ c. milk
¼ c. grated Parmesan cheese
4 eggs, separated
Mushroom Sauce

Cook broccoli according to package directions; drain. Add butter; stir until melted and all moisture is evaporated. Reserve 2 tablespoons broccoli. Blend flour and salt into remaining broccoli; stir in milk. Cook over medium heat, stirring constantly, until mixture thickens. Remove from heat; stir in cheese. Beat egg yolks until thick; beat small amount of hot broccoli mixture into egg yolks. Stir egg yolk mixture into broccoli mixture. Beat egg whites until stiff peaks form. Fold broccoli mixture into egg whites carefully. Pour mixture into an ungreased 1-quart souffle dish. Bake at 350 degrees for 20 minutes. Top with reserved broccoli. Bake 15 minutes longer or until a knife inserted into middle comes out clean. Serve with mushroom sauce: Yield: 4-6 servings.

Mushroom Sauce:

1 6-oz. can sliced mushrooms, drained
¼ c. butter or margarine, melted
2 tbsp. all-purpose flour
Dash of salt and pepper
1 chicken bouillon cube

Saute mushrooms in butter until lightly browned. Blend in flour, salt and pepper. Add 1 cup water and bouillon cube. Cook until sauce is boiling, stirring constantly. Cook for 1 to 2 minutes longer. Yield: 2 cups.

Janice Baggett, Henry County Jr. H. S.
McDonough, Georgia

BROCCOLI-CORN CASSEROLE

2 pkg. frozen broccoli
2 cans cream-style corn
1 egg, beaten
1 c. bread crumbs or cracker crumbs
1 c. grated Cheddar cheese

Combine broccoli, corn and egg. Place in casserole. Top with bread crumbs. Bake, uncovered, at 350 degrees for 45 minutes. Sprinkle cheese on top. Bake 15 minutes longer or until cheese is melted.

Diane Intoccio, Reynoldsburg Jr. H. S.
Reynoldsburg, Ohio

BROCCOLI AND RICE

1 pkg. chopped frozen broccoli
½ c. chopped celery
½ c. chopped onions
Fresh or canned Mushrooms
2 tbsp. butter or maraarine
1 c. cooked rice
1 can cream of mushroom soup
4 oz. Cheeze Whiz
Salt and papper to taste

Cook broccoli according to package directions. Saute celery, onions and mushrooms in butter in skillet. Combine remaining ingredients with broccoli and celery mixture. Pour into casserole; cover. Bake at 350 degrees for 25 to 30 minutes. Yield: 8 servings.

Karen S. Sikes, Lamar Consolidated H. S.
Rosenberg, Texas

BROCCOLI SUPREME

1 8-oz. package frozen broccoli
1 egg, beaten
½ med. onion, chopped fine
½ can cream of mushroom soup
⅓ c. mayonnaise
¾ c. cheddar cheese, grated
4 oz. herb-seasoned stuffing mix
¼ c. butter or margarine, melted

Cook broccoli according to package directions. Combine egg, onion, soup and mayonnaise in a small bowl. Place layer of broccoli in a 1-quart casserole. Add layer of cheese. Pour a small amount of sauce over cheese. Repeat layers until all ingredients are used. Top with stuffing mix. Drizzle butter on top. Bake for 20 to 25 minutes at 350 degrees. Yield: 5-6 servings.

Diane Avery, Ingleside Middle Sch.
Phoenix, Arizona

BROCCOLI-PECAN SUPREME

3 10-oz. packages frozen chopped broccoli
4 tbsp. flour
1½ tbsp. powdered chicken stock base
Melted butter
2 c. milk
1 pkg. herb-seasoned stuffing mix
⅔ c. coarsely chopped pecans

Cook broccoli until just tender; drain. Place in 13 x 9-inch greased baking dish. Add flour and chicken base to ½ cup melted butter in medium saucepan. Add milk slowly. Cook until thickened, stirring frequently. Mix 6 tablespoons melted butter and ⅔ cup very hot water; add to stuffing mix. Add pecans; toss to mix. Place over broccoli. Bake at 375 degrees for 20 minutes. Yield: 10 servings.

Lettie Ann Boggs, Orrville Sr. H. S.
Orrville, Ohio

BROCCOLI-RICE CASSEROLE

1 c. uncooked rice
1 10-oz. can mushroom soup
1 sm. jar Cheez Whiz
½ c. chopped onion
½ stick margarine
1 pkg. frozen chopped broccoli

Cook rice according to package directions. Add soup and Cheeze Whip to hot rice. Saute onions in margarine; set aside. Pour enough boiling water over frozen broccoli to thaw; drain well. Add broccoli and rice mixture to onion and butter; mix well. Pour into 2-quart casserole. Bake at 325 degrees for 45 minutes. May be served hot or chilled. Freezes well before baking. Yield: 6-8 servings.

Cynthia Stewart, Trinity H. S.
Euless, Texas

BROCCOLI-RICE DELUXE

3 pkg. frozen chopped broccoli
1 c. cooked rice
1 can. chopped pimento
1 can water chestnuts, sliced
1 8-oz. jar Cheez Whiz
1 stick margarine, sliced
1 can celery soup
Shredded-sharp cheese

Cook broccoli according to package directions. Combine next 6 ingredients; pour into buttered casserole. Top with cheese. Bake in 350-degree oven until hot and bubbly.

Pam Lynch, Riverdale H. S.
Murfreesboro, Tennessee

MACKIE'S BROCCOLI SUPREME

1½ lb. fresh broccoli, cut into 1-in. pieces
1 can cream of chicken soup
1 tbsp. all-purpose flour
½ c.sour cream
¼ c. grated carrots
1 sm. onion, chopped
1 tsp. salt
⅛ tsp. pepper
¾ c. herb-seasoned stuffing mix
2 tbsp. melted butter or margarine

Cook broccoli until tender; drain. Blend soup and flour. Add sour cream, carrots, onion, salt and pepper. Stir broccoli into mixture. Place in 2-quart casserole. Combine stuffing mix and melted butter. Sprinkle around edge of casserole. Bake at 350 degrees for 30 to 35 minutes. Yield: 4-6 servings.

Mackie S. Randall, Rossville H. S.
Rossville, Georgia

CAROLYN'S BROCCOLI CASSEROLE

2 10-oz. packages frozen chopped broccoli
1 stick margarine
1 env. dry onion soup mix
1 8-oz. can water chestnuts, sliced
½ c. chopped pecans
1 c. cracker crumbs

Cook broccoli until just tender; drain. Melt margarine in saucepan. Add onion soup mix; stir to soften. Combine broccoli, soup mixture, water chestnuts and pecans in baking dish. Top with cracker crumbs. Bake at 350 degrees for 25 minutes, or until brown. Yield: 8 servings.

Carolyn Caviness, Blue Mountain H. S.
Blue Mountain, Mississippii

CHARLENE'S BROCCOLI CASSEROLE

2 pkg. frozen chopped broccoli, thawed
1½ c. cooked rice
1 can cream of mushroom soup
1 can cream of chicken soup
1 sm. jar of Cheez Whiz

Layer all ingredients in casserole in order listed. Bake at 375 degrees for 45 minutes or until golden brown.

Charlene Frey, Springfield Jr. H. S.
Springfield, Tennessee

DOUBLE CHEESE BROCCOLI

2 10-oz. packages chopped frozen broccoli, cooked and drained
1 can cream of chicken soup
1 c. mayonnaise
½ c. Parmesan cheese
1 c. grated sharp sheese
2 eggs, beaten
Salt and pepper to taste
Seasoned bread crumbs

Combine all ingredients except bread crumbs. Place in greased casserole. Top with bread crumbs. Bake for 45 minutes to 1 hour at 350 degrees. Yield: 6-8 servings

Bonnie Andrews, Ocean Springs H. S.
Ocean Springs, Mississippi

MICROWAVE BROCCOLI

1 pkg. frozen broccoli
1 c. grated American cheese
1 10½-oz. can cream of mushroom soup
⅓ c. evaporated milk
1 can onion rings

Place frozen broccoli in 2-quart greased glass casserole. Microwave on High for 5 or 6 minutes, covered stirring once. Drain. Sprinkle cheese over broccoli. Dilute soup with evaporated milk. Pour over broccoli and cheese. Microwave for 6 minutes on Reheat setting. Remove from oven. Sprinkle onion rings over top of casserole. Return casserole, uncovered, to oven. Microwave on High for 2½ minutes. Yield: 4 servings.

Mrs. Barbara E. Smoot, Wapahani H. S.
Selma, Indiana

TASTY BROCCOLI CASSEROLE

1 med onion, chopped
3 stalks, celery, chopped
1 stick margarine
1 10-oz. package chopped frozen broccoli
8 oz. Velveeta cheese
1 can cream of mushroom soup
1 c. milk
¼ to ½ tsp. garlic powder
1 c. bread crumbs

Cook onion and celery in margarine until tender; add broccoli. Cook until broccoli thaws. Add Velveeta cheese, soup, milk, bread crumbs and garlic powder. Cook until smooth and creamy. Pour into 3-quart casserole. Top with additional bread crumbs. Bake for 20 to 30 minutes at 375 degrees.

Dana Doster Horn, Kirby H. S.
Kirby, Arkansas

BROCCOLI WITH SOUR CREAM

1 c. sour cream
2 tbsp. brown sugar
2 tbsp. cider vinegar
¼ tsp. salt
½ tsp. mustard
1 lb. broccoli, cooked

Combine sour cream, brown sugar, vinegar, salt and mustard in saucepan; heat until brown sugar is melted. Pour over hot broccoli; serve immediately. Yield: 4 servings.

Karleen J. Moore, Happy H. S.
Happy, Texas

PARTY BROCCOLI AND ONIONS

2 pkg. frozen broccoli spears, thawed
1 pkg. frozen chopped broccoli, thawed
3 cans cream of mushroom soup
½ c. grated Cheddar cheese
2 c. whole pearl onions
½ c. slivered almonds
Bread crumbs
Butter

Place broccoli spears and chopped broccoli in casserole. Combine soup, cheese, onions and almonds; spread over broccoli. Top with bread crumbs; dot with butter. Bake in 350-degree oven for 35 minutes or until bubbly. Yield: 20 servings.

Mrs. Jamie H. White, Signal Mountain Jr. H. S.
Signal Mountain, Tennessee

EASY SCALLOPED BROCCOLI

1 10-oz. package frozen broccoli spears
¾ c. evaporated milk
¾ c. chopped onions
1 3-oz. can mushroom pieces, drained
1 tsp. salt
¼ tsp. nutmeg
⅛ tsp. pepper
3 eggs, well beaten

Cook broccoli according to package directions; drain. Combine milk, onions, mushrooms, salt, nutmeg and pepper in saucepan; simmer for 1 minute. Add small amount of hot mixture to eggs; blend well. Stir eggs into hot mixture. Place broccoli in greased small baking dish; cover with sauce. Bake at 350 degrees for 30 minutes or until firm.

Margaret Henderson, Walters H. S.
Walters, Oklahoma

SCALLOPED FRESH BROCCOLI

1 lg. bunch broccoli
¼ c. minced onion
¼ c. melted butter
¼ c. flour
1 tsp. salt
2 c. milk
1½ c. grated Cheddar cheese
½ c. buttered bread crumbs

Cook broccoli in salted water until crisp tender; drain well. Saute onion in butter until transparent; stir in flour and salt to make a paste. Add milk; cook until thickened, stirring constantly. Remove from heat; stir in cheese. Arrange alternate layers of broccoli and cheese sauce in greased 1-quart casserole; top with crumbs. Bake at 350 degrees for 20 minutes or until bubbly.

Kathleen Burchett, Flatwood H. S.
Jonesville, Virginia

CREAM OF BROCCOLI SOUP

2 10-oz. packages frozen chopped broccoli, thawed
¼ c. chopped onion
2 cans chicken broth
2 tbsp. butter
2 tbsp. flour
2 c. half and half
2 tsp. salt
⅛ tsp. mace
Dash of pepper

Combine broccoli, onion, and chicken broth in medium saucepan. Bring to a boil. Simmer for about 10 minutes or until broccoli is tender crisp. Whirl broccoli mixture in blender until very smooth. Melt butter; stir in flour. Add half and half, stirring constantly, until thickened. Add seasoning. Stir in broccoli puree. Cook over medium heat, stirring frequently until soup bubbles. Serve hot. Yield: 10 to 12 servings.

Becky Sweeney, Duncanville H. S.
Duncanville, Texas

BRUSSELS SPROUTS AND WALNUTS AUGRATIN

2 10-oz. packages frozen Brussels sprouts
1 tsp. salt
½ c. grated process sharp cheese
¼ c. butter or margarine
¼ c. packaged herbed dry bread crumbs
⅓ c. chopped walnuts

Place Brussels sprouts and salt in 1 cup boiling water in 1½-quart saucepan; simmer for 4 to 5 minutes or until tender. Drain well. Place in greased 1½-quart casserole; sprinkle with cheese. Melt butter in small frying pan; add bread crumbs and walnuts. Saute until lightly browned, stirring constantly. Sprinkle over Brussels sprouts. Bake in preheated 400-degree oven for 10 minutes or until cheese is melted. Yield: 6 servings.

Mrs. Bernadette Schoen, East Troy Community H. S.
East Troy, Wisconsin

FAVORITE BRUSSELS SPROUTS AUGRATIN

2 c. Brussels sprouts
½ c. medium white sauce
Salt and pepper to taste
½ c. shredded American cheese
½ c. buttered crumbs
1 tbsp. chopped parsley

Steam Brussels sprouts in salted water until tender; drain well. Arrange alternate layers of Brussels sprouts and white sauce in buttered casserole, seasoning each layer with salt and pepper. Sprinkle with cheese and crumbs. Bake in 350-degree oven for 20 minutes or until bubbly. Sprinkle with parsley to serve.

Marjorie Chaney, Zachary H. S.
Zachary, Louisiana

BRUSSELS SPROUTS IN CELERY SAUCE

1½ c. diced celery
1⅛ tsp. salt
6 tbsp. butter
6 tbsp. flour
Milk
Dash of pepper
2 qt. Brussels sprouts, cooked

Bring 2¼ cups water to a boil in saucepan; add celery and salt. Cook for 15 minutes or until tender; drain well, reserving celery stock. Melt butter in saucepan; stir in flour to make a smooth paste. Combine celery stock and enough milk to measure 3 cups liquid; add to paste. Cook until thickened, stirring constantly. Stir in celery; season with pepper. Place Brussels sprouts in serving dish; pour celery sauce over top. Yield: 8 servings.

Mrs. Margaret Cepelka, Clarke County H. S.
Berryville, Virginia

BRUSSELS SPROUTS WITH CHESTNUTS

2 tbsp. butter
2 tsp. flour
¾ c. chicken broth
¼ tsp. salt
Pinch of white pepper
¼ tsp. basil
3 lb. fresh Brussels sprouts
1½ c. sliced chestnuts

Melt butter in top of double boiler; stir in flour to make a smooth paste. Add broth; cook until thickened, stirring constantly. Stir in salt, pepper and basil; keep warm over simmering water. Cook Brussels sprouts in boiling salted water until crisp tender; drain well. Place Brussels sprouts in serving dish. Stir chestnuts into white sauce; pour sauce over Brussels sprouts. Yield: 8 servings.

Meroe E. Stanley, Northville H. S.
Northville, Michigan

BRUSSELS SPROUTS WITH GRAPES

2 pkg. frozen Brussels sprouts
¾ c. sour cream
½ c. slivered almonds
⅔ c. drained mushrooms
1 c. seedless white grapes
¼ c. chopped pimento
1 tsp. sugar
½ tsp. pepper
2 tsp. salt
¾ c. shredded American cheese
Paprika to taste

Cook Brussels sprouts according to package directions; drain well. Combine Brussels sprouts, sour cream, almonds, mushrooms, grapes, pimento and seasonings in double boiler. Cook for 7 minutes or until heated through. Place in serving dish; sprinkle with cheese and paprika. Yield: 8-10 servings.

Novella Mae Melton, Roswell H. S.
Roswell, New Mexico

COUNTRY-STYLE CABBAGE

1 med. cabbage, shredded
½ c. butter
½ c. light cream
½ tsp. salt

Place cabbage and butter in large saucepan. Cover; cook for 5 to 6 minutes. Stir in cream and salt; cook for 1 to 2 minutes longer or until heated through. Yield: 6 servings.

Mrs. Ruth Cudworth, Milroy School
Milroy, Indiana

BELMONT CASSEROLE

3 c. shredded cabbage, cooked
1½ c. drained canned tomatoes
Salt and paprika to taste
1 c. grated cheese
1 c. bread crumbs
1 ½ tbsp. butter

Arrange alternate layers of cabbage and tomatoes in greased casserole, sprinkling each layer with salt and paprika. Top with cheese and bread crumbs; dot with butter. Bake at 250 to 300 degrees for 15 to 20 minutes or until cheese melts. Yield: 6 servings.

Fornadia Cook, Osborne Jr. H. S.
Marietta, Georgia

BEBE'S RED CABBAGE

1 med. onion, chopped
4 tbsp. corn oil
1 head red cabbage, chopped
1 tsp. salt
2 tart apples, sliced
½ c. cider vinegar
⅓ c. (packed) brown sugar

Add onion to oil in large heavy skillet; brown. Add cabbage and salt; cover. Steam on low heat for 10 minutes. Add apples, ½ cup hot water, vinegar, and brown sugar. Simmer, covered, for 45 minutes. Yield: 4-6 servings.

Reita Ellis Wilson, Trinity Gardens Middle Sch.
Mobile, Alabama

CABBAGE FOR THE KING

2 c. coarsely chopped cabbage
2 tsp. salt
2 tbsp. butter
1 tbsp. flour
2 c. milk
¼ tsp. pepper
1 c. grated Cheddar cheese
¼ c. buttered cracker crumbs

Cook cabbage with 1 teaspoon salt in ¼ cup boiling water for 3 minutes; drain well. Melt butter in saucepan; stir in flour to make a smooth paste. Add milk, remaining 1 teaspoon salt and pepper; cook until thickened, stirring constantly. Arrange cabbage and white sauce in layers in buttered casserole; top with cheese and crumbs. Bake at 275 degrees for 1 hour or until bubbly.

Mrs. Maxine Muck, Adrian Catholic Central H. S.
Adrian, Michigan

COMPANY CABBAGE

5 c. finely shredded cabbage
1 c. finely shredded carrots
½ c. chopped green onions and tops
½ tsp. salt
⅛ tsp. pepper
1 beef bouillon cube
¼ c. butter
1 tsp. prepared mustard
⅓ c. chopped pecans
¼ tsp. paprika

Combine cabbage, carrots, green onions, salt and pepper in large heavy saucepan. Dissolve bouillon cube in ¼ cup hot water; add to cabbage mixture. Toss with fork to blend thoroughly; cover tightly. Cook over low heat for 5 minutes, stirring and turning once during cooking. Drain well; turn into warm serving dish. Melt butter in small saucepan over low heat; stir in mustard and pecans. Heat thoroughly. Pour over cabbage. Sprinkle with paprika.

Mrs. Jean C. Vandergrift, Lee Jr. H. S.
Roanoke, Virginia

CZECHOSLOVAKIAN CABBAGE SOUP

2 lb. beef bones
1 c. chopped onions
3 carrots, pared and coarsely chopped
2 cloves garlic, chopped
1 bay leaf
2 lb. beef short ribs
1 tsp. thyme
½ tsp. paprika
8 c. coarsely shredded cabbage
2 1-lb. cans tomatoes
2 tsp. salt
½ to ¾ tsp. hot pepper sauce
¼ c. chopped parsley
3 tbsp. lemon juice
3 tbsp. sugar
1 can sauerkraut
Sour cream

Place beef bones, onions, carrots, garlic and bay leaf in roasting pan. Top with short ribs. Sprinkle with thyme and paprika. Roast, uncovered, at 450 degrees for 10 minutes until meat is browned. Transfer meat and vegetables to large kettle. Add 8 cups water, cabbage, tomatoes, salt and hot pepper sauce. Bring to a boil. Cover. Simmer for 1 hour and 30 minutes. Skim off fat. Add parsley, lemon juice, sugar and sauerkraut. Cook, uncovered for 1 hour. Remove bones and short ribs from kettle. Remove meat from bones. Cut into cubes; return to kettle. Cook for 5 minutes longer. Serve with dollop of sour cream on each bowl. Freezes well. Yield: 8-10 servings.

Phyllis Pope, Medford Jr. H. S.
Medford, Ohio

SKILLET CABBAGE

4 slices bacon
¼ c. vinegar
1 tbsp. brown sugar
1 tsp. salt
1 tbsp. onion
4 c. quartered cabbage

Cook bacon until crisp; remove from skillet. Crumble. Add vinegar, brown sugar, salt and onion. Add bacon; heat thoroughly. Add ½ cup water and cabbage; cover. Steam until tender.

Bonnye Gage, Rivercrest H. S.
Bogata, Texas

SKILLET CABBAGE MEDLEY

1 tbsp. bacon drippings
1 med. onion, finely chopped
1 green pepper, finely chopped
3 stalks celery, finely chopped
1 to 2 lg. green tomatoes, finely chopped
½ med. cabbage, finely chopped
1 tsp. salt
¼ tsp. pepper

Melt bacon drippings in large skillet; add vegetables. Season with salt and pepper; mix well. Cover; cook over medium heat for 5 to 8 minutes or until cabbage is crisp, tender stirring occasionally. Yield: 4 servings.

Hilda H. Sharp, Cohn H. S.
Nashville, Tennessee

DANISH RED CABBAGE

1 3-lb. red cabbage
Vinegar
¼ c. butter
¼ c. sugar
1 tsp. salt
½ c. red currant juice or currant jelly
1 apple, cubed

Cut cabbage into quarters; cut out core. Chop cabbage fine; sprinkle with vinegar to prevent discoloration. Melt butter in kettle. Add sugar, salt and cabbage; cook, covered, for 15 minutes. Stir in currant juice, apple and 2 tablespoons vinegar; simmer, covered, for 2 hours.

Mrs. Melanie Johansen, Foslir Jr-Sr H. S.
Seattle, Washington

PENNSYLVANIA RED CABBAGE

2 tbsp. bacon drippings
4 c. shredded red cabbage
2 c. chopped unpared red apples
¼ c. (packed) brown sugar
¼ c. vinegar
1¼ tsp. salt
½ tsp. caraway seed
Dash of pepper

Heat bacon drippings in Dutch oven. Add cabbage, apples, brown sugar, vinegar, ¼ cup water, salt, caraway seed and pepper. Simmer, covered, for 15 minutes or to desired doneness, stirring occasionally. Yield: 5 servings.

Mrs. Audrey Buhl, Gaylord H. S.
Gaylord, Minnesota

SAUCY CABBAGE WEDGES

1 2-lb. cabbage
⅓ c. mayonnaise
¼ c. milk
4 tsp. vinegar
1 tsp. sugar
½ tsp. prepared mustard
Paprika to taste

Cut cabbage into 8 wedges; cook in boiling salted water for 8 to 10 minutes or until tender. Drain well. Combine mayonnaise and milk in small saucepan; stir until smooth. Add vinegar, sugar and mustard; mix well. Cook over low heat until heated through, stirring constantly. Place cabbage in serving dish; pour sauce over cabbage. Sprinkle with paprika. Yield: 8 servings.

Mrs. Billie Jean McCarroll, Slidell H. S.
Slidell, Texas

SENSATIONAL SAUERKRAUT

1 c. thin onion strips
2 tbsp. butter
1 can sauerkraut, drained
¼ c. (packed) dark brown sugar
1 tbsp. tarragon vinegar
½ tsp. salt

Saute onion strips in butter until brown. Add sauerkraut, 1 cup water and remaining ingredients; mix well. Simmer, covered, until water has evaporated and flavors have blended. Yield: 4 servings.

Mrs. Rhonda Trainor, Brewster Vocation Sch.
Tampa, Florida

UKRAINIAN-BAKED CABBAGE

1 sm. cabbage
1 sm. onion, chopped
3 tbsp. butter
½ tsp. salt
Dash of pepper
½ c. sour cream
½ c. buttered bread crumbs

Cut cabbage into small wedges; cook in boiling water for 6 minutes or until tender. Place in sieve or colander to drain thoroughly. Saute onion in butter until tender. Arrange cabbage in layers in buttered baking dish, sprinkling each layer with onion, salt and pepper. Cover with sour cream; top with buttered bread crumbs. Bake at 350 degrees for 30 minutes or until cabbage is tender and crumbs are lightly browned. Yield: 3-4 servings.

Mrs. Nadia Hamilton, Fort LeBoeuf H. S.
Waterford, Pennsylvania

BUTTERY GRATED CARROTS

2 lb. carrots, pared and grated
1 tbsp. oil
½ tsp. garlic slat
¼ tsp. salt
⅛ tsp. pepper
½ c. butter

Place carrots, oil, garlic salt, salt, pepper and 2 tablespoons water in skillet; cover tightly. Cook, covered, over medium heat for 10 to 12 minutes. Stir occasionally. Remove from heat; add butter. Toss gently until coated.

Dianne Wentzell, St. Martin H. S.
Biloxi, Mississippi

CANDIED CARROTS

1 lb. carrots
1 c. orange marmalade
1 tsp. cornstarch

Cut carrots crosswise into ¼-inch thick pieces. Place in saucepan containing a small amount of boiling water. Boil for about 5 minutes. Add marmalade; cook until carrots are tender. Remove carrots with a slotted spoon. Stir cornstarch into remaining liquid; cook until thickened, stirring constantly. Toss carrots wth marmalade sauce; serve immediately.

Alberta Hawkins, Lakeview H. S.
Battle Creek, Michigan

CARROTS WITH CELERY SEED SAUCE

8 med. carrots, sliced
4 tbsp. butter or margarine
2 tsp. flour
1 tsp. celery seed
½ tsp. salt

Cook carrots in ½ cup water in a tightly covered saucepan over medium heat for 12 to 15 minutes. Brown butter in a small frypan. Stir in flour, liquid from carrots, celery seed and salt. Cook over low heat for 1 minute, stirring constantly. Mix sauce with carrots. Serve hot. Carrots reheat without overcooking in a microwave oven.

Mrs. Marcia F. Swanson, Henry County Sr. H. S.
McDonough, Georgia

CARROTS A LA ORANGE

1 lb. small carrots
1 11-oz. can mandarin oranges
2 tbsp. butter

Scrape carrots; cut into ½-inch rings. Drain oranges; reserve juice. Cook carrots in reserved juice until tender; drain well. Add butter and oranges to carrots; heat thoroughly. Yield: 4-6 servings.

Anne Floriano, Menominee H. S.
Menominee, Michigan

CREAMED CARROTS

4 c. diced carrots
1 tsp. sugar
2 tbsp. chopped onion
½ c. heavy cream

Cook carrots in boiling salted water until crisp tender. Drain well. Combine carrots, sugar, onion and cream. Mix well. May be served hot, warm or cold. Yield: 4 servings.

Mrs. Bass Powell, Paint Creek Rural H. S.
Haskell, Texas

COPPER COINS

5 c. carrots, sliced
1 can tomato soup
½ c. salad oil
¾ c. sugar
½ c. tarragon vinegar
1 tsp. prepared mustard
1 tsp. Worcestershire sauce
1 tsp. salt
1 tsp. pepper
1 med. onion, sliced
1 green pepper, sliced

Cook carrots until tender; set aside. Heat soup, oil, sugar, vinegar, mustard, Worcestershire sauce, salt and pepper. Place carrots in casserole. Layer onion and green pepper over carrots. Pour soup mixture over vegetables. Marinate in refrigerator overnight.

Vivian B. Hicks, Corsicana H. S.
Corsicana, Texas

COPPER PENNIES

2 lb. carrots, sliced and cooked
1 med. onion, chopped
1 bell pepper, chopped
½ c. salad oil
1 c. sugar
¾ c. vinegar
1 tbsp. prepared mustard
1 tbsp. Worcestershire sauce
Salt and pepper to taste
1 can cream of tomato soup

Drain cooked carrots. Mix with remaining ingredients. Place in glass casserole. Marinate in refrigerator overnight, or longer. Keeps indefinitely.

Linda Dohnalik, Milano H. S.
Milano, Texas

CATHERINE'S MARINATED CARROTS

1 pkg. carrots, cut into sticks
½ can tomato soup
½ c. sugar
⅔ c. vinegar
¼ c. oil
Salt and pepper to taste
½ tsp. Worcestershire sauce
½ tsp. prepared mustard
1 onion, sliced in rings
Green pepper strips

Boil carrots in salted water until tender, not soft. Drain; cool. Combine next 7 ingredients. Pour marinade over carrots. Add onion and green peppers. Chill overnight.

Catherine Payne, Friendswood H. S.
Friendswood, Texas

KILA'S MARINATED CARROTS

2 lb. carrots, sliced
1 10-oz. can tomato soup
1 c. sugar
½ c. vegetable oil
¾ c. vinegar

1 tsp. salt
½ tsp. pepper
1 lg. onion, cut in rings
1 med. green pepper, cut in rings

Cook carrots until tender. Drain and cool. Combine next 6 ingredients in a saucepan. Heat until sugar dissolves. Cool. Pour over carrots, onion and pepper rings. Refrigerate at least 24 hours before serving. Keeps well in the refrigerator. Yield: 10-12 servings.

Kila Gregory, Flatwoods Combined Sch.
Jonesville, Virginia

RAE'S MARINATED CARROTS

2 lbs. carrots, peeled
1 can tomato soup
½ c. sugar
½ c. oil
¾ c. vinegar
1 tbsp. minced onion
1 bell pepper, chopped fine
2 tsp. salt
1 tsp. pepper
1 tsp. dry mustard
1 tsp. Worcestershire sacue

Cut carrots into thin slices. Cook about 20 minutes or until tender. Drain; cool. Combine remaining ingredients in saucepan. Heat to boiling point. Pour over carrots. Refrigerate overnight. Yield: 15-20 servings.

Mrs. Rae M. Boswell, Thomasville H. S.
Thomasville, Alabama

PENNIES AND RINGS

2 lb. carrots, sliced ½-inch thick
1 green pepper, cut into rings
1 onion, sliced thinly
3 stalks celery, diced
1 can tomato soup
½ c. sugar
¼ c. salad oil
¾ c. vinegar
1 tsp. mustard
1 tsp. Worcestershire sauce
Salt and pepper to taste

Simmer carrots in salted water until just tender. Drain and cool. Alternate layers of carrots, pepper rings, onion and celery in medium casserole. Combine remaining ingredients in blender. Whirl until thoroughly mixed. Pour over vegetables. Refrigerate overnight.

Sally Martin, Crestview Jr. H. S.
Huntington, Indiana

CARROTS A LA ANGIE

1 can tomato soup
½ c. oil
⅓ c. vinegar
1 c. sugar
1 tsp. Worcestershire sauce
1 tsp. dry mustard
Salt and pepper to taste
1 lb. canned or cooked carrots
1 onion, sliced
1 green pepper, sliced

Combine first 7 ingredients in a small saucepan; mix well. Bring to a boil. Layer carrots, onion and green pepper in a serving dish. Pour tomato sauce over all. Let stand for several hours for flavors to blend.

Angie Christy, Fairfield Union Jr. H. S.
Lancaster, Ohio

GUESS AGAIN CASSEROLE

2 lb. carrots, peeled and sliced
2 tbsp. margarine
1 med. onion, grated
6 to 8 oz. Cheddar cheese, grated
Salt and pepper to taste
Buttered bread crumbs (opt.)

Boil carrots until tender; mash well. Add margarine, grated onion and cheese. Season with salt and pepper. Mix to blend ingredients. Top with buttered crumbs. Bake at 350 degrees for 40 minutes. Yield: 8 servings.

Mrs. Marjorie Little, Silver Lake Regional H. S.
Pembroke, Massachusetts

LEMON-BUTTERED CARROTS

½ c. butter
½ c. sugar
2 tsp. grated lemon rind
1 tbsp. lemon juice
24 sm. carrots, cooked

Melt butter and sugar in saucepan; stir in lemon rind and lemon juice. Add carrots; simmer until glazed, turning carrots frequently. Garnish with parsley. Yield: 8 servings.

Tommi L. Gunn, Soddy-Daisy Jr. H. S.
Daisy, Tennessee

CHRISTMAS CARROT RING

2 bunches carrots, cooked and mashed
2 tbsp. sugar
4 crackers, crumbled
Salt and pepper to taste
3 tbsp. minced onion
1 green pepper, minced
½ c. minced celery
3 tbsp. butter
1 egg, beaten

Combine carrots, sugar, crackers, salt and pepper. Saute onion, green pepper and celery in butter; stir into carrot mixture. Stir in egg; spread in buttered ring mold. Place ring mold in pan of hot water. Bake at 350 degrees for 30 minutes or until firm. Invert onto serving plate; fill center with buttered peas, if desired. Yield: 6 servings.

Mrs. John E. Hillhouse, Mathiston H. S.
Mathiston, Mississippi

SAUTÉED CARROTS AND ZUCCHINI

6 med. carrots, cut into thin strips
1 bunch green onions, cut into 2 in. pieces
3 tbsp. salad oil
3 med. zucchini, cut into thin strips
1 tsp. salt

Place carrots and green onions in oil in 12-inch skillet. Cook over high heat, stirring constantly, about 3 minutes. Add zucchini and salt. Cook until tender-crisp, about 3 minutes. Yield: 6 servings.

Emily Lewis, Capitol Hill H. S.
Oklahoma City, Oklahoma

SUNSHINE CARROTS

5 med. carrots
1 tbsp. sugar
1 tsp. cornstarch
¼ tsp. ground ginger
¼ tsp. salt
¼ c. orange juice
2 tbsp. butter or margarine

Cut carrots diagonally in 1-inch chunks. Cook, covered, in boiling salted water until just tender, about 20 minutes. Drain. Mix sugar, cornstarch, ginger and salt in saucepan. Add orange juice. Cook, stirring constantly until thick and bubbly. Boil for 1 minute. Stir in butter until melted. Toss with carrots. Yield: 4 servings

Bertha Spears, Lindsay Jr. H. S.
Lindsay, Oklahoma

CAULIFLOWER A LA ROMAGNOLA

1 cauliflower, cooked
⅔ c. fine dry bread crumbs
1 tsp. grated Parmesan cheese
½ tsp. salt
¼ tsp. pepper
2 eggs, beaten
¼ c. milk

Separate cauliflower into flowerets; let cool. Combine bread crumbs, cheese, salt and pepper. Combine eggs and milk; mix well. Dip flowerets in egg mixture; dredge with crumb mixture. Fry in deep fat at 365 degrees for 2 to 4 minutes or until golden brown, turning occasionally. Drain on paper toweling; serve immediately. Yield: 4 servings.

Mrs. Catherine R. Trotter, Independence H. S.
Independence, Louisiana

CAULIFLOWER AND TOMATOES PARMESAN

1 med. cauliflower
1½ tsp. salt
1 tsp. lemon juice (opt.)
1 sm. clove of garlic, minced
2 tbsp. olive oil or cooking oil
8 to 10 tomato wedges
1 tsp. chopped parsley
2 tbsp. grated Parmesan or Cheddar cheese

Separate cauliflower into medium-sized flowerets. Place in saucepan; cover barely with water. Add 1 teaspoon salt and lemon juice. Cook, covered, for 10 minutes or until crisp tender; drain well. Saute garlic in olive oil in large skillet until browned. Add flowerets; saute lightly. Add remaining ½ teaspoon salt and tomato wedges; simmer, covered, for 2 to 3 minutes or until tomatoes are slightly soft. Pour into serving dish; sprinkle with parsley and cheese to serve.

Avis Prochaska, Glasco H. S.
Glasco, Kansas

CAULIFLOWER POLANAISE

2 pkg. frozen cauliflower
½ c. fresh coarse bread crumbs
6 tbsp. butter, melted
4 tsp. lemon juice
2 tbsp. finely chopped parsley
2 hard-cooked eggs, finely chopped

Cook cauliflower according to package directions under tender; drain well. Saute bread crumbs in butter until golden brown. Remove from heat; add lemon juice. Place cauliflower in serving dish; add bread crumbs. Mix lightly. Sprinkle with chopped parsley and eggs. Serve immediately. Yield: 6 servings.

Loraine Ranney, Plattsmouth H. S.
Plattsmouth, Nebraska

CAULIFLOWER WITH ALMOND BUTTER

1 sm. cauliflower
¼ c. slivered blanched almonds
3 tbsp. butter

Trim outer leaves from cauliflower. Cook in boiling salted water for 10 minutes or until tender; drain well. Saute almonds in butter until lightly browned. Place cauliflower in serving dish; pour butter and almonds overtop. Yield: 4 servings.

Helen Janis Hale, Somerset H. S.
Somerset, Kentucky

CAULIFLOWER WITH DILL SAUCE

1 med. cauliflower
2 tbsp. butter
1 c. sour cream
1 tsp. dillseed

Separate cauliflower into flowerets; place in pan with small amount of boiling water. Cover; bring to a boil. Reduce heat; cook until crisp tender. Melt butter in saucepan; stir in sour cream and dillseed. Cook until heated through. Do not boil. Pour over cauliflower; serve immediately.

Carolyn Carpenter, Sam Houston H. S.
Arlington, Texas

DANISH CAULIFLOWER

1 lg. cauliflower
7 tbsp. margarine
¾ c. flour
1 tsp. salt
1 ¼ c. milk
5 eggs, separated

Break cauliflower into flowerets. Cook in boiling salted water for 5 minutes; drain well. Melt margarine in saucepan; remove from heat. Stir in flour and salt to make a smooth paste. Add milk gradually. Return to heat; cook until thickened, stirring constantly. Let cool. Beat egg yolks; stir into cooled white sauce. Beat egg whites until stiff; fold into white sauce. Fold flowerets carefully into white sauce; pour into 2-quart casserole. Bake at 350 degrees for 1 hour or until set. Serve with melted butter, if desired. Yield: 6 servings.

Mrs. Martha R. Staby, Brush H. S.
Brush, Colorado

BRENDA'S FRIED CAULIFLOWER

1 head cauliflower
1 egg
Milk
Cracker crumbs

Separate cauliflower into flowerets; cook in boiling salted water until tender; drain. Beat egg with a small amount of milk. Dip cauliflower in egg mixture. Roll in cracker crumbs. Fry in deep hot fat until brown.

Brenda Bates, Meadowbrook Middle Sch.
Fort Worth, Texas

FRENCH-FRIED CAULIFLOWER

1 pkg. frozen cauliflower, cooked
1 tsp. salt
¼ c. milk
1 egg, beaten
1 c. cracker crumbs

Drain cauliflower well; season with salt. Combine milk and egg; mix well. Dip cauliflower into egg mixture; dredge with cracker crumbs. Fry in deep hot fat until golden brown. Yield: 3-4 servings.

Mrs. Donna Johns, Anna Local Sch.
Anna, Ohio

LOW-CALORIE CURRIED CAULIFLOWER

1 pkg. frozen cauliflower
½ tsp. salt
¼ tsp. curry powder

Cook cauliflower in boiling salted water until tender; drain well. Sprinkle with curry powder; serve immediately. Yield: 4 servings.

Mrs. Mary L. Weaver, Schwenksville Union Sch.
Schwenksville, Pennsylvania

SAUCY MICROWAVE CAULIFLOWER

1 lb. head cauliflower
½ c. mayonnaise
½ c. shredded cheese

1 tbsp. mustard
1 tsp. salt

Remove leaves and woody stem from cauliflower. Wrap in waxed paper; puncture paper. Microwave for 10 minutes; unwrap. Place in glass casserole. Mix together mayonnaise, shredded cheese, mustard and salt. Pour over cauliflower. Microwave uncovered, for 1 minute. Yield: 4-6 servings.

Deanna L. Irwin, Xavier H. S.
Phoenix, Arizona

SPECIAL CREAMED CELERY

1 bunch celery
3 tbsp. butter
1 tbsp. flour
½ tsp. salt
Dash of pepper
1 c. half and half
1 3-oz. package cream cheese, softened
½ c. toasted slivered almonds

Remove tough outside stalks of celery; cut remaining stalks diagonally into ¼-inch pieces. Cook celery in boiling, salted water for 5 minutes or until crisp tender. Drain well. Melt butter in saucepan; stir in flour, salt and pepper to make a smooth paste. Add half and half; cook until thickened, stirring constantly. Add cream cheese; stir until smooth. Place celery in 1½ quart buttered casserole; pour cheese sauce over celery. Sprinkle with almonds. Bake at 325 degrees for 20 to 25 minutes or until bubbly. Yield: 4-5 servings.

Mrs. Patricia Bennett, West End H. S.
Nashville, Tennessee

FRENCH-BRAISED CELERY

2 c. 1-in. pieces of celery
4 sprigs of parsley
4 slices onion
½ c. bouillon
1 tsp. salt
¼ tsp. pepper
2 strips bacon, diced
Buttered bread crumbs

Combine celery, parsley, onion and bouillon in casserole; season with salt and pepper. Sprinkle bacon over top; cover. Bake at 375 degrees for 30 minutes. Sprinkle with bread crumbs; bake, uncovered, for 10 minutes longer or until crumbs are browned. Yield: 4 servings.

Mary Ann Hribek, Giddings H. S.
Giddings, Texas

EASY SCALLOPED CELERY

3 c. sliced celery
1 c. chopped green peppers
Chopped onion to taste
½ can cream of celery soup
Salt and pepper to taste
Cracker crumbs

Boil celery, green peppers and onion until tender; drain well. Combine celery mixture, soup and seasonings; place in buttered 1-quart casserole. Top with cracker crumbs. Bake at 350 degrees until heated through.

Mrs. Jane Erickson Peterson, Ramsey Jr. H. S.
Minneapolis, Minnesota

EXOTIC CELERY

4 c. (heaping) chopped celery
¼ tsp. salt
1 can cream of chicken soup
1 sm. jar chopped pimentos and liquid
1 can water chestnuts, drained and sliced
1 c. slivered almonds
Butter

Cook celery in boiling water for 5 minutes; drain well. Combine all ingredients except almonds and butter in 2-quart casserole. Saute almonds in butter; sprinkle over celery mixture. Bake at 350 degrees for 30 minutes or until bubbly. Yield: 6 servings.

Mrs. Mary Sallee, Pocahontas Sch.
Pocahontas, Arkansas

ORIENTAL CELERY SAUTE

2 tbsp. butter
2 c. diagonally sliced celery
½ c. diagonally sliced green onions
1 4-oz. can sliced mushrooms, drained
1 5-oz. can water chestnuts, drained and sliced
1 tsp. seasoned salt
¼ tsp. seasoned pepper

Melt butter in skillet; add remaining ingredients. Saute for 2 minutes or until crisp tender, stirring constantly. Yield: 4 servings.

Mrs. Margaret Jurkiewicz,
Argos Community Jr.-Sr. H. S.
Argos, Indiana

BAKED CORN CUSTARD WITH CHEESE

2 green onions, finely chopped
3 tbsp. butter
3 tbsp. flour
½ tsp. salt
Pepper to taste
2 c. milk
1 c. grated aged cheese
1 tsp. sugar
2 tbsp. minced pimento
½ tsp. marjoram
2 eggs, beaten
2 No. 2 cans whole kernel corn, drained
½ c. bread crumbs
Paprika to taste

Saute onions in butter until golden. Stir in flour, salt and pepper. Add milk slowly, stirring constantly; cook over medium heat until thickened. Blend in cheese; add sugar, pimento and marjoram. Stir a small amount of hot cheese sauce into eggs; stir eggs into hot cheese sauce. Add corn; stir until well mixed. Pour into shallow 2-quart casserole. Sprinkle crumbs over top; sprinkle lightly with paprika. Bake at 350 degrees for 35 minutes or until done. Yield: 6 servings.

Mrs. Mary E. Morgan, Bakersfield H. S.
Bakersfield, California

BEST-EVER CORN PIE

2 med. onions, chopped
¼ c. cooking oil
2 lg. tomatoes, peeled and sliced
1 No. 2 can cream-style corn
¼ pkg. corn muffin mix
3 eggs, separated
½ lb. cheese, grated

Saute onions in oil over low heat until soft, stirring constantly. Add tomatoes; cook for 5 minutes. Combine corn and muffin mix; stir in beaten egg yolks. Stir in onion mixture and cheese. Beat egg whites until stiff; fold into corn mixture. Pour into 2-quart baking dish. Bake in preheated 300-degree oven for 1 hour or until firm.

Edith Donaldson, Gadsden H. S.
Anthony, New Mexico

BUSY-DAY CORN CASSEROLE

1 No. 303 can cream-style corn
Salt and pepper to taste
1 egg, beaten
1 sm. onion, minced
12 to 14 crackers, crushed
Butter

Pour corn into casserole; season with salt and pepper. Add egg and onion; stir in cracker crumbs. Dot with butter. Bake at 350 degrees for 45 minutes to 1 hour or until heated through.

Lynn Lankford, Carrizo Springs, H. S.
Carrizo Springs, Texas

BAKED FRESH CORN

½ c. sugar
1 tsp. salt
4 c. fresh kernel corn
2 c. milk

Combine sugar, salt and corn, tossing lightly to mix evenly. Place in lightly oiled 1½-quart casserole. Add milk; stir lightly. Cover. Bake at 350 degrees for 30 minutes. Uncover; bake for 30 minutes longer or until done. Yield: 4-6 servings.

Mrs. Jo Nita Schwarz, Central H. S.
San Angelo, Texas

BOSTON-STYLE BAKED CORN

1 tsp. dry mustard
½ tsp. salt
2 tbsp. brown sugar
1 c. catsup
1 sm. onion, diced
2 12-oz. cans whole kernel corn, drained
2 to 3 slices bacon, diced

Combine mustard, salt, brown sugar and catsup in medium bowl; add onion and corn. Mix thoroughly. Pour into greased 1½-quart casserole. Top with diced bacon. Bake in preheated 350-degree oven for 40 minutes or until bacon is cooked and corn is heated. Yield: 6-8 servings.

Cathie Miller, Saint Joseph H. S.
Jackson, Mississippi

CORN-CHEESE CASSEROLE

2 lg. cans cream-style corn
¾ c. yellow cornmeal
6 tbsp. oil
2 eggs, beaten
1 tsp. garlic salt
2 c. grated sharp Cheddar cheese
2 chopped jalapeno peppers

Combine corn, cornmeal, oil, eggs and garlic salt. Layer corn mixture with cheese and peppers, ending with corn mixture. Pour into 8 × 8-inch pan. Bake at 350 degrees for 45 to 60 minutes.

Debbie Jacoway, Crooked Oak H. S.
Oklahoma City, Oklahoma

CORN AND ONION CASSEROLE

1 3½-oz. can French-fried onions
½ c. chopped green pepper
1 tsp. butter or margarine
1 1-lb. can cream-style corn
2 tsp. chopped pimento
1 egg. slightly beaten

Crush half the onions. Saute green pepper in butter until soft. Add corn, pimento, egg and crushed onions; pour into 1 ½-quart casserole. Bake at 350 degrees for 25 minutes or until firm. Sprinkle remaining onions on top; bake for 5 minutes longer.

Mrs. Brownie S. Babington, Franklinton H. S.
Franklinton, Louisiana

CORN IN SOUR CREAM

3 strips bacon
1 can whole kernel corn
½ tsp. salt
1 c. sour cream

Fry bacon until crisp; drain and crumble. Pour off all but 2 tablespoons drippings. Stir corn, salt and sour cream into drippings; add bacon. Heat through.

Ann C. Farmer, Foust Jr. H. S.
Owensboro, Kentucky

CORN PUDDING WITH CHEESE

1 c. dry bread crumbs
2 c. cream-style corn
2 tbsp. finely chopped green pepper
1 egg, beaten
1 c. evaporated milk
1 tbsp. sugar
1 tsp. salt
½ tsp. pepper
4 oz. sliced Cheddar cheese, cut into 1½-in. strips

Reserve ¼ cup bread crumbs. Combine corn, green pepper, egg, remaining bread crumbs, milk, sugar, salt and pepper; mix well. Pour into greased casserole; arrange cheese strips over top. Sprinkle with reserved bread crumbs. Bake at 325 degrees for 1 hour or until done.

Mrs. Doveta Hunt, Pecos H. S.
Pecos, Texas

CORN SAUTE

8 ears of corn
¼ c. butter or margarine
1 c. thin onion rings
½ c. green pepper strips
1½ tsp. salt
¼ tsp. monosodium glutamate
¼ tsp. dried oregano
½ c. light cream
2 med. tomatoes, sliced and halved.

Cut enough corn from cobs to measure 1 quart. Melt butter in 10-inch heavy skillet over medium heat. Add corn, onion rings; green pepper, salt, monosodium glutamate and oregano. Cover; cook for 6 to 7 minutes, stirring occasionally with spoon. Add cream and tomato slices; simmer, uncovered, for 1 to 2 minutes or until tomatoes are heated through but still firm. Yield: 4-6 servings.

Susan Snell, Montour Joint H. S.
McKees Rocks, Pennsylvania

CRUSTY CORN SOUFFLE

¼ c. butter
3 tbsp. flour
8 oz. creamed corn
4 eggs, separated
Salt and pepper to taste
Chopped parsley
¼ c. cheese, grated

Melt butter in medium saucepan; remove from heat. Stir in flour and corn. Return to heat; stir for 1 minute. Cool. Add egg yolks, one at a time, beating well. Add salt, pepper and parsley. Whip egg whites until stiff, fold lightly into corn mixture. Pour into ungreased souffle dish. Sprinkle with grated cheese. Bake at 350 degrees for 45 minutes, or until puffy and golden brown. Serve immediately.

Holly Haddow, Camelback H. S.
Phoenix, Arizona

CRISP-TOPPED CORN

1 pkg. frozen whole kernel corn
2 tbsp. butter or margarine
½ c. herb seasoned dressing mix
2 sprigs of parsley

Cook corn in a small amount of salted water until done. Melt butter in skillet. Add dressing mix; cook until lightly browned. Sprinkle over corn when ready to serve. Garnish with parsley.

Mrs. Janice Larson, Iron River H. S.
Iron River, Michigan

EASY CORN OYSTERS

3 tbsp. flour
½ tsp. salt
½ tsp. baking powder
1 egg, slightly beaten
½ c. milk
Butter or margarine
1 c. corn

Sift flour with salt and baking powder. Add egg, milk, 1 teaspoon melted butter and corn; mix well. Fry teaspoonfuls of corn mixture in small amount of butter until brown on both sides. Yield: 6-8 servings.

Mrs. Dorothy Waugh, Strasburg H. S.
Strasburg, Virginia

FAVORITE CORN FRITTERS

1 egg
¼ c. milk
1 c. pancake mix
1 12-oz. can whole kernel corn, drained
Cooking oil

Combine egg and milk. Add pancake mix; stir just until smooth. Fold in corn. Drop by teaspoonfuls into 1-inch oil at 325 degrees. Cook for 4 minutes or until golden brown. Yield: 8-10 servings.

Mrs. D. J. Dear, Stringer H. S.
Stringer, Mississippi

FRESH CORN AU GRATIN

3 tbsp. butter or margarine
1 tbsp. flour
½ c. milk
½ c. shredded American cheese
3 c. corn
1 tsp. ground nutmeg
1 tsp. salt
⅛ tsp. pepper
½ c. soft bread crumbs

Melt 1 tablespoon butter in saucepan; blend in flour to make a paste. Add milk; cook until thick, stirring constantly. Add cheese, corn, nutmeg, salt and pepper; mix well. Turn into buttered 1-quart casserole. Melt remaining butter; mix with bread crumbs. Sprinkle over casserole. Bake in preheated 350-degree oven for 35 to 40 minutes or until crumbs are brown. Yield: 5-6 servings.

Joyce Gandy Garrison, Chesnee H. S.
Chesnee, South Carolina

MEXICAN CORN PUDDING

3 slices white bread
Milk
1 sm. can corn or 2 fresh ears corn
3 tbsp. butter, melted
⅓ bell pepper, diced finely
½ med. onion
1 whole pimento, diced
2 eggs, beaten

Soak bread in enough milk to saturate thoroughly. Beat mixture until smooth. Combine with remaining ingredients. Pour into casserole. Bake at 375 degrees for 30 minutes.

Marie R. Duggan, Johnson County H. S.
Wrightsville, Georgia

GREEN CORN TAMALE PIE

12 lg. ears of corn
½ c. margarine
Minced garlic to taste
1 sm. can green chili peppers, chopped
Milk
Salt to taste
1 lb. Cheddar cheese, grated

Cut corn from cobs; scrape cobs. Saute corn in margarine in heavy skillet until tender, stirring frequently. Stir in garlic and chili peppers; stir in enough milk to moisten, if needed. Season with salt. Place half the corn mixture in buttered baking dish; sprinkle with half the cheese. Add remaining corn mixture; top with remaining cheese. Bake at 350 degrees for about 1 hour or until heated through and bubbly. Yield: 12 servings.

Willie Mae Cornwell, Midway H. S.
Waco, Texas

HERBED ROASTING EARS

6 ears of corn
½ c. soft butter or margarine
1 tsp. dried rosemary
½ tsp. dried marjoram
1 head romaine

Remove husks and silk from corn. Combine butter and herbs; mix well. Spread on corn. Wrap each ear in 2 or 3 leaves of romaine; place in shallow baking dish. Cover tightly. Bake at 450 degrees for 20 to 25 minutes or until corn is tender.

Betty Phillips, Scurry-Rosser Sch.
Scurry, Texas

KENTUCKY CORN PUDDING

1 c. dry bread crumbs
½ c. milk
2 eggs, separated
2 c. cream-style corn
1 tsp. cream of tartar
½ tsp. salt
¼ c. butter

Soak bread crumbs in milk until moistened. Add beaten egg yolks, corn, cream of tartar and salt; mix well. Fold in stiffly beaten egg whites. Pour in buttered casserole; dot with butter. Bake in preheated 350-degree oven for 45 minutes or until lightly browned.

Linda Midkiff, Pendleton Memorial Sch.
Falmouth, Kentucky

MEXICAN CORN

1 onion, finely minced
1 tbsp. olive oil
2 c. tomato puree
1 tbsp. diced celery
2 tbsp. chili powder
2 tbsp. butter
Salt and pepper to taste
3 c. fresh or frozen corn

Saute onion in hot oil until golden. Add remaining ingredients; mix well. Pour into casserole. Bake at 350 degrees for 1 hour or until bubbly. Yield: 6 servings.

Mrs. R. F. Schwagel, Boonsboro, H. S.
Boonsboro, Maryland

SCALLOPED CORN WITH CHEESE

1 16-oz. can cream-style corn
½ c. chopped celery
¼ c. chopped onion
⅔ c. shredded American cheese
1 tsp. salt
2 eggs, beaten
2 tbsp. butter, melted
¼ tsp. paprika
1 c. milk
1 c. crushed cracker crumbs

Combine first 4 ingredients; mix well. Stir in salt, eggs, butter, paprika and milk. Pour into 1½-quart casserole; top with cracker crumbs. Cover. Bake at 350 degrees for about 1 hour or until done.

Mrs. Alfrieda Jacobson, Granite Falls H. S.
Granite Falls, Minnesota

CUCUMBERS IN SOUR CREAM SAUCE

1 tsp. salt
1 c. sour cream
2 tbsp. lemon juice
1 tbsp. chopped onion
¼ tsp. sugar
2 tsp. chopped parsley
2 lg. cucumbers, peeled and sliced

Combine all ingredients except cucumbers; mix well. Toss cucumbers in sauce until well coated. Chill until ready to serve. Serve cold. Yield: 6-8 servings.

Alma Frerichs, Grants Pass H. S.
Grants Pass, Oregon

DIETER'S COOKED CUCUMBERS

1 chicken bouillon cube
1 tbsp. butter
2 lg. cucumbers, peeled

Place bouillon cube, butter and ¼ cup water in saucepan; bring to a boil. Boil until bouillon cube is dissolved. Cut cucumbers into 1-inch slices; add to bouillon. Simmer, covered, for 10 minutes or until cucumbers are tender. Drain; serve immediately. Yield: 2-3 servings.

Dorothy Brevoort, Home Economics Education
Beach Haven, New Jersey

FAVORITE BAKED CUCUMBERS

¼ c. chopped onion
¼ c. chopped parsley
½ c. margarine
1½ c. bread crumbs
2 c. tomato pulp
1 tsp. salt
⅛ tsp. pepper
4 lg. cucumbers, peeled and sliced

Saute onion and parsley in margarine until onion is transparent. Add remaining ingredients except cucumbers; cook for 5 minutes longer. Reserve part of onion mixture for topping. Arrange cucumber slices and remaining onion mixture in layers in greased casserole. Pour in a small amount of hot water. Spread reserved onion mixture over top. Bake at 350 degrees for 1 hour or until cucumbers are tender and top is browned. Yield. 4-6 servings.

Mrs. Dorothy W. Hayes, Lee Jr. H. S.
Roanoke, Virginia

SCALLOPED CUCUMBERS

4 med. cucumbers
1½ c. milk
1 tsp. salt
½ tsp. pepper
1 c. dry bread crumbs
¼ c. butter

Peel and dice cucumbers. Combine cucumbers, milk, salt and pepper; fold in bread crumbs. Pour into greased 1-quart casserole; dot with butter. Bake at 350 degrees for 30 minutes or until bubbly. Yield: 4-6 servings.

Mrs. Stenson Terry, San Perlita H. S.
San Perlita, Texas

BAKED PARMESAN EGGPLANT

1 eggplant, peeled and cubed
2 tbsp. butter
½ tsp. salt
¼ tsp. pepper
½ c. bread crumbs
Parmesan cheese, grated

Boil eggplant in lightly salted water until tender. Drain and mash. Combine all ingredients except Parmesan cheese; mix thoroughly. Spread in a lightly greased 8-inch square baking dish. Sprinkle with Parmesan cheese to taste. Bake for 20 minutes at 350 degrees.

Bethany J. McCulloch, Ellison H. S.
Killeen, Texas

BRENDA'S ITALIAN EGGPLANT

1 med. eggplant, peeled and cubed
1 med. onion, chopped
5 tbsp. olive oil
1 tbsp. garlic salt
1 tbsp. oregano
1 tsp. salt
Pepper to taste
1 1-lb. can tomatoes

Cover eggplant with cold salted water; let stand for about 15 minutes. Drain well. Saute onion in olive oil in large saucepan until tender. Add garlic salt, oregano, salt, pepper and eggplant. Blend tomatoes until smooth; pour into eggplant mixture. Stir in enough water to cover eggplant mixture, if needed. Simmer until eggplant is tender, adding more water if needed. Yield: 6-8 servings.

Mary Faye Slagle, Washington College Academy
Washington College, Tennessee

CAJUN-STYLE EGGPLANT FRITTERS

1 c. flour
½ tsp. salt
2 eggs, separated
1 boiled eggplant, peeled and mashed

Combine flour, salt, egg yolks and enough water to make a stiff dough. Add eggplant. Beat egg whites until stiff. Fold into eggplant mixture. Drop by heaping teaspoonfuls into hot deep fat. Cook until light brown. May be rolled in confectioners' sugar as a dessert.

Catherine Bass, Parkway H. S.
Bossier, City, Louisiana

EGGPLANT-ALMOND SOUFFLE

2 eggplant, peeled and cubed
2 tbsp. butter
½ c. bread crumbs
½ c. milk
¼ tsp. salt
¼ tsp. pepper
¼ tsp. nutmeg
1 onion, grated
3 eggs, separated
½ c. sauteed mushrooms (opt.)
2 tbsp. buttered crumbs
2 tbsp. toasted slivered almonds

Cook eggplant in boiling salted water until tender; drain and mash eggplant. Add butter, ½ cup bread crumbs and milk; season with salt, pepper and nutmeg. Stir in onion and beaten egg yolks. Fold in mushrooms and stiffly beaten egg whites; place in baking dish. Sprinkle with buttered crumbs and almonds. Bake at 400 degrees for 30 minutes or until firm. Yield: 10 servings.

Gladys Addington Brewer, Lynn View H. S.
Kingsport, Tennessee

EGGPLANT DRESSING

2 chicken bouillon cubes
¼ c. margarine
2 c. croutons
1 sm. onion, chopped
1 sm. green pepper, chopped
1 sm. eggplant, cooked and mashed
2 tbsp. chopped pimento
½ c. grated cheese

Dissolve bouillon cubes and margarine in 1 cup boiling water. Add croutons; let stand until soft. Mash thoroughly. Saute onion and green pepper in bacon fat until onion is transparent. Combine all ingredients except cheese; place in buttered 9-inch casserole. Bake at 425 degrees for 15 minutes. Reduce oven temperature to 300 degrees; bake for 30 minutes longer. Sprinkle cheese on top; serve immediately.

Mrs. Ramona Hext, Newton H. S.
Newton, Texas

EGGPLANT-OLIVE SUPREME

1 lg. eggplant
2 stalks celery, chopped
1 lg. onion, chopped
1 sm. green pepper, chopped
¼ c. butter
1 tsp. Worcestershire sauce
Dash of hot sauce
1 c. grated sharp cheese
1 c. chopped pitted ripe olives
Seasoning to taste
Cracker crumbs

Peel and dice eggplant; cook in small amount of water until tender. Saute celery, onion and green pepper in butter until onion is transparent. Add eggplant, Worcestershire sauce and hot sauce; fold in cheese and olives. Add seasoning; place in greased casserole. Cover with cracker crumbs. Bake at 375 degrees for 30 minutes or until heated through. Yield: 6 servings.

Mrs. Lucile Weaver, West Jr. H. S.
Gulfport, Mississippi

ITALIAN EGGPLANT CASSEROLE

1 egg
1 tsp. garlic salt
1 eggplant, peeled and thinly sliced
Bread crumbs
2 cans tomato sauce
1 tbsp. parsley flakes
Grated Parmesan cheese
American or Cheddar cheese slices

Beat egg with ½ teaspoon garlic salt. Dip eggplant slices into egg; dredge with bread crumbs. Fry in hot fat until golden; drain well. Place remaining ½ teaspoon garlic salt in greased saucepan; add tomato sauce. Cook for 10 minutes, stirring occasionally. Stir in parsley flakes. Place eggplant, cheeses and tomato sauce in layers in casserole; cover. Bake at 350 degrees for 20 minutes. Remove cover; bake for 10 minutes longer or until bubbly.

Mrs. Katherine Gant, White County H. S.
Sparta, Tennessee

EGGPLANT WITH SOUR CREAM

1 lg. eggplant, peeled and cubed
2 tbsp. butter
2 tbsp. Spice Islands beef stock base
1½ tsp. Italian seasoning
1 c. sour cream
1 tbsp. instant minced onion
½ tsp. salt
¼ tsp. pepper
¼ c. bread crumbs
2 tbsp. grated Parmesan cheese

Saute eggplant in butter for 5 minutes or until crisp tender. Combine ½ cup hot water, beef stock base and Italian seasoning; pour over eggplant. Simmer, covered, until eggplant is tender and liquid has evaporated. Spoon into shallow baking dish. Combine sour cream, onion, salt and pepper; spread over eggplant. Sprinkle with crumbs and cheese. Bake at 350 degrees for 20 to 25 minutes or until heated through. Yield: 6 servings.

Mrs. Helen Lipscomb, St. Petersburg H. S.
St. Petersburg, Florida

EGGPLANT PARMESAN

1 lg. eggplant
3 eggs, beaten
1 c. dry bread crumbs
¾ c. olive oil or salad oil
2 tsp. oregano
½ c. grated Parmesan cheese
½ lb. sliced mozzarella cheese
3 8-oz. cans tomato sauce

Pare eggplant; cut into ¼-inch slices. Dip slices in eggs; dredge with crumbs. Saute in hot oil until golden brown. Place eggplant in layers in 2-quart casserole with oregano, cheeses and tomato sauce, topping wth mozzarella cheese slices. Bake at 350 degrees for 30 minutes or until cheese is melted and sauce is bubbly. Yield: 6 servings.

Homoiselle House, Hempstead H. S.
Hempstead, Texas

JANET'S FRIED EGGPLANT

1 sm. eggplant
2 tsp. salt
2 eggs, beaten
1 c. packaged dry bread crumbs
Salad oil

Cut eggplant into strips ½-inch thick. Sprinkle with salt. Place in collander in bowl; set aside. Dip each piece into beaten egg; roll in bread crumbs. Heat oil 1-inch deep in electric skillet to 375 degrees. Fry eggplant for 2 minutes or until brown. Drain. Yield: 6-8 servings.

Janet K. Townsend, Jarman Jr. H.S.
Midwest City, Oklahoma

MARIE'S EGGPLANT CASSEROLE

2½ lb. eggplant, peeled
¼ c. onion, grated
2 c. milk
2 eggs, beaten
2¾ c. bread crumbs
5½ tbsp. butter or margarine
1 tsp. salt
¾ tsp. pepper
2 tsp. sugar
2 c. buttered bread crumbs

Cook eggplant in salted water until tender. Drain. Mash eggplant. Combine with next 8 ingredients. Place in casserole. Bake at 350 degrees for 30 minutes. Cover top with bread crumbs. Bake 15 minutes longer. Yield: 10 servings.

Marie R. Duggan, Johnson County H. S.
Wrightsville, Georgia

PAN-FRIED EGGPLANT

1 eggplant, peeled
Cornmeal
Salt and pepper to taste
Sugar to taste
Cooking oil

Slice eggplant crosswise into ⅛-inch slices; cover with cold salted water. Let stand for about 20 minutes. Drain well. Combine cornmeal with salt, pepper and sugar. Dredge eggplant slices with cornmeal mixture; fry in hot oil until golden brown. Drain on paper toweling; serve immediately.

Mrs. Laura H. Wilkins, Pickens County H. S.
Reform, Alabama

RATATOUILLE

2 tbsp. butter or olive oil
2 med. onions, chopped
1 med. eggplant, peeled and cubed
2 med. summer squash, cubed
2 green peppers, thinly sliced
2 lg. tomatoes, peeled and cubed
2 cloves of garlic, crushed
½ bay leaf, crushed
Salt and pepper to taste
2 tbsp. brown sugar (opt.)

Melt butter in skillet; saute onions until golden. Arrange eggplant, squash, onions, green peppers and tomatoes in layers in large casserole, seasoning each layer with garlic, bay leaf, salt, pepper and brown sugar. Cover tightly. Bake at 250 degrees for about 2 hours or until vegetables are tender. Remove cover; bake for about 15 minutes longer.

Mrs. Rosie Hurd, Thompson Jr. H. S.
Lubbock, Texas

SAVORY EGGPLANT CASSEROLE

1 med. eggplant, cooked and mashed
1 egg, beaten
1 c. bread crumbs
1 tsp. each sage, salt, parsley flakes, and
    oregano
½ tsp. pepper
2 tbsp. chopped onion
½ c. grated cheese

Combine eggplant with remaining ingredients; mix gently. Place in 1½-quart casserole. Bake at 325 degrees for 25 to 30 minutes or until heated through.

Mrs. Marjorie Wilks, Tomball H. S.
Tomball, Texas

SCALLOPED EGGPLANT

1 med. eggplant, peeled
2 tbsp. lemon juice
3 tbsp. butter
3 tbsp. flour
1½ c. milk
1 c. grated sharp cheese
1 can tomato soup
½ tsp. salt
Dash of pepper
½ c. buttered crumbs

Cut eggplant into ½-inch cubes; cook in boiling salted water with lemon juice for 10 minutes or until tender. Drain well. Melt butter in saucepan; stir in flour to make a smooth paste. Add milk; cook until thickened, stirring constantly. Add cheese; cook and stir until melted. Combine eggplant, soup and cheese sauce; season with salt and pepper. Pour into greased 2-quart casserole; sprinkle with buttered crumbs. Bake at 350 degrees for 15 minutes.

Nan Lindsey, Wade Hampton H. S.
Greenville, South Carolina

CHEESE-STUFFED EGGPLANT

1 med. eggplant
4 tbsp. lemon juice

½ tsp. salt
1 8-oz. can tomato sauce
¼ tsp. oregano leaves, crushed
1 tbsp. butter
½ c. chopped onion
½ lb. cooked ham, cut into sm. pieces
⅓ c. coarsely grated carrot
¼ c. finely chopped celery
2 c. shredded Cheddar cheese

Cut eggplant in half lengthwise. Scoop out center, leaving ½-inch around edge. Bring 2 cups water, 2 tablespoons lemon juice and salt to a boil in 3-quart saucepan. Place eggplant shells in boiling water; cover. Parboil about 5 minutes. Drain; set aside. Chop eggplant pulp. Mix eggplant, tomato sauce, 2 tablespoons lemon juice and oregano in 2-quart saucepan. Heat to boiling point. Melt butter in large skillet; add onion. Cook until tender. Remove from heat. Stir in ham, carrot, celery and cheese. Spoon in ⅔ of the tomato mixture in 1½-quart buttered baking dish. Arrange eggplant shells on top. Fill eggplant shells with ham and cheese mixture; pour over remaining tomato sauce. Bake in preheated 375-degree oven for 25 to 30 minutes or until hot.

Photograph for this recipe see page 121.

STUFFED EGGPLANT PALERMO

2 lg. firm eggplant
2 4½-oz. cans artichoke hearts, drained
2 4-oz. cans mushrooms, drained
½ tsp. garlic powder
½ c. butter
1½ tsp. oregano
1 tsp. sweet basil
2 tbsp. minced onion
1 tsp. salt
2 sm. green peppers, chopped
2 sm. fresh tomatoes, chopped
1 c. grated Parmesan cheese

Cut eggplant in half lengthwise; scoop out centers leaving ½-inch shells. Place shells in boiling salted water; cook until just tender. Drain well. Place shells in baking dish, cut side up. Dice eggplant; set aside. Cut artichoke hearts in half. Saute mushrooms with garlic powder in butter. Add eggplant; saute until golden. Stir in oregano, basil, onion, salt, green peppers, tomatoes and artichokes; simmer for 3 to 4 minutes or until heated through. Stir in ¾ cup Parmesan cheese. Spoon into eggplant shells; sprinkle with remaining ¼ cup Parmesan cheese. Bake at 350 degrees for 20 minutes or until heated through.

Sandra Hartman, Norte Vista H. S.
Riverside, California

BUSY-DAY GREEN PEPPER CASSEROLE

1 c. cooked chopped green peppers
1½ c. milk
1 c. cracker crumbs
2 tbsp. butter, melted
Salt and pepper to taste
1 c. shredded Cheddar cheese

Combine all ingredients in casserole. Bake at 350 degrees for about 30 minutes or until heated through.

Doris C. Mountjoy, Stanford H. S.
Stanford, Kentucky

CORN-STUFFED GREEN PEPPERS

4 med. green peppers
1½ c. corn
1 c. diced tomato
¼ c. finely chopped celery
1 tbsp. finely chopped onion
2 tbsp. melted butter
2 eggs, slightly beaten
1¼ tsp. salt
⅛ tsp. pepper
½ c. soft bread crumbs
1 tsp. sugar (opt.)

Cut tops from green peppers; set aside. Remove seeds carefully, keeping green peppers whole. Parboil in salted water for 3 to 5 minutes; drain well. Combine remaining ingedients, adding sugar if canned corn is used. Stuff green peppers with corn mixture; replace tops. Place in greased casserole; add a small amount of water. Cover. Bake at 350 degrees for about 1 hour or until well done.

Mrs. May Calicutt, Elysian Fields H. S.
Elysian Fields, Texas

ITALIAN-STYLE PEPPER SAUTE

1 tbsp. olive oil
2 onions, sliced
3 green peppers, sliced
½ lb. fresh mushrooms, sliced
1 tsp. salt
⅛ tsp. crushed dried red pepper
⅛ tsp. oregano

Heat oil in skillet. Add onions; saute for 5 minutes. Add green peppers; saute for 3 minutes. Add mushrooms, salt, red pepper and oregano; cook over medium heat for 5 minutes, stirring frequently. Yield: 6 servings.

Mrs. Irene Wells, Grant County Rural H. S.
Ulysses, Kansas

SAUCY GREEN PEPPER CASSEROLE

4 or 5 green peppers, chopped
1 tsp. butter
2 tbsp. flour
1 c. milk
¾ c. grated cheese
½ c. cracker crumbs

Cook green peppers in small amount of water until tender. Drain well. Melt butter in saucepan; blend in flour to make a smooth paste. Add milk gradually; cook until thickened, stirring constantly. Add cheese; stir until melted. Stir in green peppers; pour into baking dish. Cover with crumbs. Bake at 350 degrees until bubbly and crumbs are browned. Yield: 5-6 servings.

Mrs. Martha Young, Franklin-Simpson H. S.
Franklin, Kentucky

HERB-GRILLED VEGETABLES

½ c. butter or margarine, melted
1 tbsp. onion powder
1 tbsp. parsley flakes
1 tsp. crumbled basil
1 tsp. garlic powder
½ tsp. salt
⅛ tsp. pepper
2 med. zucchini, halved lengthwise
1 med. eggplant, cut in ½ in. slices
2 med. tomatoes, halved crosswise

Melt butter; add next 6 ingredients to melted butter. Brush vegetables with melted butter mixture. Grill zucchini and eggplant over hot charcoals for 5 minutes. Turn zucchini and eggplant. Place tomatoes on grill cut side up. Grill vegetables for 5 minutes or until done, brushing occasionally with butter mixture.

Sandy Kopin, Aiken H. S.
Cincinnati, Ohio

MIXED VEGETABLES IN WINE SAUCE

1 lb. fresh broccoli, cut up
1 sm. cauliflower, cut up
3 fresh carrots, sliced
3 celery stalks, cut up
1 tbsp. butter
1 tbsp. flour
¼ tsp. salt
¼ tsp. white pepper
1½ c. white wine
½ c. grated Swiss Cheese
¼ c. grated Gruyere cheese
Wheat germ

Steam vegetables in a vegetable steamer until tender. Melt butter in small saucepan. Stir in flour and seasonings. Add wine. Stir over medium heat until thickened. Add grated cheese; stir over low heat until melted. Place vegetables in a casserole. Cover with sauce. Top with wheat germ. Bake at 350 degrees until heated through.

Cheryl C. Elsberry, Westland H. S.
Galloway, Ohio

CLUB MUSHROOM CASSEROLE

1 lb. fresh mushrooms, sliced
½ c. butter
⅓ c. flour
3 c. milk
2 tsp. Worcestershire sauce
1½ tsp. salt
¼ tsp. pepper
4 hard-cooked eggs, sliced
½ c. diced green pepper
1 4-oz. can pimentos, diced
2 c. shredded process cheese

Saute mushrooms in butter until golden; push aside. Stir in flour to make a paste. Add milk gradually; cook until thickened, stirring constantly. Add remaining ingredients except cheese; stir gently. Place in greased casserole. Bake at 350 degrees for 30 minutes or until heated through. Top with cheese; bake until cheese is melted. May serve over rice or toast, if desired. Yield: 6-8 servings.

Jean Capling, Cousino H. S.
Warren, Michigan

MUSHROOMS WITH SOUR CREAM AND BACON

2 lb. sm. fresh mushrooms
¼ c. butter
3 green onions, minced
1 tbsp. flour
1 c. sour cream
1 tsp. salt
½ tsp. pepper
1 tbsp. minced parsley
3 strips bacon, cooked and crumbled

Remove stems from mushrooms; saute stems and caps in butter for several minutes or until golden. Add onions; simmer, covered, for 15 minutes. Sprinkle flour over mushrooms; stir lightly. Add sour cream, salt and pepper; heat through. Do not boil. Place mushroom mixture in serving bowl; sprinkle with parsley and bacon. Serve immediately. Yield: 6 servings.

Mrs. Elizabeth L. Jeffries, South Jr. H. S.
Johnson City, Tennessee

GOURMET STUFFED MUSHROOMS

1 lb. fresh mushrooms
1 tbsp. butter or margarine
¾ c. finely chopped onions
Salad oil
Seasoned salt
3 slices bread with crusts removed
1 tbsp. dried parsley flakes
½ tsp. salt
⅛ tsp. pepper
¼ tsp. marjoram
¼ tsp. thyme
1 tsp. Worcestershire sauce
3 tbsp. Sherry or bouillon
1 egg, slightly beaten
¼ c. toasted slivered almonds

Remove stems from mushrooms; mince stems. Melt butter in saucepan. Add minced stems and onions; saute until onions are transparent. Remove from heat. Brush outsides of mushroom caps with oil; place, hollow side up, in shallow 8 x 12-inch baking dish. Sprinkle insides of caps with seasoned salt. Cut bread into cubes. Stir bread cubes and remaining ingredients into onion mixture; toss gently to mix stuffing. Fill mushroom caps with stuffing. Bake at 425 degrees for about 15 minutes or until mushrooms are tender but not limp. Yield: 8-10 servings.

Mrs. Virginia Mullen, Lake Oswego H. S.
Lake Oswego, Oregon

HOLIDAY MUSHROOMS WITH BLEU CHEESE

2 lb. large fresh mushrooms
½ c. crumbled bleu cheese
1 c. dry bread crumbs
⅛ tsp. minced chives
2 tbsp. butter
¼ c. Sherry
½ c. heavy cream

Remove stems from mushrooms; set aside for future use. Place a small amount of cheese in each mushroom cap. Saute crumbs and chives in butter until golden; stir in any remaining cheese. Place a layer of crumb mixture in buttered casserole; place mushroom caps on crumb mixture, hollow side up. Sprinkle with Sherry and remaining crumb mixture; pour cream over top. Bake, covered, at 375 degrees for 25 minutes or until bubbly. Yield: 6 servings.

Vivian I. Reagan, Millvale H. S.
Pittsburgh, Pennsylvania

MUSHROOM GARDEN BAKE

1 lb. fresh mushrooms, halved
1 lb. cherry tomatoes
¼ lb. zucchini or yellow squash, sliced ½-inch
    thick
1 tsp. Italian seasoning
1 tsp. onion powder
¼ tsp. garlic powder
1 tsp. salt
⅛ tsp. ground pepper
3 tbsp. olive oil
2 tbsp. melted butter

Line a 10 x 8 x 2-inch baking dish with aluminum foil. Place mushrooms, tomatoes and zucchini in foil. Mix Italian seasoning, onion powder, garlic powder, salt and pepper. Sprinkle over vegetables. Combine oil and butter; sprinkle over seasoned vegetables. Cover with second sheet of foil, sealing edges. Bake in a preheated 350-degree oven for 25 to 30 minutes. Remove foil cover. Toss lightly and serve. Yield: 6 servings.

Jewell T. Johnson, Westover H. S.
Albany, Georgia

OLD-FASHIONED SOUTHERN GUMBO

2 or 3 sm. slices salt pork
1 c. corn
1 c. green limas
2 c. fresh and sliced okra
6 tomatoes, quartered
Sugar to taste
Salt and pepper to taste

Fry salt pork in large skillet over medium heat until most of the oil disappears. Add corn, limas and ¾ cup water. Cook for 10 minutes, stirring occasionally. Add okra, tomatoes and seasonings. Reduce temperature to simmer; cover. Cook for 30 to 40 minutes, stirring occasionally. Serve over rice or as a separate vegetable dish. Yield: 4 servings.

Mrs. Dorothy W. Reese, C. L. Harper H. S.
Atlanta, Georgia

FRENCH-FRIED OKRA

1 lb. fresh okra, cut into ½-in. pieces
½ c. flour or fine cornmeal
Seasoning to taste

Dredge okra with flour; fry in deep hot fat until lightly browned. Drain on paper toweling. Season as desired; serve immediately. Yield: 4-6 servings.

Myrtis L. McAlhany, Saint George H. S.
Saint George, South Carolina

FRITTER-FRIED OKRA

1 c. flour
3 tsp. baking powder
½ tsp. salt
2 eggs, well beaten
⅓ c. milk
5 c. thinly sliced okra

Sift flour with baking powder and salt. Combine eggs and milk; stir into flour mixture until smooth. Add okra; mix gently. Drop by spoonfuls into deep hot fat; fry until golden brown. Drain on paper toweling; serve immediately. Yield: 6-8 servings.

Mrs. Patsy Cooper, Goree H. S.
Goree, Texas

OKRA CREOLE

2 doz. young tender okra pods
1 sm. onion, minced
1 clove of garlic, minced
½ sm. green pepper, minced
2 tbsp. butter or bacon drippings
2 fresh tomatoes, coarsely chopped
½ tsp. salt
⅛ tsp. pepper

Cut ends from okra pods. Saute onion, garlic and green pepper in butter for about 6 minutes. Add tomatoes, okra and seasonings; simmer for 10 minutes or until okra is tender. Yield: 6 servings.

Edna S. Ewing, Seventy-First Street H. S.
Fayetteville, North Carolina

OKRA-ONION CASSEROLE

2 c. sliced okra
1 sm. onion, chopped
1 c. buttered bread crumbs
½ c. shredded Cheddar cheese
2 tbsp. melted butter or margarine
1 egg, beaten
½ tsp. salt
½ tsp. pepper
¼ c. shredded, mozzarella cheese, (opt.)

Combine all ingredients except ¼ cup buttered bread crumbs and cheese. Spoon into lightly greased 1½-quart casserole. Bake at 350 degrees for 30 minutes. Sprinkle with reserved bread crumbs and cheese. Bake for 5 additional minutes. Serve hot. Yield: 4 servings.

Joan Richards, Stratford H. S.
Nashville, Tennessee

OKRA GUMBO

1 lb. okra, cut into ½ in. pieces
1 lg. onion, chopped
1 No. 303 can tomatoes or 4 fresh tomatoes
Salt and pepper to taste

Saute okra and onion; add tomatoes. Season to taste. Cook covered over low heat for 25 minutes. Add water if necessary.

Mrs. Tennie Isbell, Hillsboro H. S.
Hillsboro, Texas

OKRA ETOUFFE

3 c. sliced okra
¼ c. cooking oil
1 c. chopped canned tomatoes
1 med. onion, chopped
1 med. green pepper, chopped
Salt and pepper to taste
Red pepper to taste
¼ c. cracker crumbs or crushed potato chips

Spread okra in greased casserole; cover with oil, tomatoes, onion, green pepper and seasonings. Cover loosely with foil. Bake at 400 degrees for 1 hour or until tender, stirring occasionally. Uncover; top with crumbs. Bake until lightly browned. Yield: 3-4 servings.

Mrs. Guy Mitchell, Chataignier H. S.
Chataignier, Louisiana

SAVORY OKRA AND TOMATOES

3 c. ½-in. slices okra
1 No. 2 can tomatoes
1 sm. can tomato paste
1 env. dry onion soup mix
3 tbsp. bacon drippings
2 tsp. sugar
Salt and pepper to taste

Combine all ingredients in heavy saucepan; bring to a boil, stirring constantly. Cover; simmer for 15 to 20 minutes, stirring occasionally. Yield: 8-10 servings.

Mrs. Jeanne C. Hinton, Mainland Jr. H. S.
Daytona Beach, Florida

SCALLOPED OKRA AND CORN

2 lb. fresh okra
4 tbsp. butter

1 can corn, drained
Salt and pepper to taste
2 tbsp. flour
1 c. milk
¼ lb. sharp cheese, grated
1 c. fine dry bread crumbs

Fry okra in 2 tablespoons butter for 10 minutes, stirring frequently. Arrange okra and corn in layers in greased baking dish, seasoning each layer with salt and pepper. Melt remaining 2 tablespoons butter in saucepan; stir in flour to make a smooth paste. Add milk; cook until thickened, stirring constantly. Add cheese; stir until melted. Pour over corn; sprinkle with crumbs. Bake at 350 degrees until bubbly and browned. Yield: 4 servings.

Mrs. Audrey Shaw, Springhill H. S.
Springhill, Louisiana

BAKED ONION RINGS

2 lb. white onions, sliced
8 slices buttered toast
¼ lb. American cheese, shredded
2 eggs
2 c. milk
½ tsp. salt
⅛ tsp. pepper
1 tbsp. butter
Paprika (opt.)

Cook onions in boiling salted water until tender; drain well. Place half the toast in baking dish; arrange layer of half the onions and layer of half the cheese over toast. Repeat layers. Beat eggs slightly. Add milk, salt and pepper. Pour over cheese. Dot with butter; sprinkle with paprika. Bake at 350 degrees for 40 minutes or until done. Yield: 8 servings.

Mrs. Ron Havenstein, Regina H. S.
Iowa City, Iowa

CREAMED ONIONS WITH PECANS

18 to 20 sm. onions
1½ tsp. salt
¼ c. butter or margarine, melted
¼ c. flour
1½ c. milk
1 c. shredded cheese
½ c. chopped pecans

Place onions, ½ cup water and 1 teaspoon salt in 1½-quart saucepan. Cover; bring to a boil over high heat. Reduce heat; simmer for 15 minutes or until tender. Drain well. Melt butter in saucepan; stir in flour to make a smooth paste. Add milk and remaining ½ teaspoon salt; cook until thickened, stirring constantly. Add cheese; stir until melted. Add onions; heat through, stirring gently. Place in serving dish; sprinkle pecans over onions. Yield: 4-6 servings.

Mrs. Juanita Patton, Inola H. S.
Inola, Oklahoma

FRENCH-FRIED ONIONS

6 med. Bermuda onions, thinly sliced
Milk
2 egg whites or 2 eggs
Flour
Salt and pepper to taste

Separate onion slices into rings. Cover rings with milk; let stand for 30 minutes. Drain thoroughly. Beat egg whites until stiff; season flour with salt and pepper. Dip onion rings into egg whites; dredge with seasoned flour. Fry in deep fat at 375 degrees until light brown. Drain on paper toweling. Serve immediately.

Bert Hearn, Caldwell Parish H. S.
Columbia, Louisiana

HOLIDAY GLAZED ONIONS

20 sm. onions
6 tbsp. butter or margarine
3 tbsp. sugar
1 tbsp. brown sugar
½ tsp. salt
1½ tsp. prepared mustard
1 tsp. lemon juice
Dash of paprika

Peel onions; make crosswise cuts at root ends. Place in saucepan; add a small amount of water. Bring to a boil. Reduce heat; simmer until onions are tender. Drain well; place in baking dish. Melt butter in saucepan; stir in sugars, salt, mustard and lemon juice. Mix well; pour over onions. Sprinkle with paprika. Bake at 375 degrees for 15 minutes or until onions are glazed, basting frequently.

Mrs. Marjorie Balestri, Farwell H. S.
Farwell, Texas

ONIONS WITH SAGE STUFFING

6 lg. onions, peeled
4 c. dry bread cubes
3 tbsp. melted butter
½ tsp. chopped parsley
1 tsp. sage

1 tbsp. chopped celery
½ tsp. salt

Boil onions in salted water for 10 minutes or until just tender. Drain well, reserving stock. Add water to stock to measure 6 tablespoons, if needed. Hollow out onions, leaving ¾-inch shells. Set shells aside. Chop onions; add remaining ingredients. Add enough reserved stock to moisten stuffing. Spoon stuffing into onion shells; place in baking dish. Bake at 325 degrees for 30 minutes or until heated through.

Mrs. Ruth Williams, Mount Sterling H. S.
Mount Sterling, Kentucky

SCALLOPED ONIONS WITH ALMONDS

4 c. ½-in. thick onion slices
½ c. slivered almonds
1⅓ cans cream of mushroom soup
1 tsp. salt
½ c. corn flake crumbs
2 tbsp. melted margarine

Cook onions in boiling salted water until tender; drain well. Arrange layers of onions, almonds and soup in greased 1-quart baking dish, sprinkling each layer with salt. Combine corn flake crumbs and margarine; sprinkle over top. Bake at 350 degrees for 20 minutes or until heated through and top is browned. Yield: 6-8 servings.

Mrs. Clark Hudson, East Coweta H. S.
Senoia, Georgia

HONEY-GINGER ONIONS

1 No. 2½ can white onions or 16 uniform
    onions, cooked
¼ c. honey
2 tbsp. butter
1 tbsp. paprika
½ tsp. salt
¼ tsp. ginger

Drain onions; place in buttered shallow baking dish. Combine honey, butter, paprika, salt and ginger in saucepan; cook for 5 minutes. Pour over onions. Bake at 325 degrees for 10 minutes or until well glazed. Yield: 8 servings.

Mrs. Velma Shaffer, Home Economics Education
Little Rock, Arkansas

CARAMELIZED ONIONS

12 sm. onions, peeled
½ c. (packed) brown sugar
Salt and pepper to taste
2 tbsp. butter, melted

Place onions in casserole. Combine brown sugar, salt, pepper, butter and 2 tablespoons water; mix well. Pour over onions. Bake at 375 degrees for 45 minutes or until onions are tender and glazed. Yield: 4 servings.

Jean Passino, Keewatin-Nashwauk Jr. H. S.
Keewatin, Minnesota

ONION-CHEESE PIE

1½ c. finely chopped soda crackers
Melted butter
2½ c. sliced onions
1½ c. milk
3 eggs, well beaten
1 tsp. salt
¼ tsp. pepper
½ lb. cheese, grated

Combine crackers and ½ cup melted butter; press in 9-inch pie pan. Saute onions in additional butter until light brown; place in pie crust in layers. Scald milk; add slowly to eggs, stirring constantly. Add salt, pepper and cheese; pour over onions. Bake at 350 degrees for 40 to 45 minutes or until set. Garnish center with parsley. Yield: 6-8 servings.

Mrs. Ann Edwards, Corsicana H. S.
Corsicana, Texas

CANDIED PARSNIPS

6 med. parsnips
⅔ c. (packed) brown sugar
1 tsp. salt
1 tbsp. lemon juice
⅓ c. butter or margarine

Boil parsnips in salted water for 20 minutes or until crisp tender; drain and slice. Arrange parsnips in layers in greased casserole, sprinkling each layer with brown sugar, salt and lemon juice. Dot with butter. Bake at 375 degrees for 25 to 30 minutes or until glazed. Yield: 6 servings.

Mrs. Effie G. Hoyle, Warwick H. S.
Newport News, Virginia

PAN-FRIED PARSNIPS

1 lb. fresh young parsnips
½ c. butter or margarine

Peel parsnips; cut into ¼-inch thick slices. Melt butter in 300-degree electric skillet. Place parsnips in butter; cover. Cook for 10 minutes. Turn parsnips; cover and cook until tender. Remove cover; turn parsnips. Cook until browned. Yield: 6 servings.

Mrs. Bud Gaulke, Riddle H. S.
Riddle, Oregon

PARSNIPS IN ORANGE SAUCE

12 sm. parsnips, cooked
½ c. orange juice
2 tbsp. brown sugar
2 tbsp. light syrup
½ tsp. salt
⅛ tsp. paprika
2 tbsp. butter
Grated orange peel

Place parsnips in shallow 9 x 12-inch casserole. Combine orange juice, brown sugar, syrup, salt and paprika; pour over parsnips. Dot with butter; sprinkle with orange peel. Bake at 400 degrees for 20 minutes or until bubbly. Yield: 6 servings.

Mrs. Bette Eckre Johnson, Raymond H. S.
Raymond, Minnesota

COWBOY BLACK-EYED PEAS

1 No. 303 can black-eyed peas
1 med. onion, sliced
½ tsp. Worcestershire sauce
2 tbsp. butter

Drain half the liquid from peas; pour remaining liquid and peas in saucepan. Add remaining ingredients; heat through. Serve hot.

Colleen Stevenson, Alexander H. S.
Neroosa, Wiscomsin

QUICK FRENCH PEAS

1½ tbsp. butter or margarine, melted
½ c. thinly sliced mushrooms
1½ c. fresh peas
1 sm. onion, thinly sliced
½ tsp. salt

Combine all ingredients in saucepan; add 2 tablespoons water. Cover; cook over medium heat for 12 to 16 minutes or until peas are tender, shaking pan occasionally to mix ingredients.

Kaye Bain, Bird City Rural H. S.
Bird City, Kansas

CITRUS HONEY PEAS

1½ tsp. grated orange rind
1½ tsp. grated lemon rind
2 tbsp. butter
Juice of 1 orange
Juice of 1 lemon
¼ c. honey
1 No. 303 can early garden peas, drained
¼ c. chopped pimento

Saute rinds in butter for 2 to 3 minutes; stir in juices and honey. Cook rapidly for several minutes or until thickened. Add peas and pimento; heat through. Yield: 4 servings.

Mrs. Marie Hayes, St. Paul Park H. S
St. Paul Park, Minnesota

HOPPING JOHN

1 8-oz. package black-eyed peas
½ lb. ham bone
1 sm. onion, chopped
1 tsp. salt
¼ tsp. pepper
1 c. instant rice
1 1-lb. can tomatoes (opt.)

Cover peas with boiling water; add ham bone, onion, salt and pepper. Cook for 1 hour and 15 minutes. Sprinkle rice over peas; add enough water to cover rice. Bring to boiling point. Cover; remove from heat. Let stand until rice is cooked. Stir in tomatoes; heat through. Yield: 6 servings.

Mrs. Malta O. Ledford, Jupiter H. S.
Jupiter, Florida

DEVILED PEAS

1 No. 2 can English peas, drained
1 sm. can chopped pimentos, drained
1 green pepper, finely cut
1 c. grated cheese
1 tsp. Worcestershire sauce
1 sm. can mushroom pieces, drained
1 can tomato soup
1 c. finely chopped celery
½ c. chili sauce
6 hard-cooked eggs, sliced
1½ c. white sauce or 1 can cream of
    mushroom soup
Cracker crumbs (opt.)
Butter (opt.)

Combine first 9 ingredients; mix gently. Arrange layers of peas mixture, sliced eggs and white sauce in greased casserole. Top with additional grated cheese and cracker crumbs; dot with butter. Bake at 350 degrees for 20 to 30 minutes or until bubbly.

Mrs. Doris Griffith, Elmore County H. S.
Eclectic, Alabama

ENGLISH PEAS A LA ORANGE

2 pkg. frozen English peas
3 tbsp. orange juice
1 orange, sectioned

Cook peas according to package directions; drain partially. Add orange juice; cook for 3 minutes longer. Place in serving dish; top with orange sections.

Jean Ray, H. V. Jenkins H. S.
Savannah, Georgia

CLASSIC FRENCH PEAS

6 lettuce leaves
2 lb. shelled peas
6 sm. onions
½ tsp. salt
¼ tsp. thyme
1 tsp. sugar
1 tbsp. butter

Line saucepan with lettuce leaves; place peas on lettuce. Add remaining ingredients except butter; pour in ¼ cup water. Cover; simmer for about 25 minutes or until peas are tender. Place peas and onions in serving dish; dot with butter. Serve immediately. Yield: 4 servings.

Mrs. Betty Helen O'Connell, Incarnate Word H. S.
San Antonio, Texas

GREEN PEAS AU GRATIN

2 pkg. frozen peas
2 5-oz. cans water chestnuts
1 can cream of mushroom soup
1½ c. grated sharp Cheddar cheese

Cook peas according to package directions; drain well. Drain and slice water chestnuts. Combine peas, water chestnuts and soup; mix gently. Stir in cheese; place in lightly greased casserole. Bake at 350 degrees for 25 to 30 minutes or until bubbly. Yield: 6-8 servings.

Mrs. Joyce Niedenthal, Parkway Jr. H. S.
Fort Lauderdale, Florida

GREEN PEAS IN SOUR CREAM

1 10-oz. package frozen green peas
3 green onions
1 c. sliced mushrooms
2 tbsp. butter or margarine
¾ tsp. salt
Dash of pepper
½ c. sour cream
1 tbsp. flour
Paprika (opt.)

Let peas stand at room temperature until partially thawed. Cut onions in half lengthwise; cut into 2½-inch lengths. Saute mushrooms in butter until lightly browned. Combine peas, onions, mushrooms, 2 tablespoons water, salt and pepper in saucepan; cover. Cook for 5 minutes or until peas are tender. Combine sour cream and flour; stir into peas mixture. Heat thoroughly, stirring gently. Sprinkle with paprika to serve.

Mrs. Lucille Reid Marker, Robertsdale H. S.
Robertsdale, Alabama

HERBED FIELD PEAS

½ c. sliced green onions
2 tbsp. butter
2 10-oz. packages frozen field peas
½ tsp. sugar
½ tsp. salt
⅛ tsp. pepper
¼ tsp. basil
1 tbsp. parsley flakes

Saute onions in butter until soft. Add frozen peas and ¼ cup water; bring to a boil. Stir in remaining ingredients. Simmer, covered, for 10 minutes or until done. Yield: 4-6 servings.

Sister Mary Albertus, S.S.N.D., Tyler Catholic H. S.
Tyler, Texas

PEAS CONTINENTAL

1 c. drained canned sliced mushrooms
¼ c. minced onion
2 tbsp. butter or margarine
¼ tsp. salt
Dash of pepper
¼ tsp. nutmeg
⅛ tsp. dried marjoram
2 c. cooked or canned peas

Saute mushrooms and onion in butter until onion is transparent. Add salt, pepper, nutmeg and marjoram; stir in hot peas. Serve immediately.

Alberta Ball Bickerdike, East Pike Sch.
Milton, Illinois

PARTY GREEN PEAS

1 can cream of mushroom soup
2 c. shredded Velveeta cheese
1 sm. can pimentos, diced
1 c. diced mushrooms
2 pkg. frozen green peas, cooked
1 lg. green pepper, chopped
1 onion, chopped
1 clove of garlic, minced
½ c. butter or margarine

Combine soup, cheese, pimentos, mushrooms and drained peas in saucepan; heat until cheese is melted, stirring frequently. Saute green pepper, onion and garlic in butter until onion is transparent. Stir carefully into peas mixture; pour into casserole. Bake at 350 degrees until bubbly.

Mrs. Peggy Sisk Maddox, Koffman Jr. H. S.
Hopkinsville, Kentucky

PEAS AND ONIONS AMANDINE

1 c. diagonally sliced celery
½ c. slivered almonds
½ c. melted butter
1 sm. can whole onions
1 10-oz. package frozen English peas, cooked
Salt and pepper to taste

Cook celery in small amount of boiling salted water until crisp tender; drain. Saute almonds lightly in butter. Combine onions, peas, celery and almonds in saucepan; season with salt and pepper. Heat through. Serve hot.

Mrs. Marie M. Hubbard, Palestine H. S.
Palestine, Texas

PEAS SUPREME

3 strips bacon
½ c. chopped onion
½ c. diced celery
1 c. cracker crumbs
1 c. tomato soup
1 tsp. Worcestershire sauce
1 can button mushrooms, drained
1 can English peas, drained
½ c. grated sharp cheese

Fry bacon until crisp; drain and crumble. Saute onion and celery in bacon drippings until transparent. Remove onion mixture from drippings; place in mixing bowl. Add bacon and remaining ingredients except cheese; mix gently. Place in greased casserole; top with cheese. Bake at 350 degrees for 20 to 30 minutes or until bubbly.

Mrs. Miriam Bobo Templeton, Hickory Tavern H. S.
Gray Court, South Carolina

PEAS PAGODA

1 No. 303 can early garden peas
1 5-oz. can water chestnuts,
1 3-oz. can sliced mushrooms
1½ tsp. Spice Islands chicken seasoned stock
    base
¼ tsp. ginger
½ tsp. sugar
1 tbsp. salad oil
1½ tsp. cornstarch
1 tbsp. soy sauce

Drain peas; reserve liquid. Drain and slice water chestnuts. Drain mushrooms. Place peas, water chestnuts and mushrooms in saucepan; add ½ cup reserved liquid and remaining ingredients except cornstarch and soy sauce. Mix gently; cover. Heat through. Combine cornstarch and soy sauce; stir gently into peas mixture. Cook until thickened, stirring carefully. Serve hot.

Phyllis L. Barton, Fort Hunt H. S.
Alexandria, Virginia

BELGIAN SMOTHERED POTATOES

½ c. butter
6 lg. potatoes, peeled and quartered
3 tbsp. dry white wine
1 tsp. onion powder
¾ tsp. salt
¼ tsp. coarsely ground pepper
1 tbsp. freeze-dried chives

Melt butter in a heavy skillet. Add potatoes and remaining ingredients, except chives. Cover tightly. Cook over low heat for 45 minutes. Remove cover. Add chives. Yield: 6 servings.

Rebecca Nix, Aldine Jr. H. S.
Houston, Texas

BAKED SHOESTRING POTATOES

4 med. baking potatoes, peeled
3 tbsp. butter
1½ tsp. salt
⅛ tsp. pepper
½ c. grated sharp process American cheese
2 tbsp. chopped parsley
½ c. cream

Cut potatoes into thin strips; place in baking dish. Dot with butter; sprinkle with salt, pepper, cheese and parsley. Cover with cream. Bake, covered, at 375 degrees for 1 hour or until done. Yield: 4 servings.

Mrs. Pauline W. Ferrell, Marion H. S.
Marion, Kansas

BROWNED PAPRIKA POTATOES

8 med. baking potatoes, pared
Butter
1 c. corn flake crumbs
½ tsp. paprika
½ tsp. salt

Brush pared potatoes with melted butter. Mix corn flake crumbs, paprika and salt in plastic bag. Place one potato at a time into bag; shake to coat completely. Place in greased 1½-quart baking dish; cover. Bake in 425-degree oven for 45 minutes. Yield: 8 servings.

Billie R. Bacon, Hixson H. S.
Hixson, Tennessee

CHEESE HERB FRENCH FRIES

1 1-lb. package frozen French-fried potatoes
¼ c. shredded American cheese
½ tsp. celery salt or onion salt
Summer savory or basil to taste

Bake frozen potatoes at 450 degrees for 20 minutes or until golden brown. Sprinkle with cheese, celery salt and savory. Serve immediately. Yield: 3-4 servings.

Mrs. LeNora Hudson, Oklahoma School for Deaf
Sulphur, Oklahoma

CONFETTI POTATO PUFF

1 3-oz. envelope instant mashed potatoes
¼ c. chopped pimento
¼ c. chopped green onions
1 clove of garlic, minced
2 tsp. salt
2 c. cottage cheese
1 c. sour cream
3 eggs, separated
2 tbsp. butter

Prepare potatoes according to package directions; combine with pimento, onions, garlic, salt, cottage cheese, sour cream and well-beaten egg yolks. Fold in stiffly beaten egg whites; place in greased 2-quart casserole. Dot with butter. Bake at 350 degrees for about 1 hour. Yield: 8 servings.

Mrs. Frances Bowyer, Fayetteville H. S.
Fayetteville, North Carolina

DUCHESS POTATOES

3 c. hot mashed potatoes
Butter
6 tbsp. milk

1½ tsp. salt
⅛ tsp. pepper
3 eggs, separated

Combine potatoes with 3 tablespoons butter, milk, salt, pepper and egg yolks; mix well. Fold in stiffly beaten egg whites. Place mixture in pastry bag with star tube; form rosettes on a greased baking sheet or shape border around meat or fish. Brush with melted butter. Bake at 425 degrees for 5 minutes or until brown. Yield: 6-8 servings.

Mrs. Charlene Strickland, Madison County H. S.
Danielsville, Georgia

FOILED POTATOES

3 lg. baking potatoes, sliced ¼ in. thick
1 tsp onion salt
1 tsp. celery salt
Dash of pepper
⅓ c. grated Parmesan cheese
⅓ c. butter or margarine

Spread potato slices on 20 x 18-inch piece of foil; sprinkle with seasonings and cheese. Arrange seasoned slices in overlapping rows; dot with butter. Close foil securely. Cook on outdoor grill until potatoes are tender. May bake in 350-degree oven for 30 to 45 minutes, if desired.

Mrs. Virginia Hearne, Marsh Jr. H. S.
Fort Worth, Texas

HASHED BROWN CASSEROLE

1 2-lb. bag frozen hashed brown potatoes
1 can cream of chicken soup
2 tbsp. chopped onion
2 tbsp. pimento
2 tbsp. bell pepper
1 8-oz. carton sour cream
1 stick butter, melted

Combine potatoes, soup, onion, pimento, bell pepper, sour cream and melted butter. Place in greased casserole. Bake in 325-degree oven for 2 hours. May be prepared the night before and refrigerated.

Betsy Mowery, Pine Tree H. S.
Longview, Texas

HOLIDAY POTATO DISH

4 lb. unpared potatoes, cooked and drained
1½ c. shredded Cheddar cheese
1 c. chopped onion
Butter
1 10¾-oz. can cream of celery soup

1 pt. sour cream
½ c. crushed corn flakes
Pimento strips
Chopped fresh parsley

Remove skins from potatoes; shred into bowl. Mix cheese with potatoes. Sauté onion in ¼ cup melted butter until tender. Remove from heat. Stir in soup and sour cream. Pour over potatoes and cheese; mix well. Turn into greased 13 x 9 x 2-inch baking dish; cover. Refrigerate overnight. Sprinkle with corn flakes. Drizzle with 3 tablespoons melted butter. Bake in 350 degree-oven for 1 hour. Garnish with pimento and parsley. Yield: 12 servings.

Peggie McColloch, Warren County Jr. H. S.
McMinnville, Tennessee

MICROWAVE SCALLOPED POTATOES

4 c. potatoes, pared and sliced
¼ c. chopped onion
¾ tsp. salt
⅛ tsp. pepper
1 10½-oz. can cream of celery soup
½ c. milk
Paprika

Place half the potatoes in greased 2-quart glass casserole. Top with half the onion. Repeat layers; sprinkle with salt and pepper. Blend soup and milk; pour over potato mixture. Cover. Microwave on High setting for 20 minutes, stirring every 5 minutes. Sprinkle with paprika. Let stand 5 minutes before serving.

Pamela Vaughan, Clarksville H. S.
Clarksville, Texas

MOTHER'S SCALLOPED POTATOES

4 c. diced potatoes
1 green pepper, chopped (opt.)
2 pimentos, chopped (opt.)
Salt and pepper to taste
1 can celery soup
½ c. grated cheese

Cook potatoes for 5 minutes in water to cover; add green pepper and pimento. Season with salt and pepper to taste. Pour into a well-greased baking dish. Cover with soup and cheese. Bake at 350 degrees for 50 minutes. Yield: 6 servings.

Ruth Ann Eckel, Star Spencer H. S.
Spencer, Oklahoma

NEW POTATO CURRY

1½ tbsp. chopped onion
2 tbsp. butter or margarine
¾ tsp. curry powder
1½ tbsp. flour
¾ tsp. salt
1½ c. milk
3 lb. cooked new potatoes, peeled

Saute onion in butter until tender. Blend in curry powder, flour and salt to make a paste. Add milk gradually; cook until thickened, stirring constantly. Place potatoes in greased 2-quart casserole; pour sauce over potatoes. Bake at 375 degrees for 30 minutes or until heated through and bubbly. Yield: 8 servings.

Mrs. Merle Brotherton, Lockney H. S.
Lockney, Texas

POTATO CASSEROLE

6 potatoes
½ c. margarine, melted
1 8-oz. carton sour cream
1 bunch fresh green onions, chopped
1 c. grated cheese

Boil potatoes in jackets until just tender. Cool and peel. Grate cooked potatoes into mixing bowl. Add melted margarine, sour cream, chopped onions and grated cheese; mix well. Place in 2-quart casserole. Bake at 300 degrees for 45 minutes or until lightly browned. Yield: 6 servings.

Mrs. James F. Holloway,
W. C. Yates Vocational Center
Franklin, Tennessee

POTATO CASSEROLE DELUXE

2 lb. frozen hashed brown postatoes, defrosted
Margarine, melted
½ c. chopped onion
2 8-oz. cartons sour cream
1 can cream of chicken soup
10 oz. Cheddar cheese, grated
2 c. crushed corn flakes

Combine potatoes and ½ cup melted margarine in large bowl. Add onion, sour cream, soup and cheese. Pour into greased 9 x 13-inch Pyrex dish. Mix ¼ cup melted margarine with corn flakes. Sprinkle over potato mixture. Bake at 350 degrees for 45 minutes. Yield: 16 servings.

Mrs. Kay Brigham, Stewart County H. S.
Dover, Tennessee

POTATOES AU GRATIN

3 lb. potatoes, peeled and sliced
½ tsp. salt
¼ tsp. pepper
⅛ tsp. nutmeg
½ c. butter or margarine
1 c. grated Cheddar cheese
1 c. grated Swiss cheese
½ c. beef broth

Toss potatoes gently with salt, pepper and nutmeg. Alternate layers of potatoes, ¾ cup Cheddar cheese and Swiss cheese. Pour beef broth over all. Sprinkle ¼ cup Cheddar cheese over top. Cover with foil. Bake at 400 degrees for 45 minutes.

Joan W. Harmon, Bleckley County, H. S.
Cochran, Georgia

POTATOES ROMANOFF

5 c. cooked diced potatoes
2 tsp. salt
2 c. creamed cottage cheese
1 c. sour cream
¼ c. finely minced green onions
1 sm. clove of garlic, crushed
½ c. shredded American cheese
Paprika to taste

Sprinkle potatoes with 1 teaspoon salt. Combine cottage cheese, sour cream, onions, garlic and remaining 1 teaspoon salt; fold in potatoes. Pour into buttered 2½-quart casserole; top with cheese. Sprinkle with paprika. Bake at 350 degrees for about 45 minutes or until heated through and brown. Yield: 10-12 servings.

Dorothy Boen, Muskogee Central Sch.
Muskogee, Oklahoma

POTATO PANCAKES

3 c. finely grated potatoes
1 c. sifted flour
2 tsp. salt
2 tsp. baking powder
⅛ tsp. white pepper
2 eggs, beaten
1 c. milk
¼ c. melted margarine
2 tbsp. grated onion

Grate potatoes just before using to prevent discoloration. Sift flour, salt, baking powder and pepper together. Stir into potatoes. Add remaining ingredients; place in large mixer bowl. Beat at medium speed of electric mixer until well blended. Drop by spoonfuls into hot fat; spread out with back of spoon to make pancakes. Fry until brown. Turn to brown other side. Drain on paper toweling. Yield: 10 servings.

Mrs. Robert Gould, Porter H. S.
Maryville, Tennessee

SCALLOPED POTATOES SUPREME

2 qt. thinly sliced pared potatoes
¼ c. chopped green pepper
¼ c. minced onion
1 can cream of mushroom soup
1 c. milk
2 tsp. salt
Dash of pepper

Alternate layers of potatoes, green pepper and onion in greased 11 x 7 x 1½-inch baking dish or 2-quart casserole. Combine remaining ingredients. Pour over potato mixture. Cover. Bake at 350 degrees for 45 minutes. Bake, uncovered, for 20 to 30 minutes longer or until potatoes are tender. Yield: 8 servings.

Betty Ray, Union Grove Sch.
Gladewater, Texas

QUICK POTATO DINNER

1 can mushroom soup
1 can Cheddar cheese soup
1 c. milk
6 potatoes, peeled and sliced
2 med. onions, thinly sliced
Gourmet pepper to taste
Salt to taste
Bread crumbs (opt.)

Dilute mushroom soup and cheese soup each with ½ cup milk. Layer mushroom soup, potato slices, cheese soup and onion slices in a 1½-quart casserole. Season to taste. Continue layering until all ingredients are used, ending with layer of cheese soup. Top with bread crumbs. Bake at 350 degrees for 1 hour or until potatoes are tender.

Gail Rankin, David Crockett H. S.
Jonesboro, Tennessee

TEXAS TATERS

3 10-oz. packages frozen hashed browns
1 med. onion, finely chopped
1 tsp. salt
¼ tsp. pepper
1 can cream of chicken soup
1 sm. carton sour cream

½ c. melted butter
2 c. crushed corn flakes

Combine first 6 ingredients with ¼ cup melted butter; mix well. Place in large greased casserole. Mix corn flakes and ¼ cup melted butter. Spread over potatoes. Bake at 350 degrees for 40 minutes.

Sue Lawson, Haworth Sch.
Haworth, Oklahoma

TUNA-STUFFED POTATOES

4 baking potatoes, baked
1 c. mayonnaise
½ c. grated Cheddar cheese
¼ c. chopped green pepper
¼ c. chopped pimento
¼ c. chopped scallion
2 cans tuna, drained

Scoop centers from shells while still hot. Toss lightly with remaining ingredients. Spoon back into shells. Bake for 20 minutes at 400 degrees.

Mrs. Ruth Goyne, Dublin Middle Sch.
Dublin, Ohio

TWICE-BAKED POTATOES

3 lg. baking potatoes
2 tsp. butter
¼ c. Parmesan cheese
⅓ c. sour cream
⅓ c. cottage cheese
½ c. milk
½ tsp. Worcesterchire sauce
2 tsp. freeze-dried chives
¾ tsp. salt
⅛ tsp. pepper
Chopped parsley (opt.)
Paprika (opt.)

Bake potatoes at 425 degrees for 45 minutes. Remove from oven; cut potatoes in half lengthwise. Let cool. Scoop out centers, leaving skins intact. Mash potatoes with butter. Add next 8 ingredients; mix well. Spoon mixture into shells. Sprinkle tops with parsley and paprika. Place on baking sheet. Bake at 425 degrees for 10 to 15 minutes, or until golden brown.

Joan W. Burson, Mt. Zion H. S.
Mt. Zion, Georgia

RATATOUILLE

1 med. eggplant, peeled and cubed
1 med. zucchini, sliced
1 green pepper, sliced
1 onion, sliced
2 c. cubed tomatoes
1 clove of garlic, finely chopped
½ tsp. dried basil
1 tsp. salt
¼ tsp. pepper
¼ c. salad oil

Combine vegetables in 2-quart casserole. Mix garlic, basil, salt and pepper with oil. Stir into vegetables; cover. Bake in 350-degree oven until eggplant is tender, about 40 minutes. May be cooked in a saucepan over medium low heat for about 30 minutes. Yield: 6-8 servings.

Darlene Caddell, Central Jr. H. S.
Lawton, Oklahoma

RATATOUILLE WITH SPANISH OLIVES

1 med. eggplant, pared and cut in 3 × ½ in.
  strips
2 zucchini, cut in ¼ in. slices
2 tsp. salt
½ c. olive oil
2 onions, thinly sliced
2 green peppers, thinly sliced
2 cloves garlic, minced
3 tomatoes, peeled and cut in strips
1 c. sliced pimento-stuffed olives
¼ c. chopped parsley
¼ tsp. pepper

Toss eggplant and zucchini with 1 teaspoon salt; let stand 30 minutes. Drain on paper towels. Heat ¼ cup oil in large skillet. Brown eggplant strips lightly; add zucchini slices. Remove with slotted spoon; set aside. Heat remaining oil in skillet. Cook onions and green peppers until tender. Stir in garlic. Place tomato strips on top; cover. Cook for 5 minutes. Stir in eggplant, zucchini, olives, parsley and remaining salt and pepper. Simmer, covered, for 20 minutes; uncover. Cook for 5 minutes longer. Baste with juices from bottom of pan. Serve hot or cold. Garnish with additional parsley. Yield: 6-8 servings.

Joyce Fogle, Cypress Creek H. S.
Houston, Texas

RUTABAGA MAGIC

1½ to 2 lb. rutabagas
1½ tsp. Worcestershire sauce
¼ tsp. onion powder
¼ c. sugar
1 tsp. salt
3 to 4 drops of Tabasco sauce
Butter to taste

Peel rutabagas; cut into small pieces. Place in saucepan. Add Worcestershire sauce, onion powder, sugar, salt and Tabasco sauce; cover with water. Bring to a boil; cook until tender. Add butter; mash with a fork. Serve immediately.

Mrs. Anne Sutphen Welch, Bearden H. S.
Knoxville, Tennessee

EASY SPINACH RING

3 c. drained cooked spinach
½ c. coarse bread crumbs
1 tsp. onion juice
1 tbsp. chopped celery
¼ tsp. salt
¼ tsp. pepper
2 tbsp. butter or margarine, melted
3 eggs, beaten

Combine all ingredients; mix well. Spread in buttered ring mold; place mold in pan of hot water. Bake at 300 degrees for 30 minutes or until set. Unmold onto serving platter. Fill center with creamed cauliflower or mashed potatoes; surround ring with buttered carrots, if desired. Yield: 6 servings.

Martha June Graber, New Paris H. S.
New Paris, Indiana

SPINACH-BROCCOLI CASSEROLE

1 pkg. frozen, chopped spinach
1 pkg. frozen, chopped broccoli
1 c. shredded Cheddar cheese
1 pt. large-curd cottage cheese
3 eggs, beaten
3 tbsp. flour
Salt to taste
Dry bread crumbs
Butter

Thaw spinach and broccoli; drain well. Combine cheeses, eggs and flour. Add to spinach and broccoli. Season to taste; mix well. Place mixture in well-buttered 1-quart souffle dish. Sprinkle dry bread crumbs evenly on top; dot with butter. Bake at 350 degrees for 1 hour. Yield: 6 servings.

Debbie Hopkins, Arp H. S.
Arp, Texas

BAKED SPINACH WITH SOUR CREAM

3 10-oz. packages frozen chopped spinach
1 pkg. dry onion soup mix
1 pt. sour cream

Cook spinach according to package directions; drain well. Combine onion soup mix and sour cream; mix well. Stir sour cream mixture into spinach; place in baking dish. Bake, covered, at 350 degrees for 30 minutes or until bubbly. Yield: 8 servings.

Mrs. Mable Wallmark, Mead H. S.
Mead, Washington

SPINACH CASSEROLE

2 pkg. frozen, chopped spinach
1 8-oz. package cream cheese
½ c. margarine or butter
1 c. coarse bread crumbs
⅛ tsp. salt
⅛ tsp. pepper
⅔ tsp. sage

Cook spinach according to package directions; drain. Add cream cheese and ¼ cup margarine; stir until blended. Mix ¼ cup margarine, bread crumbs, salt, pepper and sage. Pour spinach mixture into greased casserole. Sprinkle bread crumb mixture over top. Bake at 350 degrees for 20 minutes.

Mrs. Martha R. Swann, Saltillo H. S.
Saltillo, Mississippi

SPINACH-CHEESE BAKE

1 10-oz. package frozen, chopped spinach
1 c. cooked rice
1½ c. shredded sharp American cheese
2 eggs, slightly beaten
2 tbsp. soft butter or margarine
⅓ c. milk
2½ tbsp. chopped onion
½ tsp. Worcestershire sauce
1 tsp. salt
¼ tsp. crushed rosemary or thyme

Cook and drain spinach. Mix in remaining ingredients. Pour into a 10 x 6 x 1½-inch baking dish. Bake at 350 degrees for 20 to 25 minutes, or until knife inserted into center comes out clean. Yield: 6 servings.

Karen Orsak, Hull H. S.
Hull, Massachusetts

SPINACH SOUFFLE

¼ c. butter
1 tbsp. minced onion

1 tbsp. minced green pepper
1 tbsp. minced celery
3 tbsp. flour
½ tsp. salt
⅛ tsp. pepper
1 c. milk
4 eggs, separated
2 c. cooked spinach, drained

Melt butter in saucepan. Add onion, green pepper and celery; cook until soft but not brown. Stir in flour salt and pepper to make a paste. Add milk; cook until thickened, stirring constantly. Beat egg yolks until thick and lemon colored; stir part of the hot white sauce into egg yolks. Stir egg yolks into white sauce. Stir in spinach. Beat egg whites until stiff; fold into spinach mixture. Turn into buttered 1-quart casserole; place casserole in pan of hot water. Bake at 350 degrees for 50 minutes or until souffle is firm and dry on top. Yield: 6 servings.

Toni Guast, Lackawanna Trail Joint Sch.
Factoryville, Pennsylvania

TASTY SPINACH BALLS

2 c. drained, cooked chopped spinach
2 tbsp. butter, melted
1 tsp. salt
¼ tsp. pepper
2 eggs
Bread crumbs
2 tbsp. grated onion
2 tbsp. grated cheese
¼ tsp. oregano
⅛ tsp. allspice

Combine spinach, butter, salt, pepper, 1 beaten egg, 1 cup bread crumbs, onion, cheese and spices. Let stand for 10 minutes. Shape into balls. Combine remaining egg and ¼ cup water. Dredge spinach balls with bread crumbs. Dip in egg mixture; dredge again with bread crumbs. Fry in deep fat at 375 degrees until brown; drain on paper toweling. Yield: 6 servings.

Mrs. Reva Bishop, North Hardin H. S.
Vine Grove, Kentucky

CRUNCHY MICROWAVE SQUASH

2 acorn squash
4 tsp. butter or margarine
4 tbsp. brown sugar
¼ c. crushed pecans
¼ c. coconut

Cut squash in half; remove seeds. Add 1 teaspoon butter and 1 tablespoon brown sugar to each half. Sprinkle with pecans and coconut. Place in glass baking dish. Microwave for 5 to 6 minutes or until sugar bubbles.

Trellis H. Baker, Henderson Jr. H. S.
Jackson, Georgia

ACORN SQUASH WITH ORANGE-WHEAT STUFFING

4 sm. acorn squash
½ lb. link sausages
½ c. chopped onion
¾ c. cracked wheat
1 tsp. dried leaf sage
1¼ c. orange juice
Salt
Pinch of sugar
Pepper to taste

Boil squash in large kettle of water for 20 minutes or until tender. Brown sausages in skillet; transfer to a paper towel to drain. Remove all but 2 tablespoons fat. Add onion to skillet; cook for 2 minutes. Add wheat. Cook for 5 minutes longer. Add sage, orange juice and ½ teaspoon salt; cover. Cook over low heat for 25 minutes or until liquid is absorbed. Slice sausages; add to skillet. Cut off 1-inch slice from pointed ends of the squash. Remove seeds and fibers. Cut a thin sliver from the flat ends so the squash stand evenly. Sprinkle inside of squash with a pinch of sugar and salt and pepper to taste. Spoon in stuffing. Arrange squash in a buttered baking dish. Replace lids. Bake in a 355 degree oven for 45 minutes. Yield: 4 servings.

Photograph for this recipe on page 149.

GOURMET ACORN SQUASH

3 acorn squash, halved and seeded
⅔ c. diced celery
1½ c. diced unpeeled apples
¼ c. butter or margarine
1½ c. soft bread crumbs
1 c. shredded American cheese
½ tsp. salt
⅛ tsp. pepper

Place squash, cut side down, in shallow baking dish with small amount of water. Bake at 400 degrees for 20 to 30 minutes or until just tender. Saute celery and apples in butter for 5 minutes. Stir in remaining ingredients; mix well. Fill squash with apple mixture; place in baking dish. Bake for 10 to 15 minutes longer or until squash is tender.

Mrs. Mary Jo Lyle, Putnam County H. S.
Eatonton, Georgia

BUTTERNUT SQUASH DELIGHT

1 2-lb. butternut squash
3 tbsp. butter
3 tbsp. brown sugar
3 tbsp. orange juice
½ tsp. grated lemon peel
¾ tsp. salt

Place whole unpeeled squash in saucepan in boiling water. Cover; cook for 45 minutes or until tender. Remove from water; split lengthwise. Remove seeds; scoop out squash. Mash squash. Add remaining ingredients; mix well. Serve hot. Yield: 6 servings.

Mrs. Marijo W. Rawlings, Flower Grove H. S.
Ackerly, Texas

CORN CHIP SQUASH

4 or 5 med. squash, diced
¼ c. minced onion
1 tbsp. minced pimento
Salt and pepper to taste
1 tbsp. butter
1 ¾-oz. package corn chips, crushed

Cook squash in small amount of water until tender. Combine drained squash, onion and pimento; season with salt and pepper. Place in buttered baking dish; dot with butter. Sprinkle corn chips over top. Bake at 350 degrees for 25 to 30 minutes or until heated through.

Vera Mays, Gillett Jr. H. S.
Kingsville, Texas

CROOKNECK SQUASH SUPREME

3 c. cubed crookneck squash
1 can cream of chicken soup
½ c. chopped toasted almonds
2 tbsp. diced pimento
2 tbsp. butter
¼ c. buttered bread crumbs

Cook squash in salted water for 5 minutes; drain. Arrange alternate layers of squash, soup, almonds and pimento in buttered casserole; dot with butter. Cover with bread crumbs. Bake at 375 degrees for 20 minutes or until browned. Yield: 6 servings.

Mrs. Mildred Rivers, Wilson Jr. H. S.
Charlotte, North Carolina

FRENCH-FRIED SUMMER SQUASH

3 eggs, beaten
½ c. milk
1 tsp. salt
4 med. summer squash, thinly sliced
2 c. cornmeal

Combine eggs, milk and salt to make a batter. Dip squash in batter; dredge with cornmeal. Fry in hot deep fat until crisp and golden. Yield: 6 servings.

Mrs. Frances W. Banner, Castlewood H. S.
Castlewood, Virginia

SQUASH CASSEROLE DELUXE

5 c. yellow squash, sliced
2 tsp. salt
½ c. chopped onion
1 c. grated carrots
1 pkg. herb-seasoned stuffing mix
1 carton sour cream
1 can cream of celery soup
½ c. melted margarine

Boil squash in salted water with the onion for 5 minutes. Drain; set aside. Mix carrots, half the stuffing mix, sour cream, soup and ¼ c. melted margarine. Layer squash and carrot mixtures in a 9 x 12-inch baking dish. Spread remaining stuffing mix on top; drizzle with ¼ cup margarine. Bake at 350 degrees for 20 minutes. Yield: 6-8 servings.

Sandra Vincent, Forsyth, H. S.
Forsyth, Missouri

EASY SQUASH CASSEROLE

2 lb. yellow squash, sliced
1 med. onion, chopped
Margarine
1 egg, beaten
¼ c. milk
1 c. grated sharp Cheddar cheese
Bread crumbs

Cook squash and onion in small amount of salted water; drain. Mash; add ⅓ stick margarine. Add egg, milk and cheese to squash. Place in casserole. Top with bread crumbs; dot with margarine. Bake at 350 degrees for 30 minutes or until crumbs are brown and mixture is bubbly.

Imogene D. Crawford, Flat Rock Jr. H. S.
Flat Rock, North Carolina

SQUASH DELICIOUS

1 c. sour cream
1 can cream of chicken soup
1 carrot, grated
1 stick butter or margarine, cut in half
2 lb. yellow squash, sliced
1 med. onion, chopped
½ pkg. Pepperidge Farm stuffing mix

Combine sour cream, chicken soup, grated carrot and ½ stick butter. Cook over low heat for 10 minutes. Do not let mixture boil. Boil squash in small amount of water with onion and ½ stick butter until fork tender. Drain. Layer squash, sauce and stuffing mix in 3-quart casserole, ending with stuffing mix. Bake at 350 degrees until bubbly. Yield: 8 servings.

Nita De Grand, Nacogdoches H. S.
Nacogdoches, Texas

PARTY SQUASH RING

6 c. ½-inch pieces of yellow squash
1 med. onion, diced
½ med. green pepper, diced
1 clove of garlic, diced
1 tsp. salt
2 tbsp. sugar
¼ c. butter, melted
1 tbsp. Worcestershire sauce
½ tsp. pepper
½ tsp. Tabasco sauce
1 c. bread crumbs
3 eggs, well beaten
½ c. milk

Cook squash, onion, green pepper and garlic in water until tender; drain well. Combine remaining ingredients; mix well. Stir into squash mixture; place in greased 1½-quart ring mold. Place mold in pan of hot water. Bake at 350 degrees for 40 minutes or until firm. Unmold; fill center with buttered green lima beans or English peas, if desired. Garnish with small whole pickled beets.

Mrs. Ernestine E. Hodson, Grand Prairie H. S.
Grand Prairie, Texas

SQUASH CHILI VERDE

2 tbsp. butter
6 to 8 sm. yellow squash, sliced
1 med. onion, sliced
1 to 3 hot green chili peppers
Salt and pepper to taste
4 slices American cheese

Melt butter in electric skillet. Add squash and onion; cook, covered, at 200 degrees for 30 minutes or until tender and slightly browned, stirring about four times. Add chili peppers and seasonings; cook for 15 minutes longer. Pour into casserole; cover with cheese. Bake at 350 degrees until cheese is melted. Yield: 8 servings.

Martha A. Matthews, Colorado H. S.
Colorado City, Texas

SUMMER SQUASH CASSEROLE

2 lbs. summer squash sliced
1 onion, sliced
½ c. margarine
⅓ c. flour
1 c. milk
1 sm. box Velveeta cheese, cubed
3 or 4 oz. slivered almonds

Cook squash and onion in small amount of salted water; drain. Melt margarine in saucepan. Add flour; stir until smooth. Add milk gradually; cook until thick. Add cheese; stir over low heat until melted. Add slivered almonds. Combine with squash in casserole. Bake at 350 degrees for 20 to 30 minutes. Yield: 8 servings.

Elenor Rollins, Riverdale H. S.
Fort Myers, Florida

SWEET POTATO-HONEY BALLS

2½ c. mashed cooked sweet potatoes
¾ tsp. salt
Dash of pepper
4 tbsp. butter melted
½ c. miniature marshmallows
⅓ c. honey
1 c. chopped pecans

Combine sweet potatoes, salt, pepper and 2 table-spoons butter; stir in marshmallows. Chill thoroughly. Shape into balls, using ¼ cup sweet potato mixture for each ball. Combine 1 tablespoon butter and honey in small heavy skillet; cook just until syrupy. Add balls, one at a time; turn to coat with glaze, using 2 forks and working carefully but quickly. Roll in pecans; place in greased shallow casserole. Do not let balls touch. Drizzle with remaining 1 tablespoon butter. Bake at 350 degrees for 15 to 20 minutes or until heated through. Yield: 10 servings.

Mrs. Adeline H. Kirk, Central H. S.
San Angelo, Texas

BRANDIED SWEET POTATOES

2 tbsp. cornstarch
½ tsp. nutmeg
2 tsp. salt
½ c. sugar
1 tbsp. lemon juice
⅓ c. Brandy
6 lg. sweet potatoes, cooked
Miniature marshmallows

Combine cornstarch, nutmeg, salt and sugar in 1-quart saucepan; stir in 1 cup water. Cook until clear, stirring constantly. Stir in lemon juice and Brandy. Peel potatoes; cut crosswise into ¼ to ½-inch thick slices. Place in buttered shallow casserole; cover with Brandy sauce. Cover. Bake in preheated 375-degree oven for 30 minutes or until glazed, basting occasionally. Sprinkle with marshmallows; place under broiler. Broil until golden brown. Yield: 8 servings.

Jeanne C. Conner, Greenwood H. S.
Greenwood, Delaware

CALIFORNIA-CANDIED YAMS

6 med. yams, cooked
⅓ c. (packed) brown sugar

⅓ c. sugar
Salt to taste
2 tbsp. cornstarch
1 c. orange juice
2 tsp. grated orange rind
¼ c. butter or margarine
¼ c. Sherry

Peel yams; cut into halves or thick slices. Arrange in baking dish. Combine sugars, salt and cornstarch in saucepan; stir in orange juice, orange rind and butter. Simmer for 5 minutes or until smooth and thickened, stirring constantly. Remove from heat; stir in Sherry. Pour over yams; cover. Bake at 350 degrees for 20 minutes. Remove cover; bake for 10 to 15 minutes longer or until glazed.

Mrs. Mary Lou Hayes, Altamont H. S.
Altamont, Utah

CREAMED SWEET POTATOES

1 lg. sweet potato, cooked
¾ c. margarine
1½ c. sugar
1 c. milk
1 tsp. grated orange rind
Dash of salt
1 egg

Mash sweet potato. Add margarine; mix well. Add sugar, a small amount at a time, beating after each addition. Add remaining ingredients; beat thoroughly. Place in baking dish. Bake at 350 degrees for 45 minutes or until done. Serve with ham or pork. Yield: 6 servings.

Sue Henry Calhoun, Downsville H. S.
Downsville, Louisiana

HARVEST SWEET POTATOES

¼ c. butter
⅓ c. (packed) brown sugar
¼ tsp. salt
½ c. orange marmalade
¼ c. Sherry
¼ c. raisins
1 1-lb. can sweet potatoes, drained

Combine butter, brown sugar, salt, marmalade and Sherry in saucepan; bring to a boil, stirring occasionally. Cook for 3 minutes. Add raisins. Arrange sweet potatoes in buttered shallow casserole. Pour Sherry sauce over sweet potatoes; cover. Bake at 325 degrees for 40 to 45 minutes or until heated through. Yield: 5 servings.

Mrs. Charles Thorp, Madison Jr. H. S.
Abilene, Texas

HAWAIIAN SWEET POTATOES

9 oz. grated pineapple
2 lb. cooked or canned sweet potatoes, sliced
2 tbsp. butter
1 lg. banana, sliced
Confectioners' sugar
⅛ tsp. salt

Combine pineapple and sweet potatoes in buttered baking dish; dot with butter. Dredge banana slices with sugar; sprinkle with salt. Arrange over sweet potato mixture. Bake at 350 degrees for 30 minutes or until heated through and browned. Yield: 8 servings.

Florence Tustison, Sentinel H. S.
Sentinel, Oklahoma

SWEET POTATO-ALMOND CROQUETTES

4 med. sweet potatoes, boiled
¼ c. butter
Dash of white pepper
3 tbsp. brown sugar
½ c. chopped blanched almonds
Bread crumbs or crushed corn flakes
2 eggs, slightly beaten
1 tbsp. milk

Peel and mash sweet potatoes. Add salt, butter, pepper and brown sugar; beat until fluffy. Chill thoroughly. Shape sweet potato mixture into 12 patties; roll in almonds and bread crumbs. Chill thoroughly. Mix eggs and milk together. Dip patties in egg mixture; roll again in bread crumbs. Fry in deep fat at 375 degrees until golden brown. Yield: 12 patties.

Maggie Johnson, Varnado Sch.
Varnado, Louisiana

SWEET POTATOES IN ORANGE CUPS

2 oranges, halved
4 sweet potatoes
¾ tsp. salt
4 tsp. butter or margarine
4 tsp. sugar or brown sugar
¼ c. orange juice
4 marshmallows

Remove pulp and membrane from orange halves; reserve shells. Place sweet potatoes in saucepan. Add 1 cup boiling water and ½ teaspoon salt; cover. Boil for 20 minutes or until sweet potatoes are tender. Peel and mash sweet potatoes. Add butter, sugar, orange juice and remaining ¼ teaspoon salt; beat until light and fluffy. Fill reserved orange shells with sweet potato mixture; top each orange cup with a marshmallow. Place in baking pan. Bake at 350

degrees for 15 minutes or until heated through and slightly glazed.

Virginia St. John, George Vance Jr. H. S.
Bristol, Tennessee

SWEET POTATO CASSEROLE

Melted butter or margarine
3 c. cooked, mashed sweet potatoes
1 c. sugar
2 eggs, beaten
1 tsp. vanilla extract
⅓ c. milk
½ c. (firmly packed) brown sugar
¼ c. all-purpose flour
½ c. chopped nuts

Combine ½ cup melted butter with next 5 ingredients in a mixing bowl; mix well. Pour into 2-quart casserole. Combine brown sugar, flour, 2½ tablespoons melted butter and nuts in a small mixing bowl; mix well. Sprinkle topping over sweet potato mixture. Bake at 350 degrees for 30 to 40 minutes. Yield: 8 to 10 servings.

Joni Sturm, Muenster Public Sch.
Muenster, Texas

SWEET POTATO SOUFFLE

3 c. mashed sweet potatoes
1 c. sugar
½ tsp. salt
2 eggs, beaten
⅓ stick butter, melted
1½ c. milk
1 tsp. vanilla extract
¼ tsp. nutmeg
¾ tsp. cinnamon
1 c. (firmly packed) brown sugar
1 c. chopped nuts
⅓ c. flour

Combine first 8 ingredients and ¼ teaspoon cinnamon; mix well. Pour into well-greased casserole. Combine remaining ingredients for topping. Spread over potato mixture. Bake at 350 degrees for 35 minutes. Yield: 6-8 servings.

Deborah Z. Alford, Putnam County Middle Sch.
Eatonton, Georgia

BROILED TOMATOES NAPOLI

4 lg. tomatoes
1 c. fresh bread crumbs
¼ c. melted butter
2 tbsp. grated Parmesan cheese
½ tsp. Italian herb seasoning

Cut stem portion from tomatoes; cut tomatoes into thick slices. Place in large broiler pan. Combine remaining ingredients; mix well. Spread over tomato slices. Broil 10 inches from the source of heat for 4 to 5 minutes or until heated through and crumbs are browned. Serve immediately.

Mrs. Barbara Hammerberg, Hortonville H. S.
Hortonville, Wisconsin

CURRIED TOMATOES AND ONIONS

1 c. diced onions
2 tbsp. butter
¼ c. flour
2 c. cooked tomatoes
1 tsp. salt
¼ tsp. curry powder

Saute onions in butter until transparent; sprinkle flour over onions, stirring lightly. Add tomatoes and salt; cook until thickened, stirring constantly. Add curry powder. May serve over rice if desired. Yield: 4 servings.

Reva Wilson, Drummond H. S.
Drummond, Montana

DANISH TOMATOES

Fresh tomatoes
Sugar to taste
Salt to taste
Buttered croutons
Crumbled bleu cheese

Make cuts from blossom end almost to stem end of each tomato to form petals. Place tomatoes in baking pan; spread out petals to make flowers. Season with sugar and salt. Bake at 375 degrees for 10 minutes. Sprinkle with croutons and cheese; bake until cheese bubbles.

Rosemary Martine, Gridley Jr. H. S.
Erie, Pennsylvania

CREOLE-FRIED TOMATOES

1 clove of garlic, minced
1 tbsp. chopped parsley
½ tsp. salt
Dash of pepper
1 onion, minced
1 tbsp. vegetable oil
2 lg. red or green tomatoes, thickly sliced
1 c. cornmeal

Combine garlic, parsley, salt, pepper, onion and oil. Spread mixture on tomato slices; sprinkle with cornmeal. Saute in lightly oiled skillet until heated through and browned. Yield: 4 servings.

Doris Y. Burnette, Fort Defiance H. S.
Fort Defiance, Virginia

FRIED GREEN TOMATOES

4 or 5 green tomatoes
⅓ c. flour
¾ tsp. salt
Dash of pepper (opt.)
¼ c. shortening

Remove stem ends from tomatoes; cut into ½-inch slices. Combine flour, salt and pepper; dredge tomato slices with flour mixture. Saute quickly in hot shortening until brown on one side; turn. Reduce heat; cook until soft. Remove to hot platter; serve immediately.

Mrs. Patricia D. Chappell, Spalding Jr. H. S.
Griffin, Georgia

MARINATED TOMATOES

6 med. ripe tomatoes, peeled and sliced
½ tsp. oregano
¼ c. salad oil
1 tbsp. lemon juice
½ tsp. minced garlic
½ tsp. salt

Place tomatoes in shallow dish. Combine remaining ingredients; mix well. Pour over tomatoes. Refrigerate, covered, for several hours until well chilled. Yield: 12 servings.

Becky Burns Drone, Page H. S.
Franklin, Tennessee

STEWED TOMATOES WITH PEAS AND CELERY

1 tbsp. cornstarch
1 1-lb. can stewed tomatoes
1 tsp. instant minced onion
1 8-oz. can sm. green peas, drained
½ c. finely diced green celery
¼ tsp. salt
White pepper to taste
Dried basil or minced fresh basil to taste

Dissolve cornstarch in small amount of tomato juice. Combine tomatoes with juice, cornstarch mixture and onion in saucepan; cook until thickened, stirring constantly. Stir in remaining ingredients; heat through. Serve hot. Yield: 6 servings.

Carol L. Sheldon, Boonsboro H. S.
Boonsboro, Maryland

CORN BREAD-STUFFED TOMATOES

1 c. cornmeal
1 egg, beaten
Salt
½ tsp. soda
1 c. thick buttermilk
6 med. tomatoes
1 med. onion, minced
Pepper to taste
Butter

Combine cornmeal, egg, ½ teaspoon salt, soda and buttermilk; mix well. Pour into greased small baking pan. Bake at 350 degrees for 25 to 30 minutes or until corn bread tests done. Let cool; crumble. Scoop out centers of tomatoes; set shells aside to drain. Combine tomato pulp, corn bread and onion; season with salt and pepper. Stuff tomato shells with corn bread mixture; top with butter. Bake at 350 degrees for 30 minutes or until heated through.

Mrs. Nelle B. Underwood, Flomaton H. S.
Flomaton, Alabama

TOMATO-CHEESE BAKE

4 med. tomatoes, peeled
1 tsp. sugar
Dash of pepper
2 c. shredded sharp process American cheese
½ c. finely chopped celery
¼ c. finely chopped onion
1 c. soft bread crumbs
2 tbsp. margarine, melted

Slice tomatoes into fourths. Sprinkle with sugar and pepper. Toss cheese, celery and onion in bowl. Place half the tomato slices in 10 × 6 × 1¾-inch baking dish. Sprinkle half of the cheese mixture over tomato slices. Repeat layers. Toss bread crumbs with margarine; sprinkle over casserole mixture. Bake at 350 degrees for 25 to 30 minutes. Yield: 4-6 servings.

Paula Pope, Franklin Heights H. S.
Columbus, Ohio

TOMATOES SAINT GERMAIN

6 lg. tomatoes
Salt and pepper to taste
5 tsp. lemon juice
3 c. cooked English peas
3 tbsp. instant minced onion
½ tsp. Worcestershire sauce
2 tbsp. butter, melted
3 tbsp. bread crumbs

Cut tops from tomatoes; scoop out pulp. Invert shells to drain. Chop tomato pulp. Season insides of shells with salt and pepper; sprinkle with 3 teaspoons lemon juice. Combine tomato pulp, remaining 2 teaspoons lemon juice, peas, onion and Worcestershire sauce; season with salt and pepper. Spoon into tomato shells; place shells in baking dish. Mix butter and bread crumbs together; sprinkle over stuffed tomatoes. Bake at 300 degrees for 15 minutes or until heated through. May place tomatoes under broiler to brown, if desired.

Mrs. Frances Jones, Littlefield H. S.
Littlefield, Texas

TOMATO-ZUCCHINI SCALLOP

6 or 7 zucchini squash sliced
4 or 6 med. tomatoes, sliced
1 lg. onion, sliced
Salt and pepper to taste
1 to 2 c. croutons
1 c. grated cheese

Slice zucchini into ¼-inch slices. Slice tomatoes and onions. Layer zucchini, onion, tomatoes, salt and pepper in greased 1½-quart casserole. Sprinkle with croutons. Repeat layers. Top with tomato slices; cover. Bake at 350 degrees for 1 hour. Uncover; sprinkle with grated cheese. Return to oven to melt cheese. Yield: 6-8 servings

Clarabel Tepe, Fort Towson Sch.
Fort Towson, Oklahoma

TURNIP CUPS

6 sm. white turnips
1 tbsp. lemon juice
3 med. beets, cooked
4 tsp. butter, melted

Peel turnips. Cook whole turnips in water with lemon juice until tender; cool slightly. Scoop out centers, leaving shells intact; set shells aside. Dice beets and turnips; mix with butter. Stuff turnip shells with turnip mixture. Serve garnished with parsley. Reheat in oven, if necessary.

Mrs. Bert Johnson, Bruce H. S.
Bruce, Mississippi

WHIPPED TURNIP PUFF

4 c. mashed cooked turnips
2 c. soft bread crumbs
½ c. melted margarine
2 tbsp. sugar
2 tsp. salt

¼ tsp. pepper
4 eggs, well beaten

Combine all ingredients; spoon into greased 6-cup casserole. Spread top with a small amount of additional melted maragarine. Bake at 375 degrees for 1 hour. Yield: 8 servings.

Mrs. Willa Mae Scroggs, Sylva-Webster H. S.
Sylva, North Carolina

CALIFORNIA VEGETABLE BAKE

1 pkg. frozen California Mix vegetables
1 can Cheddar cheese soup

Place frozen vegetables in glass casserole. Pour soup over the vegetables. Microwave for 12 to 15 minutes, stirring and turning several times.

Carol Zwolanek, Chippewa Falls H. S.
Chippewa Falls, Wisconsin

CREAM VEGETABLES

1 can green beans
1 can cream of mushroom soup
Salt and pepper to taste
1 can onion rings

Drain vegetables. Mix in soup. Season to taste with salt and pepper. Place in casserole. Bake at 350 degrees until bubbly. Top with onion rings. Garnish with bits of pimento or green pepper.

Brenda L. LeJune, Aldine Jr. H. S.
Houston, Texas

LAYERED VEGETABLE CASSEROLE

3 med. yellow squash, sliced
Dash of salt
1 lb. mushrooms, sliced and washed
1 tbsp. butter
10 oz. spinach
2 lg. slices mozzarella cheese
¼ c. grated Parmesan cheese

Place squash in saucepan with small amount of water and salt. Cook until just tender; drain. Saute mushrooms in butter; set aside. Cook spinach in a small amount of water in separate saucepan; drain. Place squash, 1 slice mozzarella cheese, mushrooms, 1 slice mozzarella cheese and spinach in casserole in order listed. Sprinkle with Parmesan cheese. Bake at 400 degrees for 20 to 25 minutes, or until hot and bubbly.

Mary Scullion Carter, Bradley H. S.
Cleveland, Tennessee

MARINATED VEGETABLES

1 16-oz. can whole green beans
1 pkg. frozen broccoli, thawed
1 pkg. frozen Brussels sprouts, thawed
1 pkg. frozen cauliflower, thawed
1 lg. bottle Italian dressing

Drain all vegetables in colander. Place in plastic container. Pour Italian dressing over all; seal tightly. Refrigerate for 24 hours. Turn container every 2 or 3 hours to mix. Serve, drained, in large clear bowl.

Kay Moyers, Pine Tree H. S.
Longview, Texas

SALLY'S VEGETABLE CASSEROLE

20 oz. frozen mixed vegetables
1 c. chopped celery
½ c. chopped onion
1 c. grated cheese
¾ c. mayonnaise
1 stick margarine, melted
¼ lb. crackers, crushed

Cook vegetables according to package directions; drain. Add celery, onions, cheese and mayonnaise. Place vegetable mixture in greased casserole. Mix margarine and crackers together. Place over vegetables. Bake at 350 degrees until bubbly, about 20 minutes.

Sally Grimmer Mace, Hendersonville H. S.
Hendersonville, Tennessee

MIXED VEGETABLE CASSEROLE

2 pkg. frozen mixed vegetables
4 hard-cooked eggs
1 sm. can asparagus, chopped
¾ c. mayonnaise
1 sm. onion, chopped
1 tsp. Worcestershire sauce
1 tsp. Tabasco sauce
1 tbsp. mustard

Cook mixed vegetables according to package directions; drain. Set aside to cool to room temperature. Separate hard-cooked eggs. Chop egg whites; grate egg yolks. Combine all ingredients except egg yolks. Place in casserole. Sprinkle grated egg yolks over top. Serve at room temperature. Yield: 6 servings.

Patricia Hudnall, Stratford H. S.
Nashville, Tennessee

THREE-VEGETABLE MEDLEY

1 10-oz. package frozen Brussels sprouts
1 med. carrot, sliced
5 green onions, chopped
¼ c. margarine
1 tsp. sugar
¼ tsp. ground thyme
¼ tsp. salt
Pepper to taste

Combine all ingredients in a saucepan with 2 tablespoons water. Cook over low heat until vegetables are tender. Yield: 6 servings/95 calories per serving.

Lee Ann Babbitt, Duncanville H. S.
Duncanville, Texas

MIXED VEGETABLE MEDLEY

2 cans mixed vegetables
Milk
2 tbsp. butter
2 tbsp. flour
¼ tsp. nutmeg
½ tsp. salt
Dash of garlic powder
Bread crumbs

Drain vegetables, reserving liquid. Add enough milk to measure 2 cups. Melt butter in saucepan. Stir in flour slowly; then slowly add liquid. Bring sauce to a boil, stirring constantly until thickened. Add remaining ingredients except bread crumbs. Place vegetables in baking dish. Pour sauce over all; top with bread crumbs. Bake at 325 degrees for 20 to 25 minutes.

Dorothy R. Trodahl, De Soto County H. S.
Arcadia, Florida

SAVORY VEGETABLE CASSEROLE

2 env. instant cream of mushroom soup mix
½ c. sour cream
½ c. grated Swiss cheese
2 1-lb. cans mixed vegetables, drained
1 c. finely rolled cracker crumbs
3 tbsp. melted butter or margarine
1 tsp. marjoram
½ tsp. onion powder

Place soup mix in medium bowl; stir in 1 cup boiling water. Blend in sour cream and cheese. Add vegetables. Pour into 1½-quart oblong baking dish. Combine next 4 ingredients; sprinkle over top of vegetable mixture. Bake in a preheated 350-degree oven for 30 to 35 minutes, or until bubbly. Yield: 6 servings.

Mrs. Loretta Spurlock, Lookout Valley H. S.
Chattanooga, Tennessee

TRIO VEGETABLE CASSEROLE

1 10-oz. package frozen green peas
1 10-oz. package frozen French-style green beans
1 10-oz. package frozen baby limas
1 tbsp. Worcestershire sauce
1 tsp. prepared mustard
Juice of ½ lemon
1 sm. purple onion, grated
1 can water chestnuts, sliced and drained
1½ c. mayonnaise
Bread crumbs, buttered

Cook vegetables separately; drain. Combine vegetables with next 6 ingredients. Place in buttered casserole. Sprinkle with buttered bread crumbs. Bake at 350 degrees for 30 minutes. Yield: 10 servings.

Elizabeth Miller, Shelby Sr. H. S.
Shelby, North Carolina

VARIETY VEGETABLE CASSEROLE

2 med. eggplant, peeled and sliced ½-inch thick
Salt
Oil
2 lg. zucchini, sliced
½ lb. mushrooms, sliced
1 lg. green pepper, seeded and diced
2 lg. tomatoes, sliced
1 bunch fresh spinach, washed
2 c. grated asiago or Parmesan cheese
3 lg. tomatoes, chopped
Oregano
Salt and freshly ground pepper

Sprinkle eggplant generously with salt. Place in colander; let stand 30 minutes. Rinse well; pat dry. Heat 3 tablespoons oil in large skillet. Saute eggplant slices until lightly browned, adding oil if necessary. Layer half the eggplant, zucchini, mushrooms, green pepper, sliced tomatoes, spinach, cheese and chopped tomatoes in greased 6-quart casserole. Sprinkle generously with oregano, salt and pepper. Repeat layers with remaining ingredients. Bake, uncovered, in preheated 375-degree oven for 30 to 40 minutes, or until vegetables are tender. Yield: 12-16 servings.

Mrs. Marian Tidwell, Woodville H. S.
Woodville, Texas

VEGETABLE GUMBO

2 tbsp. bacon drippings
1 med. onion, chopped
2 c. cut up fresh okra
2 fresh tomatoes, peeled and cut up
Salt and pepper to taste

Melt bacon drippings in 10-inch skillet. Saute onion until soft. Add okra; cover. Steam over low heat for 5 minutes. Add tomatoes, salt and pepper. Steam, covered, for 5 to 10 minutes. Do not stir.

Virginia Richards, Huntsville H. S.
Huntsville, Texas

VEGETABLE SOUFFLE

1 lg. can French-style string beans
1 sm. can diced carrots
1 sm. can peas
1 onion, chopped
Salt and pepper to taste
2 c. milk
¼ square butter
4 slices bread, cubed and trimmed
3 eggs, beaten
½ c. grated Tillamook cheese

Mix vegetables, onion, salt and pepper in buttered pan. Scald milk and butter. Add bread; remove pan from heat. Add beaten eggs. Pour over top of vegetables. Cover with grated Tillamook cheese. Bake for 45 minutes at 375 degrees.

Doris Waller, Chino H. S.
Chino, California

CHEESY ZUCCHINI BAKE

2 c. bread crumbs
1 clove of garlic, crushed
1 tsp. sweet basil
1 tsp. rosemary
1 tsp. parsley
½ tsp. salt
¼ tsp. pepper
5 sm. zucchini, thinly sliced
1 c. grated Parmesan cheese
½ c. oil

Mix bread crumbs, garlic, sweet basil, rosemary, parsley, salt and pepper in a medium bowl. Place half the zucchini slices in a greased 9-inch square pan. Top with a layer of bread crumbs mixture and half the cheese. Sprinkle with 4 tablespoons oil. Repeat layers, ending with remaining oil. Bake at 375

degrees for 1 hour to 1 hour and 30 minutes, or until golden brown. Yield: 6 servings.

Deborah Z. Block,
Plymouth Carver Intermediate Sch.
Plymouth, Massachusetts

COLORFUL ZUCCHINI CASSEROLE

1 lb. zucchini, cubed
1 12-oz. can whole kernel corn, drained
2 med. cloves of garlic, crushed
2 tbsp. salad oil
1 tsp. salt
¼ tsp. pepper
½ c. shredded mozzarella cheese

Combine all ingredients except cheese in a large skillet; cover. Cook over medium heat, stirring occasionally, for about 10 minutes, or until zucchini is crisp-tender. Stir in cheese; heat through.

Barbara Porter, Paradise Valley H. S.
Phoenix, Arizona

CURRIED ZUCCHINI

1 sm. zucchini, sliced thin
1 sm. green or white scallop squash, sliced thin
2 sm. onions, sliced
1 green tomato, sliced
½ green pepper, diced
2 to 3 tbsp. butter
1 tsp. curry powder
1 tsp. salt

Place all vegetables in skillet with butter and small amount of water. Add seasonings; cover. Cook over medium heat until vegetables are just tender.

Marian L. Earnhart, Morgan H. S.
McConnelsville, Ohio

PANNED ZUCCHINI WITH DILL

1 sprig fresh dill
½ sm. onion, chopped
2 tbsp. bacon drippings
4 c. sliced zucchini
½ tsp. salt
Pepper to taste

Saute dill and onion in hot drippings until golden. Add zucchini, salt and pepper. Cover; simmer for 10 minutes or until just tender, adding ¼ cup water, if needed. Yield: 4 servings.

Polly J. Hanst, Northern Garrett Sch.
Accident, Maryland

ZESTY ZUCCHINI

1 med. onion, chopped
1 clove of garlic, chopped
Cooking oil
1 med. zucchini, thinly sliced
1 12-oz. can stewed tomatoes, drained
⅛ tsp. oregano
⅛ tsp. Italian seasoning
¼ tsp. salt
1 c. shredded cheese

Sauté onion and garlic in small amount of oil. Add zucchini; sauté until tender. Add tomatoes and seasonings; mix well. Bake at 400 degrees for 15 minutes. Add cheese. Bake until cheese melts. Serve hot. Yield: 8 servings.

Kimberly C. Travis, Grove City H. S.
Grove City, Ohio

ZUCCHINI AU GRATIN

4 tbsp. butter
¼ c. chopped onion
1 clove of garlic, crushed
2 lbs. zucchini, cut in ½ inch chunks
½ tsp. salt
⅛ tsp. white pepper
16 cherry tomatoes, cut in half
4 oz. Cheddar cheese
½ c. soft bread crumbs

Melt 2 tablespoons butter in frypan. Saute onion and garlic. Add zucchini, salt and white pepper. Cook for 5 minutes. Layer zucchini mixture in buttered 1½-quart baking dish with tomatoes and cheese. Combine crumbs with 2 tablespoons melted butter. Sprinkle over casserole. Bake at 350 degrees for about 25 minutes. Yield: 6 servings.

Martha Love, R. B. Worthy H. S.
Saltville, Virginia

TASTY ZUCCHINI CASSEROLE

6 c. zucchini, sliced
½ c. chopped onion
1 can cream of chicken soup
1 c. sour cream
1 c. shredded carrots
Salt and pepper to taste
8 oz. package herb-seasoned stuffing mix
2 tbsp. margarine, melted

Cook zucchini and onions together over low heat for 5 minutes; drain. Combine soup, sour cream and carrots. Fold into squash and onion. Add salt and pepper. Combine stuffing mix and margarine. Spread ⅔ stuffing mixture in bottom of 9 x 13-inch pan. Add vegetable mixture. Sprinkle remaining stuffing mixture over top. Cover with foil. Bake at 350 degrees for 45 minutes, or until bubbly.

Florence Hodges, Corsicana H. S.
Corsicana, Texas

ZUCCHINI SUPREME

2 med. zucchini, washed and sliced
1 med. onion, diced
½ green pepper, diced
1 tsp. salt
1 8-oz. can tomato sauce
½ c. bread crumbs
½ c. grated cheese

Place zucchini in saucepan. Add onion, green pepper, salt, tomato sauce and 1 cup water. Cook, covered, until tender, 5 to 10 minutes. Pour into greased 1-quart casserole. Sprinkle with bread crumbs and cheese. Bake at 350 degrees for 25 to 30 minutes. May be frozen and reheated. Yield: 6-8 servings.

Barbara G. Harper, Copperas Cove H. S.
Copperas Cove, Texas

ZUCCHINI IN CREAM

6 sm. zucchini, cut in ½-in. slices
⅔ c. sour cream
1 tbsp. butter or margarine
6 tbsp. grated sharp Cheddar cheese
½ tsp. seasoned salt
3 tbsp. fresh bread crumbs

Simmer zucchini in water to cover for 10 minutes; drain well. Place in 8-inch baking dish. Combine sour cream, butter, 4 tablespoons cheese and salt in small saucepan; cook until well blended, stirring constantly. Pour over zucchini; top with bread crumbs and remaining 2 tablespoons cheese. Bake in preheated 375-degree oven for 10 minutes or until heated through and crumbs are golden. Let stand for 5 minutes before serving. Yield: 4 servings.

Ardis D. East, Ysleta H. S.
El Paso, Texas

ZUCCHINI WITH SOUR CREAM

3 med. zucchini
½ c. sour cream
2 tbsp. butter
2 tbsp. grated cheese
Salt and pepper to taste
Paprika to taste

1 tbsp. chopped chives
Bread cumbs

Slice unpared zucchini into thin rounds. Simmer zucchini in water to cover for 6 to 8 minutes. Shake pan frequently; drain. Combine sour cream, butter, cheese, salt, pepper and paprika in a saucepan. Stir over low heat to melt cheese. Remove from heat; mix in chives. Add zucchini; toss lightly to coat with sour cream mixture. Place in greased 1-quart baking dish. Top with crumbs, dot with additional butter. Sprinkle with additional grated cheese. Bake at 375 degrees for 10 minutes. Yield: 4 servings.

Ann Edwards, Duncanville High
Duncanviile, Texas

VEGETABLE TIMBALE

6 eggs, beaten
1 tsp. salt
2 oz. butter or margarine, melted
1 pt. milk
3 c. chopped vegetables, cooked

Combine eggs, salt, butter and milk; add vegetable. Turn into a 5 x 9-inch buttered pan; set pan in hot water. Bake at 325 degrees for 1 hour and 30 minutes or until firm. Test with silver knife. Turn out of pan; cut into twelve 2 x 5-inch portions. Serve with cheese sauce. Spinach, broccoli or asparagus may be used. Yield: 10 servings.

Elizabeth G. Voland, Franklin Comm. H. S.
Franklin, Indiana

LEBANESE GRAPE LEAF ROLLS

50 fresh grape leaves
1 c. uncooked rice
1 lb. uncooked ground beef or lamb
2 tsp. salt
4 lamb bones or 6 chicken wings or necks
Juice of 2 lemons

Soak grape leaves in hot water for 15 minutes to soften; remove from water. Squeeze out moisture; remove stems. Combine rice, ground beef and 1 teaspoon salt. Place 1 tablespoon stuffing on each leaf; fold end of leaf and roll. Place lamb bones in pan. Arrange stuffed leaves in rows in pan, alternating direction of each row. Sprinkle 1 teaspoon salt over stuffed leaves; press leaves down with inverted dish. Cover with water. Cover and cook on low heat for 35 minutes or until tender. Add lemon juice during last 10 minutes of cooking. Rhubarb stalks on bottom of pan add a delicious variation. Yield: 6 servings.

Mrs. Margaret Doyle, Wellsville H. S.
Wellsville, Ohio

VEGETABLE PLATTER

1 sm. cauliflower, cooked
1 can seasoned French-cut green beans, cooked
1 bunch carrots, cut lengthwise and cooked
1 can frozen shrimp soup
¼ c. evaporated milk
½ c. grated cheese
½ c. sliced almonds

Place cauliflower on round serving platter; alternate small portions of beans and carrots around cauliflower. Heat soup with milk and cheese; pour over vegetables. Sprinkle with almonds. Yield: 6 servings.

Helen F. Cade, Marengo County H. S.
Thomaston, Alabama

TURNIP GREENS WITH CORNMEAL DUMPLINGS

Turnip greens
½ c. sifted flour
1 tsp. baking powder
½ tsp. garlic salt
½ c. yellow cornmeal
⅛ tsp. pepper
1 egg
¼ c. milk
1 tbsp. melted butter

Cook turnips until done using plenty of liquid; remove turnips. Sift dry ingredients into mixing bowl; add egg, milk and butter. Stir until batter is well mixed. Drop dumplings by teaspoonfuls into simmering broth. Cover tightly; simmer for 15 minutes. Do not lift cover while dumplings cook. Chicken broth may used instead of turnip broth. Yield: 4 servings.

Mrs. Thelma L. Fowler, South Side Sch.
Counce, Tennessee

WATERCRESS SOUP

2 c. finely diced cooked pork
⅓ c. soy sauce
2 10½-oz. cans beef broth
1 bunch watercress, chopped
Sliced water chestnuts

Marinate pork in soy sauce for 2 hours, stirring occasionally. Blend broth and 2 broth cans water. Place pork in pan; add broth. Cover; bring to a gentle boil. Cook 15 to 20 minutes. Add watercress; stir to blend. Cook 5 minutes longer. Serve hot. Garnish with slices of water chestnuts. Yield:4-5 servings.

Mrs. Barbara Brannen, Lincoln-Sudbury H. S.
Sudbury, Massachusetts

Appetizers

Appetizers are all those delectable little hot and cold "finger foods" that you could nibble at for hours and still not get enough. But, that's the whole reason for appetizers! They are meant only to pique the appetite before a good meal, and not to satisfy it.

Hors d'oeuvres and canapes, the most typical appetizers can be served hot or cold, and include tiny open-faced sandwiches, bite-sized kabobs, crackers with meat and cheese spreads or dips, as well as olives, relishes, pickles, and salted nuts. When choosing before-dinner hors d'oeuvres, try not to use the same ingredients that will appear on the main menu. If the meal is hearty, select light appetizers; serve the more substantial ones before a light dinner.

Imagination plays the largest role in creating appetizers which are both tasty and colorful. The look of the hors d'oeuvres can be varied by different garnishing techniques—a twist of pimento here, a lemon slice there, a sprinkling of fresh herbs, a touch of colorful, candied fruit.

First course appetizers are served not so much to perk up the appetite, but rather to "take the edge off" so your diners can relax, eat slowly, and enjoy the fellowship. Wise selections might include avocado slices with grapefruit sections or seafood, a light soup such as French onion, tomato, vichyssoise, or cream soup, as well as a fruit, seafood, or yogurt cocktail.

Accompaniments call to mind the word "relish", meaning any number of nice things such as pleasure, enjoyment, zest, or an attractive quality. That is what accompaniments bring to a meal in the form of relishes, preserves, conserves, jams and jellies. Vegetable relishes are prepared from chopped or whole vegetables, and in addition to being sweet or sour, spiced or unspiced, they can be very colorful additions to a plate. Fruit relishes consist of chopped or small, whole fruits usually preserved with sugar, spices, or vinegar.

If you have never made any of your own preserves or relishes, and feel inspired to be creative in the kitchen, try some of the following recipes from Home Economics Teachers. The pleasurable result will be a shining array of jars on your pantry shelf. And, try your artistry with these appetizers from Home Economics Teachers. You will take pride in serving these delightful appetizers and accompaniments as often as possible.

BACON ROLL-UPS

1 loaf fresh bread
1 3 oz. package cream cheese, softened.
1 lb. bacon, cut in half

Trim edges from bread; cut in half. Spread with softened cream cheese. Roll up. Wrap with ½ slice bacon. Secure with toothpick. Bake at 300 degrees until brown on one side; turn and brown on the other side. Serve immediately. Yield: 24 servings.

Mary H. McMillin, Ripley H. S.
Ripley, Mississippi

KAREN'S CHEESE BALL

2 8-oz. packages cream cheese, softened
1 8-oz. can crushed pineapple, drained
½ c. diced green pepper
1 tsp. minced onion
1 tsp. seasoning salt
Fresh chopped parsley
2 c. chopped pecans

Combine cream cheese, pineapple, green pepper, onion, salt and enough parsley for color; mix well. Form into a ball. Roll in pecans. Refrigerate at least 24 hours before serving. Serve with favorite crackers.

Karen Sikes Lamar, Consolidated H. S.
Rosenberg, Texas

CAROLYN'S COLD CUT APPETIZERS

1 8-oz. package cream cheese, softened
1 8-oz. package bologna, or ham

Spread cream cheese on individual cold cut slices. Roll up. Wrap in plastic wrap. Chill for several hours or overnight. Cut into ¾ inch slices before serving. Garnish tops with pimento or parsley.

Carolyn S. Lovett, Lawton H. S.
Lawton, Oklahoma

COPONATINI

2 med. eggplant, cubed
Salt
Cooking oil
1 can tomato sauce
1 lg. onion, finely chopped
2 celery, stalks, finely chopped
1 clove of garlic, finely chopped
10 green olives, quartered
1 tsp. vinegar
Sugar to taste

Combine eggplant and 1 tablespoon salt; let stand for about 30 minutes. Squeeze out moisture lightly. Saute eggplant in 3 tablespoons hot cooking oil until tender. Stir in tomato sauce. Saute onion, celery, garlic and olives in small amount of hot oil until onion is transparent; stir in vinegar. Add to eggplant mixture; season with salt and sugar. Cook until flavors are blended. Serve as spread with crackers.

Mrs. Ted Trotter, Independence H. S.
Independence, Louisiana

EGGPLANT IN PASTRY

Salt
1 c. cooking oil
4½ c. (about) flour
1 med. eggplant, peeled and diced
¼ c. olive oil
1 sm. onion, chopped
1 med. tomato, diced
½ med. green pepper, chopped (opt.)
Pepper to taste
Sugar to taste
1 tbsp. minced parsley
1 egg, beaten
Sesame seed (opt.)

Combine 1 cup water, 1 teaspoon salt and cooking oil in large mixing bowl. Add enough flour to make a dough the consistency of pie pastry. Cover bowl; set aside. Place eggplant in bowl of salted water. Heat olive oil in large skillet. Add onion; saute until transparent. Drain eggplant well. Add to onion; simmer, covered, for 15 minutes, stirring occasionally. Stir in tomato and green pepper; season with salt, pepper and sugar. Stir in parsley. Simmer, covered, until eggplant is tender, stirring frequently. Pinch off small pieces of dough; roll out in circles 2½ inches in diameter and ⅛ inch thick. Place 1 tablespoon eggplant mixture in each circle; fold over dough to form half circles. Press edges together firmly. Place on cookie sheet; brush tops with egg. Sprinkle with sesame seeds. Bake in preheated 375-degree oven until lightly browned. Serve immediately.

Mrs. Carole O'Donnell, Weldon Valley Sch.
Weldona, Colorado

FESTIVE FRUIT KABOBS

½ grapefruit
Melon balls
Whole strawberries
Pineapple chunks
Banana chunks

Place grapefruit, cut side down, on serving plate. Place a melon ball, strawberry, pineapple chunk and banana chunk on each skewer; insert skewers into grapefruit. May be used as centerpiece, if desired.

Mrs. Ralph Shipman, Paris H. S.
Paris, Texas

HIGH HAT MUSHROOMS IN WINE SAUCE

16 fresh mushrooms
½ lb. ground sausage
1 cup tomato sauce
1 c. white wine
½ clove of garlic, mashed
⅛ tsp. oregano

Remove stems of mushrooms; set caps aside. Chop stems; mix with sausage. Stuff caps with sausage mixture, rounding stuffing into high crown; place in baking dish. Bake in 350-degree oven for 30 minutes. Remove from oven. Heat tomato sauce, wine, garlic and oregano in chafing dish, mixing well. Add mushrooms; cover. Let mushrooms heat through in wine sauce. Serve with toothpicks.

Mrs. Katheryn Chambers, Wayne City Sch.
Wayne, Nebraska

LEBANESE APPETIZERS

1 19-oz. can garbanzos, well drained
1 tsp. salt
1 clove of garlic
½ c. olive oil or salad oil
1 tbsp. lemon juice

Combine garbanzos, salt and garlic in blender container; process until pureed. Add olive oil in a fine stream with blender running; process until thickened. Blend in lemon juice. Serve as a spread with crackers; garnish with chopped parsley and paprika.

Mrs. Jeanne Bundi, Van Buren Sch.
Van Buren, Ohio

MOCK OYSTERS ROCKEFELLER

1 onion, finely chopped
Margarine
1 lg. can mushrooms, drained and minced
1 can cream of mushroom soup
1 pkg. chopped broccoli, cooked
1 roll garlic cheese
Hot sauce to taste

Saute onion in margarine until transparent. Add remaining ingredients; heat through. Serve hot with crackers.

Mrs. Lucille Gelpi, Hahnville H. S.
Hahnville, Louisiana

SAUSAGE BALLS

3 c. Bisquick
1 lb. hot sausage
1 lb. sharp cheese, grated

Combine Bisquick, sausage and grated cheese; mix into soft dough. Roll into balls the size of walnuts. Bake at 350° until lightly browned, about 15 minutes. Serve hot. Yield: 40 balls.

Jo Ann Glass, Meade County Middle Sch.
Brandenburg, Kentucky

COCKTAIL SPINACH BALLS

2 10-oz. packages frozen chopped spinach
2 c. herb-seasoned dressing mix, crushed
1 c. grated Parmesan cheese
6 eggs, slightly beaten
¾ c. softened butter
Salt and pepper to taste

Cook spinach; drain. Combine all ingredients; mix well. Shape into walnut-sized balls. Place on ungreased cookie sheets. Bake for 10 minutes at 350°. Serve hot with toothpicks. May be made ahead and frozen. Yield: 50 balls.

Marilyn M. Cipov, Winona Sr. H. S.
Winona, Minnesota

POPEYE BALLS

2 c. chopped cooked spinach
2 tbsp. margarine, melted
Salt and pepper to taste
2 eggs
Bread crumbs
2 tbsp. grated onion
2 tbsp. grated cheese
⅛ tsp. allspice

Combine spinach, melted margarine, salt, pepper, 1 well beaten egg, 1 cup bread crumbs, onion, cheese and allspice; mix well. Allow to stand for 10 minutes. Shape into walnut-sized balls. Combine remaining egg and ¼ cup water; beat until well blended. Roll balls in bread crumbs; dip in egg mixture, then in bread crumbs. Fry in hot deep fat until golden brown. Drain on paper towels. Serve immediately.

Johnna R. Husarek, Rosepine H. S.
Rosepine, Louisiana

TASTY SPINACH BALLS

3 eggs, beaten
1 c. Pepperidge farm dressing mix
1 onion, chopped
⅜ c. melted butter
½ tsp. garlic salt
¼ tsp. thyme
¼ tsp. pepper
¼ c. Parmesan cheese
1 pkg. chopped spinach, cooked and drained

Combine all ingredients in order listed; mix well. Chill for at least 3 hours or overnight. Shape into 1½-inch balls. Place on ungreased cookie sheet. Bake in 350-degree oven for 20 minutes.

Mrs. Robert Crowell, Nauset Middle Sch.
Orleans, Maine

SPINACH QUICHE

½ c. margarine
3 eggs
1 c. flour
1 c. milk
½ tsp. salt
1 tsp. baking powder
½ lb. Monterey Jack cheese, grated
4 c. fresh, uncooked chopped spinach

Melt margarine in 9 x 13-inch pan. Beat eggs with flour, milk, salt and baking powder. Add cheese and spinach; mix well. Pour into pan. Do not stir. Bake at 350 degrees for 35 minutes. Cool for 30 minutes before cutting. Yield: 48 servings.

Arlene Gallipeau, Falmouth H. S.
Falmouth, Massachusetts

SPICED PINEAPPLE PICKUPS

1 No. 2½ can pineapple chunks
¾ c. vinegar
1¼ c. sugar
Dash of salt
6 to 8 whole cloves
1 4-in. stick cinnamon

Drain pineapple; reserve ¾ cup syrup. Combine pineapple syrup and remaining ingredients in saucepan; bring to a boil. Simmer for 10 minutes. Add pineapple chunks; return to a boil. Let cool; chill in refrigerator until ready to serve. Remove pineapple chunks from syrup; serve with toothpicks.

Cheryle DeVan, Rio Vista Joint Union H. S.
Rio Vista, California

STUFFED CELERY

2½ c. grated Cheddar cheese
2 tbsp. mayonnaise
1 sm. clove of garlic, chopped fine
1 jar pimentos, chopped
1 bunch celery

Combine cheese, mayonnaise, garlic and pimentos; mix well. Set aside. Remove leaves from outer celery stalks; trim wide ends. Cut stalks into about 3-inch pieces. Chill in ice water for 1 hour. Drain well. Fill centers with cheese mixture.

Mrs. D. J. Dear, Stringer H. S.
Bay Springs, Mississippi

BLENDER AVOCADO DIP

2 avocados, chopped
2 hard-cooked eggs, chopped
Juice of 1 lg. onion
Juice of 1 lemon
3 tbsp. salad dressing
Tabasco sauce to taste
Salt to taste

Place avocados and eggs in blender container; process until pureed. Add remaining ingredients; process to mix well.

Mrs. Joel Ferrell, Brinkley H. S.
Brinkley, Arkansas

FAVORITE AVOCADO DIP

1 c. mashed avocado
1 8-oz. package cream cheese, softened
¼ c. lemon juice
1 tsp. salt
½ tsp. grated onion or onion salt
¼ tsp. steak sauce

Mix avocado and cream cheese together until smooth. Stir in remaining ingredients; mix well. Serve with crackers or potato chips.

Clarinda A. Britt, Maiden H. S.
Maiden, North Carolina

GREEN GODDESS DIP

1 ripe avocado
1 c. sour cream
¼ c. mayonnaise
½ tsp. salt
½ tsp. seasoned salt

½ c. finely chopped parsley
¼ c. finely chopped green onions

Mash avocado. Stir in sour cream and mayonnaise; mix well. Add salt and seasoned salt; fold in parsley and onions. Serve with potato chips or crackers. Yield: 2½ cups.

Mrs. Marie Lovil, McLeod H. S.
McLeod, Texas

BROCCOLI DIP

1 pkg. frozen chopped broccoli
1 med. onion, chopped
1 c. chopped celery
1 lg. can mushrooms
1 roll garlic cheese spread, cubed

Prepare broccoli according to package directions. Sauté onion, celery and mushrooms in hot oil until clear and tender. Drain. Add to drained broccoli. Add garlic cheese. Melt at low temperature in a double boiler. Serve hot with fresh vegetables.

Mrs. Kay Moyers, Pine Tree H. S.
Longview, Texas

CARROT DIP

3 carrots
3 dill pickles
1 sm. jar pimentos
2 green peppers
1 sm. onion
3 hard-cooked eggs, chopped
Salt and pepper to taste
Mayonnaise

Put carrots, dill pickles, pimentos, green peppers and onion through food chopper; drain well. Add eggs to carrot mixture; season with salt and pepper. Stir in enough mayonnaise to hold mixture together and moisten as desired.

Mrs. Jane Wisdom, Hillsboro H. S.
Hillsboro, Illinois

CONFETTI DIP

1 pkg. dry onion soup mix
1 pt. sour cream
¼ c. finely chopped green pepper
¼ c. finely chopped cucumber
¼ c. finely diced pimento

Combine all ingredients; chill for at least 1 hour to blend flavors. Serve with assorted crackers or chips.

Mrs. Vada Belle Zellner, South San Antonio Sr. H. S.
San Antonio, Texas

CUCUMBER DIP

½ c. shredded unpeeled cucumber
1 8-oz. package cream cheese, softened
¼ tsp. Worcestershire sauce
Dash of garlic salt

Drain cucumber well. Combine cream cheese and cucumber; mix well. Stir in Worcestershire sauce and garlic sauce. Serve with potato chips.

Mrs. Grace E. Kukuk, Negaunee H. S.
Negaunee, Michigan

HOT MUSHROOM DIP

1 lb. fresh mushrooms, sliced
1 clove of garlic, crushed
1 sm. onion, grated
2 tbsp. butter
¼ tsp. Accent
⅛ tsp. mustard
½ tsp. soy sauce
⅛ tsp. paprika
⅛ tsp. salt
⅛ tsp. pepper
1 tbsp. flour
1 c. sour cream

Saute mushrooms, garlic and onion in butter until golden. Combine Accent, mustard, soy sauce, paprika, salt, pepper and flour; stir in enough sour cream to make a smooth paste. Stir into mushroom mixture; mix well. Stir in remaining sour cream; cook over low heat until thickened, stirring constantly. Do not boil. Serve hot with crackers or potato chips. Yield: 2 cups.

Annie Lillian Brewton, Escambia H. S.
Pensacola, Florida

FRUIT DIP

¼ c. strawberry jam
1 3-oz. package cream cheese
1 c. Cool Whip

Cream jam and cream cheese together thoroughly. Fold in Cool Whip. Chill. Thin with milk if dip becomes too thick. Serve with chunks of fresh fruit such as strawberries, bananas, apples and pears.

Cheryl C. Elsberry, Westland H. S.
Galloway, Ohio

JICAMA STICKS AND DIP

1 lg. jicama, peeled
Assorted raw vegetables
1 recipe onion dip

Cut jicama into finger-sized sticks. Arrange with assorted raw vegtables on platter. Prepare onion dip. Serve with vegetables.

Barbara Smith, Corona del Sol H. S.
Tempe, Arizona

SOUR CREAM VEGETABLE CHUTNEY

1 c. sour cream
1 c. yogurt
¼ c. chopped chives
¼ c. chopped onion
1 c. chopped celery
1 med. cucumber, chopped
1 lg. tomato, chopped
¼ c. chopped ripe olives
1 tbsp. horseradish
1 tsp. sugar
1 tsp. salt
1 tsp. pepper

Combine all ingredients; mix well. Chill until needed. Serve as a dip with vegetables or potato chips. May be served as an accompaniment with corned beef brisket. Yield: 3 cups.

Mrs. Maureen O'Neill, Belmont Community Sch.
Belmont, Wisconsin

TEXAS CAVIAR

2 No. 2 cans black-eyed peas, drained
⅓ c. peanut oil
⅓ c. wine vinegar
1 clove of garlic
¼ c. finely chopped onion
½ tsp. salt
Freshly ground pepper to taste

Combine all ingredients in mixing bowl; mix well. Cover; chill in refrigerator for at least 24 hours. Remove garlic before serving. Will keep for 2 weeks.

Mrs. Rachel Pearce, Castleberry H. S.
Fort Worth, Texas

CAROL'S FRESH VEGETABLE DIP

1 c. mayonnaise
Salad Supreme Seasoning to taste
Celery sticks

Carrots sticks
Cherry tomatoes
Bell pepper slices
Mushrooms
Cauliflower

Mix mayonnaise and salad seasoning; chill. Wash and dry vegetables. Arrange on platter. Serve with dip. Recipe can be doubled.

Carol Stallard, Monroney J. H. S
Midwest City, Oklahoma

RUTH ANN'S VEGETABLE DIP

1 pkg. Hidden Valley Ranch-style salad
    dressing mix
1 c. mayonnaise
1 c. milk

Mix all ingredients together. Serve with any raw vegetables. One small carton creamy cottage cheese may be substituted for mayonnaise and milk.

Ruth Ann Eckel Star, Spencer H. S.
Spencer, Oklahoma

VEGETABLE CONFETTI DIP

1 green pepper, finely chopped
1 tomato, finely chopped
1 bunch green onions, finely chopped
1 8-oz. package cream cheese, softened
½ c. sour cream
1 tsp. dry mustard
1 tsp. salt
½ tsp. pepper

Combine all ingredients in small bowl. Blend well. Chill for several hours. Serve with broccoli, cauliflower, celery, cherry tomatoes, cucumber slices and green peppers.

Janet R. Boroff, Elmwood Jr. H. S.
Cygnet, Ohio

VEGETABLE MIX

1 pkg. Good Seasons Italian dressing mix
Cauliflower, cut up
Broccoli, cut up
Carrots, diagonally sliced

Prepare dressing mix according to package directions. Pour over fresh vegetables. Marinate overnight. Serve as an hors d'oeuvres.

Jenny L. Curtis, Orrville H. S.
Orrville, Ohio

BAKED STUFFED MUSHROOMS

24 lg. mushrooms
Lemon juice
Butter
¼ c. grated Swiss cheese
Bread crumbs
Salt and pepper to taste
¼ c. minced parsley
1 clove of garlic, minced
2 tbsp. minced onion
¼ c. Sherry

Remove stems from mushrooms, leaving caps intact. Sprinkle each mushoom cap with several drops of lemon juice; set aside. Mince stems; saute in 3 tablespoons butter until golden. Combine cheese and ½ cup bread crumbs; season with salt and pepper. Add parsley, garlic, onion, Sherry and mushroom stems; mix well. Pile stuffing into mushroom caps; sprinkle with bread crumbs. Dot with butter. Place in baking dish. Bake in 350-degree oven for 15 minutes or until heated through. Serve as an accompaniment or as an appetizer.

Mrs. Jo Anne Sandager, Stillwater Jr. H. S.
Stillwater, Minnesota

PRUNE CATSUP

9 c. coarsely ground fresh prunes
4 c. sugar
1 c. vinegar
3 tsp. cinnamon
1½ tsp. cloves

Combine all ingredients in kettle; cook over medium heat until mixture reaches desired thickness. Pour into sterilized jars; seal. Process in hot water bath for 10 minutes to complete seal. Yield: 7 pints.

Lucille Cook, Wilmer-Hutchins H. S.
Hutchins, Texas

TOMATO CATSUP

20 lb. tomatoes, peeled and chopped
6 onions, peeled and chopped
4 sweet red peppers, seeded and chopped
2 c. vinegar
1½ c. sugar
2 tbsp. salt
¼ c. paprika
2 tsp. celery seed
1 tsp. whole allspice
1 tsp. whole cloves
3 oz. cinnamon sticks

Combine tomatoes; onions and red peppers in kettle; cook until mushy. Press through strainer. Pour juice into kettle; add vinegar, sugar, salt and paprika. Tie remaining spices in cloth bag; place in kettle. Mix well; bring to a boil. Simmer until mixture reaches desired thickness. Remove cloth bag; pour catsup into sterilized jars. Seal. Process in hot water bath for 10 minutes to complete seal.

Beatrice Campbell, Leland Consolidated Sch.
Leland, Mississippi

APPLE CHILI SAUCE

12 tomatoes, ground
12 apples, ground
8 onions, ground
12 sm. sweet red peppers, ground
2 c. vinegar
5 tsp. salt
4 c. sugar

Combine all ingredients in kettle; simmer for 45 minutes or until thick. Pour into sterilized jars; seal. Process in hot water bath for 10 minutes to complete seal. Yield: 6 pints.

Mrs. Ellen Morgan Schenck, Wilson Area H. S.
West Lawn, Pennsylvania

TASTY CHILI SAUCE

4 qt. chopped peeled ripe tomatoes
2 c. chopped onions
2 c. chopped sweet red or green peppers
1 hot red pepper, minced
1 c. sugar
3 tbsp. salt
3 tbsp. mixed pickling spices
1 tbsp. celery seed
1 tbsp. mustard seed
2 c. vinegar

Combine tomatoes, onions, sweet peppers, hot pepper, sugar and salt in kettle; simmer for 45 minutes. Tie spices in cheesecloth bag; add to tomato mixture. Cook for 45 minutes or until thick, stirring frequently to prevent sticking. Add vinegar; simmer until mixture reaches desired thickness. Pour into sterilized jars, leaving ⅛-inch head space. Adjust caps; seal. Process in hot water bath for 10 minutes to complete seal. Yield: 6 pints.

Avis Elizabeth Mullins, Franklin H. S.
Meadville, Mississippi

CHUTNEY SUPREME

3 tbsp. whole allspice
12 apples, ground
12 green tomatoes, ground
12 onions, ground
3 green peppers, ground
2 sweet red peppers, ground
3 c. sugar
3 tbsp. salt
3 c. vinegar
1 tsp. (scant) ground cloves
1 tsp. (scant) red pepper

Tie allspice in cloth bag. Combine all ingredients in kettle; bring to a boil. Simmer for 30 minutes or until thickened, stirring occasionally. Remove cloth bag. Pour chutney into sterilized jars; seal. Process in hot water bath for 10 minutes to complete seal.

Mrs. Peggy Hendrickson, Lone Jack H. S.
Fourmile, Kentucky

PEAR CHUTNEY

6 c. chopped pears
1½ c. raisins
1 onion, chopped
1 sm. cabbage, ground
4 stalks celery, ground
1½ c. (packed) brown sugar
3 tbsp. salt
1 tsp. dry mustard
1 tsp. turmeric
1 qt. vinegar

Combine pears, raisins, onion, cabbage, celery, brown sugar, salt and spices in kettle; pour vinegar over top. Simmer for 45 minutes, stirring occasionally. Pack into sterilized jars; seal. Process in hot water bath for 10 minutes to complete seal. Yield: 5 pints.

Mrs. Eva Herbert, Beaumont H. S.
Beaumont, Texas

CINNAMON APPLE BUTTER

3 qt. canned applesauce
10 c. sugar
½ c. vinegar
1 c. cinnamon candies

Combine all ingredients in kettle; simmer for 20 to 25 minutes or until candies dissolve and mixture is thick, stirring frequently. Pour into sterilized jars; seal. Process in hot water bath for 10 minutes to complete seal. Yield: 6 pints.

Susan Holbrook, Blackford H. S.
San Jose, California

HEAVENLY CONSERVE DELIGHT

6 c. sliced fresh peaches
3 c. halved white seedless grapes
2 c. diced pineapple
2 c. diced peeled red plums
2 lemons, peeled, seeded and diced
1 c. orange juice
9 c. sugar

Combine all ingredients; let stand for several hours or overnight. Cook ⅓ of the mixture at a time until thick, stirring frequently. Pour into sterilized jars; seal. Process in hot water bath for 10 minutes to complete seal. Yield: 7 pints.

Mrs. Marjorie Hall, Normantown H. S.
Normantown, West Virginia

PEACH AND CANTALOUPE CONSERVE

2 c. diced peaches
2 c. diced cantaloupe
Grated rind and juice of 2 lemons
⅔ c. chopped blanched English walnuts

Combine all ingredients except walnuts in saucepan; cook until thick and clear, stirring frequently. Stir in walnuts. Pour into sterilized jars; seal. Process in hot water bath for 10 minutes to compelete seal. Yield: 3 pints.

Sister Mary Carmelito, Regis H. S.
Cedar Rapids, Iowa

PEAR CONSERVE ROYALE

3 c. sliced peeled pears
2½ c. sugar
1 c. seedless raisins
Chopped rind of ½ orange
Juice of 1 orange
Juice of 1 lemon
1 c. chopped nuts

Combine pears and sugar; let stand overnight. Combine pears, raisins, orange rind, orange juice, lemon juice and nuts in saucepan; bring to a boil. Simmer for 30 to 35 minutes or until thick. Pour into sterilized jars; seal. Process in hot water bath for 10 minutes to complete seal. Yield: 2 pints.

Mrs. Charles Yount, Bandys H. S
Catawba, North Carolina

PEARS HARLEQUIN

4 lb. pears, peeled and thinly sliced
1 No. 2½ can crushed pineapple
3 oranges, thinly sliced
12 c. sugar
1 c. maraschino cherries

Combine pears, pineapple, oranges and sugar in kettle; let stand overnight. Simmer for 1 hour and 20 minutes, stirring frequently. Add cherries; cook for 10 minutes longer. Pour into sterilized jars; seal. Process in hot water bath for 10 minutes to complete seal. Yield: 7 pints.

Marie A. Yenne, North Kitsap H. S.
Poulsbo, Washington

TUTTI-FRUTTI CONSERVE

3 c. chopped pears
1 lg. orange, seeded and chopped
¾ c. drained crushed pineapple
½ c. maraschino cherries
½ c. lemon juice
½ c. chopped nuts
1 c. coconut
1 pkg. powdered pectin
5 c. sugar

Combine pears, orange, pineapple, cherries, lemon juice, nuts and coconut in large heavy saucepan; stir in pectin. Bring to a boil over high heat, stirring constantly. Add sugar. Bring to a rolling boil; boil hard for 1 minute, stirring constantly. Remove from heat. Skim off foam; stir for 5 minutes. Pour into hot sterilized jars; seal. Process in hot water bath for 10 minutes to complete seal.

Sallie P. Satterly, Hitchins H. S.
Hitchins, Kentucky

DILLED ONION RINGS

1 lg. Spanish onion
½ c. sugar
½ tsp. dillseed
2 tsp. salt
½ c. white vinegar

Slice onion; separate into rings. Place onion rings in bowl. Combine remaining ingredients in saucepan; stir in ¼ cup water. Bring to a boil. Pour over onion rings; let stand overnight. Serve as an accompaniment.

Mrs. Madra Fischer, Mendota H. S.
Mendota, Illinois

GOLDEN MARMALADE

1 lb. dried apricots, cup up
1 1-lb. 4-oz. can crushed pineapple
½ c. lemon juice
8 c. sugar

Combine apricots, pineapple, lemon juice, 4 cups water and sugar in saucepan; blend well. Cook over medium heat for 25 minutes or until mixture comes to a rolling boil, stirring frequently. Boil for 35 minutes or until thick. Ladle into hot sterilized jars; seal with paraffin. Yield: Twelve 8-ounce glasses.

Margery M. Bartlett, Zilwaukee Jr. H. S.
Saginaw, Michigan

HOLIDAY JAM

2 10-oz. packages frozen strawberries
2 c. fresh cranberries
4 c. sugar

Thaw strawberries. Place half the cranberries in blender container; cover. Process at high speed, turning control on and off several times to chop cranberries. Empty into saucepan. Chop remaining cranberries; place in saucepan. Add strawberries and sugar. Bring to a boil. Boil until thick, stirring frequently. Pour into sterilized glasses; seal with paraffin. Yield: Five 8-ounce glasses.

Sister Mary Cordia, Academy of Our Lady
Chicago, Illinois

PEACH-WALNUT JAM

4 c. chopped peaches
½ c. chopped walnuts
¼ c. lemon juice
7 c. sugar
½ bottle liquid fruit pectin

Combine peaches, walnuts, lemon juice and sugar in large heavy saucepan; bring to a rolling boil. Boil hard for 1 minute, stirring constantly. Remove from heat; stir in fruit pectin immediately. Skim off foam, using metal spoon. Stir for 5 minutes or until slightly cooled to prevent fruit from floating. Skim well. Ladle jam quickly into sterilized glasses; cover with ⅛-inch layer of hot paraffin.

Clara Barrows, Groton H. S.
Groton, South Dakota

DIETETIC STRAWBERRY JAM

4 c. strawberries
3 to 4 tsp. liquid sweetener
1 ¾-oz. package powdered fruit pectin
1 tbsp. unsweetened lemon juice
½ tsp. ascorbic acid (opt.)

Crush strawberries in 1½-quart saucepan. Stir in liquid sweetener, fruit pectin and lemon juice. Add ascorbic acid. Bring to a boil; boil for 1 minute. Remove from heat. Continue to stir for 2 minutes. Pour into freezer containers; cover. Freeze. Thaw before serving. Store in refrigerator after opening. Jam will be slightly thinner in consistency than regular jams. Can be used as sauces or topping. Yield: 2⅝cups.

Mary Jane Miller, Miller City H. S.
Miller City, Ohio

FREEZER STRAWBERRY JAM

1¾ c. crushed fresh strawberries
4 c. sugar
2 tbsp. lemon juice
½ bottle fruit pectin

Place strawberries in large bowl; stir in sugar. Let stand until sugar is dissolved. Combine lemon juice and pectin; stir into strawberries. Stir continuously for 3 minutes. Ladle into jars; cover tightly. Let stand until jam is set. Store in freezer.

Vivian Delene, Baraga H. S.
Baraga, Michigan

FRESH STRAWBERRY PRESERVES

4 c. fresh strawberries
1 tbsp. vinegar
4 to 5 c. sugar

Boil strawberries and vinegar in large kettle for 1 minute. Add sugar; boil for 20 minutes, stirring frequently. Let stand in kettle until cool. Pour into sterilized jars; seal with paraffin. Yield: 2 pints.

Margaret Sloop, South Rowan H. S.
China Grove, North Carolina

MOCK STRAWBERRY JAM

6 c mashed fresh figs
3 c. sugar
2 pkg. strawberry gelatin

Combine all ingredients in large kettle; bring to a boil over medium heat. Reduce heat; simmer for 45

minutes, stirring frequently. Pour into sterilized glasses; seal with paraffin. Yield: 4-5 pints.

Mrs. Irvin Derangeo, Sunset H. S.
Sunset, Louisiana

WHOLE STRAWBERRY JAM

2 c. large firm strawberries
2 c. sugar

Place layer of strawberries in saucepan; top with layer of sugar. Repeat layers until all ingredients are used. Let stand overnight. Bring to a boil; boil for 10 minutes. Pour into bowl; let stand overnight. Fill sterilized glasses; seal with paraffin. Yield: 2 cups jam.

Mrs. Diana Ulbricht, Freeland H. S.
Freeland, Michigan

HOT PEPPER JELLY

¼ c. chopped hot green peppers
¼ c. chopped sweet green peppers
6½ c. sugar
1½ c. cider vinegar
1 6-oz. bottle fruit pectin
Red or green food coloring

Combine peppers, sugar and vinegar in saucepan; bring to a rolling boil. Boil for 10 minutes. Remove from heat; add fruit pectin and food coloring. Pour into sterilized baby food jars; seal with paraffin.

Mrs. Estelle Hottel, Dimmitt H. S.
Dimmitt, Texas

NO-COOK RASPBERRY JELLY

2½ qt. ripe raspberries
6 c. sugar
1 pkg. powdered pectin

Crush raspberries. Place in jelly bag; squeeze out juice. Add sugar; mix well. Combine ¾ cup water and pectin in saucepan; bring to a boil. Boil for 1 minute, stirring constantly. Stir into juice; stir for 3 minutes. Pour into jars; cover with tight lids. Let stand at room temperature for 24 hours. Store in freezer. Yield: Eight 8-ounce jars.

Britt Wedin, Patrick Henry H. S.
Minneapolis, Minnesota

ORANGE JUICE JELLY

1 6-oz. can frozen orange juice concentrate
1 box fruit pectin
3½ c. sugar

Thaw orange juice concentrate. Combine pectin and 2 cups water in saucepan; bring to a rolling boil. Boil hard for 1 minute, stirring constantly. Reduce heat to low. Add orange juice concentrate and sugar; stir until sugar is dissolved. Do not boil. Remove from heat; skim off foam. Pour quickly into sterilized glasses; seal with ⅛-inch layer of paraffin.

Lacquita Olson, Washington H. S.
Sioux Falls, South Dakota

PARADISE JELLY

5 lb. Jonathan apples or tart apples
2½ lb. quinces
1 lb. cranberries
Sugar

Dice apples and quinces; place in kettle. Add a small amount of water; cook until tender. Place in jelly bag; strain well to remove all juice. Cook cranberries in small amount of water in saucepan until tender. Place in jelly bag; strain to remove all juice. Combine juices; measure into kettle. Bring to a boil. Add equal amount of sugar; cook for 15 to 20 minutes or until jelly sheets from a spoon. Pour into sterilized glasses; seal with paraffin.

Mrs. Frances Steube, Groveport-Madison H. S.
Groveport, Ohio

PEAR-PINEAPPLE HONEY

6 c. chopped pears
2 No. 2½ cans crushed pineapple and juice
1 6-oz. bottle maraschino cherries, chopped
2 lemons, diced
2½ c. sugar

Combine all ingredients in kettle; simmer for 3 hours or until thick, stirring frequently. Pour into sterilized jars; seal. Process in hot water bath for 10 minutes to complete seal. Yield: 6 pints.

Mrs. Elizabeth S. Richardson, Orangeburg H. S.
Orangeburg, South Carolina

CANTALOUPE PICKLES

2 med. cantaloupes
1 qt. white vinegar
2 sticks cinnamon, broken
½ tsp. mace
15 whole cloves
4 c. sugar

Remove rind and seeds from cantaloupes; cut into 1 x 3-inch chunks. Bring 2 cups water and vinegar to a rolling boil; add cinnamon. Tie mace and cloves in cheesecloth bag; add to vinegar solution. Pour over cantaloupe; let stand in refrigerator overnight. Drain solution from cantaloupe; bring to a rolling boil. Add sugar, stirring until dissolved. Add cantaloupe chunks; cook for 20 to 30 minutes or until transparent. Remove bag of spices. Pack cantaloupe into sterilized jars. Add hot syrup; seal. Process in hot water bath for 10 minutes to complete seal. Yield: 3½ pints.

Mrs. Sallie Beville Fisher, Lee Davis H. S.
Mechanicsville, Virginia

CHERRY OLIVES

2 lb. fresh Bing cherries
1 c. vinegar
1 tbsp. sugar
3 tbsp. salt

Pack cherries into 6 sterilized pint jars. Combine 3 cups water and remaining ingredients in saucepan; cook until sugar and salt have dissolved, stirring constantly. Let cool. Pour syrup over cherries; seal jars. Process in hot water bath for 10 minutes to complete seal.

Mrs. Patsy Howsley Mayer, Kermit H. S.
Kermit, Texas

ALABAMA CUCUMBER PICKLES

3 gal. cucumbers
1 c. salt
3 tbsp. alum
8 c. sugar
8 c. vinegar
3 tbsp. mixed pickling spices

Place cucumbers in stone crock; add salt and enough boiling water to cover. Let stand for 7 days. Drain off brine; prick each cucumber twice with a fork. Place in crock. Add alum; cover with boiling water. Let stand for 24 hours. Drain; cover with boiling water. Let stand until cold. Pack in 8 sterilized quart jars. Combine remaining ingredients in large saucepan; bring to a boil. Pour over pickles; seal. Process in hot water bath for 10 minutes to complete seal.

Mildred Mason, Cherokee Vocational H. S.
Cherokee, Alabama

BREAD AND BUTTER PICKLES

6 qt. sliced cucumbers
6 med. onions, sliced
6 sweet green peppers, sliced
1 c. salt
6 c. vinegar
6 c. sugar
½ c. mustard seed
1 tsp. celery seed
1 tsp. turmeric

Combine cucumbers, onions, sweet peppers and salt in ice water to cover; let stand for 3 hours. Combine vinegar, sugar, mustard seed, celery seed and turmeric in kettle; bring to a boil. Add drained sweet peppers, onions and cucumbers; simmer for 5 minutes. Pack cucumber mixture into sterilized jars; cover with vinegar mixture. Seal. Process in hot water bath for 10 minutes to complete seal.

Mrs. Alice K. Ray, East H. S.
Memphis, Tennessee

CUBED MUSTARD PICKLES

12 6-in. long cucumbers
1 cauliflower, cut up
1 bunch celery, cut into ½-in. pieces
4 sweet green peppers, diced
4 sweet red peppers, diced
1 qt. small pickling onions
½ c. salt
1½ qt. cider vinegar
1½ c. sugar
2 tsp. white mustard seed
2 tsp. celery seed
½ c. flour
1 tsp. (heaping) turmeric
1 tsp. (heaping) dry mustard
¼ c. white vinegar

Cut cucumbers into chunks. Combine cucumbers, cauliflower, celery, green peppers, red peppers and onions in large bowl. Sprinkle with salt; cover with water. Let stand for 3 hours. Drain well; place cucumber mixture in large kettle. Combine cider vinegar, sugar, mustard seed and celery seed in saucepan; bring to a slow boil. Mix flour, turmeric and mustard together. Combine white vinegar and ¼ cup water; stir enough vinegar mixture into flour mixture to make a thin paste. Add paste to cider vinegar mixture; mix well. Stir into cucumber mixture; bring to a boil. Simmer for 15 minutes. Pack into sterilized jars; seal. Process in hot water bath for 10 minutes to complete seal.

Mrs. Joyce Shull, Clare H. S.
Clare, Michigan

CUCUMBER SPECIAL

24 lg. sour cucumber pickles
5 lb. sugar
1 tsp. salt
2 cloves of garlic
2 tsp. tarragon vinegar
2 oz. pickling spices

Cut pickles into ½-inch slices. Place alternate layers of pickles, sugar, seasonings and spices in gallon crock. Stir each day for 7 days. May seal in sterilized jars, if desired.

Lorene Featherstone, Northside Sch.
Jackson, Tennessee

DILL DANDIES

24 lg. cucumbers
Powdered alum
Cloves of garlic
Fresh dill
Hot red pepper (opt.)
4 c. cider vinegar
1 c. coarse salt
Grape leaves (opt.)

Cover cucumbers with cold water; let stand in cool place overnight. Pack cucumbers in sterilized jars. Add ⅛ teaspoon powdered alum, 1 clove of garlic, 2 heads dill and 1 strip hot red pepper to each jar. Combine vinegar, salt and 6 cups water; bring to a boil. Fill jars with hot vinegar solution; top each with fresh grape leaf. Seal immediately. Process in hot water bath for 10 minutes to complete seal. Store in cool place for 6 weeks before using.

Mrs. Milton McNea, Huntley Project H. S.
Worden, Montana

SUPER DILL PICKLES

Cucumbers
Garlic cloves (opt.)
Fresh dill
1 qt. vinegar
1 c. salt

Pack cucumbers in sterilized quart jars with 1 garlic clove and 1 head dill per jar. Combine 2 quarts water, vinegar and salt in saucepan. Bring to a boil. Pour over cucumbers to within ½ inch of jar top. Seal immediately. Let stand 4 to 6 weeks before serving. Yield: 4-6 quarts.

Mrs. Fred Herron, C. E. King H. S.
Houston, Texas

SWEET CUCUMBER PICKLES

2 c. slaked lime
7 lb. cucumbers
2 qt. vinegar
1 tbsp. salt
1 tsp. cloves
1 tsp. celery seed
1 tsp. mixed picking spices
4½ lb. sugar

Combine lime and 2 gallons water in crock. Add cucumbers; let soak for 24 hours, stirring occasionally. Drain and rinse cucumbers. Combine remaining ingredients in kettle; cook until sugar dissolves. Place cucumbers in syrup; let stand overnight. Bring to a boil; boil for 40 minutes. Pack in sterilized jars; seal. Process in hot water bath for 10 minutes to complete seal.

Mrs. Theresa J. King, Wellman H. S.
Wellman, Texas

FIG PICKLES

5 qt. firm ripe figs
8 c. sugar
2 c. vinegar
1½ tbsp. whole cloves
1½ tbsp. whole allspice
1½ sticks cinnamon

Wash and drain figs. Dissolve 4 cups sugar in 2 quarts water in kettle. Add figs; cook until tender. Add remaining 4 cups sugar, vinegar and spices; cook until figs are clear. Let stand overnight in refrigerator. Bring syrup and figs to boiling point. Sterilize pint jars, rings and lids. Fill hot jars with figs; fill with syrup. Add rings and hot lids. Tighten lids; process in 180 to 190 degree-water bath for 30 minutes. Remove from water bath; let cool away from draft. Remove rings; test for complete seal by gently lifting up on edge of lid. Replace rings on jars.

Mrs. Ruth L. Thorne, Imperial Jr. H. S.
Ontario, California

GREEN TOMATO PICKLES

9 lb. green tomatoes
3 c. slaked lime
5 lb. sugar
3 pt. apple cider vinegar
2 tsp. salt
2 sticks cinnamon
1 tsp. whole cloves
1 tsp. whole allspice

Cut tomatoes into ⅜ to ¼-inch slices. Dissolve lime in 2 gallons water. Add tomato slices; let stand for 24 hours. Drain off brine. Cover with clear water; let stand for 4 hours longer, changing water every hour. Drain well. Combine sugar, vinegar, salt and cinnamon in large saucepan. Tie cloves and allspice in cloth bag; place in sugar mixture. Bring to a boil. Pour over tomato slices; let stand overnight. Bring tomato mixture to a boil; boil slowly for 1 hour. Remove cinnamon sticks and cloth bag; place tomato pickles in sterilized jars. Seal. Process in hot water bath for 10 minutes to complete seal. Yield: 15 pints.

Mrs. Sallie Dorroh, Whitmire H. S.
Whitmire, South Carolina

HOT PICKLED OKRA

3 lb. okra
5 cloves of garlic
5 pods of hot peppers
1 qt. white vinegar
6 tbsp. salt
6 tbsp. celery seed
6 tbsp. mustard seed
½ tsp. hot red pepper

Place okra in 5 sterilized pint jars; add 1 clove of garlic and 1 pod of pepper to each jar. Combine ½ cup water and remaining ingredients in saucepan; bring to a boil. Pour over okra; seal jars. Process in hot water bath for 10 minutes to complete seal. Let stand for 2 weeks before using.

Bertie Joe Womack, Andrew Jackson H. S.
Jacksonville, Florida

PICKLED PEACHES

½ bushel sm. ripe peaches
5 lb. sugar
1 pt. cider vinegar
1 tsp. whole cloves
4 oz. cassia buds or 3 oz. cinnamon bark

Remove skins from peaches; place peaches in a large kettle. Combine remaining ingredients in large saucepan; bring to a boil. Boil for 5 minutes. Pour syrup over peaches; let stand overnight. Heat through; place peaches in 7 sterilized quart jars. Pour in syrup. Seal. Process in hot water bath for 10 minutes to complete seal.

Mrs. Evelyn Tompkins, Shelby H. S.
Shelby, Michigan

SPICED PICKLED CRAB APPLES

1 qt. white vinegar
4 c. sugar
1 tbsp. cinnamon
1 tbsp. cloves
1 tsp. mace
1 tsp. allspice
½ to ¾ gal. red crab apples

Combine vinegar, 1 cup water, sugar and spices in kettle; bring to a boil. Let cool. Add crab apples; heat through slowly to keep skins from bursting. Let crab apples stand in syrup overnight. Pack cold apples and syrup in sterilized jars, filling to ½-inch from top. Seal. Process in hot water bath for 20 minutes to complete seal. Unsealed jars may be kept in refrigerator for 2 to 3 weeks. Yield: 5 pints.

Mrs. Katy Jo Powers, Haysi H. S.
Haysi, Virginia

SWEET MIXED CAULIFLOWER PICKLES

2 qt. cauliflowerets
1½ c. sugar
2½ c. white vinegar
2 tbsp. salt
1 tbsp. white mustard seed
1 tbsp. celery seed
2 green peppers, cut into ¼-in. strips
2 sweet red peppers, cut into ¼-in. strips
1½ lb. onions, quartered

Cook cauliflowerets in a small amount of water for 5 minutes; drain well. Combine sugar, vinegar, salt, mustard seed and celery seed in kettle. Cover; bring to a boil. Add cauliflowerets and remaining vegetables; return to a boil. Cook, uncovered, for 2 minutes. Place in 5 sterilized pint jars; seal. Process in hot water bath for 10 minutes to complete seal.

Melba Lee Moore, State Department of Education
Little Rock, Arkansas

SQUASH PICKLES

6 qt. squash, sliced
½ c. salt
2 or 3 onions, sliced
2 sweet peppers, sliced
5 c. sugar
1½ tsp. turmeric powder
1½ tsp. celery seed
2 tsp. mustard seed
3 c. vinegar

Place squash, salt, onions and sweet peppers in container. Cover with ice. Refrigerate for 3 hours.

Drain. Combine sugar, turmeric powder, celery seed, mustard seed and vinegar in a saucepan. Bring to a boil. Simmer for 15 minutes. Pack squash into hot sterilized jars. Pour hot mixture over squash to within ½-inch of jar top. Seal immediately.

Mrs. Bobbie Sharpe, Warren County Jr. H. S.
McMinnville, Tennessee

WATERMELON PICKLES

7 lb. peeled cut watermelon rind
7 c. sugar
1 pt. mild vinegar
½ tsp. oil of cloves
½ tsp. oil of cinnamon

Soak rind overnight in kettle in salted water to cover. Drain off brine. Add fresh water; cook until rind is tender but not soft. Drain. Combine remaining ingredients in large saucepan; bring to a boil. Pour over rind; let stand overnight. Reheat syrup. Pour over rind; let stand overnight. Repeat, letting rind stand one more night. Bring rind and syrup to a boil; place in 7 sterilized pint jars. Seal. Process in hot water bath for 10 minutes to complete seal.

Hazel I. Coatsworth, Pueblo H. S.
Tuscon, Arizona

BEAN RELISH

2 c. chopped green tomatoes
2 c. chopped sweet green or red peppers
2 c. diced peeled cucumbers
2 c. chopped onions
½ c. salt
2 c. chopped celery
2 c. diced carrots
1 can lima beans
1 can kidney beans
1 can wax beans
3 c. sugar
¾ qt. vinegar
1 tbsp. dry mustard

Combine tomatoes, green peppers, cucumbers, onions, salt and 2 quarts water; let stand overnight. Drain well. Place in kettle; add celery, carrots and water to cover. Bring to a boil; boil for 30 minutes. Drain well. Add remaining ingredients; bring to a boil, stirring gently. Place in hot sterilized jars; seal. Process in hot water bath for 10 minutes to complete seal. Yield: 10 pints.

Sara Lee Greeley, Preston H. S.
Preston, Minnesota

BEET RELISH

2 c. chopped boiled beets
2 c. chopped cabbage
2 stalks celery, diced
½ c. grated horseradish or 1 tbsp. dried
  horseradish
¼ tsp. white pepper
Pinch of red pepper
½ tsp. salt
¾ c. sugar
1 c. vinegar

Combine all ingredients in saucepan; heat through. Pour into hot sterilized jars; seal. Process in hot water bath for 10 minutes to complete seal. Yield: 3-4 pints.

Mrs. Marguerite S. Darnall,
Mount Empire Jr.-Sr. H. S.
Campo, California

EASY CORN RELISH

4 c. sugar
4 c. vinegar
1 tbsp. salt
1 tbsp. celery seed
1 tsp. turmeric
4 c. chopped onions
4 c. chopped tomatoes
4 c. chopped cucumbers
4 c. fresh corn
4 c. chopped cabbage

Combine sugar, vinegar, salt, celery seed and turmeric in large Dutch oven; bring to boiling point. Add remaining ingredients. Cook, uncovered, for 25 minutes, stirring occasionally. Pack in hot, sterilized jars; seal. Process in hot water bath for 10 minutes to complete seal. Yield: 6 pints.

Oleta Hayden, Milford H. S.
Milford, Texas

FAVORITE CORN RELISH

12 ears corn
1 box dry mustard
1 tbsp. turmeric
2 lb. sugar or to taste
2 tsp. salt
2 qt. vinegar
2 bunches celery, diced
6 onions, diced
3 sweet red peppers or pimentos, diced
3 green peppers, diced

Cut corn from each cob. Dissolve mustard, turmeric, sugar and salt in vinegar. Place all ingredients in kettle; bring to a boil. Simmer until thick, stirring frequently. Pack into sterilized jars; seal. Process in hot water bath for 10 minutes to complete seal.

Helen D. Stephens, Tallulah Falls Sch.
Tallulah Falls, Georgia

HOT DOG RELISH

5 c. coarsely ground, peeled seeded cucumbers
2 c. coarsely ground green peppers
1 c. coarsely ground red peppers
3 c. coarsely ground onions
3 c. coarsely ground celery
¾ c. salt
1 qt. white vinegar
3 c. sugar
1 tbsp. celery seed

Combine first 5 ingredients in kettle; stir in salt and 1½ cups water. Let stand overnight. Drain well. Stir in remaining ingredients; bring to a boil. Simmer for 10 minutes. Pack into sterilized jars; seal. Process in hot water bath for 10 minutes to complete seal.

Mrs. Margaret Busch, Magnolia Public Sch.
Magnolia, Minnesota

INDIAN RELISH

12 green tomatoes
6 sweet red peppers
6 sweet green peppers
4 lg. onions
1 tbsp. celery seed
2 tbsp. salt
1½ lb. sugar
3 c. vinegar

Grind tomatoes, peppers and onions coarsely; drain well. Combine all ingredients in kettle; stir in 1 cup water. Bring to a boil; boil for 25 minutes. Pour into hot sterilized pint jars; seal. Process in hot water bath for 10 minutes to complete seal. Yield: 6-7 pints.

Mrs. Ralph W. Downs, Pequannock H. S.
Pompton Plains, New Jersey

CARROT RELISH

3 carrots
1 lg. lemon, seeded
½ c. (scant) sugar

Grind carrots and lemon, using fine blade of food chopper. Add sugar. Store in jar in refrigerator for several hours or overnight to blend flavors. Serve with fish or meat salads.

Dorothy E. Kinsman, Ishpeming H. S.
Ishpeming, Michigan

PEAR RELISH

3 qt. ground pears
12 onions, ground
12 green peppers, ground
4 lg. cans pimentos, chopped
3 pods of hot peppers
¼ c. prepared mustard
2 tbsp. turmeric
8 c. sugar
1 qt. vinegar
2 tbsp. salt

Combine all ingredients in kettle; simmer for 1 hour and 30 minutes, stirring frequently. Fill hot sterilized jars; seal. Process in hot water bath for 10 minutes to complete seal.

Mrs. Margaret Lee, Tylertown H. S.
Tylertown, Mississippi

PICCALILLI

1 qt. chopped cabbage
1 qt. chopped green tomatoes
2 sweet red peppers, chopped
2 sweet green peppers, chopped
2 lg. onions, chopped
¼ c. salt
1½ c. vinegar
2 c. (firmly packed) brown sugar
1 tsp. dry mustard
1 tsp. turmeric
1 tsp. celery seed

Combine vegetables and salt; let stand overnight. Drain vegetables; press in cloth to remove all liquid. Combine remaining ingredients in saucepan; stir in 1½ cups water. Bring to a boil. Boil for 5 minutes. Stir into vegetables in kettle; bring to a boil. Pour into sterilized jars; seal immediately. Process in hot water bath for 10 minutes to complete seal.

Mrs. Verda E. McConnell, Adams City H. S.
Commerce City, Colorado

SPICY PICKLE RELISH

12 lg. cucumbers
8 green peppers, seeded
10 med. onions
4 tbsp. salt
5 c. sugar
5 c. vinegar
3 tbsp. celery seed
6 tbsp. mustard seed

Peel cucumbers; cut lengthwise to remove seeds. Grind cucumbers, green peppers and onions, using coarse blade of food chopper. Place in kettle; stir in salt. Let stand overnight. Drain well. Combine remaining ingredients; pour over cucumber mixture. Bring to a boil; simmer for 20 minutes. Pour into hot sterilized jars. Process in hot water bath for 10 minutes to complete seal. Yield: 8 pints.

Mrs. Revia C. Munch, Branford H. S.
Branford, Florida

SWEET PEPPER RELISH

12 sweet green peppers, finely chopped
12 sweet red peppers, finely chopped
3 hot peppers, finely chopped (opt.)
3 lg. onions, finely chopped
3 tbsp. salt
2 pt. vinegar
2 c. sugar

Combine peppers and onions in kettle; cover with boiling water. Let stand for 10 minutes. Drain well. Cover again with boiling water; bring to a boil. Remove from heat; let stand for 10 to 15 minutes. Drain dry. Stir remaining ingredients into pepper mixture; bring to a boil. Pack hot relish into sterilized jars. Seal. Process in boiling water bath for 10 minutes to complete seal.

Mrs. Rebecca McGaughy, Montevallo H. S.
Montevallo, Alabama

BEST-EVER CHOW CHOW

8 qt. green tomatoes
Salt to taste
2 qt. sweet green and red peppers
2 qt. onions
2 lg. cabbages
¼ c. white mustard seed
2 tbsp. allspice
2 tbsp. celery seed
2 tbsp. ground cloves
1 sm. box dry mustard
1 lb. brown sugar
3 to 4 c. sugar
1 jar pimentos, chopped
1 sm. hot pepper, chopped
½ gal. vinegar

Cut tomatoes in halves; sprinkle with salt. Place salted tomatoes in layers; let stand overnight. Drain well. Grind tomatoes, sweet peppers, onions and cabbages coarsely; place in kettle. Add remaining ingredients; mix well. Bring to a boil; simmer for 4 hours. Place in sterilized jars; seal. Process in hot water bath for 10 minutes to complete seal.

Mrs. Vivian Bain, Brackenridge H. S.
San Antonio, Texas

GREEN TOMATO RELISH

24 green tomatoes
8 carrots
12 lg. onions
8 sweet green or red peppers
6 hot red peppers
½ cabbage
1 qt. apple cider vinegar
3 c. sugar
6 tbsp. salt
1 tbsp. celery seed

Grind vegetables, using medium blade of food chopper. Place in kettle; cover with boiling water. Let stand for 5 minutes. Drain well. Combine remaining ingredients in saucepan; bring to a boil. Pour over tomato mixture. Bring to a boil; simmer for 15 minutes. Place in sterilized jars; seal. Process in hot water bath for 10 minutes to complete seal.

Mrs. Marshall J. King, Gatesville H. S.
Gatesville, Texas

RIPE TOMATO GARDEN SPECIAL

6 sweet peppers, chopped
1 qt. chopped celery
1 qt. sliced onions
3 tbsp. salt
2 tbsp. sugar
4 qt. peeled, sliced ripe tomatoes

Combine all ingredients except tomatoes in kettle; add 4 cups water. Bring to a boil; simmer for 20 minutes. Add tomatoes; return to a boil. Pour into sterilized jars; seal. Process quart jars in hot water bath for 30 minutes or pint jars for 25 minutes to complete seal. Yield: 12 pints.

Mrs. Nancy Putney, Sunapee Central Sch.
Sunapee, New Hampshire

SPECIAL OCCASION ARTICHOKE HEARTS

Juice of 1 lemon
6 lg. artichokes
6 lg. onions, thinly sliced
½ c. olive oil
Salt to taste
¾ tsp. monosodium glutamate

Pour half the lemon juice in bowl of cold water. Cut stems from artichokes; peel off tough outer leaves. Cut off 1 inch or more from top of each artichoke, leaving only tender portion of leaves. Cut each artichoke in half lengthwise; remove choke portion. Place halves in lemon water as finished. Saute onions in oil until transparent; place artichoke halves on onions, cut side down. Add ½ cup water and remaining lemon juice; sprinkle with salt and monosodium glutamate. Cover; simmer for about 45 minutes or until artichokes are tender. Chill until ready to use. Serve cold as an accompaniment or as an appetizer.

Mrs. Mildred Callahan, Thomas Jefferson Jr. H. S.
Miami, Florida

SVENGALI TOMATOES

1 1-lb. can tomatoes, cut up
¼ c. cranberry-orange relish
2 tbsp. light raisins
1 tbsp. sugar
½ tsp. ginger
½ tsp. salt
¼ tsp. cayenne pepper

Combine all ingredients in saucepan; simmer for 8 to 10 minutes, stirring occasionally. Serve warm or cold.

Mrs. Janet Stark Halvorson, St. Charles H. S.
St. Charles, Minnesota

TASTY SANDWICH SPREAD

6 lg. onions, ground
11 sweet red peppers, ground
11 sweet green peppers, ground
6 green tomatoes, ground
Vinegar
2 c. sugar
3 tbsp. salt
6 tbsp. flour
3 tbsp. prepared mustard
1 qt. salad dressing

Combine vegetables; cover with boiling water. Let stand for 10 minutes. Drain well, pressing out all liquid; place in kettle. Add 3 cups vinegar, sugar and salt; bring to a boil. Boil for 5 minutes, stirring occasionally. Combine flour, mustard and enough vinegar to make a thin paste; stir into vegetable mixture. Boil for 5 minutes longer or until thickened. Stir in salad dressing; bring to boiling point. Pour into sterilized jars; seal. Process in boiling water bath for 10 minutes to complete seal. Yield: 4 pints.

Mrs. Iris S. Nelson, Franklin H. S.
Franklin, West Virginia

STIR-FRY SUMMER VEGETABLES

2 tbsp. butter or margarine
2 tbsp. salad oil
2 chicken bouillon cubes
1 med. clove of garlic, minced
1 lb. zucchini, thinly sliced
½ lb. fresh mushrooms, sliced
4 green onions, cut in 2-inch pieces
1 sm. red or green pepper, cut in ½-inch
    squares
Grated rind and juice of ½ lemon

Melt butter with oil, bouillon cubes and garlic in large skillet. Add zucchini and mushrooms; stir-fry over medium-high heat for 3 minutes. Add green onions and pepper. Cook 2 minutes longer or until vegetables are tender-crisp. Stir in lemon peel and juice. Yield: 6 servings.

Photograph for this recipe on page 136.

SAVORY CORN ON THE COB

Corn on the cob, cooked
Fresh lemon wedges
Butter or margarine, softened
Seasoned salt

Cook corn in microwave oven on high. Remove husks from 4 ears of corn. Wrap each ear in waxed paper. Cook until tender-crisp. 7 to 8 minutes for 4 ears. Let stand 2 minutes. Rub with lemon wedge. Spread with butter. Sprinkle with seasoned salt.

Photograph for this recipe on page 136.

TUNA MOUSSAKA

1 med. eggplant
⅓ c. chopped onion
3 tbsp. dry white wine or 3 tbsp. water and 1
    tsp. lemon juice
2 tbsp. cornstarch
2 c. skim milk
½ tsp. salt
⅛ tsp. pepper
¼ tsp. cinnamon
Dash of nutmeg
1 can tuna
2 eggs
1 c. cottage cheese
½ c. grated Parmesan cheese, divided

Pare eggplant; cut into slices about ⅜ inch thick. Cook in boiling water to cover for 3 or 4 minutes. Drain thoroughly on paper towels. Place onion and wine in medium saucepan; cover. Cook over moderate heat for 5 minutes. Mix cornstarch with about ¼ cup milk; stir until smooth. Add to saucepan with remaining milk, salt, pepper, cinnamon and nutmeg. Cook, stirring constantly, until mixture thickens and comes to a boil. Remove from heat. Drain tuna and mix with ½ cup onion sauce. Beat eggs in medium bowl. Add cottage cheese and remaining onion sauce; mix well. Place layer of half the eggplant slices in bottom of 8 × 8 × 2-inch baking dish. Cover with tuna mixture; sprinkle with ¼ cup grated Parmesan cheese. Add layer of remaining eggplant slices. Pour egg and cottage cheese mixture over all; sprinkle with remaining ¼ cup cheese. Bake uncovered in 350-degree oven for 50 to 55 minutes, or until custard topping is set. Remove from oven; let stand 10 minutes. Cut into squares to serve. Yield: 6 servings.

Photograph for this recipe on page 135.

TUNA RAMEKINS CHASSEUR

¼ lb. mushrooms, sliced
¼ c. chopped onion
¼ c. dry vermouth, white wine or water
2 cans tuna
3 eggs
1½ c. buttermilk
¼ tsp. salt
½ tsp. dried leaf basil
¼ c. chopped parsley
¾ c. grated Parmesan cheese
1 lg. tomato, peeled and cut into 6 slices.

Cook mushrooms and onion in vermouth in small saucepan, over medium heat, covered, for 5 minutes. Uncover and cook until vermouth is evaporated. Drain tuna. Layer with mushroom mixture in 6 individual ramekins. Beat eggs with buttermilk, salt, basil, parsley and ½ cup cheese. Pour over tuna and mushrooms. Top each ramekin with 1 slice tomato. Sprinkle with remaining ¼ cup cheese. Bake in 325-degree oven for 20 to 25 minutes or until set. Yield: 6 servings.

Photograph for this recipe on page 135.

TUNA-STUFFED CABBAGE ROLLS

12 large cabbage leaves
2 cans tuna
1 c. cooked rice
1 c. finely chopped celery with leaves
½ c. finely chopped onion
¼ c. chopped parsley
1 egg, slightly beaten
1 tbsp. Dijon-style mustard
2 tsp. caraway seed, (opt.)
½ tsp. salt
2 tsp. lemon juice
4 chicken bouillon cubes

½ c. buttermilk or skimmed milk
1 tbsp. cornstarch
¼ tsp. nutmeg
⅛ tsp. pepper
2 tbsp. prepared horseradish
1 tsp. sugar

Remove 12 leaves from large cabbage carefully. Cook in boiling water to cover for 2 minutes. Drain leaves well. Cut lengthwise about 2 inches through heavy vein of each leaf. Drain tuna; flake in large bowl. Add rice, celery, onion, parsley, egg, mustard, caraway seed, ¼ teaspoon salt and lemon juice; mix well. Place ¼ cup mixture on each cabbage leaf. Roll up, tucking in ends securely, and fasten with wooden picks. Place rolls in large skillet with 3 cups water and chicken bouillon cubes. Cover; simmer 15 to 20 minutes, or until rolls are tender. Remove rolls to a warm serving platter; cover. Keep warm. Mix buttermilk with cornstarch until smooth; gradually stir into hot liquid in skillet. Add remaining ¼ teaspoon salt, nutmeg, pepper, horseradish and sugar. Cook, stirring constantly, until sauce thickens and comes to a boil. Simmer 2 or 3 minutes. Pour sauce over cabbage rolls. Yield: 6 servings.

Photograph for this recipe on page 135.

SPRING VEGETABLE RING

2 lb. new potatoes
6 tbsp. butter or margarine
2 cloves of garlic, minced
1½ lb. fresh green beans, cut into 1½-inch
    pieces
3 lg. tomatoes, peeled and chopped
1½ tsp. dried leaf basil
1¼ tsp. salt
⅛ tsp. pepper
1 tbsp. fresh lemon juice

Scrub new potatoes. Remove a strip of peel around center of each potato. Cook potatoes in boiling salted water to cover until just tender, about 20 minutes. Melt 4 tablespoons butter in large skillet. Add garlic, green beans, tomatoes, basil, salt and pepper; cover. Cook over medium heat, stirring occasionally about 20 minutes or until beans are tender-crisp. Drain cooked potatoes. Melt remaining 2 tablespoons butter in saucepan. Add lemon juice; pour over potatoes. Place green bean and tomato mixture in center of a shallow bowl. Surround with ring of buttered new potatoes. Yield: 6 servings.

Photograph for this recipe on page 102.

ARTICHOKES WITH HOLLANDAISE SAUCE

4 artichokes
1 lemon, sliced
1 tsp. salt
1 tsp. ground coriander
Hollandaise sauce

Cut stem of artichoke close to the base. Pull off loose leaves from the bottom. Snip off sharp leaf tips with scissors. Bring 2 to 3 inches water to boil in a large saucepan or kettle. Add lemon, salt, coriander and prepared artichokes. Simmer 30 to 40 minutes or until stem is fork-tender and a leaf pulls easily from the base. Turn upside down to drain. Serve with Hollandaise Sauce. Yield: 4 servings.

Hollandaise Sauce

3 egg yolks
½ tsp. salt
Dash of cayenne pepper
½ c. butter or margarine, melted
2 tbsp. fresh lemon juice
1 tsp. chopped fresh parsley

Beat egg yolks until thick and lemon colored. Mix in salt and cayenne pepper. Blend in 3 tablespoons melted butter gradually, beating constantly. Beat in remaining butter alternately with lemon juice. Sprinkle with parsley. Yield: 1 cup.

Photograph for this recipe on page 102.

GRAPEFRUIT HOT BEAN SALAD

2 tbsp. butter or margarine
½ c. chopped onion
1 tbsp. cornstarch
1 c. Florida grapefruit juice
2 tbsp. cider vinegar
1 tbsp. soy sauce
¼ c. (firmly packed) brown sugar
2 c. diagonally sliced celery
1 20-oz. can kidney beans, drained
1 20-oz. can chick-peas, drained
1 16-oz. can cut green beans, drained
2 c. grapefruit sections

Melt butter in large skillet. Add onion; cook until tender. Mix cornstarch and grapefruit juice in medium bowl. Add to skillet with cider vinegar, soy sauce and brown sugar; mix well. Bring to a boil. Cook until sauce is thickened, stirring constantly. Stir in celery, kidney beans, chick-peas and green beans. Cook over low heat 10 minutes. Add grapefruit sections; heat thoroughly. Yield: 6 servings.

Photograph for this recipe on page 68.

STIR-FRY ASPARAGUS

2 lb. fresh asparagus
¼ c. butter or margarine
½ tsp. salt
⅛ tsp. pepper
½ tsp. dried leaf thyme

Cut asparagus into 2-inch diagonal pieces. Melt butter in large skillet. Add asparagus; sprinkle with seasonings. Cover and cook over medium high heat about 5 minutes, stirring occasionally until lower part of stalk is just tender-crisp. Yield: 4-6 servings.

Photograph for this recipe on page 102.

HOT GRAPEFRUIT, HAM AND CABBAGE SALAD

2 tbsp. butter or margarine
⅓ c. chopped onion
1½ tbsp. flour
1 tbsp. sugar
1 tsp. salt
¼ tsp. pepper
1 tbsp. prepared mustard
1 c. grapefruit juice
2 tbsp. cider vinegar
2 c. diced cooked ham
1 c. chopped walnuts
4 c. thinly shredded cabbage
2 c. grapefruit sections

Melt butter in large skillet. Add onion; cook until tender. Blend in flour, sugar, salt, pepper and mustard. Stir in grapefruit juice, vinegar and ¼ cup water. Bring to a boil over medium heat, stirring constantly. Stir in ham, walnuts and cabbage; cook 10 minutes. Add grapefruit sections; heat thoroughly. Yield: 4 servings.

Photograph for this recipe on page 68.

GRAPEFRUIT HOT POTATO SALAD

1 lb. Italian sweet sausage, cut in 1-inch slices
½ c. chopped onion
¼ c. chopped parsley
4½ tsp. flour
4 tsp. sugar
½ tsp. salt
⅔ c. grapefruit juice
2 tbsp. vinegar
4 c. sliced pared cooked potatoes
2 c. grapefruit sections

Brown sausage in a large skillet over medium heat. Add onion and parsley; cook until onion is tender.

Blend in flour, sugar and salt. Stir in grapefruit juice, vinegar and ½ cup water. Bring to a boil, stirring constantly. Add potatoes; cook over low heat 15 minutes. Add grapefruit sections and heat. Yield: 4 servings.

Photograph for this recipe on page 68.

FRESH ASPARAGUS SUPREME

4 lb. asparagus
2 tbsp. butter or margarine
2 tbsp. flour
2 c. light cream
1 c. diced cooked ham
2 tsp. fresh lemon juice
¼ tsp. salt
⅛ tsp. nutmeg
¼ c. shredded Swiss cheese

Wash asparagus; break off each stalk as far down as it snaps easily. Cook, covered, in 1 inch boiling water in a large skillet until tender, 5 to 8 minutes. Melt butter in medium saucepan. Blend in flour. Remove from heat; stir in cream. Return to heat and cook, stirring constantly, until mixture thickens and comes to a boil. Add ham, lemon juice, salt, nutmeg and Swiss cheese; heat until cheese melts. Drain asparagus. Serve immediately with sauce. Yield: 8 servings.

Photograph for this recipe on page 101.

GREEN BEANS PROVENCAL

4 slices bacon
½ c. chopped fresh onion
½ c. chopped celery
1 lb. fresh green beans, diagonally sliced
1 tsp. salt
⅛ tsp. pepper
½ tsp. dried leaf oregano
2 tomatoes, peeled and cut in wedges

Cook bacon in large skillet until lightly browned. Remove bacon, drain, crumble and reserve. Pour off bacon fat except for 2 tablespoons. Add onion and celery to skillet; cook until tender. Add green beans, salt, pepper and oregano. Cover and cook 10 minutes, stirring occasionally. Add tomatoes; cook 5 minutes longer. Sprinkle with bacon before serving. Yield: 4 servings.

Photograph for this recipe on page 101.

VEGETABLE-STUFFED ARTICHOKES

4 artichokes
¼ c. butter or margarine
¼ c. chopped pared carrot

¼ c. chopped fresh onion
¼ c. chopped celery
¼ lb. fresh mushrooms, chopped
1½ tsp. salt
⅛ tsp. pepper
2 tsp. fresh lemon juice
¼ tp. dried dillweed

Cut off stems of artichokes. Cut off tips of leaves with scissors. Pull off tough outside leaves around base of each artichoke and discard. Carefully open center leaves with scissors, turn the artichoke over on a board and press down firmly at the base to spread leaves open. Turn artichoke right side up and pull out yellow leaves from the center. Scrape out fuzzy and prickly portion from the heart, with a spoon. Melt butter in large skillet. Add carrots, onion and celery; cook until tender. Add mushrooms, 1 teaspoon salt, pepper, lemon juice and dillweed. Cook until mushrooms are tender, about 10 minutes. Sprinkle remaining ½ teaspoon salt over cavities of artichokes. Place ⅓ cup mixture in the center of each artichoke. Place in baking pan; add water to cover bottom of pan. Cover and bake in 375 degrees oven 45 minutes. Yield: 4 servings.

Photograph for this recipe on page 101.

SCALLOPED POTATOES AND TOMATOES

2 tbsp. butter or margarine
1 onion, sliced
1 clove of garlic, minced
1 tsp. salt
⅛ tsp. pepper
¼ tsp. dried leaf basil
¼ tsp. dried leaf thyme
2 tomatoes, peeled and sliced
2 c. thinly sliced pared potatoes
¼ c. grated Parmesan cheese

Melt butter in large skillet. Add onion and garlic; cook until tender. Stir in salt, pepper, basil and thyme. Add tomatoes and potatoes. Mix gently until coated with seasonings. Turn into greased 1-quart baking dish. Sprinkle with Parmesan cheese. Bake in 400-degree oven 40 minutes, until potatoes are tender. Yield: 4 servings.

Photograph for this recipe on page 101.

TRIPLE B SALAD

1 pkg. frozen baby lima beans
5 slices bacon
¼ c. vinegar
2 tbsp. sugar
½ c. sour cream
4 c. torn head lettuce
2 c. torn leaf lettuce

2 hard-cooked eggs, sliced
1 can diced beets, drained
½ c. sliced celery
½ c. crumbled blue cheese

Cook lima beans; drain and cool. Cook bacon until crisp; crumble and set aside. Reserve 2 tablespoons drippings; stir in vinegar and sugar. Blend in sour cream until smooth with a wire wisk. Refrigerate until serving time. Toss together head and leaf lettuce; place in salad bowl. Arrange rows of beans, eggs, beets and celery on greens. Sprinkle blue cheese over beets, and bacon over beans. Chill, covered, until serving time. Serve with sour cream dressing. Yield: 6-8 servings.

Photograph for this recipe on page 67.

TROPICAL FRUIT PLATTER

¼ c. confectioners' sugar
Lime juice
Dash of salt
1¼ c. sour cream
1½ c. shredded Cheddar cheese
32 pecan halves
8 slices avocado
8 slices cantaloupe
4 slices fresh pineapple, cut in half
Leaf lettuce

Fold sugar, 1 tablespoon lime juice and salt into 1 cup sour cream. Chill. Whip together Cheddar cheese and ¼ cup sour cream in a small mixing bowl. Using a scant tablespoon for each, shape into 16 cheese balls. Press each ball between 2 pecan halves; chill. Dip avocado slices in lime juice. Arrange cheese balls on a large platter; alternate cantaloupe, avocado slices, pineapple and leaf lettuce. Garnish tray with fresh strawberries and watercress, if desired. Serve dressing separately. Yield: 8 servings.

Photograph for this recipe on page 67.

LEMON ROLLS

¼ c. butter
1 tbsp. (firmly packed) light brown sugar
1 tbsp. grated lemon peel
1 tbsp. lemon juice
1 pkg. refrigerator buttermilk biscuits

Whip together butter, brown sugar, lemon peel and juice in a small mixing bowl until light and fluffy. Roll each biscuit into a 2½-inch circle. Spread about 1 teaspoon butter mixture on each biscuit. Cut each into 6 triangles. Place 3 triangles in each cup of a miniature muffin pan. Bake in preheated 400-degree oven for 9 to 11 minutes. Yield: 20 rolls.

Photograph for this recipe on page 67.

TUNA-FRUIT SALAD PLATTER

1 c. strawberries
2 oranges, peeled and sliced
2 bananas, sliced
1 avocado, peeled and sliced
1 sm. bunch green grapes
1 sm. bunch dark grapes
2 cans tuna
Poppy seed dressing
Orange-Ginger dressing

Arrange fruit and tuna chunks on a large platter. Garnish with fresh mint sprigs. Serve with Poppy Seed Dressing or Orange-Ginger Dressing. Yield: 4 to 6 servings.

Poppy Seed Dressing:

½ tsp. dry mustard
1 tsp. salt
1 tsp. grated onion
⅓ c. honey
2 tbsp. cider vinegar
¾ c. salad oil
2 tsp. poppy seed

Mix mustard, salt and grated onion in a 2 cup measuring cup. Beat in honey, vinegar and oil. Add poppy seed and stir. Serve over Tuna Fruit Salad. Yield: 1¼ cup dressing.

Orange-Ginger Dressing:

½ c. sour cream
⅓ c. mayonnaise
¼ tsp. grated orange rind
2 tbsp. orange juice
1 tbsp. finely chopped candied ginger

2 tsp. sugar
⅛ tsp. salt

Mix all ingredients in a small bowl. Chill for 1 hour. Serve over Tuna-Fruit Salad. Yield: 2 cups dressing.

Photograph for this recipe on page 34.

FRESH FRUIT COMBO WITH JEWEL DRESSING

¼ c. fresh squeezed orange juice
1½ env. unflavored gelatin
¾ c. mayonnaise or sour cream
1 env. blue cheese salad dressing mix
1 tbsp. fresh squeezed lemon juice
1 tsp. fresh grated orange peel
3 tbsp. parsley, finely snipped
Orange cartwheels
Peach slices
Whole strawberries
Melon balls
Watermelon chunks
Salad greens and parsley

Mix orange juice with 1¼ cups water in medium saucepan. Sprinkle gelatin over orange juice mixture; soften 5 minutes. Heat until gelatin is dissolved, stirring constantly. Combine mayonnaise, salad dressing mix, lemon juice and grated orange peel. Stir in hot liquid gradually; blend until smooth. Chill until thickened but not set. Stir in parsley. Pour into 2⅓ cups mold or a No. 2 size can. Chill until set. Unmold onto serving platter. Surround with fruits. Garnish with salad greens and parsley. Dressing is sliced and served with fruits. Yield: 8 servings.

Photograph for this recipe on page 33.

Fruit and Vegetable Calorie Chart

FRUITS

Apples, medium, raw	1	70
Applesauce, canned, sweetened	1 cup	230
Bananas, raw, 6 by 1½ in.	1	100
Blueberries, raw	1 cup	85
Cantaloupe, raw, medium	½ melon	60
Grapefruit, raw, medium, white	½	45
Grapes, raw, American type	1 cup	65
Lemons, raw, medium	1	20
Lemon juice, fresh	1 cup	60
Lime juice, fresh	1 cup	65
Oranges, raw, 2 ⅝-in. diam.	1	65
Peaches, raw, whole, medium	1	35
Peaches, canned, halves or sliced	1 cup	200
Pears, raw, 3 by 2½ in.	1	100
Pineapple, canned, sliced	Large slice	90
Plums, raw, 2-in. diam.	1	25
Raisins, seedless, pkged., ½ oz.	1 pkg	40
Strawberries, raw, capped	1 cup	55
Watermelon, raw	1 wedge	115

VEGETABLES

Asparagus, cooked, spears	4 spears	10
Asparagus, canned	1 cup	45
Beans, lima, baby, cooked	1 cup	190
Beans, snap, green, cooked	1 cup	30
Beans, snap, canned, green	1 cup	45
Beans, snap, yellow or wax	1 cup	30
Beans, sprouted mung, cooked	1 cup	35
Beets, cooked	2 beets	30
Broccoli, cooked	1 stalk	45
Brussels sprouts, cooked	1 cup	55
Cabbage, raw, shredded	1 cup	15
Cabbage, cooked	1 cup	30
Carrots, raw, 5½ by 1 in.	1	20
Carrots, cooked, diced	1 cup	45
Cauliflower, cooked, flower buds	1 cup	25
Celery, raw, stalk, large	1 stalk	5
Corn, cooked, 5 by 1¾-in. ear	1 ear	70
Corn, canned	1 cup	170
Cucumbers, raw, pared	10 oz.	30
Lettuce, Boston type	1 head	30
Mushrooms, canned	1 cup	40
Onions, mature, raw, 2½ in.	1	40
Peas, green, cooked	1 cup	115
Peas, green, canned	1 cup	165
Potatoes, medium, baked	1	90
Potatoes, medium boiled in skin	1	105
Potatoes, mashed, milk added	1 cup	125
Sauerkraut, canned	1 cup	45
Spinach, cooked	1 cup	40
Squash, summer, diced, cooked	1 cup	30
Squash, winter, baked, mashed	1 cup	130
Sweet potatoes, baked	1	155
Tomatoes, raw, medium	1	40

NUTRITION LABELING

Modern Americans have become very diet and nutrition conscious, and in response, commercial food producers have begun to include nutrition information on the labels of their products. Nutrition Labeling is an invaluable service in many ways. There are many persons on special diets (diabetic, low-sodium, low-cholesterol) who must know the specifics of the foods they eat. However, whether the homemaker cooks for a special diet or not, Nutrition Labeling on the foods she buys helps her to know the part they play in her overall nutrition and menu planning.

The United States Food and Drug Administration has determined how much of every important nutrient is needed by the average healthy person in the United States, well known as the Recommended Daily Dietar Allowance (RDA). The United States RDA reflects the highest amounts of nutritives for all ages and sexes. Pregnant and nursing women, as well as persons with special dietary needs, should consult their doctors for any recommended increases or decreases in their daily diet.

UNITED STATES RECOMMENDED DAILY ALLOWANCE CHART

Protein . . . . .45-65 Grams
Carbohydrates . . . . 125 Grams
Vitamin A . . . . .5,000 International Units
Thiamine (Vitamin B_1) . . . . .1.5 Milligrams
Riboflavin (Vitamin B_2) . . . . .1.7 Milligrams
Vitamin B_6 . . . . 2 Milligrams
Vitamin B_{12} . . . . 6 Micrograms
Folic Acid (B Vitamin) . . . . .0.4 Milligrams
Pantothenic Acid (B Vitamin) . . . . 10 Milligrams
Vitamin C (Ascorbic Acid) . . . . .55-60 Milligrams
Vitamin D . . . . 400 International Units
Vitamin E . . . . 30 International Units
Iron . . . . 18 Milligrams
Calcium . . . . .1 Gram
Niacin (Nicotinic Acid) . . . . .13-20 Milligrams
Magnesium . . . . 400 Milligrams
Zinc . . . . 15 Milligrams
Copper . . . . 2 Milligrams
Phosphorus . . . . .1 Gram
Iodine . . . . 150 Micrograms
Biotin (Vitamin H) . . . . .0.3 Milligrams

IMPORTANT NUTRIENTS YOUR DIET REQUIRES

PROTEIN

Why? Absolutely essential in building, repairing and renewing of all body tissue. Helps body resist infection. Builds enzymes and hormones, helps form and maintain body fluids.

Where? Milk, eggs, lean meats, poultry, fish, soybeans, peanuts, dried peas and beans, grains and cereals.

CARBOHYDRATES

Why?   Provide needed energy for bodily functions, provide warmth, as well as fuel for brain and nerve tissues. Lack of carbohydrates will cause body to use protein for energy rather than for repair and building.

Where? Sugars: sugar, table syrups, jellies and jams, etc., as well as dried and fresh fruits. Starches: cereals, pasta, rice, corn, dried beans and peas, potatoes, stem and leafy vegetables, and milk.

FATS

Why?   Essential in the use of fat soluble vitamins (A, D, E, K), and fatty acids. Have more than twice the concentrated energy than equal amount of carbohydrate for body energy and warmth.

Where? Margarine, butter, cooking oil, mayonnaise, vegetable shortening, milk, cream, ice cream, cheese, meat, fish, eggs, poultry, chocolate, coconut, nuts.

VITAMIN A

Why?   Needed for healthy skin and hair, as well as for healthy, infection-resistant mucous membranes.

Where? Dark green, leafy and yellow vegetables, liver. Deep yellow fruits, such as apricots and cantaloupe. Milk, cheese, eggs, as well as fortified margarine and butter.

THIAMINE (VITAMIN B_1)

Why?   Aids in the release of energy of foods, as well as in normal appetite and digestion. Promotes healthy nervous system.

Where? Pork, liver, kidney. Dried peas and beans. Whole grain and enriched breads and cereals.

RIBOFLAVIN (VITAMIN B_2)

Why?   Helps to oxidize foods. Promotes healthy eyes and skin, especially around mouth and eyes. Prevents pellagra.

Where? Meat, especially liver and kidney, as well as milk, cheese, eggs. Dark green leafy vegetables. Enriched bread and cereal products. Almonds, dried peas and beans.

VITAMIN B_6

Why?   Helps protein in building body tissues. Needed for healthy nerves, skin and digestion. Also helps body to use fats and carbohydrates for energy.

Where? Milk, wheat germ, whole grain and fortified cereals. Liver and kidney, pork and beef.

VITAMIN B_{12}

Why?   Aids body in formation of red blood cells, as well as in regular work of all body cells.

Where? Lean meats, milk, eggs, fish, cheese, as well as liver and kidney.

FOLIC ACID

Why?   Aids in healthy blood system, as well as intestinal tract. Helps to prevent anemia.

Where? Green leaves of vegetables and herbs, as well as liver and milk. Wheat germ and soybeans.

PANTOTHENIC ACID

Why?   Aids in proper function of digestive system.

Where? Liver, kidney and eggs. Peanuts and molasses. Broccoli and other vegetables.

VITAMIN C (ASCORBIC ACID)

Why?   Promotes proper bone and tooth formation. Helps body utilize iron and resist infection. Strengthens blood vessels. Lack of it causes bones to heal slowly, failure of wounds to heal and fragile vessels to bleed easily.

Where? Citrus fruits, cantaloupe and strawberries. Broccoli, kale, green peppers, raw cabbage, sweet potatoes, cauliflower, tomatoes.

VITAMIN D
Why? Builds strong bones and teeth by aiding utilization of calcium and phosphorus.
Where? Fortified milk, fish liver oils, as well as salmon, tuna and sardines. Also eggs.

VITAMIN E
Why? Needed in maintaining red blood cells.
Where? Whole grain cereals, wheat germ, and beans and peas, lettuce and eggs.

IRON
Why? Used with protein for hemoglobin production. Forms nucleus of each cell, and helps them to use oxygen.
Where? Kidney and liver, as well as shellfish, lean meats, and eggs. Deep yellow and dark green leafy vegetables. Dried peas, beans, fruits. Potatoes, whole grain cereals and bread. Enriched flour and bread. Dark molasses.

CALCIUM
Why? Builds and renews bones, teeth, other tissues, as well as aiding in the proper function of muscles, nerves and heart. Controls normal blood clotting. With protein, aids in oxidation of foods.
Where? Milk and milk products, excluding butter. Dark green vegetables, oysters, clams and sardines.

NIACIN
Why? Helps body to oxidize food. Aids in digestion, and helps to keep nervous system and skin healthy.
Where? Peanuts, liver, tuna, as well as fish, poultry and lean meats. Enriched breads, cereals and peas.

MAGNESIUM
Why? Aids nervous system and sleep.
Where? Almonds, peanuts, raisins and prunes. Vegetables, fruits, milk, fish and meats.

ZINC
Why? Needed for cell formation.
Where? Nuts and leafy green vegetables. Shellfish.

COPPER
Why? Helps body to utilize iron.
Where? Vegetables and meats.

PHOSPHORUS
Why? Maintains normal blood clotting function, as well as builds bones, teeth and nerve tissue. Aids in utilization of sugar and fats.
Where? Oatmeal and whole wheat products. Eggs and cheese, dried beans and peas. Nuts, lean meats, and fish and poultry.

IODINE
Why? Enables thyroid gland to maintain proper body metabolism.
Where? Iodized salt. Saltwater fish and seafood. Milk and vegetables.

BIOTIN (VITAMIN H)
Why? Helps to maintain body cells.
Where? Eggs and liver. Any foods rich in Vitamin B.

CAN SIZE CHART

8 oz. can or jar ....1 c.
10 1/2 oz. can (picnic can) ....1 1/4 c.
12 oz. can (vacuum) ....1 1/2 c.
14-16 oz. or No. 300 can ....1 1/4 c.
16-17 oz. can or jar
   or No. 303 can or jar ....2 c.
1 lb. 4 oz. or 1 pt. 2 fl. oz.
   or No. 2 can or jar ....2 1/2 c.

1 lb. 13 oz. can or jar
   or No. 2 1/2 can or jar ....3 1/2 c.
1 qt. 14 fl. oz. or 3 lb. 3 oz.
   or 46 oz. can ....5 3/4 c.
6 1/2 to 7 1/2 lb.
   or No. 10 can ....12-13 c.

EQUIVALENT CHART

3 tsp. ....1 tbsp.
2 tbsp. ....1/8 c.
4 tbsp. ....1/4 c.
8 tbsp. ....1/2 c.
16 tbsp. ....1 c.
5 tbsp. + 1 tsp. ....1/3 c.
12 tbsp. ....3/4 c.
4 oz. ....1/2 c.
8 oz. ....1 c.
16 oz. ....1 lb.
1 oz. ....2 tbsp. fat or liquid
2 c. ....1 pt.

2 pt. ....1 qt.
1 qt. ....4 c.
5/8 c. ....1/2 c. + 2 tbsp.
7/8 c. ....3/4 c. + 2 tbsp.
1 jigger ....1 1/2 fl. oz.(3 tbsp.)
2 c. fat ....1 lb.
1 lb. butter ....2 c. or 4 sticks
2 c. sugar ....1 lb.
2 2/3 c. powdered sugar ....1 lb.
2 2/3 c. brown sugar ....1 lb.
4 c. sifted flour ....1 lb.
4 1/2 c. cake flour ....1 lb.

3 1/2 c. unsifted whole wheat flour ....1 lb.
8 to 10 egg whites ....1 c.
12 to 14 egg yolks ....1 c.
1 c. unwhipped cream ....2 c. whipped
1 lb. shredded American cheese ....4 c.
1/4 lb. crumbled blue cheese ....1 c.
1 chopped med. onion ....1/2 c. pieces
1 lemon ....3 tbsp. juice
1 lemon ....1 tsp. grated peel
1 orange ....1/3 c. juice
1 orange ....about 2 tsp. grated peel
1 lb. unshelled walnuts ....1 1/2 to 1 3/4 c. shelled
1 lb. unshelled almonds ....3/4 to 1 c. shelled
4 oz. (1 to 1 1/4 c.) uncooked macaroni ....2 1/4 c. cooked
7 oz. spaghetti ....4 c. cooked
4 oz. (1 1/2 to 2 c.) uncooked noodles ....2 c. cooked
28 saltine crackers ....1 c. crumbs
4 slices bread ....1 c. crumbs
14 square graham crackers ....1 c. crumbs
22 vanilla wafers ....1 c. crumbs

SUBSTITUTIONS FOR A MISSING INGREDIENT

1 square *chocolate* (1 ounce) = 3 or 4 tablespoons cocoa plus 1/2 tablespoon fat.
1 tablespoon *cornstarch* (for thickening) = 2 tablespoons flour.
1 cup sifted *all-purpose flour* = 1 cup plus 2 tablespoons sifted cake flour.
1 cup sifted *cake flour* = 1 cup minus 2 tablespoons sifted all-purpose flour.
1 teaspoon *baking powder* = 1/4 teaspoon baking soda plus 1/2 teaspoon cream of tartar.
1 cup *sour milk* — 1 cup sweet milk into which 1 tablespoon vinegar or lemon juice has been stirred; or
    1 cup buttermilk (let stand for 5 minutes).

SUBSTITUTIONS FOR A MISSING INGREDIENT

1 cup *sweet milk* = 1 cup sour milk or buttermilk plus 1/2 teaspoon baking soda.
1 cup *canned tomatoes* = about 1 1/3 cups cut-up fresh tomatoes, simmered 10 minutes.
3/4 cup *cracker crumbs* = 1 cup bread crumbs.
1 cup *cream, sour, heavy* = 1/3 cup butter and 2/3 cups milk in any sour milk recipe.
1 cup *cream, sour, thin* = 3 tablespoons butter and 3/4 cup milk in sour milk recipe.
1 cup *molasses* = 1 cup honey.
1 teaspoon *dried herbs* = 1 tablespoon fresh herbs.
1 *whole egg* = 2 egg yolks for custards.
1/2 cup *evaporated milk* and 1/2 cup *water* or 1 cup *reconstituted nonfat dry milk* and 1 tablespoon
       butter = 1 cup whole milk.
1 package *active dry yeast* = 1 cake compressed yeast.
1 tablespoon *instant minced onion, rehydrated* = 1 small fresh onion.
1 tablespoon *prepared mustard* = 1 teaspoon dry mustard.
1/8 teaspoon *garlic powder* = 1 small pressed clove of garlic

METRIC CONVERSION CHARTS FOR THE KITCHEN

VOLUME

1 tsp.	4.9 cc	2 c.	473.4 cc
1 tbsp.	14.7 cc	1 fl. oz.	29.5 cc
1/3 c.	28.9 cc	4 oz.	118.3 cc
1/8 c.	29.5 cc	8 oz.	236.7 cc
1/4 c.	59.1 cc	1 pt.	473.4 cc
1/2 c.	118.3 cc	1 qt.	.946 liters
3/4 c.	177.5 cc	1 gal.	3.7 liters
1 c.	236.7 cc		

CONVERSION FACTORS:

Liters	X	1.056	=	Liquid Quarts
Quarts	X	0.946	=	Liters
Liters	X	0.264	=	Gallons
Gallons	X	3.785	=	Liters
Fluid Ounces	X	29.563	=	Cubic Centimeters
Cubic Centimeters	X	0.034	=	Fluid Ounces
Cups	X	236.575	=	Cubic Centimeters
Tablespoons	X	14.797	=	Cubic Centimeters
Teaspoons	X	4.932	=	Cubic Centimeters
Bushels	X	0.352	=	Hectoliters
Hectoliters	X	2.837	=	Bushels
Ounces (Avoir.)	X	28.349	=	Grams
Grams	X	0.035	=	Ounces
Pounds	X	0.454	=	Kilograms
Kilograms	X	2.205	=	Pounds

WEIGHT

1 dry oz.	28.3 Grams
1 lb.	454 Kilograms

LIQUID MEASURE AND METRIC EQUIVALENT

(NEAREST CONVENIENT EQUIVALENTS)

CUPS SPOONS	QUARTS OUNCES	METRIC EQUIVALENTS
1 teaspoon	1/6 ounce	.5 milliliters / 5 grams
2 teaspoons	1/3 ounce	.10 milliliters / 10 grams
1 tablespoon	1/2 ounce	.15 milliliters / 15 grams
3 1/3 tablespoons	1 3/4 ounces	.50 milliliters
1/4 cup (4 tablespoons)	2 ounces	.60 milliliters
1/3 cup (5 1/3 tablespoons)	2 2/3 ounces	.79 milliliters
1/3 cup plus 1 tablespoon	3 1/2 ounces	.100 milliliters
1/2 cup (8 tablespoons)	4 ounces	.118 milliliters
1 cup (16 tablespoons)	8 ounces	.1/4 liter / 236 milliliters
2 cups	1 pint / 16 ounces	.1/2 liter less 1 1/2 tablespoons / 473 milliliters
2 cups plus 2 1/2 tablespoons	17 ounces	.1/2 liter
4 cups	1 quart / 32 ounces	.946 milliliters
4 1/3 cups	1 quart, 2 ounces	.1 liter / 1000 milliliters

CONVERSION FORMULAS:

To convert Centigrade to Fahrenheit: multiply by 9, divide by 5, add 32.

To convert Fahrenheit to Centigrade: subtract 32, multiply by 5, divide by 9.

DRY MEASURE AND METRIC EQUIVALENT

(MOST CONVENIENT APPROXIMATION)

POUNDS AND OUNCES	METRIC	POUNDS AND OUNCES	METRIC
1/6 ounce	.5 grams	1/4 pound (4 ounces)	.114 grams
1/3 ounce	.10 grams	4 1/8 ounces	.125 grams
1/2 ounce	.15 grams	1/2 pound (8 ounces)	.227 grams
1 ounce	.30 grams (28.35)	3/4 pound (12 ounces)	.250 grams
1 3/4 ounces	.50 grams	1 pound (16 ounces)	.454 grams
2 2/3 ounces	.75 grams	1.1 pounds	.500 grams
3 1/2 ounces	.100 grams	2.2 pounds	.1 kilogram / 1000 grams

Index

Photography Credits

Cover and Illustrations: Designer—Lee Hamblen;
The McIlhenny Company; United Fresh Fruit and
Vegetable Association; Florida Department of
Citrus; Tuna Research Foundation; American
Dairy Association; Sunkist Growers, Inc.

Favorite Recipes®
of Home Economics Teachers
COOKBOOKS

Add to
Your Cookbook Collection
Select from These ALL-TIME
Favorites

BOOK TITLE	ITEM NUMBER
Dieting To Stay Fit (1978) 200 Pages	01449
Desserts—Revised Edition (1962) 304 Pages	01422
Our Favorite Meats (1966) 384 Pages	70114
*Salads * Vegetables* (1979) 200 Pages	05576
Quick and Easy Dishes—Revised Edition (1968) 256 Pages	00043
Money-Saving Cookbook (1971) 256 Pages	70092
Americana Cooking (1972) 192 Pages	70351
Poultry Cookbook (1973) 192 Pages	70319
New Holiday (1974) 200 Pages	70343
Canning, Preserving and Freezing (1975) 200 Pages	70084
Life-Saver Cookbook (1976) 200 Pages	70335
Foods From Foreign Nations (1977) 200 Pages	01279

FOR ORDERING INFORMATION
Write to:
Favorite Recipes Press
P. O. Box 77
Nashville, Tennessee 37202

BOOKS OFFERED SUBJECT TO AVAILABILITY.